Diplomacy
and
Deception

Diplomacy and Deception

The Secret History of Sino-Soviet Diplomatic Relations, 1917-1927

Bruce A. Elleman

M.E. Sharpe
Armonk, New York
London, England

Library of Congress Cataloging-in-Publication Data

Elleman, Bruce A. 1959–
Diplomacy and deception: the secret history of Sino-Soviet diplomatic relations,
1917–1927 / by Bruce A. Elleman.
p.   cm.
Includes bibliographical references and index.
ISBN 0-7656-0142-7 (cloth : alk. paper)
1. Soviet Union—Foreign relations—China.
2. China—Foreign relations—Soviet Union.
3. Soviet Union—Foreign relations—1917–1945.
4. China—Foreign relations—1912–1949.
I. Title.
DK68.7.C6E44   1997
327.47051—dc21
97-3075
CIP

Printed in the United States of America

The paper used in this publication meets the minimum requirements of the
American National Standard for Information Sciences—
Permanence of Paper for Printed Library Materials,
ANSI Z 39.48-1984.

BM (c)   10   9   8   7   6   5   4   3   2   1

To my parents

Contents

List of Documents

List of Maps

List of Abbreviations

CCP	Chinese Communist Party
CER	Chinese Eastern Railway
Comintern	Communist International
FER	Far Eastern Republic
KMT	Kuomintang
Narkomindel	People's Commissariat of Foreign Affairs (Soviet)
Waichiaopu	Chinese Ministry of Foreign Affairs
WCTA	Wai-chiao Tang-an (Peking government's foreign ministry archives, Academia Sinica, Taipei, Taiwan)

Acknowledgments

Many people helped me with this project, but I would like to thank in particular my spouse, Sarah C. M. Paine, and our two children, Anna Virginia Elleman and Steven Moyers Elleman. At Texas Christian University history department, I owe a debt of gratitude for the support of the chairman, Spencer Tucker, and to all the other faculty and staff, especially Gene Smith and Barbara Pierce. Yin Shih-tsung, at the Taipei Language Institute, helped check my translations of handwritten documents in grass writing and Yu Miin-ling, at Taiwan's Institute of Modern History at Academia Sinica, kindly proofread the Chinese text that appears in this manuscript.

I would like to acknowledge those who influenced me at various stages of my education. For the intellectual foundation, I am extremely indebted to Stephen Cohen, Milan Hauner, John LeDonne, Martin Malia, Nicholas Riasanovsky, and Allen Whiting. At Columbia University, I must mention Thomas Bernstein, Carol Gluck, Marc Raeff, Michael Tsin, Mark von Hagen, and Madeleine Zelin. At Stanford University, I would especially like to thank Robert Conquest, Gerald Dorfman, John Dunlop, Thomas Henricksen, Tetsuya Kataoka, Thomas Metzger, Ramon Myers, Mark Peattie, and Richard Staar. At M.E. Sharpe, I greatly benefited from the advice of Patricia Kolb, Ana Erlic, and Elizabeth Granda.

This work could not have been completed without the help of many language teachers who taught me how to read modern and classical Chinese, grass writing, Russian, and Japanese. I therefore owe a deep debt to dozens of language teachers at the University of California at Berkeley, Columbia, the Middlebury College Russian School, the National Normal University in Taipei, the Taipei Language Institute, and International Christian University in Tokyo.

Beyond the help of these individuals, I was also fortunate to receive financial assistance from the following organizations: the Committee on Scholarly Communication with the People's Republic of China with support from the United States Department of Education funded twelve months of research in Beijing and Nanjing in 1990; the Pacific Cultural Foundation funded research in Taipei during ten months in Taiwan during the 1991-92 academic year; and the Hoover Institution on War, Revolution and Peace funded writing and publication of this research during the 1993-94 academic year under the Discretionary Grant Program, U.S. Department of State, Soviet-Eastern European Research and Training Act of 1983 (Public Law 98-164, Title VIII, 97 Stat. 1047-50), and during the 1994-95 academic year under the National Fellowship program.

I would also like to express my gratitude to the organizations and staff that made their archival collections available to me: I am especially grateful to the staffs at the Academia Sinica and the Kuomintang Archives (both in Taipei), the Lenin Library in Moscow, the Number Two Historical Archives in Nanjing, the Foreign Ministry Archives in Tokyo, and the Butler library and archives at Columbia University in New York, all of which so generously shared their extensive collections of documents on foreign relations. In particular, I would like to thank Chen San-ching, Director of the Institute of Modern History at Academia Sinica, the Japanese Foreign Ministry Archives, and the Hoover Institution Archives for granting me permission to reprint selected archival documents in this volume. The number of librarians and archivists who have assisted me in my research is also long, but I would like to extend a special thanks to Frances LaFleur at Columbia, Molly Molloy at Stanford, and Elena Danielson and Carol Leadenham at the Hoover Institution Archives. Finally, this book could not have been completed without the heroic efforts of Joyce Martindale at the interlibrary loan office, Mary Couts Library, Texas Christian University.

I would also like to extend my appreciation to the editors, publishers, and anonymous reviewers who helped revise my research findings for publication in article form, and in particular Winston Yang at *The American Asian Review*; Charles Schlacks Jr. at *The Soviet and Post-Soviet Review;* Richard Gunde at *Modern China*; Ian D. Slater at *Pacific Affairs*; David Buck, Jeff Kinkley, and Gladys Bovee at *The Journal of Asian Studies*; Coonoor Kripalani-Thadani at the *Journal of Oriental Studies;* Stephen Averill at *Republican China*; Denis Sinor at the *Journal of Asian History*; and G. D. Armstrong and Erik Goldstein at *Diplomacy & Statecraft*. Portions of this manuscript were derived from these articles and are included with the permission of the above-mentioned journals. Sections of Chapter 4, in particular, are reprinted with permission of the Association for Asian Studies, Inc.

Needless to say, I could not have completed my graduate education without the assistance and support of my parents, Charlotte Ann Elleman and Thomas S. Elleman, and of my mother-in-law, Henrietta N. Paine.

I alone am responsible for the interpretations presented in this work and for all shortcomings contained therein.

Technical Note

The transliteration system used for Russian is the Library of Congress system minus the diacritical marks. For Chinese, the Wade-Giles system has been used, except for those names which have entered into common usage by another romanization, for example: Sun Yat-sen, Sinkiang. Words in Cyrillic have been spelled according to the rules of the new orthography, while Chinese characters appear in both their simplified and their complicated forms, depending largely on whether the source was published before or after 1949. All Chinese characters have been reproduced as in the original sources.

The term *Outer Mongolia* refers to the northern portion of Greater Mongolia that roughly corresponds to modern-day Mongolia. *White Russians* refers generally to all Russians who fled to China in the aftermath of the 1917 revolutions, irrespective of whether they supported the tsarist government, the provisional government, or some other faction. *Soviet Russia* is used to refer to the Bolshevik state prior to 1922, while *Soviet Union* or *USSR* is used after 1922. Finally, the *Peking government* refers to the internationally recognized central government in Peking, now Beijing, while the Canton government refers to Sun Yat-sen's opposition government in the southern Chinese city of Canton, now Guangzhou. Similary, the Kuomintang refers to Sun Yat-sen's political party, also spelled Guomindang.

All Chinese personal names are written with surname first, then given name.

China

Center for Cartographic Research and Spatial Analysis
Michigan State University

Diplomacy
and
Deception

Introduction

After World War I, Soviet Russia and China were thrust together by a little-known but important event, commonly called the "Shantung question." In short, the Shantung question refers to the 1919 Versailles Peace Treaty decision to transfer Germany's 200-square-mile concession in Kiaochow harbor, Shantung, indirectly from Germany to Japan and then to China instead of being transferred directly from Germany to China. A common interpretation of the Paris Peace Conference's resolution was as a "betrayal of Chinese interests."[1] President Woodrow Wilson was criticized for backing this decision, with some historians describing his support for China as "wavering," while others have concluded that Wilson "sacrificed China."[2] Thereafter, it was the Chinese peoples' "dissatisfaction and bitterness" over America's actions that "Bolshevik-controlled Russia sought to exploit in its first diplomatic overtures toward the Peking government."[3]

Archival documents now prove that Wilson did not sacrifice China. In fact, he worked diligently to negotiate terms that led to the return of the Shantung concession to China in 1922, a full seventy-five years before Germany's treaty had stipulated. Wilson also convinced Japan to set aside all political rights in Shantung, which Tokyo had gained by means of the 1915 Twenty-one Demands and a 1918 secret agreement signed with Peking. But China refused to compromise, deeming it beneath her dignity and a loss of face to deal with Japan, thus undermining and ultimately delaying the return of the Shantung concession.

Instead of betraying China, Wilson did everything in his power to help her. The main obstacle impeding success was not his lack of sympathy for China's plight, but a myriad of agreements and treaties that China had herself negotiated with Japan from 1915 to 1918. But when even Wilson's lengthy negotiations with Japan proved insufficient to release China completely from her obligations under international law, the Chinese delegation at Paris turned on their staunchest defender and tried to make Wilson culpable for China's own botched diplomacy.

The resulting myth that America turned its back on China in her hour of need convinced many Chinese to turn to Soviet Russia instead; they hoped that the Bolsheviks would grant to China the equal treatment that the nations at Paris had apparently forsworn. Even more important, Chinese officials tried to make use of the illusion of friendly Sino-Soviet relations to exert diplomatic pressure on the Western nations and Japan. This outwardly fraternal facade was made possible by a series of secret agreements that camouflaged the actual animosity underlying Sino-Soviet relations. This book will discuss the terms of these secret agreements as well as their effect on the most important issues surrounding Sino-Soviet relations, including the United Front Policy, Outer Mongolia, the Chinese Eastern Railway, the Boxer Indemnity, territorial concessions, extraterritoriality, and the formation of the Chinese Communist Party.

The Diplomatic Situation Prior to 1919

To understand what happened at Paris in 1919, one must start with the German seizure of Kiaochow harbor, in the province of Shantung, China, in 1897. After receiving assurances from Russia that it would not interfere, the German government responded to the murder of two German missionaries in Shantung on November 1, 1897, by occupying Kiaochow and forcing China to agree to a ninety-nine year lease, beginning on March 6, 1898. In addition to ceding Germany land around Kiaochow harbor for its concession at Tsingtao, German interests were permitted to develop several railway lines in Shantung, and were given mining rights on all land within ten miles of the railway lines. Finally, German businesses were to be approached first if China wished to develop Shantung, which meant that Shantung became an exclusive German sphere of influence.[4]

This arrangement continued unchanged for sixteen years. After the beginning of World War I, however, Japan sought to fulfill her obligations to Great Britain under their mutual 1902 alliance by demanding that Germany vacate Shantung. Japan's August 15, 1914 ultimatum specifically called for Germany to "unconditionally hand over the territory [of Kiaochow] to Japan which she intended to restore to China."[5] After a two-month siege, Japanese troops occupied Kiaochow on November 7, 1914. Even though Tokyo had promised to restore Kiaochow to China, Peking retained diplomatic relations with Germany until 1917, as well as protested Japan's seizure of the Shantung concession.

The Japanese government and people were proud of their contribution to the war effort. Dr. Toyokichi Iyenaga, formerly a member of the Japanese Foreign Office, and later a lecturer at Columbia University, explained this pride[6]:

> [Japan] destroyed at one stroke the German power in the Far East by the reduction of the fortress of Tsingtao, hunted out the enemy warships roving the adjoining seas; patrolled the South Sea, the Indian and Pacific Oceans during the whole period of the war; convoyed the troops of Australia and New Zealand to the battlefields of Europe and Asia; co-operat[ed] on the Mediterranean with the allied fleets in their operations against the enemy submarines; prevented the [in]filtration of German influence and the spread of Bolshevism into East Siberia; subscribed to the allied loans to the full extent of her financial capacity; provided the Entente [Allied] powers with munitions and other war materials; and stood ever ready to respond to the call of her allies in case of necessity.

After the war, Japan expected to retain proof of her victory over Germany; it was particularly important to Japan's national honor to assume control over the territory that her armed forces had taken in battle. In this regard, Japan did not differ from her European allies, most of whom made similar financial and territorial claims for German and Austrian territory and colonies after the war.

In January 1915, Tokyo presented Peking with the Twenty-one Demands, which sought to define Japan's new position in China. In a list divided into five groups, Tokyo demanded the right to dispose of Germany's concession in Shantung as she saw fit; to increase her influence in Manchuria and Inner Mongolia; to receive special mining and commercial privileges along the Yangtse River; to stop China from leasing additional coastal bays or harbors to other powers; and, in the highly disputed fifth group, to give Japan a wide range of political rights in China proper, including exclusive rights to sell arms to China and to develop Fukien province, across the straits from the Japanese colony of Taiwan.

The United States government criticized the Twenty-one Demands on March 13, 1915. Its protest stated that it "could not regard with indifference the assumption of political, military, or economic domination over China by a foreign power," and requested Japan to refrain from "pressing upon China an acceptance of proposals that would, if accepted, exclude Americans from equal participation in the economic and industrial development of China and would limit the political independence of that country."[7] On March 30, Secretary of State William J. Bryan specifically criticized Japan for trying to force Japanese advisers on the Chinese government, as well as claiming exclusive rights to sell arms and manage Japanese police forces in Manchuria and Inner Mongolia.[8]

As a result of America's dissatisfaction, Japan modified her demand to make China accept Japanese police, and she also retracted the demand to make Fukien province an exclusive zone for Japanese development. On April 28, the Japanese government announced that it had even offered to restore Kiaochow Bay to China in exchange for opening the port of Tsingtao to foreigners, allowing a Japanese concession as well as an international settlement, and turning the German public buildings and property over to Japan.[9] Japan also asked for permission to build three railway lines from Nanchang to Hangchow, from Kiukiang to Nanchang, and from Nanchang to Chaochow, but reported that to her "surprise and disappointment . . . the Chinese Government, instead of showing any disposition to listen to these fair and reasonable representations of the Japanese Minister, flatly refused to consider the proposal."[10]

In the end, Japan pressured China to accept her terms, prompting another American protest. Washington stated on May 13, that "it cannot recognize any agreement or undertaking which has been entered into or which may be entered into between the Governments of Japan and China impairing the treaty rights of the United States and its citizens in China, the political or territorial integrity of the Republic of China, or the international policy relative to China commonly known as the 'Open Door Policy'."[11] Nevertheless, Peking signed treaties with Tokyo on May 25, 1915, even though Japan's demands had been significantly reduced as a result of Washington's earlier protests.

The United States continued to refuse to recognize Japan's Twenty-one Demands and urged China to end diplomatic relations with Germany and join the Allies, as an important first step in having these provisions reversed. On March 14,

1917, China broke with Germany, and then on August 14, she declared war. Tokyo foresaw the problems that China's actions might cause to Japan's position in Shantung, however, and so in early 1917 signed secret agreements with Great Britain, France, Italy, and Russia that guaranteed her rights to the German concession in Shantung.[12] Finally, in November 1917, the United States recognized Japan's "geographical propinquity" in China in the Lansing-Ishii agreement.[13] Although this agreement fell far short of recognizing Japan's Twenty-one Demands, it did tacitly admit that Japan's economic interests in China were legitimate.

These already complex arrangements were further complicated on September 24, 1918, when Peking signed a separate secret agreement with Tokyo (see Document 1). In return for withdrawing the Japanese civil administration from Shantung and turning this responsibility back over to China, Peking agreed to manage the former Tsingtao-Chinan railway line as a joint Sino-Japanese company. Included in this agreement was the provision that Japanese policemen could patrol this railway. Peking then accepted a Japanese loan of twenty million yen as an advance on this railway agreement. It later proved difficult for China to show that this agreement had been forced on her by Japan, since the Chinese Minister to Tokyo, Chang Tsung-hsiang, wrote to the Japanese government at the time: "I beg to acquaint you in reply that the Chinese gladly agree."[14]

When the Paris Peace Conference convened in 1919 and addressed the Shantung question, it was faced with the prospect of untangling not only China's 1898 treaty with Germany, but China's 1915 and 1918 treaties with Japan, as well as Japan's secret agreements with Great Britain, France, Italy, and Russia. The Shantung question, which seemed deceptively simple to many outsiders, actually involved eight countries: China; Germany; Japan; Great Britain; France; Italy; Russia; and, finally, the United States. Of these, the United States alone had not signed any agreements recognizing the 1915 and 1918 treaties, making it the only reasonably objective party concerned with the negotiations. Considering the complexity of this problem, it should come as no surprise that the final solution satisfied no one, least of all the Chinese.

The Chinese Delegation's Proposals

China's expectations going into the Paris Peace Conference were very high. When China entered World War I on the side of the Allies during 1917, many Chinese intellectuals assumed that this meant that China would be treated as an equal after the war was over. But this assumption ignored the continuing impact of China's treaties and agreements, which, according to international law, could not be unilaterally rescinded. China's obligations, in fact, could only be altered by the mutual consent of all parties involved; it quickly became evident that the Chinese delegation was not willing to participate in this kind of dialogue.

Tokyo, September 24, 1918

Monsieur le Ministre,

I have the honour to inform you that the Imperial
Government, in view of the feeling of good neighbourhood
existing between our two countries, and in the spirit of
mutual accomodation, have deemed it fitting, and have accordingly decided to propose to your Government, to settle various
questions relating to the Province of Shantung in manners as
below set forth.

1. To concentrate at Tsingtao all the Japanese troops
stationed along the Tsingtao-Tsinan Railway, excepting a
contingent to be left at Tsinan.

2. The Chinese Gouvernment to provide for guarding the
Tsingtao-Tsinan Railway and to organize a police force for the
purpose.

3. The Tsingtao-Tsinan Railway to contribute an appropriate
sum of money towards defraying the expenses of such police
force.

4. Japanese to be employed at the head quarters of the
police force, the principal railway stations and the training
stations of police forces.

5. Chinese to be employed on the Tsingtao-Tsinan Railway.

6. Upon determination of the ownership of the Tsingtao-
Tsinan Railway, to run it as a joint Chino-Japanese undertaking .

7. The civil administration now in force to be withdrawn.

In acquainting you with the above, the Japanese Government desire to be advised of the disposition of your Government regarding the proposals.

Accept, etc, etc, etc,

(Signed) Shimpei Goto.

His Excellency
  Mr. Tsung-hsiang Chang,
    Etc, etc, etc.

Document 1
September 24, 1918 Sino-Japanese Secret Agreement

It should be remembered that China had joined the Allies at a very late date in the war and, unlike Japan, never sent troops into action or took part in the fighting. While 100,000 Chinese helped the Allies in Europe by working on the docks, in construction, and digging trenches, many of these men were recruited before China declared war; by and large, these Chinese workers were lured by the generous wages, free food and clothing, and the chance to travel to Europe *gratis*. Considering that China never had to spend money on the war, nor shed blood as a combatant, the Chinese delegation actually held a weak hand when it arrived at the Paris Peace Conference. Furthermore, after joining the Allied war effort, China had already been rewarded once by the outright cancellation of the German and Austrian twenty percent share of the Boxer Indemnity. In addition, the Allies had agreed to defer payments on the majority of the remaining Boxer Indemnity for five years (see Chapter 5).

After the war, China hoped that her status as an Ally would be sufficient to convince the nations attending the Paris Peace Conference to agree to eliminate almost a century of international treaties between China and various powers. China now claimed that these treaties were to her disadvantage. The Chinese delegation's main purpose in going to Paris, therefore, was to present a series of proposed reforms, divided into three groups: 1) territorial integrity, 2) preservation of sovereign rights, and 3) economic and fiscal independence.

Territorial integrity included the return of all foreign concessions in China and a cancellation of special foreign rights pertaining to police, taxation, public domain, etc. This proposal would also have done away with all leased territories as well, including the immediate return of Port Arthur, Kiaochow, and Kowloon. Guaranteeing China's sovereignty included the elimination of all legation guards, the removal of all foreign troops stationed in China, and the abolition of extraterritorial rights. Finally, fiscal independence included the full restoration to China of its right to regulate and administer tariffs, which were then under foreign management to ensure that China met her debt payments promptly.[15]

In November 1918, immediately prior to the convening of the Paris Peace Conference, V. K. Wellington Koo, China's minister to the United States and one of the delegates to Paris, met with President Wilson in Washington, at which time Koo told him of China's proposals.[16] Even before the conference had started, Wilson warned Koo that China's 1915 treaty with Japan would be difficult to circumvent, but that he would try to help. Wilson, however, was not told about China's 1918 secret treaty with Japan; even Koo did not know about this agreement until January 1919.[17]

Since Koo could not provide Wilson with all of the facts, Wilson's promise to help the Chinese delegation was actually elicited under false pretenses. Likewise, in December 1918, when Secretary of State Robert Lansing offered Koo his support, he also did not know about Peking's new secret agreement with Tokyo. Even without this knowledge, Lansing still cautioned Koo that all participants at the Paris Peace Conference would have to be considered.[18]

Wilson and Lansing were careful not to raise China's hopes because she had signed official treaties that turned the German concession in Shantung over to Japan. Although the Chinese delegation later argued that these agreements had been forced, coercion could not explain why the Peking government accepted a twenty million yen advance from Japan in 1918; the transfer of funds meant that reversing these agreements would be difficult, if not impossible. Peking tacitly acknowledged this fact, ordering its delegation in Paris not to be the first to bring up the Shantung issue. But, once the Paris Peace Conference convened, the Japanese delegation took the initiative by presenting copies of the two agreements that she had signed with China in 1915 and 1918, as well as her treaties with Great Britain, France, Italy, and Russia.

Faced with these six official agreements, Wilson tried to convince the Japanese delegation to allow Shantung to be made a trusteeship of the five main powers that were meeting at Paris, but this solution was not acceptable to Tokyo. Wilson then approached the Chinese delegation and asked whether it was better for China to cede Japan the rights Germany had formerly held in Shantung, or whether China's recent treaties with Japan were less onerous; the Chinese delegation refused to choose, insisting that both were unacceptable.[19] Stymied, Wilson had to find a compromise solution that would, on the one hand, protect China's sovereignty, while on the other hand, cede Japan economic benefits that she had not only wrested from Germany in World War I, but had then consolidated by signing official treaties with China. Wilson hit upon a solution in the midst of almost two weeks of intensive talks with the Chinese and Japanese delegations at Paris.

Wilson's Compromise Solution

The most important decisions at Paris were made by the United States, Great Britain, and France, three of the four great allies in World War I (Italy's delegate, Vittorio Orlando, had temporarily withdrawn from the conference in a dispute over Fiume). While Wilson represented the United States, David Lloyd George represented Great Britain, and George Clemenceau represented France. These three men met with the Chinese and Japanese delegations separately, since, in the opinion of one of the Japanese delegates, Baron Nobuaki Makino, the issues at stake were "difficult to discuss with people who had preconceived ideas."[20] To make matters worse for Wilson, both Lloyd George and Clemenceau stated at the very beginning that they felt obliged to support Japan, since both leaders considered their 1917 secret agreements with Japan to be still in effect. For this reason, it fell on Wilson alone to determine a suitable compromise, a goal that he achieved in a series of meetings with the Japanese delegation between April 22 and 30, 1919.

The Allies were well aware that a generally acceptable solution to the Shantung question might prove to be impossible. Prior to the talks, Lloyd George approached the leader of the Japanese delegation, Viscount Sutemi Chinda, and requested that Japan delay negotiations on Shantung altogether. Chinda refused, however, explaining that Japan had a "duty to perform to China," and that if the Shantung question was not decided, then the "Japanese Delegates were under an expressed instruction from their government that unless they were placed in a position to carry out Japanese obligations to China, they were not allowed to sign the Treaty." As a result of this order, Chinda warned Lloyd George that the Japanese delegation "had no power to agree [to] a postponement of this question."[21]

Once it became clear that the Japanese delegates would not postpone talks on Shantung and that they would boycott the peace negotiations if there were a delay, the three leaders had little choice but to address the issue. The greatest single problem was China's two treaties ceding Japan economic and political rights in Shantung. Great Britain and France had then concluded separate agreements with Japan that supported her rights. As Lloyd George was quick to point out, these obligations could not simply be ignored, since "the war had been partly undertaken in order to establish the sanctity of treaties." This meant that so far as Great Britain was concerned, "they had a definite engagement with Japan, as recorded in the note of the British Ambassador at Tokyo, dated 18th February 1917."[22]

The United States had refused to recognize the validity either of Japan's Twenty-one Demands, or of the later 1918 agreement. Negotiating records show that on April 22, 1919, Wilson urged Japan to forego these agreements for the good of peace in the Far East[23]:

> President Wilson pointed out that in the circumstances he was the only independent party present. He would like to repeat a point of view which he had urged on the Japanese Delegation a few days before.

> He was so firmly convinced that the Peace of the Far East centered upon China and Japan, that he was more interested from this point of view than any other. He did not wish to see complex engagements that fettered free determination. He was anxious that Japan should show to the world, as well as to China, that she wanted to give the same independence to China as other nations possessed, that she did not want China to be held in manacles. What would prejudice the Peace in the Far East was any relationship that was not trustful.

> It was evident that there was not that relationship of mutual trust that was necessary if peace was to be ensured in the Far East. What he feared was that Japan, by standing merely on her treaty rights, would create the impression that she was thinking more of her rights than of her duties to China.

The only possible way out, as Wilson saw it, was to find an equitable solution to the Shantung question that would not be based on the Twenty-one Demands or on the 1918 agreement. Specifically, Wilson agreed with Lloyd George that he "did not wish to interfere with treaties," but that the "validity of treaties could not be called in question if they were modified by agreements between both sides."[24] In other words, Wilson hoped to negotiate a new agreement that would modify Japan's and China's mutual relations over the Shantung concession.

The starting point for any new arrangement would have to take into account Japan's four primary preconditions to China for returning Shantung, published in the *Japanese Chronicle* on November 8, 1917: "1) The whole of Kiaochow Bay to be opened as a commercial port; 2) A concession under the exclusive jurisdiction of Japan to be established at a place to be designated by the Japanese Government; 3) If the foreign powers desire it, an international concession may be established; 4) As regards the disposal to be made of the buildings and properties of Germany and the conditions and procedures relating thereto, the Japanese Government shall arrange the matter by mutual agreement [with China] before the restoration."[25]

On December 16, 1918, the American Chamber of Commerce in China had warned that if Japan was granted these conditions, then it would result in the "absolute control of Tsingtao and its hinterland." They cautioned that this might equal the "outright annexation of the Port and to the virtual annexation of the Province by the Japanese Government." Accordingly, in the opinion of some of the top American businessmen in China, it was best either to internationalize completely the port of Tsingtao, or to restore it to China.[26]

On April 23, 1919, the Japanese delegation publicly defended its agreements with China, which were intended to restore Kiaochow to China under "conditions, none of which can be regarded in any sense as unjust or unfair, considering the part Japan took in dislodging Germany from Shantung Province." In Japan's view, China's 1917 declaration of war had no effect on the 1915 agreement, especially since "the articles of September 1918, which were made more than one year after China's declaration of war, could not have been entered into without presupposing existence and validity of the Treaty of May 1915." That the 1918 agreement was acknowledged by China was shown by the fact that "China has actually received [an] advance of twenty million yen according to terms of above arrangement." For these reasons, the Japanese delegation concluded that "full justice" should be accorded to Japan, based "upon her sacrifices and achievements and upon the fact of actual occupation, involving [a] sense of national honor."[27]

Based on these arguments, the Japanese delegation proposed that Germany transfer to Japan its rights over its "territory of Kiaochow, Railways, Mines, and Submarine cables," which Germany had received as a result of its March 6, 1898 treaty with China. Furthermore, all railway "stations, shops, fixed materials, and rolling stock," should be transferred to Japan, as well as all of Germany's movable and immovable property. Finally, Japan wanted to acquire Germany's underwater telegraph and telephone cables, running from Tsingtao to Shanghai, as well as from Tsingtao to Chefoo. Japan also proposed that its citizens be granted the same extraterritorial rights at the Germans had enjoyed before them, as well as the right to have their own Japanese-controlled police force.[28]

On April 29, 1919, Wilson expressed his concern that Japan might assume Germany's former political rights in Shantung. He went so far as to ask Baron Makino detailed questions, first about the underwater cables, then about the railways and mines, to make sure that Japan was not being given more rights than Germany had previously enjoyed. Wilson was especially concerned about Japan's contention that her citizens should enjoy extraterritorial rights along the railway lines in Shantung, even warning the Japanese delegates that: "He must say frankly that he could not do this. He asked the Japanese representatives to cooperate with him in finding a way out. He wanted to support the dignity of Japan, but he thought that Japan gained nothing by insisting on these leased rights being vested in the government."[29] As for Japan's insistence on using Japanese police along the railways, Wilson clarified that "he did not mind Japan asking for these rights, but what he objected to was their imposing them."[30]

What Wilson hoped to do was convince Japan to forego the Twenty-one Demands and develop her relations with China based on respect for China's sovereignty: "President Wilson said that one of the worst features in [the] whole of these transactions had been the unfortunate Twenty-one Demands and these had included a demand for police instructors, although, of course, on a much wider basis. This had caused the greatest irritation, as it was an invasion of Chinese political and administrative independence. It was impossible to divorce transactions of this kind from the public impression they made. The present arrangement was, in public intimation, tied up with the impression made by the Twenty-one Demands. He admitted that the police point in itself was a minor one, but in its implications, both in China and the United States . . . it was very unfortunate."[31] Wilson's proposal for circumventing the Twenty-one Demands called for Japan to make a statement respecting China's sovereignty, and he recommended the following wording: "Surrender to China of all rights of sovereignty and retention with regard to the railway and the mines only of the economic rights of a concessionaire; to retain however privilege of establishing a non-exclusive settlement at Tsingtao."[32]

After deliberation, the Japanese delegation agreed to Wilson's suggestion and, on April 30, 1919, formally announced Japan's goals with regards to Shantung[33]:

> In reply to questions by President Wilson, Japanese delegate declared as follows:–the policy of Japan is to hand back the Shantung peninsula in full sovereignty of China, retaining only the economic privileges granted to Germany and the right to establish a settlement under the usual conditions at Tsingtao.

The owners of the railway will use special police only to insure security for traffic. They will be used for no other purpose.

The police force will be composed of Chinese and such Japanese instructor[s] as the directors of the railway may select and will be appointed by the Chinese Government.

By phrasing Japan's position in such as way, Wilson had convinced the Japanese delegation to retain certain economic rights in Shantung, but no military or political rights; even the Japanese police instructors would have to be approved by the Chinese government. Most important, this solution completely avoided referring back to, and thereby recognizing, the 1915 and 1918 Sino-Japanese agreements' infringement on China's sovereignty. In effect, Wilson had convinced Japan to wipe the slate clean, and build her relations with China on the basis of equality and good will.

The Japanese delegation fully admitted that this new arrangement was not based on Japan's former agreements with China. But, it warned, if China failed to accept this new arrangement, such as by refusing "to cooperate in the formation of the police force or to admit the employment of Japanese instructors," then this would leave Japan with no recourse but to "fall back, in the last resort, on the Sino-Japanese agreements of 1915 and 1918." Wilson expressed his hope that this would not happen, and urged that "in the event of such failure on the part of China, Japan, instead of appealing to agreements, should voluntarily apply for mediation by the Council of the League of Nations."[34]

In accordance with Wilson's compromise, Japan acknowledged that her much stricter treaties with China would be referred to only as a last resort and that she would attempt to base her relations with China on the public declaration that had been drafted with Wilson's help. In an attempt to eliminate Japanese encroachments on Chinese sovereignty, Wilson supported this solution as the only plan that might work. Wilson was later said to have complained that the Shantung problem had been settled "in a way which seems to me as satisfactory as could be got out of the tangle of treaties in which China herself was involved."[35]

Wilson also had other weighty matters to consider. According to one reminiscence, in the week prior to Wilson's final discussions with Japan, Italy had left the Paris Peace Conference in a huff over her failure to be ceded the city of Fiume, which had been given to the Yugoslavs instead.[36] Since Wilson was concerned about alienating Japan, he compromised on the Shantung problem not because he was giving up his high ideals, but because the danger of pushing Japan away from international cooperation would have been a much greater threat to these ideals: "[Wilson] knew his decision would be unpopular in America, that the Chinese would be bitterly disappointed, that the Japanese would feel triumphant, that he would be accused of violating his own principles, but nevertheless, he must work for world order and organization against anarchy and a return to the old militarism."[37] Another observer reported that Wilson felt sorry that he could not do more for China, but that he was compelled to work with Japan in order to "save the League of Nations," which required Japan's support if it was to be accepted by the Versailles Peace Conference.[38] All these accounts are consistent in showing that Wilson tried to find the best solution possible under the circumstances.

The Versailles Treaty's Shantung Resolutions

In the end, the Paris Peace Conference did decide on China's behalf that Germany must give up to China "all the buildings, wharves and pontoons, barracks, forts, arms and munitions of war, vessels of all kinds, wireless telegraphy installations and other public property." It also ordered Germany to return the ancient astronomical instruments that German troops had taken from Peking in 1901.[39] The key exceptions were the economic privileges of the Shantung concession itself, which were ceded to Japan. Although Japan promised to respect China's sovereignty in Shantung, Japan also clearly relished the position of superiority that this decision gave her over China. The reverse applied to China: while many Chinese had applauded Japan's victory over Germany in 1914, acknowledging Japan's rights over Shantung, even if they were only partial economic rights, was an entirely different matter.

In the heat of the moment, it was largely forgotten that the Treaty of Versailles gave China many other benefits, such as terminating all of Germany's and Austria's unequal treaties with China, returning all of Germany's property in Tientsin and Hankow, and reaffirming the total abolition of the German and Austrian shares of the Boxer Indemnity. In addition, the compromise solution Wilson worked out with Japan meant that the Paris Peace Conference never recognized Japan's 1915 and 1918 treaties with China, which meant that the special rights and economic privileges that Japan actually received were much smaller than China's own treaties specified. But these positive points were overshadowed by Versailles Peace Treaty's decision to turn Germany's former concession in Shantung over to Japan, which the Chinese delegation portrayed as an affront to Chinese sovereignty and to China's self-esteem.

According to a public statement made on May 3, 1919, the Chinese delegation received news of Wilson's compromise with "disappointment and dissatisfaction." But, the Chinese delegation did not even attempt to explain why Peking had accepted twenty million yen from Tokyo the previous year. Instead, the Chinese delegation falsely implied that Japan was gaining control of all of Shantung, recalling that "Shantung is China's holy land, packed with memories of Confucius and Mencius, and hallowed as [the] cradle of her civilization."[40] On May 4, 1919, Lou Tseng-hsiang, the leader of China's delegation, presented Peking's real arguments in a confidential three-page letter to Wilson (see Document 2).

SECRET
DECLASSIFIED

AMERICAN COMMISSION TO NEGOTIATE PEACE.

S-H Bulletin No. 238.

Paris, May 4, 1919.

Sir:

The Rt. Hon. Arthur J. Balfour, on behalf of the Council of Three, verbally informed the Chinese Delegates on May 1, 1919, of the settlement arrived at by the Council in regard to the Kiaochow-Shantung question. They were given to understand that the clause to be inserted in the Peace Treaty would be very general, to the effect that Germany should renounce all her rights in Kiaochow-Shantung to Japan, that the conclusions reached by the Council of Three regarding Kiaochow-Shantung was that all political rights formerly enjoyed by Germany were to be restored to China, and to Japan were given only the economic rights such as a settlement at Tsingtao, the railway already built (Tsingtao-Chinan railway), the mines connected therewith, and two other railways to be built.

* * * * * * *

If the Shantung peninsula is to be restored in full sovereignty, according to the proposed settlement to China, the reason does not appear clear why recourse should be had to two steps instead of one, why the initial transfer should be made to Japan and then leave it to her to "voluntarily engage" to restore it to China.

* * * * * * *

The Chinese Delegation feel it to be their duty to register a formal protest with the Council of Three Against the proposed settlement of the Kiaochow-Shantung question.

I have the honour to be

Sir,

Your most obedient.

Humble Servant.

Signed   Lou Tsengtsiang.

To the President
  The Council of Three
    Peace Conference, Paris.

Document 2
Excerpt from May 4, 1919 Chinese Letter to Woodrow Wilson

In this document, Lou not only acknowledged that all political rights in Shantung would be returned to China and that Japan would retain only economic rights; he further admitted that Japan had agreed to return the Shantung concession as soon as Germany formally ceded it to Japan. What Lou actually opposed, therefore, was the indirect method for restoring Shantung to China: "If the Shantung peninsula is to be restored in full sovereignty, according to the proposed settlement to China, the reason does not appear clear why recourse should be had to two steps instead of one, why the initial transfer should be made to Japan and then leave it to her to 'voluntarily engage' to restore it to China."[41]

In this secret protest Lou brushed aside the controversy over the September 1918 Sino-Japanese agreements, which were the single strongest evidence that the Japanese delegates had presented at Paris to back their case. Lou dismissed them by claiming that officials in the "Chinese Government were obliged to exchange the 1918 notes" with Japan. Describing the final Shantung resolution as a "grievous disappointment" to China, Lou concluded by blaming Wilson for China's defeat: the Chinese delegation had come to Paris naively relying on Wilson's Fourteen Points, on the "spirit of honorable relationship between states," and on the "justice and equity of her case."[42]

The Japanese point of view on the Shantung question was quite different, of course, since Japan's offer to return the Shantung concession would ensure that China regained this important territory more than seventy-five years before Germany's former lease came due. Accordingly, one of Japan's supporters wondered: "I am at a loss to understand all this fuss about the Shantung settlement. I cannot but take it as the result of either ignorance or of 'deliberate exaggeration' to serve some purpose. This outcry seems to have originated in a large measure by the mixing up of Kiaochow and Shantung. The latter is a big province the size of Illinois, while Kiaochow has a land area of 200 square miles." This author called the general misconception that Shantung's 55,000 square miles and its thirty-six million population had been turned over to Japan "sheer nonsense," and concluded: "The Shantung settlement does not infringe upon the territorial integrity of China or her independence, rather does it serve to recover China's sovereignty which Germany had overrun at Kiaochow—for Japan proposes to restore the leasehold to China."[43]

In fact, to understand the Sino-Japanese conflict over Shantung, one must refer to the Chinese term called "face."[44] Even though Japan had formally promised to hand back the Shantung concession "in full sovereignty" to China, this decision placed Japan in a superior position to China. China's subsequent displeasure with this solution was due, in part, to the historical relationship between China and Japan. In this relationship China had traditionally played the dominant role, even deprecatingly referring to the Japanese as "wo-kou," or "midget pirates," in its history books.[45]

Sun Yat-sen, the leader of the Chinese opposition government in Canton, later discussed this relationship in a 1924 speech. Sun referred to Japan as China's "younger brother," and stated: "It is our hope that Japan, as the younger brother, will assist the elder brother in his efforts to abolish these Unequal Treaties, and to secure emancipation from his serfdom."[46] From China's point of view, therefore, it was bad enough that the Europeans had forced concessions out of China, but now other Asian powers were being allowed to do the same. This further insult merely increased the frustration that Chinese felt at foreign mistreatment.

But, unfortunately for China, her own internationally recognized Republican government in Peking had signed treaties, as well as accepted money, in exchange for transferring economic rights in Shantung to Japan. These actions solidly supported Japan's position. Therefore, delegates at the Paris Peace Conference felt that they had little choice but to recommend that the Shantung concession be turned over to Japan, lest Japan claim that she was being treated differently only because of racial prejudice.

Since Japan formally promised to return control of this area to China, which she subsequently did in 1922, the end result was actually the same. The intense emotions that were raised in China, however, cannot be understood without referring to China's particular cultural characteristics, such as the concept of face. A similar diplomatic agreement with a European country or the United States would probably have generated a far less severe public reaction, since it would have been the end result that was emphasized; in China, the end result was not in question, it was the methods that were considered to be most important.

The May Fourth Movement

News of the transfer of the Shantung concession to Japan was initially released on April 30, 1919, although Japan's statement of intent was not widely published.[47] In China, public demonstrations and student protests indicated that dissatisfaction with this solution was widespread, as student groups marched through the foreign legation quarter on May 4, and left protests at the American, British, French, and Italian embassies. When the police arrested thirty-two students, one student was mortally wounded, which caused further demonstrations.[48] By May 20, the "May Fourth Movement" had expanded, and students from middle schools and universities in Peking went on strike. The students spearheaded efforts to organize boycotts of Japanese goods, and in early June another thousand students were arrested. The center of the movement then shifted from Peking to Shanghai, where a general strike reportedly paralyzed Shanghai.[49]

During June 1919, Peking ignored these public demonstrations when it instructed the Chinese delegation in Paris to sign the Versailles Treaty. The student union in Peking once again led the public protest, as hundreds of representatives from different groups opposing the treaty stood outside of the president's office for two days and nights to put pressure on him to change his mind. President Hsu reluctantly sent a telegram to Paris to rescind his previous order, but did not expect it to arrive before the scheduled time for the signing. Wellington Koo was one of the most important representatives of the Peking government in the Chinese delegation, while another important American-trained Chinese diplomat, representing Sun Yat-sen's opposition government in Canton, was Wang Cheng-t'ing, better known as C. T. Wang.[50]

On June 28, the day the peace treaty was to be signed, Chinese students and workers surrounded the Chinese delegation at their hotel in Paris to stop them from leaving to attend the ceremony. Even though the Chinese delegation in Paris had not yet received President Hsu's new order not to sign, they had already been sent thousands of telegrams from Chinese students and workers in France who opposed the terms of the treaty. Under this intense public pressure, the Chinese delegation took the unusual step of unanimously refusing to sign the treaty as written; Wang seems to have been the most vigorous in opposing the treaty, with Koo joining later.[51] The delegation's decision not to sign the Versailles Treaty later gave these American-trained diplomats enormous prestige, as well as giving them almost a free hand in determining the Peking government's foreign policy.[52] In fact, according to one of Wellington Koo's later biographers: "This Anglo-American group was in control of China's foreign policy for almost the entire span of the Republican governments, be it a warlord government in Peking or the Nationalist Government in Nanking and Taiwan."[53]

On July 28, 1919, the *Peking Daily News* published a letter from the Chinese delegation to the U.S. Senate. This communication was intended to bypass Wilson altogether by calling upon Congress to refuse to ratify the Treaty of Versailles. Even though Wilson had warned China in 1918 that it was her own treaties with Japan that had so complicated the Shantung problem, the Chinese delegation now fully blamed Wilson: "[The] President's counsel finally brought about China's entry into war. On him, as trustee of American honor, China rested hope of settlement enabling her to live untrammeled and unthreatened by Japanese imperialism."[54]

On August 3, 1919, Wilson answered China's accusation. He denied that his compromise solution with Japan was "in any way dependent upon the execution of the agreement of 1915." As for his compromise solution: "Indeed, I felt it my duty to say that nothing that I agreed to must be construed as an acquiescence on the part of the government of the United States in the policy of the notes exchanged between China and Japan in 1915."[55]

As long as China refused to sign the Versailles Peace Treaty, then Japan could not transfer the Shantung concession to China. It was China's own intransigence, therefore, that delayed the ultimate return of this territory to China until 1922. On October 19, 1921, Japan even complained to China about these delays: "[M]ore than twelve months have elapsed since when the Japanese Government invited the Chinese Government to enter into negotiations on this subject."[56] Furthermore, with the failure of the Chinese delegation to take advantage of Wilson's compromise, it became clear that China was determined to make Wilson the scapegoat for her own mismanaged diplomacy with Japan.

The Versailles Treaty and Soviet Russia

Perhaps the greatest historical importance of the Chinese delegation's refusal to sign the Versailles Peace Treaty was that it was brought about, in part at least, because of the huge outpouring of Chinese public disapproval at the terms transferring Germany's former concession to Japan. Although the Chinese delegation's refusal to sign the Versailles Peace Treaty temporarily ended the May Fourth Movement in China, the Chinese anger at the settlement remained. One good example of this was Ch'en Tu-hsiu, later to become the first leader of the Chinese Communist Party, who had initially supported declaring war with the hope that this action would enhance China's world standing. Ch'en saw the terms of the Versailles Peace Treaty as a national humiliation, and his disillusionment was subsequently directed against the Western capitalist countries and Japan, as well as against the Chinese central government in Peking, which was perceived as having failed in its efforts to gain equal treatment for China.[57]

The May Fourth experience turned many Chinese intellectuals against Western democracy. The united action by students, workers, and many other sections of society during 1919 forged a new unity among the Chinese people, which included some of China's most famous intellectuals, such as Ch'en Tu-hsiu, Li Ta, Li Ta-chao, Lu Hsun, and Hu Shih. As a result, following the decision of the Paris Peace Conference, many Chinese intellectuals became more receptive to reports about the Bolsheviks' political, economic, and social reforms, reports that first began to be published in China during the second half of 1919.

To take advantage of the Chinese people's dissatisfaction with Versailles, the embattled Soviet government issued the Karakhan Manifesto during the summer of 1919. In this declaration, the Bolsheviks offered equal treatment to China by promising to abolish all the former unequal treaties between Russia and China. In a widely circulated propaganda pamphlet entitled *China and Soviet Russia,* which reprinted this manifesto in full, a whole chapter was entitled "China and the Lessons of Versailles." It made a harsh comparison between the friendly offers the Soviet government were making to China and the poor treatment China had received at the Paris Peace Conference at the hands of "America, Great Britain, and France." This same pamphlet then went so far as to propose that China should redeem herself through revolution, and offered the Russian proletariat's help in urging "forward and accelerating the beginning of revolutionary movements in the Far East."[58]

As a reaction to public disappointment with Versailles, Arif Dirlik has determined that by 1920, "Chinese publications turn[ed] to the systematic study of the Russian Revolution and its ideology."[59] James Sheridan has also commented on the importance of the Bolsheviks' promises in spurring on Chinese intellectuals and students to oppose foreign interference in China: "Marxism found a sympathetic hearing among the May Fourth youth who had been radicalized by the iconoclasm of the age and by the agitation against the Versailles settlement of the Shantung question. This sympathy was intensified after March 1920, when news reached China that the Soviet Union had unilaterally relinquished all of the privileges of the 'unequal treaties' concluded between China and tsarist Russia. This declaration by the new Russian Communist regime seemed a concrete manifestation of Leninist hostility to imperialism, the most attractive element of the Marxist-Leninist package to anti-imperialistic young Chinese."[60]

It was the Soviet promises of immediate and unconditional equality that made Wilson's efforts at Paris look like a betrayal of China, since suddenly Wilson was being measured by a new standard. But, this new standard proved illusive: for example, as this work will discuss in greater detail below, the author of the Karakhan Manifesto and the Soviet Union's first ambassador to China, Lev Karakhan, later justified Moscow's January 20, 1925 convention with Tokyo, which tacitly redivided control of the Manchurian railways between the USSR and Japan, by accusing the Peking government of ignoring agreements that China had earlier concluded with Japan. Specifically, Karakhan referred to China's 1915 treaty with Japan, the infamous Twenty-one Demands. In the end, the United States remained alone among the major nations in the world by refusing to recognize the Twenty-one Demands' infringements on China's sovereignty and territorial integrity.

Conclusions

Woodrow Wilson succeeded in achieving a compromise solution at Paris in which the most onerous political terms of Japan's 1915 and 1918 agreements with China were circumscribed and whereby Japan agreed to retain only a portion of Germany's former rights in Shantung. The Chinese delegation rejected Wilson's compromise, however, and the subsequent portrayal of Wilson as betraying China convinced many Chinese to turn away from Western democracy and capitalism. Instead, Chinese diplomats and intellectuals early on turned to Soviet Russia in order to try to gain many of the same goals that the Chinese delegation had apparently failed to achieve at Paris.

The Paris Peace Conference's 1919 decision on the Shantung question, and the resulting May Fourth demonstrations that followed in China, marked the first stage in the competition to win over the Chinese people between Western democracy and Soviet-style socialism. If the Versailles Peace Treaty had satisfied the Chinese people at the expense of Japan, then the goal of forming closer links with the Bolsheviks might never have grown into such an important national issue. But, for the world leaders at Paris to have done so would have meant overlooking no fewer than six internationally recognized treaties and thereby would have called into question the Allies' support for the sanctity of treaties. This, Woodrow Wilson refused to do.

Once the terms of the Versailles Peace Treaty convinced China to turn elsewhere in her search for equal treatment, however, the Bolsheviks quickly put themselves in that role by initiating a propaganda campaign aimed at forming closer diplomatic and political ties with China. Soviet Russia's eventual goal was to draw China away from the United States and the other capitalist powers, and to promote a socialist revolution in China. The widely accepted myths that Wilson betrayed China and that the Bolsheviks treated China equally were to play a crucial role in this campaign's later success. It is the debunking of this second myth that will be at the heart of this work and that will be discussed at greater length below.

Notes

1. Maurice Meisner, *Li Ta-chao and the Origins of Chinese Marxism*, 58.

2. Chow Tse-Tsung, *The May 4th Movement: Intellectual Revolution in Modern China*, 89; Immanuel C. Y. Hsu, *The Rise of Modern China*, 505.

3. Robert C. North, *Moscow and the Chinese Communists*, 41.

4. Russell H. Fifield, *Woodrow Wilson and the Far East*, 7.

5. The Japanese Ministry of Foreign Affairs has a total of six large volumes on the Shantung negotiations at Versailles, as well as almost a dozen volumes concerning the Twenty-one Demands, Archives of the Gaikō Shiryōkan (外務省外交史料館), Tokyo (hereafter Gaimushō). Gaimushō, 2.3.1-3.1.

6. Toyokichi Iyenaga, "Iyenaga Decries Shantung Charge," *New York Times,* August 1, 1919.

7. Gaimushō, 2.1.1-32.2.

8. *Ibid.*, 2.1.1-32.3.

9. *Ibid.*

10. *Ibid.*

11. *Ibid.*, 2.1.1-32.2; according to Sir Harold Parlett, Wellington Koo cited China's internal weakness as the main reason that Peking had been coerced into signing Japan's Twenty-one Demands: "History records scarcely another instance in which demands of such a serious character as those which Japan presented to China in 1915, have, without even pretense of provocation, been suddenly presented by one nation to another nation with which it was at the time in friendly relations" (*A Brief Account of Diplomatic Events in Manchuria*, 87-88).

12. Ray Stannard Baker, *Woodrow Wilson and World Settlement*, Vol. 1, 59-62; Vol. 2, 244.

13. Hsu, 502.

14. Chow, 187.

15. Chu Pao-chin, *V. K. Wellington Koo: A Case Study of China's Diplomat and Diplomacy of Nationalism*, 15; The Paris Peace Conference decided not to discuss these points, but hoped instead that the League of Nations would address them once it was formed. Instead, many of these issues were discussed at the 1921-22 Washington Conference.

16. Ku Wei-chun, better known simply as Wellington Koo, received his B.A., M.A., and Ph.D. from Columbia University. After the Paris Peace Conference, Koo was appointed China's representative to the Washington Conference. During the months from September until December 1922, he then held the post of foreign minister when Adolf Joffe, the first fully empowered Soviet representative to China, was in Peking. Finally, Koo was

reappointed minister of foreign affairs from April 1923 all the way through September 15, 1924, during which time he worked closely with Lev Karakhan to sign the May 31, 1924 treaty opening official relations between China and the Soviet Union. *The China Yearbook* 1925-26 "Who's Who," 1248.

17. Russell H. Fifield interviewed Wellington Koo on October 31, 1951, and discovered that when Koo talked to Wilson in late 1918, neither was cognizant of Peking's secret agreement with Tokyo, signed only months before. Furthermore, the acting foreign minister in Peking openly expressed his wish that the 1918 secret agreement had never become known. Fifield, 145, 187.

18. Chu, 16-17.

19. Roy Watson Curry, *Woodrow Wilson and Far Eastern Policy 1913-1921*, 268- 70.

20. Gaimushō, 2.3.1-3.4.

21. *Ibid.*

22. *Ibid.*

23. *Ibid.*

24. *Ibid.*, 2.3.1-3.6.

25. *Ibid.*, 2.3.1-3.1.

26. Japan's four points were listed in a letter written by the American Chamber of Commerce in China to the American government; reprinted in the March 21, 1919 *Peking Leader*, in the article "Is Japan's Promise to Return Kiaochow Camouflage?" The president of the American Chamber of Commerce in China was J. Harold Dollar, of the Robert Dollar Company; the Vice-President was W. C. Sprague, of the Standard Oil Company; and the Treasurer was J. W. Gallagher, of the U.S. Steel Products Company; Gaimushō, 2.3.1-3.1.

27. *Ibid.*

28. *Ibid.*

29. *Ibid.*, 2.3.1-3.4.

30. *Ibid.*

31. *Ibid.*

32. *Ibid.*, 2.3.1-3.1.

33. *Ibid.*

34. *Ibid.*, 2.3.1-3.2.

35. Curry, 279.

36. Baker, Vol. 1, 30; the Paris Peace Conference's opposite decisions on Fiume and Shantung have often been portrayed as signs of indecisiveness. In fact, Italy was not ceded the city of Fiume because the Yugoslavs had received assurances at the beginning of World War I that it would be returned to them; likewise, Japan had received similar promises regarding the Shantung concession.

37. Baker, Vol. 2, 266.

38. Curry, 280.

39. *The Treaty of Versailles and After*, 287-88.

40. Gaimushō, 2.3.1-3.1.

41. "Communication from M. Lou Tseng-tsiang, protesting for the Chinese Delegation against the proposed settlement of the Kiaochow-Shantung question," May 4, 1919, Stanley K. Hornbeck Papers, Hoover Institution Archives, Box 383; stamped "Secret" and then "Declassified."

42. *Ibid.*

43. Toyokichi Iyenaga; misrepresentations of the Shantung solution were commonplace, with the Hearst papers running headlines: "SOLD 40,000,000 People" (Thomas A. Bailey, *Wilson and the Peacemakers*, 283).

44. For a better understanding of how this concept of "face" influenced Chinese politics in the 1920s, see: Andrew J. Nathan, *Peking Politics, 1918-1923: Factionalism an the Failure of Constitutionalism*; and S. C. M. Paine, *Imperial Rivals: China, Russia, and Their Disputed Frontier*, 54-57.

45. History texts published in Taiwan as late as the 1950s still used this derogatory term. Wu Hsiang-hsiang (吳相湘). 俄帝侵略中國史 (*History of Imperial Russia's Aggression in China*).

46. From a speech given by Sun Yat-sen on November 28, 1924, at the Oriental Hotel in Kobe. As reprinted in Sun Yat-sen, *The Vital Problem of China*, 161.

47. The opinion of one observer at Paris is particularly relevant: "Perhaps the greatest shortcoming of the Peace Conference was the inability or unwillingness–it was both–of the chief conferees to dramatize their day's work; to take the publics of the world along with them as they met their problems, and to explain clearly why they were forced to make the decisions they did. No one person can be blamed for this condition, and no one person, at this stage of development in world relations, could have much changed it; but the fact remains that each important decision made by the conferees, and presented baldly, without its background or proper setting, came to the world with a kind of shock." Ray Stannard Baker, "How Japan Forced Shantung Clause," (*New York Times,* August 17, 1919).

48. Chow, 113-114.

49. Wang Shih-han, "May 4th Movement," *China Reconstructs,* 64.

50. C. T. Wang studied law at Yale University. Afterward, he became a delegate to the Paris Peace Conference on behalf of the Kuomintang government in South China. In March 1922, Wang became the Chinese commissioner for the settlement of the Shantung question, overseeing the return of Shantung from Japan to China. Afterward, Wang was named the director-general of the Commission for Sino-Russian Affairs in March 1923, a position that put him in almost daily contact with the Soviet diplomats until March 1924, when Koo took over the negotiations. After acting as foreign minister in the fall 1924, Wang was once more appointed director-general in charge of Sino-Russian Affairs to negotiate new treaties with the Soviet Union. Wang then became the foreign minister of the Kuomintang's unified Chinese government in 1928. (*The China Yearbook* 1925-26, "Who's Who," 1282a).

51. Chow, 165-66; See footnote w, where Chow discounts a later claim by Koo that Wang was originally willing to sign the treaty.

52. In the midst of the constant cabinet changes that the Peking government went through between 1912 and 1928, there were forty-five changes in the Peking government's cabinet but only nineteen changes of foreign ministers (Nathan, 67).

53. Chu, 2.

54. Gaimushō, 2.3.1-3.3.

55. *Ibid.,* 2.3.1-3.3.

56. *Ibid.,* 2.3.1-3.6.

57. Lee Feigon, *Chen Duxiu Founder of the Chinese Communist Party,* 105, 110; Joseph R. Levenson has discussed how Liang Ch'i-ch'ao also supported World War I, and

how the war, "which so profoundly shook the West's belief in its own traditional values, came as a godsend to those Chinese who had been reluctantly reexamining the Chinese values" (*Liang Chi'i-ch'ao and the the Mind of Modern China,* 153).

58. Vladimir Dmitrievich Vilenskii-Sibiriakov (Владимир Дмитриевиц Виленский-Сибиряков), *Китай и Советская Россия* (*China and Soviet Russia*), 3, 12.

59. Arif Dirlik, *The Origins of Chinese Communism,* 41.

60. James E. Sheridan, *China in Disintegration: The Republican Era in Chinese History, 1912-1949,* 142.

1
The Opening of Sino-Soviet Diplomatic Negotiations

The Soviet government's diplomatic isolation and military weakness in the years following the October Revolution forced it to rely heavily on propaganda and diplomatic maneuvering to achieve its foreign policy goals: a prime example of this was Soviet Russia's determined efforts to establish formal diplomatic relations with China between 1917 and 1924. Beginning in early 1918 the Soviet government repeatedly denounced secret diplomacy, condemned the imperialist powers' poor treatment of China, and promised to treat China as an equal. The Bolsheviks' real aspirations were quickly revealed to Chinese officials once Sino-Soviet negotiations began, however, as Soviet officials emphatically denied that any such promises had ever been made.

A study of Soviet Russia's earliest attempts to open Sino-Soviet diplomatic negotiations reveals the Soviet government's treatment of China was disingenuous from the very beginning. Contrary to Bolshevik protestations that the Siberian-based Far Eastern Republic (FER) was an independent entity, the Bolshevik leader Leon Trotsky personally ordered its formation on February 18, 1920, in order to allow this buffer state to open diplomatic negotiations with the nations of the Far East. Thereafter, the FER became Moscow's secret proxy to secure China's diplomatic recognition, thereby breaking Soviet Russia out of its political isolation in the Far East.

The FER's first hurtle was to open its own diplomatic negotiations with the Peking government. To facilitate this action, the FER denied any connection with the Bolshevik government in Moscow and insisted that it was an elected democratic government. International reaction to the FER was mixed: while White Russians–Russians who had fled Soviet Russia and continued to oppose the Bolsheviks–warned that it was a trick, Paul S. Reinsch, the American minister to China, openly favored the Peking government establishing diplomatic relations with the FER.[1] When the FER's foreign ministry sent its own mission to Peking, under the leadership of Ignatii L. Iurin, to negotiate directly with the Chinese government, Moscow succeeded in using Washington's support for the FER to circumvent Allied efforts to isolate the Bolshevik regime.[2]

An important part of Iurin's mission to Peking was to convince the Chinese Ministry of Foreign Affairs officials that he was working solely for the best interests of the FER, and that Moscow's views were important only so far as they affected his own government's attempts to secure its borders and open trade with its neighbors. That Iurin succeeded in keeping his links with Moscow secret is best shown by the constant questioning he underwent at the hands of these Chinese officials, who at almost every meeting grilled him about the exact nature of the FER's relations with Moscow.[3]

During the next two and a half years Iurin carried out talks with the Chinese Ministry of Foreign Affairs, ostensibly to sign a commercial treaty, but in fact he consistently worked to further Soviet diplomatic interests. By the end of 1921 he had convinced the Peking government to allow a Soviet mission into China on terms of equality. This was a decisive diplomatic victory for the Bolsheviks at a time when their diplomatic successes in Asia were few and far between.

An unforeseen result of the secrecy that surrounded Iurin's mission has been that historians have previously overlooked his important role in the establishment of Sino-Soviet diplomatic relations. Mainly because Iurin's commercial negotiations with Peking were never completed prior to Soviet Russia's absorption of the FER in the fall of 1922, historians have generally dismissed Iurin's mission to China. One criticized Iurin for serving merely as a negative example to later Soviet negotiators.[4] Another, while giving Iurin due credit for "paving the way for the Soviet mission," also characterized Iurin's mission as a failure.[5] These negative assessments of Iurin's mission are in fact the highest tributes, albeit unintended tributes, to Iurin's abilities as Soviet Russia's first secret representative in China.

The Karakhan Manifesto

On July 25, 1919, only a month after the end of the May Fourth Movement, the Soviet government's Assistant People's Commissar of Foreign Affairs Lev Karakhan issued a manifesto addressed to the Peking government and the Chinese people. This manifesto promised to abolish all of tsarist Russia's so-called unequal treaties, abandon all Russian territorial concessions, eliminate extraterritoriality, and cancel Russia's share of the Boxer Indemnity. Most important, it promised to return the Chinese Eastern Railway (CER) without compensation.

The Karakhan Manifesto was clearly an attempt to capitalize on the May Fourth Movement: even the order of the Soviet promises matched China's proposals at the Paris Peace Conference, divided into: 1) territorial integrity, 2) preservation of sovereign rights, and 3) economic and fiscal independence. As such, the Karakhan Manifesto appeared to fulfill willingly all the requests that China had just had rejected by the Paris Peace Conference.

The Karakhan Manifesto's most valuable promise was to return the CER to China free of charge (see Document 3). It stated: "The Soviet government restores to the Chinese people without exacting any kind of compensation, the CER, as well as all concessions of minerals, forests, gold, and others that were seized from them by the government of Tsars, the government of Kerensky, and the brigands Horvath, Semenov, Kolchak, the former generals, merchants, and capitalists of Russia." Karakhan ended his manifesto with a warning to China that its only "allies and brothers" in the struggle for liberty from imperialism were the "Russian worker and peasant and the Red Army of Russia."[6]

THE CHINESE TELEGRAPH ADMINISTRATION

TELEGRAMS FOR ALL TELEGRAPH STATIONS IN THE WORLD

JOURNAL No. 2068

PEKING STATION.

REMARKS

1 0

TELEGRAM No. 55/05   Class   Words.

Station from:

GOUVERNEMENT QU ELLES VOUDRONT ADOPTER CHEZ ELLES.

ALINEA. LE GOUVERNEMENT DES SOVIETS RESTITUE AU

PEUPLE CHINOIS SANS EXIGER AUCUNE ESPECE DE

COMPENSATION VIRGULE LE CHEMIN DE FER CHINOIS

DE L EST, VIRGULE AINSI QUE TOUTES LES

CONCESSIONS MINIERES, VIRGULE FORESTIERES, VIRGULE

AURIFERE, ET AUTRES QUI LUI FURENT ARRACHEES

PAR LE GOUVERNEMENT DES TZARS, VIRGULE LE

GOUVERNEMENT KERENSKY ET LES BRIGANDS KHORVAT,

VIRGULE SEMENOFF, VIRGULE KOLTCHAK, VIRGULE LES EX-

GENERAUX, VIRGULE LES NEGOCIANTS ET LES CAPITALI-

STES RUSSES, ALINEA LE GOUVERNEMENT DES SOVIETS

RENONCE A LA CONTRIBUTION DUE PAR LA CHINEE

POUR L INSURRECTION DES BOXEURS DE 1900. POINT

IL SE VOIT

Document 3
The Karakhan Manifesto's Promise on the CER

The Karakhan Manifesto was not only an attempt to obtain the Chinese people's sympathy for the diplomatically isolated Soviet state, but it was also the first step in opening diplomatic negotiations with the Peking government. The later controversy between the Soviet Union and China over the Karakhan Manifesto revolved around the fact that when this July 25, 1919 document was published in the Soviet press under the title "Обращение Советская России к Китаю" ("Appeal from Soviet Russia to China"), the August 26, 1919 *Izvestiia* edition did not contain the crucial sentence about returning the CER without compensation; Soviet diplomats later used this second version initially to demand payment for the CER, and then to refuse to return the railway to China altogether.

But, in addition to the original Soviet telegram, a 1919 pamphlet published under the name of a Bolshevik Foreign Ministry official, Vladimir Vilenskii, confirmed that the original version of the Karakhan Manifesto's promise to return the CER free of charge.[7] A third published document from the April 24, 1921 *Bulletin of the Far Eastern Secretariat of the Comintern* also conforms to these other two sources, stating: "The Soviet government renounces all mining and lumber concessions in Manchuria, and returns to China without compensation the Chinese Eastern Railway and everything that was forcibly seized by the tsarist government, the brigands Kolchak and Semenov and the Russian bourgeoisie."[8]

These three sources–the original telegram, the Vilenskii pamphlet, and the version published in the Communist International's Siberian journal in 1921–are convincing proof that Soviet Russia did initially offer to return the CER to China without compensation. Scholars have argued about the authenticity of the two versions of the Karakhan Manifesto ever since Allen Whiting pointed out this discrepancy, which he explained by examining the Soviet military situation during 1919. In the early part of July, Whiting claimed, it looked as if the Red Army would not be able to take back the CER, while by the middle of August, the Red Army had succeeded in defeating most of the White forces.[9]

Whiting's interpretation was that the second version of the Karakhan Manifesto merely took this new situation into account as "responsible officials realized that regaining a foothold in the Far East was now an actual possibility, to be treated more cautiously than in so sweeping a renunciation of the highly strategic railroad."[10] Whiting's conclusions, however, do not explain why the original Karakhan Manifesto continued to be used to support Soviet Russia's propaganda efforts in China long after August 1919, as shown by its appearance in the Communist International's Siberian journal as late as 1921.

Sow-theng Leong's work on Sino-Soviet relations repeats much of Whiting's argument, but he concludes that Soviet foreign policy makers were divided into two camps–the "realists" and the "idealists"–and that it was the "idealists" who decided to make the offer to return the CER to China without compensation. Their goal was to cement an alliance with China by returning "the most concrete symbol of tsarist aggression." According to Leong, these "idealists" believed that "an alliance with 'revolutionary China' was worth any price," while the "realists" later decided to retain title over the CER.[11] Although this explanation is worth considering, Leong does not identify who the "idealists" and the "realists" were, nor does he document how or why two conflicting copies of the Karakhan Manifesto were circulated and continued to be circulated through 1921.

While both Whiting and Leong have presented complex theories to explain the two versions of the Karakhan Manifesto, there is a much more simple explanation. That there were two versions of the Karakhan Manifesto cannot be questioned. That the Soviet government repeatedly presented the more liberal manifesto to the Chinese government and populace between 1919 and 1921, and then the less generous manifesto after 1921, also cannot be denied. This suggests that the Soviet government made two versions of the Karakhan Manifesto on purpose–one to satisfy its propaganda requirements and the other to satisfy its diplomatic requirements–and then proceeded to pick and choose the manifesto that best suited its purposes.

The primary reason for promising to return the CER to China was to provide Soviet officials–in this case, Ignatii Iurin–with potent bait to lure the Peking government into quickly opening diplomatic negotiations with Soviet Russia, a goal that was achieved in 1921. But, in addition, the Soviet government's generous promises helped attract Chinese intellectuals to Marxism-Leninism. This resulted in the organization of the Chinese Communist Party during 1921, and the formation of the United Front Policy with Sun Yat-sen's Kuomintang party in 1923. Once the Soviet government achieved these goals, the second version of the Karakhan Manifesto, which did not include the promise to return the CER, took the place of the original. This second version then became a stepping-stone to regaining majority control over this important railway line.

The Bolsheviks and the Open Door Policy

Perhaps no other American foreign policy has been vilified and condemned as much as the Open Door Policy in China. During the cold war, for example, it was widely accused of supporting American "economic imperialism," as one historian asserted that by means of the Open Door, the United States "could pose as the savior of China while advancing its own economic and cultural interests."[12] A second portrayed this policy as merely an attempt "to secure supremacy in Manchuria through economic penetration."[13] Finally, a third critic stated that the Open Door was simply a "viable alternative to imperialism," as it evolved from "a diplomatic tactic to its place as holy writ in the shrine of American foreign policy."[14]

These historical criticisms must be reconsidered in light of new evidence showing the important role the Open Door Policy played in protecting China's territorial integrity from Soviet expansionism. This evidence shows that while the Soviet government secretly relied on the Open Door Policy to halt Japanese expansion into Siberia, Soviet propaganda promoting Soviet Russia's expansion into China publicly condemned the Open Door as being merely a tool of American "economic imperialism." This dual policy suggests that the Bolsheviks were cognizant of the territorial guarantees that this policy provided for China. Moscow clearly hoped that by eliminating the very protection for China that it sought for itself in Siberia, Soviet Russia could increase its influence in China. This Soviet policy proved to be enormously successful.

It should be recalled that the Open Door Policy was created, in part at least, to oppose tsarist Russian expansion in Asia. During the nineteenth century, the Far East was seen as Russia's best chance for territorial expansion. During 1858-60, for example, Russia annexed the Amur region, the Maritime province, and large parts of Sinkiang.[15] The Russia government's territorial appetite was not satisfied, however, for it stated in 1862: "[I]n the event of the fall of the Empire of the Manchus our activities must be so aimed as to enable the formation of an independent domain . . . in Mongolia and Manchuria."[16]

An opportunity to carry out this expansionist policy appeared in 1896, when Russia resorted to bribery to gain permission for the construction of the Chinese Eastern Railway in northern Manchuria, giving the Russians control of over a quarter of a million acres of land–the largest foreign concession in China.[17] The CER was also one of the largest foreign-run railways in China, accounting for almost 45 percent of all such railways in the early 1920s. As a result of the CER, tsarist Russia was arguably the greatest imperialist power in China.[18]

Historians have argued that the United States, which did not have any railway or territorial concessions in China, created the Open Door Policy to halt further Russian expansion.[19] Secretary of State John Hay proposed this policy in 1899 in order to preserve China's territorial and administrative unity. One account has explained the Open Door's immediate impact: "The 'open-door' is one of the most creditable episodes in American diplomacy, an example of benevolent impulse accompanied by energy and shrewd skill in negotiation. Not one of the statesmen and nations that agreed to Hay's policy wanted to. It was like asking every man who believes in truth to stand up–the liars are obliged to be the first to rise. Hay saw through them perfectly; his insight into human nature was one of his strongest qualities."[20] Unfortunately, the most that America could do was exert subtle diplomatic pressure, since there were no sanctions for countries that continued to try to undermine China's territorial integrity.

Russia's effort to expand into Manchuria led to war with Japan. After Russia's defeat in 1905, Washington offered its services to negotiate a peace treaty. By means of the 1905 Portsmouth Treaty, Russia was persuaded to declare that it did not have "in Manchuria any territorial advantages or preferential or exclusive concessions in impairment of Chinese sovereignty or inconsistent with the principle of equal opportunity."[21] But this treaty also reaffirmed that Russia retained control over the Chinese Eastern Railway, while Japan acquired the South Manchurian Railway. In practical terms, therefore, Manchuria remained divided into competing Russian and Japanese spheres of influence.

Ignoring all attempts by the United States to enforce the Open Door Policy, Russia and Japan partitioned northern China, even signing a series of four secret agreements between 1907 and 1916 to delimit their respective spheres of influence.[22] When the 1911 revolution divided and weakened China, Russia used this opportunity in 1915 to negotiate a tripartite treaty with China and Outer Mongolia, by which Outer Mongolia became a Russian protectorate.[23] Japan carried out similar policies in southern Manchuria and Inner Mongolia, presenting China with Twenty-one Demands during 1915 that ceded to Japan a long list of territorial and economic rights. As discussed above, the United States immediately protested Japan's actions, condemning the Twenty-one Demands as a violation of the political and territorial integrity of the Republic of China.

From 1899 to 1917, the United States attempted to protect China's territorial integrity by enforcing the Open Door Policy. Although not entirely successful, this policy did help keep Outer Mongolia and Manchuria from being openly annexed by Russia and Japan. Following the 1917 October Revolution, the Bolsheviks actively lobbied Washington for help in stopping Japan's expansion into Siberia, and the United States provided this help under the auspices of the Open Door Policy. Woodrow Wilson's fourteen points included special support for the Open Door Policy in Russia, since he proposed that Russia should be given "an unhampered and unembarrassed opportunity for the independent determination of her own political development and national policy."[24] This proposal was so attractive to the Bolsheviks that they ordered 3,463,000 copies of the fourteen points to be printed and distributed.[25]

The Bolsheviks' decision to turn to Washington for territorial protection meant that the Open Door Policy continued to be a primary barrier protecting Soviet Russia's territorial integrity in the Far East from 1918 through 1920. Although the Bolsheviks were not able to convince Washington to open diplomatic relations, they did use American support for the Open Door to oppose Japan's military intervention in Siberia. On January 31, 1918, Leon Trotsky suggested to the Acting Commissar for Foreign Affairs, Grigorii Chicherin, that he should warn Japan that its actions would "have a harmful effect not only on the interests of Russia, but on the interests of other countries, in particular and especially,–the United States." Since the United States had no territorial interests in Siberia, the only interests Trotsky could be referring to would be the Open Door Policy. Trotsky suggested that a copy of this note should also be sent to the American embassy, ordering Chicherin: "Prepare a draft of this note, discuss it with Lenin."[26]

On March 5, Trotsky contacted the American representative in Russia to ask what kind of action the United States would be willing to take to stop Japan's invasion of Eastern Siberia: "Should Japan–in consequence of an open or tacit understanding with Germany or without such an understanding–attempt to seize Vladivostok and the Eastern-Siberian Railway, which would threaten to cut off Russia from the Pacific Ocean and would greatly impede the concentration of Soviet troops toward the East about the Urals–in such case what steps would be taken by the other allies, particularly and especially by the United States, to prevent a Japanese landing on our Far East and to insure uninterrupted communications with Russia through the Siberian route?"[27]

What is less well known, however, is that Trotsky invited the United States to oppose Japan in Siberia on March 8 (see Document 4). The American consul in Petrograd telegraphed President Wilson and reported that: "Trotsky desires Allied assistance, especially American. He believes Japan has taken steps in Vladivostok and Siberia to seize and control railway and territory."[28] Even more important, on March 10, 1918, a second, more urgent, telegram from Russia asked President Wilson to take control of the trans-Siberian railway, to ensure that it did not fall into Japanese hands. According to the text of this telegram: "Trotsky furthermore asserted that neither his government nor Russian people would object to America supervising all shipments from Vladivostok into Russia and virtually controlling operation of Siberian railway, but Japanese invasion would result in non-resistance and eventually make Russia a German province."[29]

Trotsky's request for American assistance was granted: when Japan deployed several gunboats and an army of 75,000 men to Siberia, Wilson responded by ordering a small contingent of American troops to Vladivostok in order to "thwart" Japan's "imperialist designs."[30] Wilson's good intentions were shown in a July 17, 1918 *aide-memoire*, which listed three reasons for American intervention in Siberia, none of them having to do with overthrowing the Bolsheviks: 1) "to guard military stores," 2) "to render such aid as may be acceptable to the Russians in the organization of their own self-defense," and 3) to help Czechoslovakian troops trapped in Siberia "to consolidate their forces."[31] One historian of the American intervention observed: "Wilson's justification for this policy was his belief that it preserved the Open Door in Siberia and Manchuria, preserved Russia's territorial integrity, and aided him in establishing his League of Nations."[32]

That America's support for the Open Door Policy in Siberia actually protected the besieged Soviet state was later shown in a secret communique, dated August 5, 1919, in which Trotsky informed the Central Committee that only the United States had kept Japan in check: "[T]he favorable conditions for our advance into Siberia were made for us by the antagonism of Japan and the United States." Trotsky further noted that Soviet Russia could rely on the continued "direct support of the Washington rascals to oppose Japan."[33] Thereafter, on January 13, 1920, Trotsky ordered the chairman of the Siberian Revolutionary Committee to contact the American representative and convince him that Japan's absorption of Siberian territories had driven the local populations to "rebellion, military action, and chaos," all of which ran counter to America's interests.[34]

During 1933, when Cordell Hull was conducting negotiations with Foreign Minister Maxim Litvinov to open Soviet-American relations, Hull described how the USSR acknowledged America's assistance in halting Japan's aggression: "A statement by Litvinov waiving any claims arising out of the activities of United States military forces in Siberia subsequent to January 1, 1918, following his examination of certain documents of the years 1918 to 1921. These latter documents made clear to Litvinov that American forces had not been in Siberia to wrest territory from Russia, but to ensure the withdrawal of the Japanese, who had a far larger force in Siberia with the intent to occupy it permanently."[35]

Petrograd,
March 8, 1918.
Recd. March 10, 2 p. m.

c o d e
Warcblstaff,

Washington.
Service No. 403
No. 244, March 8, 5 p. m.

In compliance with written instructions from ambassador, Riggs and myself
had interview with Trotzky today. He and the majority of Bolsheviks now seem
convinced that peace, even if treaty be ratified at Moscow, cannot be permanent
because of German terms with the Ukraina which provide for exports to Austria-
Hungary, Germany, of all our lus grain and other food supplies, leaving Russia to
starve. The Soviet troops still in state of war with Germany, offering resistance
in, Ukraina, with considerable numbers preparing to retake Kiev with fair prospect
of success.

Trotzky desires Allied assistance, especially American. He believes Japan has
taken steps in Vladivostok and Siberia to seize and control railroad and territory
or is about to take such action, either in understanding with Germany or with
some of the Allies. He is also apprehensive of British or French action at Mur-
mansk and Archangel. There is now a fair chance that Russia will offer considerable
resistance to Germany and any such action as outlined above should be postponed,
as effect would be bad and destroy all hope of any Russian resistance to Germany
by the Bolsheviks, the only element in Russia with power to organize an effective
resistance. Trotzky now willing to reorganize army under rigid discipline, recalling Russian Government officers and best class of Russian people but believes of first importance that United States take the necessary steps to prevent
action by Japan or other Allies at this critical time.

I most strongly concur in this and desire impress upon American authorities
most emphatically that ratifications of Germany treaty of peace at Moscow, does
not necessarily put Russia finally out of the war. It is still possible and
regarded by the Bolsheviks as inevitable that hostilities on a certain scale
will soon commence. I am to have an interview this evening with General
Bonch Bruevially head of special staff and real source of Bolshevik military
authority. Krylenko actual nominal commander-in-chief but shorn of real
power.

Pershing cabled as above.

Document 4
Leon Trotsky's Request for American Intervention in Siberia

America's Open Door Policy was crucial to the Bolshevik successful campaign to retake control of Siberia. Without American opposition, Japan might have succeeded in annexing much of eastern Siberia. The USSR's 1933 decision to drop all financial claims against the United States for the Siberian intervention was a final admission that the Bolsheviks had indeed turned to Washington for support under the Open Door Policy. In addition, the Soviet-supported Far Eastern Republic also petitioned the United States for protection.

The FER and the Open Door Policy

There is no better proof of the Bolsheviks' dual policy with regard to the Open Door than the role the FER played in conducting secret diplomatic negotiations with China. Although the FER was created mainly as a buffer state between the Red Army and the Japanese occupation forces in Siberia, it was also the diplomatic intermediary between the Bolsheviks and various East Asian governments. In this role, the FER supported the Open Door Policy, a fact that has only recently become apparent with the increasing accessibility of Asian archives. Through the medium of the FER, therefore, the Bolsheviks continued to rely on the Open Door Policy to protect their Siberian borders from 1920 to 1922, long after Soviet propaganda had condemned this policy in China.

When American troops began to withdraw from Siberia in early 1920, the Bolsheviks feared that the Red Army would come into direct conflict with the Japanese troops. On February 18, 1920, therefore, Trotsky ordered the formation of the Far Eastern Republic to act as a buffer: "The conflict between our regular troops and the Japanese will be used by them for rabid jingoistic propaganda and will give superiority to those who want to further deploy occupation forces. It is necessary to hasten the formation of a buffer so that military and diplomatic negotiations to the East of Baikal will proceed under the banner of this buffer state."[36] The following day, Lenin ordered all Bolsheviks to "revile the opponents of a buffer state," and proclaimed: "Not a single step further in Siberia."[37]

On April 6, only a week after the final American troop departure from Vladivostok, A. Krasnoshchekov, a lawyer educated in Chicago, became the prime minister of the "Independent Democratic Far Eastern Republic." On April 18, 1920, Chicherin affirmed: "It is understood, of course, that the majority of the population of this new state tends to lean towards Russia, and Russia will therefore extend her influence over it in the future, just as she is doing at present. However, we are prepared to recognize the autonomy of this state."[38]

Although Moscow officially recognized the FER, Lenin reportedly sent the following secret instructions on August 13: "The bourgeois-democratic character of the buffer is purely formal. . . . The Central Committee [of the Communist party in Moscow] will direct the policy of the Far Eastern Republic through a Bureau for the Far East whose members will be appointed from Moscow and which will be directly subordinate to the Central Committee of the party."[39] On July 16, 1920, the FER achieved one of its most important goals, when it reached an agreement with Japan defining temporary borders throughout Siberia.[40] The public subterfuge that the FER was an independent country was enhanced even more when Moscow signed official treaties with the FER on November 30, securing railway and navigation rights, and on December 15, 1920, establishing mutual borders.[41]

Since Moscow's control over the FER was kept completely secret, however, Washington also supported its creation.[42] The FER's repeated appeals to Washington for help eventually bore fruit and during May 1921, an official note to Japan stated that the United States could "neither now nor hereafter recognize as valid any claims or titles arising out of a present Japanese occupation or control, that it cannot acquiesce in any action taken by the government of Japan which might impair existing treaty rights or the political or territorial integrity of Russia."[43] Washington also sent Consul John K. Caldwell to the FER and urged "upon the government of Japan, in the most earnest and friendly manner, that all remaining troops be unconditionally withdrawn from all Russian territory."[44]

On September 20, 1921, Washington went even further by releasing an official statement upholding Russia's territorial integrity. This statement warned that: "The powers soon to send their envoys to Washington are virtually put on notice by this declaration that they are expected to cooperate in safeguarding the integrity of Russian territory in the Far East and along the Pacific." Thus, as reported by *The Washington Post*, the Open Door Policy was clearly being used to protect Russian interests, as "the United States, through Secretary [Charles] Hughes' brief but all-important declaration, proceeds upon the assumption that all the powers will respect the integrity of Russia as well as the integrity of China."[45]

The FER also carried out secret negotiations directly with Japan and China during 1921 and 1922 in which it claimed to support the Open Door Policy. The Japanese Ministry of Foreign Affairs archives in Tokyo, for example, show that the FER actively embraced the Open Door Policy in its diplomatic negotiations with Japan: on August 27, 1921, Ignatii Iurin told the Japanese representative that the FER "hopes to adopt the Open Door's equal opportunity policy in Eastern Siberia."[46] Furthermore, on April 21, 1922, the FER presented a twenty-nine point plan to open diplomatic relations with Japan, and the twentieth point agreed to "recognize the principle of the Open Door" policy.[47]

The Peking government's Foreign Ministry archives in Taipei, Taiwan, also contains evidence that Iurin used similar tactics in his negotiations with China during the spring of 1921. Although Iurin was careful not to use the word "Open Door," since Soviet propaganda had already denounced this policy in China, he presented Peking with a draft treaty of "Friendship and Commerce between the Far Eastern Republic and the Republic of China" that called for mutual relations based on: "Liberty of trade, sea and river navigation."[48] Since supporting free trade was tantamount to supporting the Open Door Policy, Iurin clearly also based his negotiations with China on this policy.

From the spring of 1920 through the winter of 1922, therefore, when the FER formally united with the USSR, the Soviet strategy of creating a Siberian buffer state and relying on the Open Door Policy to protect it worked perfectly. In response to diplomatic pressure from Washington, Tokyo pulled the final Japanese troops out of Siberia during the fall 1922. During this period the United States also sent an official envoy to the FER, promoted trade links, and even invited three nonvoting FER delegates to attend the 1921-22 Washington Conference. Finally, and most important, even while the Soviet-funded Comintern criticized the Open Door Policy in China as promoting America's economic imperialism, diplomats from the Soviet-controlled FER secretly advocated the Open Door Policy during their negotiations with both Japan and China.

Ignatii Iurin's Mission to Peking

Soon after the formation of the FER in March 1920, its Ministry of Foreign Affairs sent a telegram to the Chinese foreign minister that suggested opening "friendly political and economic relations . . . to prepare the ground for an acceptable solution of the Far Eastern and Russian problems."[49] But, in direct opposition to Soviet Russia's offer to return the CER to China, as expressed in the Karakhan Manifesto, the FER government in Verkhne Udinsk (later in Chita) asserted its sovereignty over the "territories of Transbaikal, Amur, Primorskaia, Sakalin, Kamtchatka and the right of way of the Chinese Eastern Railway."[50]

On June 12, 1920, Ignatii L. Iurin, in the position of chief of the FER's diplomatic mission to China, arrived at the Siberian border city of Kiakhta and sent a telegram to the Chinese Republic's minister of foreign affairs, stating: "This mission is going to Peking, having a commission given by our government, to acquaint your government with the aim and objects of our Republic and to establish close and friendly relations between both republics."[51] Iurin's request for permission to travel to Peking initially fell on deaf ears, however, as did a second telegram of June 24 from the FER's Ministry of Foreign Affairs, because the Peking government was concerned about antagonizing nations that continued to oppose the Bolshevik regime.[52]

But once a Chinese fact-finding mission to Siberia gave a favorable report of the FER, the Peking government decided to allow Iurin into China, as long as he came as an unofficial representative and changed his title so that he was the head of a commercial, not a diplomatic, mission.[53] This decision was communicated to Iurin on July 21, and on July 26 another telegram from the FER certified that Iurin was now the chief of this "Commercial" Mission.[54] This change in status satisfied the Chinese government, and an internal note from August 25 reported Iurin's arrival in Peking. Thus, only six months after Trotsky ordered the formation of the FER, the first Bolshevik representative had already arrived in Peking and begun to promote closer Sino-Soviet ties.

In a meeting between Iurin and the officials from the Ministry of Foreign Affairs on September 10, Iurin's credentials were examined and were found to be inadequate. Although the FER government in Chita had issued Iurin his credentials, the Peking government wanted Iurin to present written confirmation that the other Siberian provisional governments, and especially the independent government in Vladivostok, also agreed to his appointment. But this did not mean that the Ministry of Foreign Affairs was not eager to open negotiations with Iurin. A September 2 meeting of the "Committee for the Study of Russian Treaties" reported that the Peking government was looking forward to discussing in more detail the "rights and interests" that the Soviet government had renounced in the Karakhan Manifesto.[55]

In an attempt to assuage continued international concern about the Peking government opening relations with the FER, the Chinese Ministry of Foreign Affairs published a statement on September 17, announcing that Iurin would be asked to make certain guarantees, including a promise not to support "Bolshevik propaganda in China."[56] Meanwhile, an internal memo dated September 18, listed two additional preconditions: 1) the FER had to repay Chinese living in the FER's territory for their financial losses following the Bolshevik revolution, and had to guarantee their safety and property in the future; and 2) the FER had to agree that "all unequal treaties signed by the tsarist imperialist government and China should be changed or annulled."[57]

The Second Karakhan Manifesto

While Iurin was waiting for the other Siberian provisional governments to send him authorization to negotiate on their behalf, the Peking government took the controversial step of suspending all Russian rights and of ordering all diplomatic and consular representatives of the former Kerensky Provisional government to leave China. Since this action threatened the extraterritoriality and concession rights of all foreigners in China, most of the foreign ministries in Peking protested this action and many accused Peking of trying to take advantage of the Karakhan Manifesto by opening diplomatic relations with the Bolsheviks, a charge that Wellington Koo energetically rejected in his post as minister plenipotentiary to the United States.[58] Peking also denied accusations that its actions coincided with Iurin's arrival in China.[59]

The real reason behind the Peking government's decision was clarified in an October 1 telegram sent by the foreign minister, Yen Hui-ch'ing (better known as W. W. Yen), to Chinese officials in Mukden, Kirin, the Amur, and along the Chinese Eastern Railroad. In this telegram Yen reaffirmed that the Peking government would initiate border and trade talks with Iurin after his credentials were verified, which seemed to corroborate Peking 's denial that Iurin's arrival had precipitated a break in relations with the Russian Provisional government. But, Yen then went on to report that Peking had received secret information that the Soviet government would soon be sending its own representative to China. The Chinese officials in these border areas were warned that if a representative from the Russian "New Party" arrived asking for an audience in Peking, the Ministry of Foreign Affairs should be contacted immediately and the situation should be "handled carefully, so as to avoid any mistakes."[60]

This telegram flatly contradicts Koo's claim that Peking was not interested in opening relations with Moscow. It also provides convincing evidence that the Peking government broke relations with the officials of the Russian Provisional government not just for Iurin's sake, but to facilitate negotiations directly with Moscow once its representative arrived in China.

The Peking government took this opportunity to extend full control over the CER so that it could present this Soviet representative with a *fait accompli*. Soon after the Bolshevik revolution, in January 1918, the Chinese government had assumed control over the administration of the railway itself. On March 18, 1920, Peking announced that it was responsible for the entire railway zone; the Ministry of Foreign Affairs' receipt of the Karakhan Manifesto on March 26 seemed to signify Moscow's full approval. On October 2, Peking took another important step by signing a "supplementary agreement" with the Russo-Asiatic Bank, one of the largest stockholders of the CER, which gave China full control over the railway zone and administration.[61] Only the FER's claim over the CER now seemed to stand in the way of China's goal of gaining full control and full rights over this railway.

On October 2, Karakhan met with a Chinese military mission in Moscow, under the leadership of General Chang Ssu-lin, and presented him with a second manifesto, which outlined the conditions under which the Soviet government would be willing to open relations with China.[62] In light of the Chinese foreign minister's telegram from October 1, Karakhan's proposals take on a new meaning, since his terms were the opening proposal in negotiations that were already under way. Besides repeating that all former Sino-Russian treaties were now "null and void," this manifesto once again renounced the Boxer Indemnity, returned to China without compensation all Russian territorial concessions, and revoked extraterritoriality for Russians living in China.[63]

It should be kept in mind, however, that these special rights and privileges primarily benefited the White Russians who had fled to China and were still actively opposing the Bolshevik government. For example, it was widely known that the $3 million a year Boxer Indemnity supported the continued activities of the defunct Russian Provisional government's consuls in China and was suspected of also being a source of income for the Provisional government's embassy in Washington.[64] As for Soviet property, the small amount that was still in Russians hands–for example, in the Russian concession in Tientsin–was owned by those who opposed the Soviet government.[65] Other Russian property, such as consulates and embassy housing, were expected to be returned to the Soviet government anyway. Finally, the Soviet government had few qualms about revoking extraterritoriality in a country where few Soviet citizens lived, but where thousands of White Russians had fled to continue their fight against the Bolsheviks.

While all these points were of little immediate use to Moscow, the one previous promise that remained important was the offer to return the CER to China. This offer was not repeated and, instead, the Soviet government seemed to be rejecting China's recent "supplementary agreement" when it stated that it wanted to continue some control over the railway. Karakhan suggested instead that China, Russia, and the FER should jointly discuss the signing of a "special treaty on the way of working the CER with regard to the needs of the Russian Socialist Federative Soviet Republic."[66]

Although Karakhan's second manifesto was not nearly as advantageous to China as the offer made in the first Karakhan Manifesto, it was vaguely enough worded that it still appeared to be significantly better than the FER's outright claim to the CER. After receiving this letter, the Chinese Ministry of Foreign Affairs quickly decided to send a three-man delegation to Moscow. Peking requested that Iurin act as its intermediary, thus proving the usefulness of Iurin's mission in China. Specifically, Iurin was asked to telegraph a message to the Russian representatives in the FER, to inform the Soviet government that the "Chinese government would reply to the aforesaid communication upon the arrival of Mr. Chen [Kuang-ping] at Moscow."[67]

China's Negotiations with the FER

Peking's diplomatic recognition of the FER was the next important step in accelerating the process of opening talks between Moscow and Peking. In his new position as middleman between these two governments, Iurin falsely assumed that his bargaining position was enhanced and his behavior became more assertive. As a result, his relations with Peking officials quickly became acrimonious.

As soon as Iurin received all the credentials demanded by the Ministry of Foreign Affairs, with the arrival of a letter in late October from the Vladivostok Provisional government confirming that he was also their representative, Iurin submitted these letters to the Peking government with the expectation that negotiations would soon follow.[68] But Peking was now more interested in negotiating directly with Moscow, which seemed to be offering better terms on the CER, and so refrained from opening talks with Iurin.

Iurin protested these delays in two letters from November 17 and 23, 1920. In these letters, Iurin told Foreign Minister Yen that although officials of the Chinese Ministry of Foreign Affairs had privately informed him after his arrival in Peking that "China would sincerely welcome every step by the Far Eastern Republic toward rapprochement as well as toward establishing direct relations," in fact, he and the members of the FER's commercial mission had been constantly snubbed by the government authorities.[69]

Iurin then demanded privileges usually accorded only to officially recognized diplomats, by insisting that the Ministry of Foreign Affairs notify the local officials and police to allow his mission freedom of "residence, movement, and communications" and to grant him the right to communicate with his government by telegraphic code.[70] Iurin ended his second letter by stating that the three months he had spent in Peking had been a waste of time and he threatened that "the people and government of the Far Eastern Republic are prepared to do anything to stabilize the alliance between our two peoples and, by refusing to welcome friendly aspirations of both nations, the Chinese government assumes all responsibility for the consequences."[71]

Iurin's implied threat seemed to have the desired effect, for Yen wrote back the same day and invited Iurin to come to his house on November 26.[72] Although no transcript of this discussion has surfaced, a letter from Iurin to Yen on the day after the meeting shows that Yen had decided to appoint Liu Ching-jen as the official representative of the Peking government in charge of negotiating with the FER. The first meeting between Iurin and Liu was scheduled for November 30, 1920. Iurin was relieved by the Ministry of Foreign Affairs' decision to begin negotiations, announcing: "I applaud the decision of the Chinese government, so timely and necessary, to start negotiations, at the same time, I venture to express confidence that our work will be successful and that we will succeed in quickly resolving problems, both of a general and specific nature."[73]

Iurin approached his first meeting with great self-assurance and outlined an ambitious four-point plan to revise the existing Sino-Russian treaties, exchange consular representatives, sign a commercial treaty, and settle the problem of the CER.[74] But, since talks with the Soviet government had already started in Moscow, the Peking government felt that it held the upper hand with the FER. Therefore, it decided to open negotiations with the FER only in exchange for immediate concessions.

During the first meeting, Liu told Iurin that all negotiations were to be unofficial and that before discussions began Iurin and his government had to accept four preconditions: "1) To agree that no political propaganda would be allowed within China's borders and that propaganda of this type was not compatible with China's social organization; 2) to compensate all losses incurred by Chinese living in Russia following the Russian revolution, including losses due to the deflation of the ruble; 3) to protect the lives, property and rights of Chinese living throughout the Far East; 4) to control and prevent the acts of violence against Chinese living in the border areas of Sinkiang and south of Lake Baikal."[75] These preconditions were not new, but were actually a revised version of the three preconditions mentioned in the ministry's September 18 memo.

After Liu presented these four points, Iurin's first reaction was to try to relegate them to a special committee. The Chinese minutes of this meeting indicate that Iurin was then caught completely off guard as Liu emphasized that these four points were nonnegotiable and that further progress in the talks was contingent on Iurin's acceptance[76]:

> **Iurin:** With regard to Your Excellency's four points, I can only accept these points after telegraphing the situation to the government of the Far Eastern Republic. In my opinion, so as not to obstruct the talks, on the one hand, we ought to nominate investigators from both sides to devote themselves to examining these four points, while on the other hand, we should discuss the commercial matters.

Liu: I think that it is better to first decide these four points and then discuss commercial matters afterward.

Iurin: Now that we have this document that we must examine and consider, let's postpone a day and discuss it at our next meeting. Please, let's first decide a time.

Liu: Once you have had a chance to examine and consider the contents of this document, then we can discuss when the next meeting will be.

Iurin: The next time we have a meeting I intend to bring a stenography student with us so that it will be convenient to take minutes of the discussion. After it is translated into French I will present a copy to Your Excellency for his files!

Iurin not only failed to sidestep these four preconditions by consigning them to a subcommittee, but by allowing the meeting to end without insisting on a date for the next interview he allowed the Peking government to gain full control over the future progress of the negotiations. Iurin's comments reveal his frustration with the Chinese, as well as showing that he was surprised by Liu's demands. Finally, Iurin's admission that he did not even have a secretary at the meeting to transcribe the conversation is particularly noteworthy, suggesting that the Chinese transcripts of these conversations are the only written records from this early period of Sino-Soviet diplomatic relations.

Stymied, Iurin had no choice but to accept the four preconditions. On December 13, he sent a letter to Yen announcing that his government had accepted the four conditions prior to "the opening of the conference concerning the commercial and economic relations of China and the Far Eastern Republic" and he requested that Yen tell him when negotiations would begin.[77] But Iurin's hopes were once again dashed when the Ministry of Foreign Affairs accepted his acquiescence to their four preconditions, but then gave no hint when the formal negotiations might start. To add insult to injury, in December 1920, during a meeting between Iurin and Liu, Iurin was presented with a series of new requests that he later referred to as "preliminary demands" but, that were, in fact, merely a list of China's estimated losses in Siberia incurred during the Russian Civil War, which it expected the FER to repay.

Iurin finally lost all patience and wrote a lengthy letter to Yen on January 12, 1921, criticizing the unexplained delay and complaining that he had trusted in the "sincerity of Your statements, Mr. Minister, and in the statements of Mr. Liu, to the effect that negotiations would begin immediately upon receipt of my four guarantees." Iurin acknowledged that he had no proof of these statements and admitted that only his complete trust in Yen had stopped him from insisting "on a written confirmation of Mr. Liu's final statements."[78]

Iurin concluded his letter by asking four rhetorical questions in which he cast doubt on whether the Peking government really wanted to improve relations with the FER, since he was being presented with preliminary conditions and had as yet received no guarantees that negotiations would actually begin. Iurin further warned Yen that the Peking government was delaying the opening of negotiations "at a time when these delays will keep putting off decisions to questions which affect millions of people of both nations."[79] But Iurin's threats were merely interpreted as a further sign of weakness, and the Chinese Ministry of Foreign Affairs now turned once again to negotiate directly with the Soviet government through its representatives in Moscow.

China's Negotiations with Soviet Russia

On January 8, 1921, the Peking government received word that its three-man delegation had arrived safely in Moscow. Although Peking telegraphed its official reply to Karakhan's previous message through Irkutsk, this telegram apparently never reached Moscow.[80] But, it is not clear whether this break in communications was real or whether the Soviet government pretended that it had not received this telegram so as to promote face-to-face talks in Peking.

While Soviet Russia's goal was to begin diplomatic negotiations with China as soon as possible, it would do so only on terms of equality and only in Peking. To hold talks anywhere outside of Peking would be interpreted by the Chinese people as a sign of Soviet weakness, in Chinese terms a "loss of face," while carrying out negotiations in Peking would imply *de facto* recognition. Since, in fact, Soviet Russia was weak, it was even more important to the Bolsheviks to gain all the trappings of strength that negotiating in Peking would give them.

Whatever the case, on February 23, Karakhan used this opportunity to put pressure on Peking in an ultimatum that he sent via the Soviet Legation in London (see Document 5). Now that Moscow had received China's delegation, Karakhan insisted that the Peking government accept and recognize a similar Soviet representative in China: "[W]ithin a fortnight's time from the delivery of this note *verbale*, you will let us know whether the Chinese government is prepared to accept and to recognize on the territory of China those representatives we propose to send in the near future," or the Soviet government would "be obliged to request the Chinese Consulate-General at present in Moscow to leave the territory of the Russian Socialist Federal Soviet Republic."[81]

The Chinese Ministry of Foreign Affair's response arrived within the two-week time limit stipulated in Karakhan's communique. It first clarified that, although there was no objection to the "desire of the Soviet government to send unofficial representatives to Peking," it would be better to carry out these discussions with a Soviet representative somewhere else. Therefore, Peking suggested that "it would be useful to have a preliminary conversation take place in London between the Soviet Representative and the Chinese Minister there, before sending the aforesaid representatives to Peking."[82]

Moscow, 23rd February 1921.

There has now arrived at Moscow the Chinese Consulate-General consisting of the following persons:

Mr. Chen-Kon-Ping, Consul-General.
Mr. Liou-Ven, Vice-Consul.
Mr. Zin-Ian, Secretary.

As far back as the 27th October of last year, in our note to the Peking Foreign Office, we expressed our desire to have our representatives on the territory of the Chinese Republic, but not receiving a reply, on the 3rd of February, in our note No. 652/2, we again informed Mr. Chen-Koh-Ping, the Consul-General in Moscow for transmission to the Chinese Government, that, taking into consideration the importance of having mutual representatives for the purpose of closer relations between Russia and China, we considered it essential to adhere completely to the principle of mutuality, with the result that our acceptance of representatives of the Chinese Republic on the territory of Russia is possible only on the express condition that the Chinese Government accepts and recognises the representatives of the Russian Socialist Federal Soviet Republic on the territory of China.

Up to the present moment we have had no reply from the Chinese Government with reference to the admittance and acceptance of our representatives on the territory of China; in view of this we beg to ask that, within a fortnight's time from the delivery of this note verbale, you will let us know whether the Chinese Government is prepared to accept and to recognise on the territory of China those representatives we propose to send in the near future.

Should we fail to receive the reply during the period stipulated above, we shall be obliged to request the Chinese Consulate-General at present in Moscow to leave the territory of the Russian Socialist Federal Soviet Republic.

We beg urgently to communicate the above to the Chinese Government in Peking.

Please transmit the reply of the Chinese Government through our representatives in London.

(signed) KARAHAN.
Assistant to the Commissar for Foreign Affairs.

Document 5
Lev Karakhan's February 23, 1921 Ultimatum to Peking

Peking's suggestion to meet in London was an attempt to keep the Soviets at arm's length, because China did not want to accord to Moscow the tacit recognition that a Soviet delegate in Peking would have implied. When Karakhan responded, he ignored this request and announced that the composition of the Soviet delegation, its transportation route, and date of departure were being discussed with the Chinese representative in Moscow. Karakhan further stated that it was Soviet Russia's goal to enter into a full range of negotiations with Peking in order to conclude a "consular agreement, trade treaty, and to the clarification of other questions concerning the mutual relations of Russia and China."[83]

These goals were much broader than Peking was willing to consider. In a letter dated March 31, the Ministry of Foreign Affairs withdrew its invitation for a Soviet representative to come to Peking. It suggested that Soviet Russia delay sending a representative until a "more opportune moment," blaming this change on the disruption of communications and transportation in Mongolia and Manchuria, a hint that the Peking government was not happy with recent skirmishes in Outer Mongolia between the Red Army and various White Russian forces.[84]

On April 13, the Ministry of Foreign Affairs sent a memorandum to the FER's mission in which it agreed to start negotiations on the commercial treaty. But, in sharp contrast to his earlier mistake of assuming that the Peking government was as eager to negotiate as he was, Iurin cautiously requested that the plan for this treaty should first be determined: "The Mission welcomes the decision of the Chinese government to commence negotiations for the discussion of the commercial treaty, but considers it necessary for a proper order of the work and its expediency to establish, before commencing negotiations, the plan and the manner of the same. This Mission will be much indebted to the Waichiaopu [Chinese Ministry of Foreign Affairs] if the latter will advise the Mission as to how it conceives the plan of these negotiations."[85] Iurin later repeated his request directly to Liu, and emphasized that a plan would ensure that their progress would not be "hampered by an absence of clarity and concord."[86]

At the same time as Iurin was trying to become the intermediary between Moscow and Peking, both Yen and Karakhan were hardening their positions. Karakhan followed up his previous communication with a note on April 14, in which he indicated that Moscow was prepared to recognize Chen Kuang-ping as the official representative of the Chinese government and grant him the rights corresponding to his position, but this action was predicated on Peking's granting the same status to the future Soviet representative. Karakhan continued: "At the same time the Soviet government supposes that upon the principle of reciprocity similar rights and guarantees will be accorded to our representative in China, of which fact the Pekin[g] government shall correspondingly inform us. [A]s soon as we shall receive information from the Chinese government that it shares our point of view in regard to this status of reciprocal representatives Mr. Chen Kuan[g] Ping will be officially presented with the above specified rights."[87]

This suggestion was yet another transparent attempt to push the Peking government into recognizing the legitimacy of the Soviet government, an action that was diametrically opposed to Peking's desire to settle all outstanding problems in as unofficial a setting as possible. Meanwhile, the Chinese Ministry of Foreign Affairs had sent a telegram to its London embassy on April 12, crossing Karakhan's letter in the process, which ordered its embassy to pass on to the Soviet government four preconditions to negotiations, an almost exact reenactment of its negotiating strategy with Iurin[88]:

1) The proposed Soviet representative will be an unofficial agent whose mission it will be to confer with the Chinese government on trade matters and who cannot claim to succeed to the late Russian Minister either in name or in his functions;

2) The proposed Soviet representative and his suite will not be permitted to carry on propaganda of doctrines incompatible with Chinese social life, or to carry with them books or papers containing such doctrines;

3) Chinese residents in Russia shall be exempted from requisitions for service. Their merchandise shall not be sequestrated or requisitioned. Chinese labourers are free to accept employment offered and shall not be subject to compulsion or restrictions;

4) The Soviet government engages to indemnify losses sustained by Chinese residents in Russia in accordance with findings on both sides.

Iurin's rapid acceptance of four preconditions for opening talks with China undoubtedly lent credence to Peking's belief that the Soviet government would have no choice but to acquiesce to these demands. For a time it seemed that Peking was right: Chen quoted Chicherin as saying he would need reassurances that the Soviet representative in Peking would be granted diplomatic immunity and be given the right to communicate with Moscow by telegraphic code and personal dispatches, "before he would consent to the Chinese government's four points about sending an unofficial representative to Peking."[89]

But when Karakhan sent his formal response he tacitly agreed to the first two conditions by not insisting that the Soviet representative receive the title of minister and by also agreeing "that the Russian representative will not interfere in the internal affairs of China and will not conduct propaganda in any form."[90] By contrast, Karakhan absolutely refused to accept the last two points, suggesting that these questions should be discussed in more detail after the Soviet representative arrived in Peking. He further expressed his hope that these conditions would not "serve as obstacles delaying and interfering with his arrival at Peking."[91]

Iurin uses the CER as Bait

After the Chinese Ministry of Foreign Affairs decided not to invite a Soviet representative to Peking, it once again resumed negotiations with Iurin. This sudden about-face might have been connected in some way to the signing of the Anglo-Soviet trade agreement on March 16, 1921, which signaled a new willingness among the Allies to negotiate with Moscow. It is more likely, however, that it was a result of a new FER declaration indicating that it was now willing to study and revise the tsarist treaty concerning the CER during a three-way conference including the FER, Soviet Russia, and China.[92] This offer was a ploy intended to jump-start Peking's talks with Moscow: Iurin was clearly using the CER as bait, since his new offer promised to revise the previous treaty along the lines proposed by Karakhan in his second manifesto, which implied that the railway would eventually be given to China.

As the positions taken by Moscow and Peking became ever more entrenched, it was up to Iurin to find a way to break the deadlock. On May 13, Iurin asked Yen how the Peking government planned to treat the Soviet representative once he arrived in China. In response, Yen reminded Iurin that the Soviet government could discuss this topic directly with Chen Kuang-ping in Moscow.[93] Iurin then brought up the CER (see Document 6). He said that his government was now willing either to return the railway "completely" to China or to manage it jointly with China, but he implied that Moscow's approval was required. He once again proposed convening a tripartite conference to resolve the issue of the CER.[94]

Iurin's new proposal to return the CER appeared to be a dramatic shift in Peking's favor. Iurin soon received help from an unexpected quarter. In July 1921, the Russo-Asiatic Bank clarified that it was planning to take its financial claim over the CER before the Washington Conference, which was scheduled to convene in November 1921. Since the Russo-Asiatic Bank owned many of the outstanding shares of railway stock, this action threatened to take the ownership of the railway away from China. Of even greater concern to Peking was that the CER might become a matter of international debate, and would give the Western powers another opportunity to meddle in China's affairs. Therefore, it was imperative for China to reach an agreement with the FER and Soviet Russia before the conference opened, so that its claim over the railway would be hard to challenge.

A second major event that contributed to Iurin's strategy was the conclusion of the civil war in Outer Mongolia. The White leader, Baron Ungern von Sternberg, had first attacked the Mongolian capital of Urga in October 1920, been repulsed, and then returned in early February 1921. After successfully taking Urga, he declared an independent Mongolian government under his leadership. During June, however, the Soviet Red Army defeated him in a campaign that ended with the Red Army occupying Urga on July 6. In late July the Mongolian People's Revolutionary government was formed, whereupon it "requested" Moscow to continue the Red Army's presence in Outer Mongolia.

中東鉄路事

總長云赤塔政府對於中東鉄路持何意見

優林云現在通商草約尚未議商政此事于本

未向赤塔政府詢及 惟據予個人意見將來此路

或完全歸於中國或以商務性質由兩國共管

均無不可 總之遠東共和國不必完全享有俄

國舊政府對於該路之權而貴總長對於該路意

見此何予亦極願聞知

Document 6

Ignatii Iurin's May 13, 1921 Offer to Return the CER to Peking

Immediately following the founding of the pro-Soviet government in Outer Mongolia, Moscow renewed its efforts to send a representative to China. It sent a message to Peking offering to open tripartite talks with China to determine the status of Outer Mongolia. This time, the talks would include Peking, Moscow, and the new Mongolian government. The Soviet government reassured China that "it has no intention of claiming the restoration of any rights and privileges which the tsarist government has in the past acquired in Mongolia and that it renounces categorically all such rights and claims" and expressed its intention to "uphold the prerogatives of the Chinese government."[95]

In July Iurin renewed his earlier suggestion that a conference be held to determine how the railway would be returned to China, but this time Iurin claimed the FER would also represent Moscow.[96] The Chinese Ministry of Foreign Affairs was initially not convinced that Iurin was authorized to negotiate on the Soviet Russia's behalf and sent an urgent telegram to its embassy in London, instructing it to ask Soviet Russia's London representative to determine whether the "Soviet government has or has not appointed the Far Eastern Republic to be solely responsible for these two problems."[97]

By October Iurin finally broke through the impasse brought about by the stubbornness of both the Moscow and the Peking governments. Iurin first urged a rapid completion of the commercial treaty between Peking and the FER, to which Yen rejoined that they should "first expedite satisfactory negotiations on the questions of Mongolia and the CER and then the commercial treaty could be decided in a matter of two or three weeks."[98] Iurin then proposed that a commission study methods of resolving these two problems, while hinting that the real reason for Yen's concern about the CER was the upcoming Washington Conference (also called the Pacific Conference): "What then would we have to fear if this conference makes a proposal on this problem?"[99]

Yen immediately understood Iurin's implication and fired off a volley in reply, reminding him: "To make a long story short, if both of our sides first resolve the CER question then we could avoid a third party at the Pacific Conference making proposals which would not be advantageous to our interests; if we are now able to get the Russians to withdraw their troops from Mongolia and resolve the issue of the CER and complete the commercial treaty, although China would not be able actively to help the Far Eastern Republic at the Pacific Conference, she would be willing passively to help Chita, which would be no small advantage."[100] Yen's offer was little more than a direct trade: the FER's immediate cooperation in return for China's support at the upcoming Washington Conference. Yen asked Iurin to consider his proposal before their meeting the next day.

Yen's proposal depended on forcing the Soviets to withdraw their troops from Mongolia and resolving the dispute over the CER before China would begin to help the FER. Although Yen's proposal was sound, it was based upon the false assumption, long promoted by Iurin, that the FER had no connection with the Moscow government; if this were the case, then Iurin would probably have been interested in gaining China's support to strengthen the FER's position at the

Washington Conference. Since Yen seemed completely convinced that Iurin was only representing the Soviet government to achieve the FER's goals, he felt sure that Iurin would decide to support Peking against Moscow.

But Yen's assumptions were soon proved to be incorrect, as shown by Iurin's actions on the following day, when Yen opened the negotiations by stating that China wanted full ownership and control over the CER and was willing to pay in cash or with bonds in order to attain this goal.[101] Although Iurin indicated that he was now ready to consider the possibility of completely turning the CER over to the Peking government, he again suggested that a commission be formed to study how this could be carried out. When Yen expressed an interest in organizing a conference and suggested that it convene in Peking within three to five days, Iurin directed the conversation along lines that once more made the Soviet government seem essential to any successful resolution[102]:

> **Iurin:** But I don't know whether or not you have decided to discuss this matter with the Soviet government.

> **Foreign Minister:** With regard to this detail, I remember that when Mr. Iurin previously came to Peking, he made it clear that the Soviet government had already abandoned it to the Far Eastern Republic's management. Why are you bringing this up now?

> **Iurin:** At that time the Soviet government had not yet sent a representative to China–the current situation is not the same as before. Yesterday a telegram arrived from Chita [saying] that the Soviet government had commissioned the Far Eastern Republic to inquire today on its behalf how the Chinese government would receive and treat the Soviet representative. The Soviet government already wants to send a representative to China and if it is necessary to negotiate with him, then it would be best to wait for him to come to China. Now it is necessary both to organize a commission to study how to solve this problem and to communicate with the Soviet government on this matter.

> **Foreign Minister:** How many days will it take if we communicate with the Soviet government?

> **Iurin:** If we had four days, sending a message through London would be the fastest.

> **Foreign Minister:** This topic is already finished, let's discuss a different matter.

> **Iurin:** China should also make it clear what kind of treatment it plans to accord to the Soviet representative coming to China, so that I can send a telegram to Chita in response to the Soviet government.

Iurin's insistence on pushing this point was not characteristic of a disinterested third party. Instead, this discussion was one more step in the long process whereby Iurin had made the Soviet government seem indispensable to the resolution of the CER and Outer Mongolian problems.

On October 5, when Yen urged Iurin to agree to convene a conference immediately to discuss the details of their agreement on the CER, Iurin procrastinated by claiming that the FER's railway experts were still in Chita. When Yen mentioned that an agreement had to be reached quickly because the Russo-Asiatic Bank was planning to try to take control of the railway at the Washington Conference, Iurin reassured him that this could never happen and revealed for the first time that the Soviet foreign minister had already informed him that according to "an investigation of tsarist Ministry of Foreign Affairs documents in Moscow" there would be "no difficulty" in disproving the claim of the Russo-Asiatic Bank.[103] Iurin then told Yen that another telegram had just arrived from the Soviet government asking whether "the Chinese government had agreed or not to allow the Moscow delegation to come to Peking" and again offered his services to relay a message to Moscow.[104]

Iurin's sudden willingness to discuss the possibility of China's total control of the CER and then his offer to provide tsarist documents that would invalidate the Russo-Asiatic Bank's claim over the railway tipped the balance in Moscow's favor. Yen finally gave his permission for a Soviet representative to come to Peking. With the opening of the Washington Conference only a little more than a month away, Yen and Iurin agreed that the tripartite conference should convene in Manchouli, Manchuria, during November to discuss both the CER and Outer Mongolia–with a Red Army military officer stationed in Irkutsk participating as the Soviet representative.[105]

But this tripartite conference never met. On the one hand, the Manchurian warlord, Chang Tso-lin, opposed negotiating with the Soviets over the CER. On the other hand, when the Peking representative arrived in Manchouli to discuss the Mongolian problem, the FER suddenly canceled the meeting, saying that the FER's troops had already been withdrawn from Outer Mongolia and so the conference was no longer necessary.[106] As Yen later complained, the most important item under discussion was to convince the Red Army to evacuate Outer Mongolia, and the Soviet representative at Manchouli broke his promise when he refused to open talks with the Chinese representative.[107]

Iurin followed up his efforts to get a Soviet representative into China by sending a letter to Yen on October 15, reminding him that two members of the FER's mission were already on their way to participate at the Washington Conference.[108] Iurin's note seems to have prompted the hoped-for response, since the Chinese Embassy in London received a telegram from Peking on the same day ordering the Embassy to telegraph Moscow and inform Consul Chen to issue visas and passports to the Soviet mission bound for China.[109]

This telegram was distinctive in that all mention of the Peking government's previous four preconditions had been dropped. Once the Soviet government was assured that its representative had received official documents, then Lenin and Chicherin signed government credentials for Aleksandr Paikes, naming him the "Plenipotentiary Extraordinary for the Russian Socialist Federal Soviet Republic to the Republic of China concerning the Chinese Eastern Railway."[110]

Conclusions

The Soviet government ordered the creation of the FER to help open diplomatic negotiations with China. The FER, in turn, appealed to Washington for protection under the Open Door Policy. Paikes's December 14, 1921 arrival in Peking was made possible, in part at least, because of Washington's support for the territorial integrity of the FER under the auspices of the Open Door Policy. With the Paikes mission, the Bolsheviks achieved an enormous diplomatic victory in the Far East. Peking had not only dropped its four preconditions, but it had also agreed to the Soviet demands that Paikes be granted diplomatic immunity and the right to use telegraphic code to communicate with Moscow, in effect granting the Soviet mission the same rights that the other recognized ministries enjoyed in China. Finally, these negotiations were taking place in Peking, as opposed to London or Manchouli, which proved–according to Chinese thinking at least–that Peking already tacitly recognized Moscow as the legitimate government of Russia.

Although Paikes's arrival in Peking did not immediately result in the opening of formal diplomatic relations, the Paikes mission opened a new era by allowing for direct government-to-government negotiations that eventually attained this goal, a goal that might have been delayed by many months or even years if Iurin had not acted as intermediary on behalf of the Soviet government. The documents cited above show how important Iurin was in opening the door for Paikes's mission to China, which then led to later Soviet missions under Adolf Joffe and Lev Karakhan.

A crucial facet of Iurin's strategy was to make it appear that the FER was totally independent from the Soviet government in Moscow. When Iurin first arrived in Peking, the FER claimed the territory around the CER and demanded control of the railway itself. As Iurin gradually changed the FER's position to conform more closely with the Soviet government's declarations–by first offering to participate in a tripartite conference, then advocating joint FER-Chinese management of the railway, and finally agreeing to return the railway completely to China–he also gradually transferred responsibility for resolving the railway issue into Moscow's hands, claiming that the Soviet government had to approve the method for returning the railway to China.

In the end, Iurin convinced Yen that not only were the Bolsheviks willing to return the CER, but that only Moscow could provide the necessary documents to prevent the Russo-Asiatic Bank from wresting control of the CER away from China. Although this tactic was successful in opening diplomatic negotiations between Soviet Russia and China, these negotiations quickly ran aground when it became clear that the Soviet government had no intention of carrying out the promises embodied in the first and second Karakhan Manifestos. It soon became necessary for Soviet diplomats to search for allies within China to help them force Peking to allow Soviet Russia to reassert control over the former tsarist concessions. These allies eventually included the Kuomintang Party and the Chinese Communist Party. The story of how the Bolsheviks created this alliance, known as the United Front Policy, will be discussed in the next chapter.

Notes

1. "Reinsch Defends Chinese Government's Attitude," *The Washington Post*, October 1, 1920. According to Joyce Kathleen Bibber, Reinsch cautioned that at the worst Bolshevik propaganda would make the Chinese more resistant to foreign capitalists working in China ("The Chinese Communists as viewed by the American Periodical Press, 1920-1937," Quoting Paul Reinsch, "Bolshevism in Asia," *Asia* XX, April 1920); but Leo Pasvolsky, a well-known journalist, warned during January 1921 that Moscow was using "devilish cunning and craftiness" to set the stage in China for "a tragic farce of a revolution," and that the Comintern was in the process of "artificially stimulating . . . a discontent, an ambitious minority which might be won over to the idea of an experiment in communism" ("The Third International in Asia," *Saturday Evening Post,* January 29, 1921).

2. Although Iurin signed his own name "Yourin" when writing in French or English, this spelling is based on the Library of Congress transliteration system.

3. Even as late as May 1922, the Peking government's Foreign Minister, Yen Hui-ch'ing, was still carefully questioning the FER's representatives to find out exactly what their relations with Moscow were like.

4. Professor Whiting's exact words are: "Yurin's failure was of little consequence in the long run, but his experiences served as an example for later Soviet negotiators faced with essentially the same problems as was the representative of the Far Eastern Republic" (Allen S. Whiting, *Soviet Policies in China, 1917-1924,* 167).

5. Wang Yu-chun (王聿均), 中蘇外交的序幕 (*The First Phase of Sino-Soviet Diplomacy*), 209-13.

6. The Soviet government's original French-language telegram of the Karakhan Manifesto to the Peking government, March 26, 1920, is located in the Foreign Ministry Archives at the Institute for Modern History, Academia Sinica, Nankang, Taiwan (*Wai-chiao Tang-an,* or WCTA below), collection 03-32, Vol. 463(1). Previous references to this telegram have come from the 1924 *The China Yearbook*, which received a translated copy of the 1920 telegram from China's Ministry of Foreign Affairs. Moscow later disputed this version's accuracy, making the original telegram especially important.

7. Vladimir Dmitrievich Vilenskii-Sibiriakov (Бладимир Дмитриевиц Виленский-Сибиряков), *Китай и Советская Россия* (*China and Soviet Russia*), 15.

8. Бюллетени Дальне-восточного Секретариата Коминтерна (*Bulletins of the Far Eastern Secretariat of the Comintern*), no. 5, Irkutsk, April 24, 1921, 3; this journal was restricted in the USSR, becoming available at Moscow's Lenin Library only in spring 1989. The republication in 1921 of the Soviet government's 1919 promise to return the Chinese Eastern Railway to China without compensation reconfirms that the Bolsheviks not only initially made this promise, but did so repeatedly.

9. Allen Whiting was the first scholar to comment on the importance of Vilenskii's pamphlet; see: "The Soviet Offer to China of 1919," in *Far Eastern Quarterly*, X (August 1951), 355-364.

10. Whiting, *Soviet Policies,* 33.

11. Sow-Theng Leong, *Sino-Soviet Diplomatic Relations, 1917-1926*, 131-135.

12. Delber L. McKee, "Chinese Exclusion Versus the Open Door Policy 1900-1906," 216.

13. William Appleman Williams, *American Russian Relations 1781-1947,* 106.

14. Michael H. Hunt, *Frontier Defense and the Open Door*, 34, 246. Marilyn Young was more positive about the Open Door, but she has described it in terms of an American empire and concluded that the "Open Door passed into the small body of sacred American doctrine" (*The Rhetoric of Empire American China Policy 1895-1901*, 231).

15. Dietrich Geyer, *Russian Imperialism, The Interaction of Domestic and Foreign Policy, 1860-1914,* 86-100.

16. Thomas Ewing, *Between the Hammer and the Anvil? Chinese and Russian Policies in Outer Mongolia 1911-1921*, 19.

17. A three million ruble fund was used to bribe Chinese officials as well as a promise to form a secret Sino-Russian military alliance against Japan, an alliance that the Russian government later broke when it took the Liaotung peninsula. S. C. M. Paine, *Imperial Rivals: China, Russia, and Their Disputed Frontier,* 185.

18. With regard to the importance of railways in China, Noel H. Pugach has commented: "Ever since China had been opened to Western capital in the 1890s, railroad concessions and railway politics had posed the greatest threats to the Open Door" (*Paul S. Reinsch: Open Door Diplomat in Action*, 110).

19. Walter LaFeber has even suggested that the origin of the U.S.-Soviet cold war rivalry can in part be traced back to the turn-of-the-century competition over Manchuria (*America, Russia, and the Cold War*).

20. Mark Sullivan, *Our Times: The Turn of the Century*, 509; quoted in George Kennan, *American Diplomacy*, 21-22.

21. "Treaty of Peace–Russia and Japan," September 5, 1905, commonly called the Portsmouth Peace Treaty. John V. A. MacMurray, *Treaties and Agreements with and Concerning China*, 522-525.

22. Ernest Batson Price, *The Russo-Japanese Treaties of 1907-1916 Concerning Manchuria and Mongolia.*

23. "Declaration, and Accompanying Exchange of Notes, in Regard to Outer Mongolia–Russia and China," November 5, 1913; "Tripartite Agreement in Regard to Outer Mongolia–Russia, Mongolia, and China," June 7, 1915, MacMurray, 1066-1067, 1240-1245.

24. Roy Watson Curry, *Woodrow Wilson and Far Eastern Policy, 1913-1921*, 218.

25. Arno J. Mayer, *Political Origins of the New Diplomacy, 1917-1918*, 373.

26. Untitled two-page letter from Trotsky to Chicherin, Acting Commissar for Foreign Affairs, January 31, 1918; Harvard University, Houghton Library, Trotsky Archives, Document No. T6.

27. "Note from Trotsky, Commissar for War, to Colonel Robins for Transmission to the American Government Concerning the Attitude of the Allies if the Soviet Congress Should Refuse to Ratify the Brest-Litovsk Treaty," March 5, 1918, Jane Degras, *Soviet Documents on Foreign Policy*, Vol. 1, 56-57.

28. Woodrow Wilson Papers, microfilm reel 384, 1089.

29. *Ibid.*, 1079.

30. André Fontaine, *History of the Cold War*, 35.

31. William S. Graves, *America's Siberian Adventure, 1918-1920*, 5-10.

32. Betty M. Unterberger, *America's Siberian Expedition, 1918-1920*, 233.

33. Copy of a Military Report to the Central Committee of the Bolshevik Party marked "Copy. Secret." August 5, 1919, Trotsky Archives No. 2956, 1.

34. Copy of a telegram from Trotsky and Lenin to Smirnov, head of the Siberian Revolution Committee, marked "Copy. Quite Secret." January 13, 1920, Trotsky Archives No. 419.

35. Cordell Hull, *The Memoirs of Cordell Hull*, Vol. 1, 299; even though William Appleman Williams' very first footnote in his book *American Russian Relations* refers to page 292 in Vol. 1 of Hull's memoirs, he completely ignores this reference only seven pages later. Williams may have misjudged the importance of the Open Door Policy in Siberia because he apparently did not use the Trotsky archives, even though these archives were perhaps the best source of information in the United States on early Soviet-American diplomatic relations. Williams does admit, however, that Washington's goal was to "proscribe further Japanese expansion" in Siberia, which undermines his thesis that the Open Door Policy only benefited American economic expansion in Asia (*American Russian Relations*, 178).

36. Copy of a telegram from Trotsky to Smirnov in Irkutsk, marked "Copy. Secret." February 18, 1920, Trotsky Archives No. 444.

37. Copy of a telegram from Lenin to Smirnov, marked "Copy. Quite Secret." February 19, 1920, Trotsky Archives No. 446.

38. Published in the April 28, 1920 issue of *Krasnoe Znamia* from an April 18th interview in the Japanese newspaper *Osaka Mainichi*.

39. David J. Dallin, *The Rise of Russia in Asia*, 170-171.

40. Alfred L. P. Dennis, *The Foreign Policies of Soviet Russia*, 301.

41. *Сборник действующих трактатов* (*Collection of Active Treaties*), Issue 2, 78-79, 129-132,133-137.

42. That Washington was not immediately aware of the close relations between the Soviet government and the Far Eastern Republic was confirmed by John Kenneth Caldwell, who wrote that he was sent to Siberia in 1921 because "it was claimed that this new government had no official connection with the Soviet Government in Moscow and one of the main purposes of my 'observing' was to form an opinion as to the truthfulness of this allegation." Hoover Institution Archives, John Kenneth Caldwell collection, unpublished memoirs.

43. Dennis, 302.

44. Unterberger, 195, note 44.

45. "The Integrity of Russia," *The Washington Post*, September 21, 1921.

46. Gaimusho, 2.5.1.106-2, No. 123.

47. *Ibid*, 2738.

48. "A Draft of a Treaty of Friendship and Commerce Between the Far Eastern Republic and the Republic of China," WCTA, 03-32, 506(3).

49. Original English-language telegram, May 18, 1920, WCTA, 03-32, 464(1).

50. *Ibid.*

51. Original English-language telegram, June 12, 1920, WCTA, 03-32, 464(1).

52. Original English-language telegram, June 24, 1920, WCTA, 03-32, 464(1).

53. This mission was composed of primarily of foreign specialists (including B. Lenox Simpson, John C. Ferguson, and George Padoux), and their positive assessment of the FER was used by China to convince the Allied countries that opening talks with the FER did not threaten their efforts to isolate the Bolsheviks; Leong, 153-154.

54. Original English-language telegram, July 26, 1920, WCTA, 03-32, 464(3).

55. Leong, 156.

56. "China's Terms to Soviets," *The New York Times*, October 3, 1920.

57. Internal Chinese-language memo, September 18, 1920, WCTA, 03-32, 523(1).

58. "China for Harmony," *The Washington Post*, October 2, 1920.

59. American embassy memo No. 62, signed by the American minister to China, Charles R. Crane, October 5, 1920, WCTA, 03-32, 438(1). See also "Treaties with Russia Stand, Declares China," *The Washington Post*, October 9, 1920.

60. Chinese-language copy of the telegram, October 1, 1920, WCTA, 03-32, 435(1).

61. Whiting, *Soviet Policies,* 155.

62. Chinese-language copy of Karakhan's proposals, October 2, 1920. These proposals were officially declared on October 27, 1920, WCTA, 03-32, 479(1).

63. English-language translation of the original declaration provided by the Soviet Mission in Peking on December 2, 1923, and marked "True to the original"; WCTA 03-32, 481(3).

64. "U.S. Moves to Block Russian Pact in China," *The New York Tribune*, October 2, 1920.

65. In a letter from Minister Crane to W. W. Yen, he pointed out that in Tientsin, "the bulk of the property in the Russian Concession is owned not by Russians but by Americans and subjects of other nations"; October 5, 1920, WCTA, 03-32, 438(1).

66. English-language translation of the original declaration provided by the Soviet Mission in Peking on December 2, 1923, and marked "True to the original;" WCTA, 03-32, 481(3).

67. Chinese-language communication, March 7, 1921, WCTA, 03-32, 471(2).

68. Russian-language letter, October 29, 1920, WCTA, 03-32, 465(1).

69. English translation of Iurin's letter, November 17, 1920, WCTA, 03-32, 523(1).

70. *Ibid.*

71. Original Russian-language letter, No. 576/a, signed by Iurin, November 23, 1920, WCTA, 03-32, 523(1).

72. Copy of the original English-language note from November 23, 1920, WCTA, 03-32, 523(1).

73. According to two letters in Russian signed by Iurin, November 27, 1920—one to Dr. Yen and the other to Liu Ching-jen; WCTA, 03-32, 523(1).

74. Leong, 160.

75. Chinese-language minutes of the meeting, November 30, 1920, WCTA, 03-32, 473(3).

76. *Ibid.*

77. French-language letter signed and sealed by Iurin, December 13, 1920, WCTA, 03-32, 523(1).

78. Official Russian-language letter, No. 303/c, signed and sealed by Iurin on

January 12, 1921, WCTA, 03-32, 523(2).

79. *Ibid.*

80. Chinese-language communication, March 7, 1921, WCTA, 03-32, 471(2).

81. English-language copy of the Russian original provided by the Soviet Legation in London, February 23, 1921, WCTA, 03-32, 472(2).

82. Chinese-language communication, March 7, 1921, WCTA, 03-32, 471(2).

83. English-language copy of Soviet memorandum No. 898/2, March 26, 1921, WCTA, 03-32, 471(2).

84. English-language *aide-memoire* from the Chinese Legation in London, March 31, 1921, WCTA, 03-32, 472(2).

85. FER mission's answer to this memorandum in English-language letter No. 344, April 18, 1921, which is a translation of Russian-language letter No. 343, April 17, 1921, WCTA, 03-32, 523(2).

86. Russian-language letter 347c, April 22, 1921, WCTA, 03-32, 523(2).

87. English-language translation of Soviet memorandum No. 960/2, April 14, 1921, WCTA, 03-32, 462(4). I have corrected misspellings in the original.

88. English-language *aide-memoire*, June 17, 1921, which repeats the content of the Chinese-language telegram from April 12, 1921, WCTA, 03-32, 462(4) and 523(1), respectively.

89. Chinese-language telegrams, June 15, 1921 and June 17, 1921, WCTA, 03-32, 462(4) and 475(1), respectively.

90. English-language note from the Soviet embassy in London, June 27, 1921, WCTA, 03-32, 472(2).

91. *Ibid.*

92. Chinese-language copy of the original document, April 2, 1921, WCTA, 03-32, 473(3).

93. Chinese-language minutes, May 13, 1921, WCTA, 03-32, 475(1).

94. *Ibid.*, WCTA, 03-32, 524(1)

95. English-language note from the Soviet embassy in London, July 1921, WCTA, 03-32, 175(1).

96. Chinese-language minutes, July 8 and 28, 1921, WCTA, 03-32, 524(2), WCTA, 03-32, 524(2).

97. Chinese Foreign Ministry telegram to its London Embassy, August 4, 1921, WCTA, 03-32, 471(1).

98. Chinese-language minutes, October 3, 1921, WCTA, 03-32, 466(2).

99. *Ibid.*

100. *Ibid.*

101. *Ibid.*, October 4, 1921, WCTA, 03-32, 466(2).

102. *Ibid.*

103. *Ibid.*, October 5, 1921, WCTA, 03-32, 466(2).

104. *Ibid.*

105. *Ibid.*

106. Leong, 194.

107. Chinese-language minutes, December 16, 1921, WCTA, 03-32, 462(2).

108. English-language letter No. 741, October 15, 1921, WCTA, 03-32, 470(1).

109. Chinese-language telegram, October 15, 1921, WCTA, 03-32, 471(1).

110. French-language credentials, October 18, 1921, WCTA, 03-32, 474(2).

2
The Origins of the United Front Policy

The generally accepted view of the first United Front Policy[1] was that the Comintern proposed this policy in 1920, at approximately the same time that Marxist study groups were being formed into a communist party in China. According to this view, an active alliance between the Chinese Communist Party (CCP) and the Kuomintang (KMT) began in 1922, as a result of the intervention of Henk Sneevliet (Maring), an agent of the Moscow-based Comintern. These dates assume the existence of the CCP prior to the Comintern's adoption of the United Front, an interpretation that most recently published Western histories of the CCP accept.[2] Historians from the PRC and the former USSR also subscribe to this view, since to do otherwise would devalue the CCP's role.[3]

The traditional view that the CCP was integral to the United Front is contradicted by evidence showing that the Bolsheviks proposed this policy almost three years before the CCP was formed. In fact, Soviet officials first promoted an alliance with Sun Yat-sen during summer 1918, before there were any communists in China. The Comintern followed suit during spring 1919, more than a year before Marxist study groups were formed. Finally, with the Comintern's backing, in January 1921 Ch'en Tu-hsiu published an article in Canton advocating that the KMT establish closer ties with Moscow, half a year before the CCP's founding congress in July 1921.[4] These initial Bolshevik attempts to ally with Sun all predated the formation of the CCP, thus contradicting the traditional interpretation that the Comintern proposed the United Front Policy in order to help the CCP.

If the United Front Policy was adopted prior to the founding of the CCP, then its original goal could only have been to ally the Bolsheviks and Sun Yat-sen, not the CCP and the KMT. It must be remembered that Sun Yat-sen was in control–off and on–of the South China city of Canton, which opposed the central government in Peking. From Moscow's perspective, therefore, an alliance with Canton could prove useful during diplomatic negotiations with Peking. Similarly, for Sun, an alliance with Soviet Russia offered political leverage with the other foreign powers, so as to force international recognition of his opposition government. Thus, from a political as well as practical point of view, the immediate benefits that the Bolsheviks and Sun could gain by allying with each other far outweighed any benefits that might one day appear by allying the KMT with the, as yet, nonexistent CCP.

This chapter will show that the primary Soviet motive behind allying with Sun Yat-sen and the KMT was to direct Chinese public opinion against Peking. Soviet diplomats used this KMT/CCP leverage during secret negotiations with

Peking officials that enabled the Bolsheviks to consolidate their occupation of Outer Mongolia, to retake majority control over the Chinese Eastern Railway, and to regain most of tsarist Russia's territorial concessions, special rights and privileges. This interpretation also helps explain later friction in the United Front, once the KMT's post-Sun leadership realized how they had unwittingly promoted the Soviet Union's national interests at China's expense.

Early Soviet Attempts to Ally with Sun Yat-sen

The Chinese revolution of 1911 and the formal abdication of the last Ch'ing emperor in February 1912 set the stage for the first United Front, since the revolution led to the founding of an opposition government in Canton under Sun Yat-sen. As early as November 1911, a secret telegram from the tsarist Russian mission in Peking suggested that in a conflict between this opposition government and China's central government in Peking, Russia's natural ally would be Canton.[5] The rationale for this proposal was simple: preexisting friction over Outer Mongolia and the CER precluded closer ties to Peking, while Russia did not have any territorial conflicts with South China, making an alliance with Canton against Peking useful.

The geopolitics of Russo-Chinese relations did not change with Russia's October Revolution. The Bolsheviks' People's Commissar of Foreign Affairs Chicherin was of noble birth and had worked for seven years in the tsarist Ministry of Foreign Affairs.[6] An early indication of the continuity between tsarist and Bolshevik diplomatic policies in China appeared on August 1, 1918, when Chicherin sent a letter to Sun expressing hope that relations between Moscow and Canton would improve.[7] After stating that the "Russian and Chinese revolutions had common aims," Chicherin even appealed to Sun for help against the capitalist governments that were trying to "strangle the Russian revolution."[8]

It is important to reiterate that there were no Chinese communists in August 1918. China's first avowed Bolshevik supporter was Li Ta-chao, and Maurice Meisner has concluded that although "by mid-1918 Li was emotionally committed to the October Revolution," Li's writings offered "nothing to suggest that he had even begun to consider seriously Marxist theory." Only in November, four months after Chicherin's letter, did Li publish his first pro-Bolshevik article. Likewise, even Mao Tse-tung's September 1918 arrival at Peking University to study Marxism under Li Ta-chao took place a month after Chicherin's letter.[9] By no stretch of the imagination, therefore, can Chicherin's letter to Sun be misconstrued as promoting an alliance between the CCP and KMT; in fact, an alliance could only have been between the Moscow and Canton governments.

A circular from Deputy People's Commissar of Foreign Affairs Lev Karakhan provides further evidence that Chicherin's proposal to ally with Sun Yat-sen did not depend on the existence of a CCP. On December 4, 1918, Karakhan sent this letter to all Soviet deputies, warning them not to mistreat Chinese citizens living in Soviet Russia. In particular, he cautioned, Chinese should not be treated like members of the "bourgeois class," but should be handled with great care because the "Soviet government is doing everything possible to attract Asian democrats to the common struggle against imperialism."[10]

These documents suggest that by 1918 the Soviet government was already interested in allying with Sun's opposition government in Canton. Moreover, this proposal actually followed the tsarist Russian consulate's 1911 suggestion to ally with Canton against Peking, a plan that was interrupted by World War I. While the Bolsheviks' early attempts to make contact with Sun may not be a direct continuation of this tsarist Russian strategy, therefore, the historical parallels are undeniable. Contrary to the traditional view, this early stage of the United Front Policy could not have included the Chinese communists as allies, much less as equal members in the United Front.

From August 1918, when Chicherin sent his first letter to Sun, forming alliances with Chinese revolutionaries to draw them into an anti-imperialist United Front against the capitalist nations constituted a major component of the Bolsheviks' Far Eastern strategy. While the CCP only had 56 members in July 1921, Sun's KMT already claimed a membership in excess of 200,000.[11] The Comintern publicly identified Sun as their top candidate for a Chinese ally in a March 1919 *Izvestiia* article signed by Lao Hsiu-ch'ao, a Chinese delegate to the founding congress of the Comintern, in which he referred to: "The pride of China–Sun Yat-sen."[12]

Soviet publications did not attempt to deny that an alliance with Sun Yat-sen might one day lead to China's entry into an anti-imperialist United Front; for example, in a February 1919 *Izvestiia* article, Stalin predicted, that in the struggle between the socialist and capitalist camps, the "roar" of socialist revolutions could be "heard in the countries of the oppressed East."[13] Thereafter, during the summer of 1919, a pamphlet written by the Soviet official Vladimir Vilenskii stated: "Everyone is saying that the revolutionary fire in South China ought inevitably to move to the North. Then revolutionary Russia will find for itself a reliable ally in China against the imperialist predators."[14]

The Soviet government was even willing to devote its own scarce resources to train and fund Chinese revolutionaries. During August 1919, Trotsky sent a secret communique to the Central Committee of the Bolshevik party stressing the importance of Asian revolutions. To assist these revolutions, Trotsky proposed constructing a revolutionary academy in the Urals or Turkestan to provide all the necessary facilities, such as linguists and translation departments, in order to train Asia's "native revolutionaries." Trotsky then concluded by stating that colonial revolutions would soon increase, and that the "arena of the next uprisings would be in Asia."[15]

These statement by Stalin, Vilenskii, and Trotsky during 1919 are the first signs of what soon became one of the Bolsheviks' most important foreign policy initiatives during the 1920s: actively promoting anti-imperialist revolutions throughout Asia by training and funding native revolutionaries.[16] It was not a prerequisite, however, that these native revolutionaries be communists, or even conversant with Marxism. Although Comintern representatives would later hold talks with a large number of influential Chinese leaders,[17] Moscow's early efforts to make contact with Sun during 1918, as well as repeated references to him in the Soviet press during 1919, show that the Bolsheviks hoped Sun would prove to be one of China's most important "native revolutionaries." Since Sun was not only a famous revolutionary in his own right but also the leader of the Canton government, Moscow and Canton already had a common opponent in Peking, thus making this alliance even more valuable.

Soviet Motives for Forming the United Front

Before an anti-imperialist United Front with Sun Yat-sen could be formed, the Bolsheviks needed to locate pro-Soviet sympathizers in China willing to act as intermediaries. These early intermediaries were destined to become the future leaders of the CCP. Even prior to the CCP's formal creation in July 1921, Ch'en Tu-hsiu played an important role in helping Comintern officials make contact with Sun Yat-sen and the KMT. These early attempts to ally Moscow with Canton show that the Bolsheviks promoted the first United Front not to further the interests of the CCP–as Comintern propaganda was later to claim–but their own.

On March 26, 1920, newspapers all over China published the Soviet government's July 25, 1919 version of the first Karakhan Manifesto. That same day the Chinese consulate in Vladivostok noted the arrival at the train station of Gregorii Voitinskii, the twenty-seven-year-old China expert for the Comintern's Far Eastern Secretariat.[18] The timely publication of the Karakhan Manifesto was clearly intended to help Voitinskii recruit sympathetic Chinese intellectuals to carry out the United Front Policy.

Voitinskii reached Peking during April 1920, whereupon Li Ta-chao introduced him to Ch'en Tu-hsiu. One commentator has concluded that it was Li who decided Ch'en was the best candidate to organize the CCP.[19] Ch'en was a good choice, since, as editor of the journal *Hsin Ch'ing-nien* [新青年] (*New Youth*), he had become one of China's most respected intellectuals. He also became widely known when he was first imprisoned during the May Fourth Movement and then fired by Peking University. According to one scholar, the "bitter antipathy for the status quo" exhibited by Ch'en and other radicals, "was part of the cultural nexus that led many radicals to socialism and then onto Bolshevism."[20]

Philosophically, it was a confusing time for Ch'en, as he dabbled with utopianism, Wilsonian democracy, Christianity, and John Dewey's guild socialism.[21] Later, he even advocated an American-style federal government for China and urged citizen groups to promote democracy.[22] But, Ch'en did not know how to carry out this plan, complaining that he wanted "to create a new form of politics, which would not be restrained and fettered by existing politics."[23]

Voitinskii had a profound influence on Ch'en, who apparently thought Soviet Russia represented the new form of politics he had been searching for. By May

1920, Ch'en claimed that since workers constituted the most important class, they should take control over "politics, the military, and industry."[24] In August 1920, he described workers as oppressed and blamed capitalists for using "state, government, and laws," to make workers less important than "beasts of burden" or "machines." Ch'en also advocated using "revolutionary means" to create a proletariat state, emphasizing the virtues of "Lenin's dictatorship of the proletariat."[25]

However, Voitinskii's mission was not simply to spread the Bolshevik revolution to China, but also to create a pro-Soviet Chinese government to "confound attempts to encircle the Soviet Union by hostile capitalist powers."[26] To further this goal, Voitinskii met with Sun Yat-sen during the fall of 1920.[27] Following an October 1920 reorganization of the Canton government, Ch'en assumed control of its Education Committee, where he edited the newspaper the *Kuang-tung ch'un-pao* [广东群报] (the *Kuangtung Masses*). In the first edition, published on January 19, 1921, he openly espoused socialism. Most importantly, Ch'en lauded Russian-style communism, proclaiming that the only brand of socialism that had been realized was the philosophy that "bore the name of the Russian Communist Party."[28]

Ch'en Tu-hsiu's efforts to promote greater cooperation between Canton and Moscow represented an important step toward forming the United Front. In particular, the publication in Canton of Ch'en's pro-Soviet article occurred only nine months after Voitinskii's arrival in China. This proved the efficacy of relying on Chinese intermediaries to contact and promote closer ties with Sun. On August 28, 1921, Sun Yat-sen wrote a letter to Chicherin expressing interest in the United Front: "Like Moscow, I wish to lay the foundation of the Chinese Republic deeply in the minds of the young generation–the workers of tomorrow."[29] During late 1921, Maring met Sun to discuss forming the United Front Policy in league with the Chinese Communist Party. The Soviet government was now closer to fulfilling its goal set in 1918 of forming an alliance with Sun Yat-sen.

An article by the Hungarian Comintern leader, Evgenii Varga, helps explain why the Comintern promoted the United Front so ardently. Varga hypothesized that once colonial independence movements' threw off their "foreign yoke," this would "undermine the very foundation of the great powers' economic hegemony."[30] In addition, Vilenskii predicted that Moscow's allies, Chang Tso-lin in Manchuria and Sun Yat-sen in Canton, would soon take control of "middle China."[31] The Comintern's own press suggests, therefore, that the United Front was not only intended to be a direct blow against capitalism, but was also thought to be a means of increasing the influence of the USSR throughout all of China.

Although Comintern publications emphasized the value of the United Front in China's struggle against the capitalist nations, there was also an important diplomatic component not presented to the Russian or the Chinese public. As revealed in a November 7, 1922 letter from Adolf Joffe, a Soviet envoy to China, to Maring, the Soviet government hoped that the United Front would prompt Sun to change "his passive policy to an active one," and to intervene "in affairs of the central government" in Peking.[32] On November 17, 1922, Joffe even urged Maring to gain Sun's help in Moscow's ongoing negotiations with the Peking government: "Moreover, I ask you to inform Sun that I rely strongly on his support at the negotiations (especially on the Mongolian and East China railways questions)."[33]

Even before receiving these letters, Maring, writing under his Chinese pen name Sun To (孫鐸), had promised Sun Yat-sen that maintaining "friendly and affectionate" relations with anticapitalist Russia would help the KMT achieve a "glorious victory in its struggle for liberation and independence," by ridding China of foreign "aggression and exploitation." Unfortunately, Maring lamented, although the KMT was "already good friends of the new Russia," it "still did not completely understand the necessity of publicizing the goodwill which existed between China and Russia."[34]

These documents suggest that one of the Comintern's primary motives for forming the United Front was to marshal Chinese public opinion behind the Soviet diplomats in Peking. In China, public opinion (輿論) first became a "powerful instrument of public rage" under the Ch'ing, an instrument that early Chinese reformers repeatedly used to "berate the authorities."[35]   During the Republican period, it became even more important; most notably, Chinese public outrage during the May Fourth Movement prevented Peking from signing the Versailles Peace Treaty in 1919. The Comintern's assignment was to turn public opinion in China against Peking once again, but this time in support of Soviet Russia's foreign policy objectives.

Sun Yat-sen's Nationalism

In a rare case of unanimity, Soviet, PRC, and Taiwanese historians generally agree that Sun Yat-sen was a nationalist. One Soviet historian, for example, described Sun as "a steadfast fighter for a free and independent China."[36] A PRC history claimed that "Sun Yat-sen–adhered to a nationalist viewpoint, and underwent many conflicts."[37] For political reasons, Taiwanese follow Chiang Kai-shek's 1943 description of Sun as the "far-sighted Father of our Republic . . . [who] called upon the people to struggle for their nation's freedom and equality."[38]

Western historians, swayed by this uncharacteristic unity of opinion, have also claimed that Sun Yat-sen was a nationalist. One sympathetically referred to Sun as a "patriotic revolutionary," and the "father of the Chinese revolution."[39] Another asserted that it was Sun who turned to "a tougher nationalism which aimed at the unequivocal assertion of Chinese independence and equality," and that "Nationalism had become the presiding passion of their lives, and Sun embodied its militant spirit."[40] A third described Sun's 1923 alliance with the USSR and the CCP as invigorating the KMT with "fresh nationalistic fire."[41] Finally, even "Sun's death transmitted his nationalistic zeal to at least the modern elites of China, for whom Sun came to symbolize a new, stirring, selfless, patriotism."[42]

Until recently, almost all descriptions of Sun Yat-sen as a nationalist deemphasized the remarkable ideological shifts following his 1923 alliance with the USSR. But, a recent publication has explained how this alliance altered Sun's views on nationalism: "Sun's principle of nationalism, which had meant the restoration of China's national independence and pride, now became infused with Lenin's theory of imperialism, thus encouraging the Chinese to blame their country's current problems on foreigners and their wealth."[43]

Determining whether Sun Yat-sen was really a nationalist, therefore, depends on whether one relies on Western or Soviet definitions. In fact, after World War I, two radically different types of nationalism competed with each other in China. Woodrow Wilson was the most visible representative of the Western viewpoint, stressing the rights of ethnic and national groups to form sovereign states with his policy of "national self-determination." Accordingly, Wilson supported the League of Nations in the hope that mutual security would replace the pre–World War I "balance of power."[44] Wilson also upheld the inviolability of a country's sovereignty and territorial integrity, optimistically proclaiming: "The day of conquest and aggrandizement is gone by."[45]

Wilson's nationalism quickly ran afoul with that of Vladimir Lenin, however, who described "nationalism" as support for socialism in its global struggle against capitalism. In 1913, Lenin attacked Wilson's nationalism as "bourgeois nationalism," and proclaimed that it and "proletariat internationalism," were the "two irreconcilably hostile slogans that correspond to the two great class camps throughout the entire capitalist world and express the *two* policies (more than that: two world outlooks), in the national question."[46] Due to this sharp ideological disagreement, Trotsky described Wilson and Lenin as "the apocalyptic antipodes of our time."[47] The Paris newspaper, *Le Temps,* concluded: "One [was] the way of the nationalities. The other the way of classes. . . . Peace of nations or Bolshevism, between these perspectives a choice [must] be made."[48]

Not surprisingly, these two competing views of nationalism differed on many basic questions, such as national sovereignty and territorial integrity. For example, unlike Wilson, Lenin claimed that ethnicity must always yield before class.[49] Lenin also supported the formation of a socialist sphere of influence, or "camp," to oppose imperialism, a characteristic that he claimed was unique to capitalist countries. As a result, only Lenin's nationalism could enable Soviet Russia to claim that its territorial and economic expansion into China–such as the Red Army's invasion of Outer Mongolia and Soviet efforts to retake majority control over the Chinese Eastern Railway–were socialist victories against imperialism.

Sun Yat-sen's earliest speeches and writings reveal that his own definition of nationalism was not dissimilar to that which only later became associated with Wilson. For example, in 1906, Sun presented a speech in Tokyo in which he claimed that: "Nationalism does not mean hostility to other nations, but the prevention of other nations' seizing the sovereignty of my nation."[50] Thereafter, in Sun's December 1911 "Statement of Proposals by the T'ung-meng-hui" he asserted: "To be sure, our party does uphold the Principle of Nationalism," and called on "the righteous, resolute men of our party, ready to exert themselves to overcome formidable hardships in order to honor our nation and bring into full play the distinctive traits of the race!"[51]

Later, in 1918, Sun presented a more detailed definition of nationalism in his *Memoirs of a Chinese Revolutionary*. Basing his description primarily on the United States, Sun announced the following nationalist goals for China[52]:

> We shall establish an united Chinese Republic in order that all the peoples–Manchus, Mongols, Tibetans, Tartars, and Chinese–should constitute a single powerful nation. As an example of what I have described, I can refer to the people of the United States of America, constituting one great and terrible whole, but in reality consisting of many separate nationalities: Germans, Dutch, English, French, etc. The United States is an example of a united nation. Such a nationalism is possible, and we must pursue it.

To build this united Chinese Republic, Sun further advocated that China had to "satisfy the demands and requirements of all races and unite them in a single cultural and political whole, to constitute a single nation."[53]

Sun's published works show that his original definition of nationalism was similar to that advocated by Woodrow Wilson. In 1918, for example, Sun explicitly stated that once China became a united nation, all smaller nationalities would be given "the opportunity to enjoy the feeling of equality of man and man, and of a just international attitude, i.e., that which was expressed in the declaration of the American President Wilson by the words 'self-determination of nations'."[54]

By 1919, Sun had adopted an even more Wilsonian definition of nationalism in his *Three People's Principles*, explaining that it required "the Han people to sacrifice the separate nationality, history, and identity that they are so proud of and to merge in all sincerity with the Manchus, Mongols, Muslims, and Tibetans in one melting pot to create a new order of Chinese nationalism, just as America has produced the world's leading nationalism by melding scores of different people, black and white."[55] Sun continued to support Wilsonian nationalism in a later book called *China's Revolution*, published in early January 1923, when he defined nationalism as "unity and equality of races within China, and China's rights among the nations of the world."[56]

Prior to January 1923, there is little doubt that Sun Yat-sen's words and actions conformed to Wilson's definitions of nationalism. In fact, Sun attributed his own nationalist ideals to Wilson when he openly advocated that the Mongolian people should become an integral part of what he called the "united Chinese Republic." Beginning in January 1923, however, Sun appeared to abandon this position when he supported the USSR's imperialist policies in Outer Mongolia and over the CER. Sun Yat-sen's actions did not conform to commonly accepted Western definitions of nationalism, which presupposed such elements as: "Devotion to one's nation; national aspiration; a policy of national independence."[57] Sun's actions could be called nationalist, therefore, only if one used a Leninist definition, like those contained in Comintern resolutions calling on China's nationalists to struggle for independence from Western imperialism.[58]

It is important to reconsider descriptions of Sun Yat-sen as a nationalist in light of these two competing definitions.[59] It is difficult to argue that policies benefiting the USSR at China's expense conformed to Wilson's nationalism, so once Sun threw his support behind Soviet Russia, his nationalism can best be understood in terms of Lenin's anticapitalist definition. In the following discussion of Sun's public support for the Red Army's occupation of Outer Mongolia and his secret support for Moscow's plan to retake majority control over the CER, it would perhaps be more accurate to describe Sun's actions not as "nationalistic," therefore, but as "opportunistic."[60]

Sun Yat-sen's Changing Views Toward Outer Mongolia

Prior to China's 1911 revolution, Chinese sovereignty over Mongolia was never disputed, not even by tsarist Russia. Even after 1911, the international community—including Russia—continued to recognize China's claim over Mongolia.[61] But between 1912 and 1915, Russia forced China to recognize the autonomy of Outer Mongolia and turned it into a Russian protectorate. Prior to 1923, Sun Yat-sen condemned these imperialist actions and claimed that Mongolia was an integral part of China. In January 1923, however, Sun publicly agreed to allow the Red Army's continued occupation of Outer Mongolia. Sun clearly changed his position as a result of forming the United Front with the USSR.

During the early 1920s, Sun Yat-sen attempted to obtain funding and recognition from the United States, Great Britain, and Japan. These countries all refused, explaining that to support Sun's Canton government while continuing to recognize the central government in Peking would merely impede China's unification.[62] Even Soviet historians have admitted that Sun only turned to the Bolsheviks as a last resort.[63] The price for cementing an alliance with the USSR clearly included Sun's support for Soviet Russia's foreign policy goals in Outer Mongolia. For example, during the spring of 1922, the Soviet labor representative in Canton, Sergei Dalin, told Sun that the Soviet-backed government in Outer Mongolia was "a kindred spirit of the revolutionary south and the Kuomintang" and promised that "if Sun Yat-sen recognized the independence of Mongolia, then he would receive a loyal ally in the north."[64]

Although Sun refused to agree immediately to Dalin's suggestion, by the fall of 1922, he had been ousted from Canton and was a political refugee in Shanghai. It was during this period that Adolf Joffe wrote to Maring and requested that Sun Yat-sen support Moscow against Peking on the Outer Mongolian and CER questions.[65] Sun's assistance was considered especially important because Peking diplomats insisted that the Red Army must first withdraw from Outer Mongolia prior to the opening of official Sino-Soviet negotiations.

When Joffe's negotiations with Peking ground to a halt in late 1922, he excused himself by explaining that he was going to Shanghai on the order of his doctors for "treatment of my illness."[66] In fact, he met with Sun and on January 26, 1923, the two men signed a four-point agreement that formally inaugurated the United Front (see Document 7). In this joint declaration, Sun agreed to allow the Soviet military occupation of Outer Mongolia to continue: "Dr. Sun Yat-sen, therefore, does not view an immediate evacuation of Russian troops from Outer Mongolia as either imperative or in the real interest of China."[67] Sun also stated in this declaration that the Soviet military occupation of Outer Mongolia did not constitute an imperialist policy. As a result, Sun's pro-Bolshevik declaration provided Soviet diplomats with crucial leverage over Peking, since they could always threaten to open Sino-Soviet diplomatic relations with Canton instead.

Descriptions of Sun as a nationalist following his support for the USSR's military occupation of Outer Mongolia necessarily reflect a shift away from Wilson's nationalism and toward Lenin's. This shift is best shown in a 1926 book by Anatolii Kallinikov, a Soviet expert on China: "The radical revolutionaries and the proletarian elements in China consider that the very widest political independence of Mongolia does not contradict the correctly understood national interests of China; . . . the Kuomintang party, founded by the old Chinese revolutionary, the late Sun Yat-sen, who unified the radical revolutionary and socialist elements in China, is the natural ally of the Mongolian revolutionaries."[68]

Kallinikov thus denied that the USSR's military occupation of Outer Mongolia was an imperialist encroachment of China's "correctly-understood national interests." This was actually a catchword for Lenin's nationalism. If Sun Yat-sen is to be considered a nationalist after 1923, therefore, it must be in the Leninist, and not the Wilsonian, sense of the term.

Sun Yat-sen's Support for Soviet Control of the CER

While Outer Mongolia had already been occupied by Soviet troops, and so one might argue that Sun's aid to the USSR was largely *ex post facto*, the CER was wholly under Chinese management after March 1920. For this reason, Sun Yat-sen's public support for joint Sino-Soviet management, as well as his secret support for Moscow's diplomatic attempts to retake majority control over this railway, helped strip China of an economic asset worth an estimated 700 million gold rubles. It also weakened China's control over northern Manchuria, since the CER was the major transportation artery.

Although Moscow had promised to renounce all tsarist concessions and to return the CER to China without compensation, Soviet diplomats in Peking in fact worked tirelessly to regain control over it. Secret communications between Maring and Moscow even referred to a Red Army plan to invade Manchuria during fall 1922, in order to retake the CER by force.[69] On January 26, 1923, Sun Yat-sen backed Moscow over Peking when he agreed that instead of returning the railway it should be managed jointly. Sun publicly advocated a management plan in which each country would have five seats on the board of directors and decisions would be made on the basis of "true rights and special interests."[70]

國父與蘇俄派至中國特命全權大使

越飛發表關於中俄間關係之聯合宣言

一、孫逸仙博士以為共產組織甚至蘇維埃制度事實均不能引用于中國因中國並無使此項共產制度或蘇維埃制度可以成功之情況也此項見解越飛君完全同感且以為中國最要最急之問題乃在民國的統一之成功與完全國家的獨立之獲得關于此項大事業越飛君並確告孫博士中國當得俄國國民最摯熱之同情且可以俄國援助為依賴也

二、為明瞭此等地位起見孫逸仙博士要求越飛君再度切實聲明一九二〇年九月二十七日俄國對中國通牒列舉之原則越飛君因此向孫博士重行宣言即俄國政府準備且願意根據俄國拋棄帝政時代中俄條約（連同中東鐵路等合同在內）之基礎另行開始中俄交涉

三、因承認全部中東鐵路問題祇能于適當之中俄會議始克解決故孫逸仙博士以為現在中東路之管理事實上現在祇能維持現狀且與越飛同意現行鐵路管理法祇能由中俄兩政府不加成見以雙方實際之利益與權利作為改組同時孫逸仙博士以為此點應與張作霖將軍商洽

四、越飛君正式向孫博士宣稱（此點孫博士以為滿意）「俄國現政府決無亦從無意思與目的在外蒙古實施帝國主義之政策或使其與中國分立」孫博士因此以為俄國軍隊不必立時由外蒙撤退緣為中國實際利益與必要計中國北京現政府無力防止因俄兵撤退後白俄反對赤俄陰謀與敵抗行為之發生以及釀成較現在尤為嚴重之局面

越飛君與孫博士以最親摯有禮之情形相別彼將于離日本之際來中國南部然後赴北京

一九二三年一月二十六日上海孫逸仙越飛簽字

Document 7

The January 26, 1923 Sun-Joffe Pact

By agreeing to these terms, Sun tacitly acknowledged that Moscow no longer had to return the railway to China "without compensation," as it had promised to do in 1919. This position was in sharp contrast to that taken by the Peking government, which insisted that the Soviet government carry through on its public commitments and honor its promise to return the CER to China. Even though Sun publicly stated that the railway should be managed equally, Moscow actually hoped to obtain his support for regaining majority control. During February 1923, Maring visited the Manchurian warlord, Chang Tso-lin, and reported to Moscow: "I gained the strong impression that a lot can be achieved with Chang through Sun Yat-sen. This situation should be made use of."[71]

Acting on Maring's recommendation, Sun sent two KMT officials, Wang Ching-wei and Chang Chih, to talk to Chang Tso-lin about Moscow's plan to retake seven of the ten seats on the railway's board of directors. Maring later reported: "On the question of the Chinese Eastern Railway, I have received news today that Wang Ching-wei and Chang Chih have returned from Mukden without getting the 7-3 demand adopted. Chang Tso-lin has declared that first Russia wanted 5-5 and he thinks that Wu P'ei-fu [a powerful Chinese warlord who opposed Chang Tso-lin] could very easily agitate against him if he adopts 7-3."[72] Maring's reports confirm that Sun Yat-sen actively assisted Soviet attempts to regain a majority of the seats on the CER's board of directors; in other words, Sun was working to reinstate tsarist Russia's unequal treaties with China.

Sun's decision to barter away control over the CER in return for Soviet aid was never previously disclosed. In return for his help with Chang Tso-lin, Moscow provided Sun with "ideological and political" help, a loan of two million gold rubles, and "assistance in organizing an outstanding military unit" armed with "eight thousand Japanese rifles, fifteen machine-guns, four 'Oriska' guns, and two armored cars."[73] Although it has long been known that Moscow helped fund Sun's government in Canton, it was never clear what benefits the USSR received in return. Recently published archival documents have finally helped answer this important question and, in so doing, have provided compelling evidence that Sun sacrificed China's interests to further his own.

Because the Bolsheviks understood the value of gathering Chinese public opinion behind their negotiations with Peking, they secretly funded, supplied, and advised Sun in return for his support. In the Sun-Joffe agreement, Sun directly opposed Peking's diplomatic position, thereby acknowledging that the Bolsheviks no longer had to uphold the Karakhan Manifesto's generous promises. Thus, Joffe quickly gained from Sun economic and territorial concessions that Soviet diplomats had fruitlessly been trying to convince Peking to accept since the Paikes mission the previous year. Although Sun had no real authority over Outer Mongolia or the CER, the Sun-Joffe pact represented an enormous propaganda victory for the Soviet Union. Thereafter, Soviet diplomats repeatedly used Sun's declaration to marshal Chinese public opinion against Peking.

Sun Yat-sen and the United Front Policy

While Moscow's goal in signing the Sun-Joffe pact can easily be understood, it is more difficult to explain why Sun would agree to Joffe's preconditions for forming the United Front. One of Sun's biographers has suggested that perhaps Sun did not "have a clear understanding of the aims and tasks of the Soviet state's foreign policy."[74] A more reasonable explanation, however, was that just as Moscow hoped to play Canton off Peking, so Sun hoped to play the Bolsheviks off the United States, Great Britain, and Japan in his ongoing quest to obtain foreign recognition of his opposition government.

Evidence supporting this interpretation is readily available. For example, immediately after meeting with Joffe in Shanghai, Sun and his secretary, Eugene Chen, returned to Canton to form a new government. Coincidentally, they traveled on the same ship as Nelson T. Johnson, the American consul-general for the Far East. If Sun had really been committed to the Bolsheviks' anti-imperialist United Front, then his secretary should have opposed American intervention in China. But in private discussions with Johnson, Eugene Chen requested that the United States *increase* its presence by sending a representative, "who as a neutral person would be able to bring together the mutually suspicious leaders of China and make it possible for them to unite for some scheme of government."[75] In addition, Sun turned to the United States during spring 1923 and requested that it intervene in China to "save it from ultimate ruin."[76]

Repeated requests for American intervention in China contradict the generally accepted image of Sun Yat-sen as the first Chinese revolutionary to forge a true anti-imperialist alliance with the Soviet Union. In reality, just as Moscow was carrying out a self-serving policy by using its alliance with Sun and the KMT to rally Chinese public opinion against Peking, Sun hoped to reap personal benefits by using his highly publicized alliance with Moscow to pressure the United States and other foreign powers to break relations with Peking and recognize his Canton government instead.

But, since at least 1920, when the American minister to China, Charles Crane, described Sun as "an unscrupulous adventurer," Washington had considered the KMT "an organization in revolt against a Government with which the United States is in friendly relations."[77] The decision to ignore Sun's appeals was made at the highest level of government: Secretary of State Charles Hughes wrote to President Warren Harding on May 24, 1922, that Sun was "impossible as a responsible statesman."[78] Even more damning was that Joffe apparently agreed with Washington's assessment, describing Sun in a November 7, 1922 letter to Maring as only interested in pursuing a "self-seeking policy."[79]

When attempts to use an alliance with the Bolsheviks as a lever to force recognition from the capitalist powers failed, Sun then had little choice but to strengthen his ties with Moscow. Sun was even quoted as stating that "he was not unaware of the Soviet intentions in China, but in the face of British, American, and Japanese hostility toward the Canton government, his alliance with the

Soviet Union was aimed at easing pressure from the other foreign power[s]. Should the relations between the Canton government and the foreign powers improve, he saw no reason why the KMT should lean just toward the Soviet Union."[80]

Documents show that in return for his support Sun demanded Soviet military and political advisers, weapons and ammunition, and funding. What Sun really wanted was Soviet aid, not an alliance with the Chinese communists. As one Soviet historian has acknowledged, the CCP's "political significance" in the KMT's eyes depended solely on its "stable connections with the Soviet Union and the Comintern."[81] As a result, the CCP's precarious existence as matchmaker for the marriage of convenience between the KMT and the Bolsheviks continued from 1923 to 1927, but only so long as neither the USSR nor the KMT could achieve their ultimate political objectives.

Sun Yat-sen and the *Three People's Principles*

The evolution of Sun Yat-sen's revolutionary philosophy, the so-called *Three People's Principles* (*The People's Nationalism* [民族主義], *The People's Democracy* [民權主義], and *The People's Livelihood* [民生主義]), reflected his shift away from Wilsonian nationalism to Leninist nationalism and his growing support for Soviet Russia's foreign policy. In fact, Sun's published works reveal that his definition of these principles changed dramatically after January 1923, when he not only began to attack the capitalist countries as oppressors, but he also started to support the USSR's foreign policies in China.

As noted above, during 1918 and 1919, Sun Yat-sen's nationalism not only called for uniting Manchus, Mongols, Tibetans, Tartars, and Han Chinese into a single nationality, but it also included uniting "all the races inhabiting China to form one Chinese people in eastern Asia, a Chinese National State."[82] But after his alliance with Moscow, Sun's nationalism added a new anti-capitalist component. On January 23, 1924, the Kuomintang's first congress officially adopted a new definition of Chinese nationalism, i.e., the "liberation" (解放) of China from the "Great Powers" (列強), a term that included the capitalist nations but that specifically excluded the USSR, and from the "warlords" (軍閥) and "domestic and external capitalists" (国內外之资本家).[83]

This metamorphosis in Sun's nationalism can be traced to the Comintern's influence, since only two months earlier, on November 28, 1923, a Comintern resolution had declared: "Nationalism is the struggle of the Kuomintang for China's independence from world imperialism and its protégés" (Национализм-борьба гоминьдана против мирового империализма и его ставленников за независимость Китая).[84] The word "protégé" here referred to the Chinese warlords and to the Peking government, which means that the Comintern's working definition for the term nationalism in China was actually: "The struggle of the Kuomintang for China's independence from world imperialism, warlords, and the Peking government."

To understand the Kuomintang's new anticapitalist resolutions, one must again refer to Sun's adoption of Leninist concepts in his *Three People's Principles*. In 1918, Sun modeled *The People's Democracy* on the United States, calling for the adoption of "equal and direct electoral rights for all the population, . . . universal suffrage, the referendum, the initiative and the right of recall," and he even quoted President Lincoln's "Government of the people, by the people, and for the people."[85]

After 1923, however, Sun adopted a more Leninist interpretation of the term democracy. In fact, Sun's new democracy was based largely on the November 28, 1923 Comintern resolution that China's democracy should serve "the interests of the workers of China" (в интересах трудовых масс Китая) in their "struggles against imperialism" (борьбы против империализма).[86] In this resolution the Comintern also defined China's struggle against imperialism as opposition "to foreign imperialists or their protégés–the Chinese militarists" (иностранным империалиситам или их ставленникам-китайским милитаристам).[87] After adopting this Comintern interpretation, therefore, the Kuomintang's first congress warned that: "Frequently, what modern countries call democracy has become a tool for the exclusive convenience of the capitalist class to oppress the working class" and advocated that the primary goal of Chinese democracy was to struggle against imperialism.[88]

Likewise, Sun's *The People's Livelihood* had formerly advocated using foreign capital to develop China's industry: "In brief, we can easily incur debt to foreign capital, but the question is–how shall we utilize it, productively or otherwise?"[89] But on November 28, 1923, the Comintern referred to Sun's principle as "State Socialism" (государственный социализм), and advocated the Kuomintang's "nationalization of foreign firms, enterprises, banks, railways, shipping lines" (национализации иностранных фирм, предприятий, банков, железных дорог и водных путей сообщения).[90] In line with this interpretation, the Kuomintang's first congress met the Comintern halfway, calling for China to nationalize all "railways and shipping lines" (铁道，航路).[91]

Finally, basing its actions on the Comintern's anticapitalist rhetoric, the Kuomintang congress adopted a resolution calling for the immediate renegotiation of any treaty between "China and the Great Powers" (中国与列強) in which China's national interests were adversely affected.[92] Since the term "Great Powers" referred only to capitalist powers, however, the USSR alone was exempt from having to renegotiate any of its treaties infringing on China's national sovereignty or territorial integrity. Thus, Moscow's attempts to renew tsarist Russia's former sphere of influence in Outer Mongolia and Manchuria now appeared secure.

Clearly, Sun Yat-sen's new definitions of nationalism, democracy, and the people's livelihood had very little in common with his earlier philosophy, but were now premised on class conflict and support for China's struggle against the capitalist countries. In fact, under the influence of Comintern advisers, Sun's *Three People's Principles* had taken on a decidedly anticapitalist character and served as the foundation for the Kuomintang's program to drive the capitalist countries out of China. As a result, one contemporary described Sun Yat-sen's *Three People's Principles* as having changed from supporting China's equal rights among the nations of the world to little more than a "terrific arraignment of foreign imperialism."[93]

This Leninist definition of Chinese nationalism proved to be extremely important, since Sun's support for Soviet diplomats in their negotiations with Peking during 1924 could only be called "nationalism" according to the Comintern's definition.[94] Although the true meaning of Sun's new nationalism became muddled over the years, one early biographer of Sun Yat-sen described how his definition changed, and attributed this change to Russian influence[95]:

> The Russians presented a brilliantly conceived, partially true and thoroughly palatable analysis of national frustration. Russia diagnosed China's plight as due to "foreign imperialism." Not so far gone that her mind was unclear, China knew that a certain amount of the trouble was due to rampant internal militarism. But the Russians affirmed that the Chinese militarists and foreign imperialists worked hand in hand; that when the militarists wanted money, they went to the foreign Powers; that when the foreign Powers wanted privileges they supported the militarists. Looked at through Russian eyes, the evil in China was the *bete noir* [sic] of communism, the "world evil" of "imperialistic exploitation," especially of an insidious, economic kind. China, wishing to throw off the disease, followed the doctor's advice. Sun Yat-sen roused the people with the fear of racial extinction. He painted the "imperialistic powers" very black and sent China on a crusade for "national independence."

In fact, what Sun's new definition of nationalism did was to replace Wilson's ethnically based with Lenin's class-based nationalism. Basing nationalism solely on class helped obscure Soviet violations of China's territorial integrity and sovereignty. For example, once Sun's definition of nationalism changed, the KMT's public support for the Soviet actions in Outer Mongolia and along the CER could be justified as nationalism, since the Bolsheviks claimed that imperialism was a characteristic that existed only in capitalist countries. As a result, Chinese nationalism began to oppose the capitalist countries while simultaneously supporting the renewal of tsarist Russia's territorial concessions, special rights, and privileges in Outer Mongolia and Manchuria.

Sun Yat-sen's new definition of nationalism soon led to the Kuomintang's adoption of anticapitalist economic policies. In particular, China's fight for liberation from foreign interference came to be associated only with the struggle against the capitalist countries. This distinction was extremely important, because while Wilsonian nationalism could be applied equally against capitalist or socialist nations, Sun's new nationalism could be directed solely against the capitalists.

The Chinese revolutionaries' complete acceptance of Sun's nationalism helps explain, therefore, how they could ignore the USSR's imperialist policies in Outer Mongolia and Manchuria through 1927, when Chiang Kai-shek finally broke with the KMT's former Soviet ally and purged the Chinese communists.

The Kuomintang's Foreign Policy Platform

Mikhail Borodin, the Comintern's main adviser in China, arrived in Canton in October 1923, carrying a letter from the USSR's new envoy to Peking, Lev Karakhan. In this letter, Karakhan requested that Sun Yat-sen support Moscow's efforts to open diplomatic relations with Peking.[96] Sun was not pleased with these negotiations, because they implied that Peking was China's legitimate government, not Canton.[97] But, Borodin convinced Sun that Peking's recognition of Moscow would also give the Comintern greater freedom to help the KMT, since Soviet advisers could more easily gain access into China.[98]

Borodin's activities in Canton coincided exactly with Karakhan's negotiations with Peking and their frequent communications continued the close working relationship between the Comintern agents and Soviet diplomats in China.[99] Initially, Karakhan even tried to obtain immediate dividends from the United Front by threatening Peking that he might begin negotiations with Canton: the November 14, 1923 edition of the *North China Herald* reported that Karakhan was tired of waiting for Peking to recognize Moscow and quoted him as claiming that he could always go south in order to open diplomatic relations. This was clearly an attempt to jump-start talks with Peking.

Meanwhile, Borodin's responsibilities included reorganizing the KMT, a job started by Maring.[100] As a result of Borodin's efforts, the KMT called a party congress and on January 23, 1924, adopted its first foreign policy program. The first three resolutions of this program stated that the KMT supported: 1) abolishing "all unequal treaties concerning foreign concessions and extraterritorial rights"; 2) granting most favored nation status to those countries that abolished treaties interfering with China's sovereignty; 3) renegotiating any treaty "between China and the Great Powers" in which China's interests had been harmed.[101]

Although these resolutions appear reasonable enough, in fact, China had lost the right in Outer Mongolia "to make laws . . . to impose and collect taxes . . . to make war or peace . . . to form treaties of alliances," all essential rights for sovereignty.[102] By relying on their own definition of sovereignty (see Chapter 3), Soviet diplomats claimed that the USSR already met the conditions contained in the KMT's first two resolutions. Although the third resolution stated that any treaty that adversely affected China's "interests" had to be renegotiated, it specified that this applied only to "great powers," which meant the capitalist powers; the USSR, therefore, was technically not in violation of the KMT's third resolution.

While Borodin's wording made it appear that the USSR had complied with the KMT's foreign policy resolutions, Moscow was actually exempt from having to give up the terms of tsarist Russia's unequal treaties with China. In fact, Borodin had drafted the KMT's resolutions so that they would apply to almost every country *but* the USSR. So long as this state of affairs remained unclear, however, then Moscow's alliance with Canton provided Soviet diplomats with leverage to force Peking to accept terms that ultimately harmed China's national interests.

The final step in the Comintern's strategy of using the United Front to support Moscow's negotiations with Peking took place on March 16, 1924, when Sun Yat-sen signed KMT directive twenty-four. This directive specified that every KMT member had to sign a pledge to uphold the KMT's foreign policy resolutions. As part of this directive, pledge books were prepared and distributed.[103] But, by agreeing to follow the KMT's foreign policy resolutions, KMT members unwittingly pledged their support to the Soviet diplomats in Peking, since the USSR was the only country that claimed that it had abolished its unequal treaties with China and so fulfilled the KMT's criteria.

The best evidence of the close coordination of the Comintern agents and Soviet diplomats was that on the very day that Sun signed directive twenty-four Karakhan delivered a three-day ultimatum to C. T. Wang (see Document 8). In this ultimatum, Karakhan stated that: "I am prepared to wait for three days, beginning with today, for confirmation on the part of the Chinese government of the agreements signed by you and me. Upon the expiration of these three days, I will not consider myself bound by them."[104] In effect, Karakhan was giving Peking a choice: either accepting the recently initialed draft Sino-Soviet treaty without revision, or breaking off all negotiations and ending any hope of opening relations between Moscow and Peking. Karakhan's ultimatum smacked of the same pressure tactics that the Bolsheviks had previously condemned tsarist diplomats for employing in China.

To support the ultimatum, Comintern agents arranged for the publication of the text of the March 14 draft Sino-Soviet treaty. Although this draft stated that all Russo-Chinese unequal treaties would be abolished, a protocol counteracting this promise remained secret. Since knowledge of this secret protocol was most likely also kept from the KMT's leadership, Sun's directive had the unintentional effect of supporting the renewal of the terms of the Russo-Chinese unequal treaties, instead of promoting a new era of equal diplomatic relations between the Soviet Union and China.

The publication of the Sino-Soviet draft treaty subjected Peking to enormous public pressure to sign it: demonstrations in Peking demanded the treaty be ratified[105]; forty-seven Peking University professors, including Li Ta-chao, urged recognition of Moscow[106]; and on April 1, 1924, Sun Yat-sen was reported as being "in favor of reassuming relations with Russia upon the preliminary terms as agreed between Dr. C. T. Wang and L. Karakhan."[107] The KMT's support ultimately helped Soviet diplomats retain control over Outer Mongolia; regain majority control over the CER; and renege on promises to abolish tsarist Russia's concessions, special rights, and privileges. By 1925, therefore, Moscow's secret diplomacy had allowed it to reclaim almost the exact same imperialist privileges and concessions that the 1919 Karakhan Manifesto had renounced.

ВЕ ПОЛНОМОЧНОЕ ПРЕДСТАВИТЕЛЬСТВО
ТСКИХ СОЦИАЛИСТИЧЕСКИХ РЕСПУБЛИК
В КИТАЕ.

ИRY PLENIPOTENTIARY MISSION OF
OF SOVIET SOCIALIST REPUBLICS
TO CHINA.

No. 1011

Пекин ___ 16 Марта ___ 4
Peking .... 192___

Милостивый Государь

Доктор Ван,

14 Марта утром мной от имени Правительства
Союза Советских Социалистических Республик и Вами
от имени Китайского Правительства были подписаны
соглашения о восстановлении нормальных отношений
между обоими странами. В течении того же дня мы
должны были подписать заново, переписанные каллиг-
рафами документы для замены подписанных предвари -
тельных текстов.

Ныне стало известно, что после подписания
Вами соглашении, Китайское Правительство постанови-
ло Вашей подписи не утверждать и не позволило Вам
подписать на бело переписанные экземпляры.

Настоящим я имею честь поставить Вас в из -
вестность и просить Вас передать об этом Китайскому
Правительству, что я готов в течении трех дней, на -
чиная с сегодняшнего дня, ждать подтверждения со
стороны Китайского Правительства, подписанных мной
и Вами соглашений. По истечении этих трех дней, я
не буду считать себя ими связанным.

Вместе с тем я имею честь сообщить, от имени
моего Правительства, что оно будет считать единствен-
но ответственным за разрыв переговоров и срыв соглашения, Китайское Правительство, на которое оно воз-
лагает также ответственность за все будущия послед-
ствия.

Пользуясь случаем, прошу принять уверения в
моем совершенном уважении. -

Управления

Китайским
договорам

С.Т.ВАНУ.

Document 8
Karakhan's March 16, 1924 Three-day Ultimatum to Peking

With the signing of the May 31, 1924 Sino-Soviet Treaty, Chinese public opinion appeared to be firmly behind Moscow. Soviet officials quickly condemned the capitalist countries for not copying Moscow's outwardly friendly relations with China; the new Soviet ambassador, Lev Karakhan, even advocated that all the capitalist countries' treaties "should not only be revised, they should be torn asunder, [and] abolished because they strangle China and because China cannot live under them."[108] But what all these denunciations failed to acknowledge, of course, was that Moscow had already succeeded in using the United Front with Sun Yat-sen to regain most of tsarist Russia's territorial and economic concessions.

Arguably, these Soviet victories would have been more difficult, if not impossible, without Sun's support; during 1924, Sun delivered a series of public lectures on the *Three People's Principles* demonstrating this support. For example, in January 1924, Sun called on the USSR to lead the world's oppressed nations against the capitalist countries, while in February 1924, he lamented that the Han Chinese had formerly been slaves of the Manchus, but were now little more than slaves of the capitalist powers.[109] In May 1924, Sun claimed that, "China under the oppression of the Powers has lost her national standing," while in November 1924, he asserted that the East employed "humanity, righteousness, and moral superiority," while the West used "military force" to achieve its ends.[110] Finally, in November 1924, Sun told cadets at the Whampoa academy that the "revolutionary method of the Russian Revolution should serve as an excellent model to us."[111]

In tandem with Sun's increasingly harsh denunciations of capitalism were his calls for the Western countries to give up their territorial and economic concessions in China, declaring during the fall of 1924: "The Chinese are determined that the concessions must be returned."[112] Thereafter, following Sun's death on March 12, 1925, his deathbed declaration, known as his political *will,* was published. It proclaimed that "the victims of imperialism will inevitably achieve emancipation from that international regime whose foundations have been rooted for ages in slavery, wars, and injustice." Sun also ordered the Kuomintang to continue its alliance with Moscow in the struggle for the "final liberation of China and other exploited countries from the yoke of imperialism."[113]

After Sun Yat-sen's death, Moscow worked diligently to promote the myth that Sun was China's greatest nationalist leader, hoping to use Sun's nationalism to rally the Chinese people against capitalism. For example, Gregorii Zinoviev, the head of the Comintern, proclaimed that China's nationalist revolution was of "great significance for world history," and called Sun the "greatest leader of the national revolutionary movements of the East." He also stated that, unlike India's nationalist leader, Gandhi, who appeased the British, Sun refused to compromise and so could truly be considered "a military ally of the world proletariat."[114] Karl Radek, a well-known Soviet theorist on China, praised Sun for being the first Asian leader not only to understand Lenin's thinking, but to "do all that was possible to bring it to reality."[115] Finally, Joseph Stalin bluntly stated that "Sun Yat-sen's doctrine" struck "terror in the enemies of the Chinese people."[116]

Conclusions

From the middle of 1918, when Chicherin sent his first letter to Sun Yat-sen, the Soviet government's China policy included an alliance with Sun and the Canton government. In order to construct this United Front, the Comintern sponsored the formation of the CCP to serve as an intermediary, and then later ordered the CCP to join the KMT (see Chapter 8). Unlike previous scholarship that has dated the founding of the CCP to some time before the adoption of the United Front, therefore, the evidence presented here suggests that this policy predated the CCP. But if the United Front Policy existed before the CCP, then this would necessarily imply that the United Front was originally intended to benefit Soviet Russia, since it could in no way benefit the nonexistent CCP.

Sun Yat-sen's apparent willingness to support the transfer of enormous territorial and economic concessions to the USSR has never before been explained. It has been suggested that Sun did not understand the Bolsheviks' real goals. But, Sun's early published works undermine this explanation, since they clearly reveal that he was cognizant of tsarist Russia's long history of imperialism and its relentless encroachment on Chinese sovereignty; by extension, therefore, Sun should have understood the danger represented by the USSR's expansionist policies. In his 1917 book *The Vital Problem of China*, Sun even described how "Russian influence extends over Outer Mongolia, Sinkiang, and North Manchuria, representing approximately 42 percent of the whole of China." By comparison, Sun estimated Great Britain's sphere of influence as a much smaller 28 percent, France's and Japan's spheres of influence as 5 percent apiece, and Germany's former sphere of influence as 2 percent. Moreover, Sun strongly condemned these foreign spheres of influence, stating, it can only be supposed, ironically: "If we desire further encroachments upon our land, we might as well proclaim to the whole world that we are offering it for sale."[117]

Given that Sun Yat-sen early opposed tsarist Russian territorial concessions in China, it seems almost unimaginable that he would later willingly agree to help the Bolsheviks rebuild tsarist Russia's sphere of influence there. Instead, convincing evidence exists to support the view that Sun agreed to ally with the USSR mainly to gain outside influence in his personal political struggle to take power in China. If true, this interpretation would help explain why Sun appeared so oblivious to the negative consequences of his actions; perhaps Sun planned to regain his losses *vis-à-vis* the USSR after he forced the other foreign powers out of China. This view would lead one to suspect that Sun intended all along to break with Moscow once he achieved his political goals, as his successor, Chiang Kai-shek, later did in 1927. With Sun's premature death in 1925, however, at the age of fifty-eight, he was prevented from carrying out this plan himself.

In the end, whether Sun Yat-sen was serious in his support for the USSR or not, his redefinition of such value-laden terms as "nationalism" had an enormous impact on the later course of the Chinese revolution. Sun's decision to grant Moscow his public support—no matter how temporarily—against China's own internationally recognized government in Peking eventually resulted in untold damage to China's sovereignty and territorial integrity. Future KMT leaders would live to regret Sun's pro-Soviet policies, particularly after Nationalist China went to war with the USSR during 1929 in a vain attempt to retake control of the CER. Thereafter, when the USSR agreed to sell the CER to Japan in 1935, Moscow even signed a secret protocol with Tokyo transferring the benefits of its 1924 secret diplomacy to Japan (see Appendix C). Finally, during 1945, the USSR not only pressured the KMT to recognize Outer Mongolia's full independence from China, but it regained control over the CER and the other tsarist concessions in Manchuria; from this vantage point, Soviet troops could threaten virtually all of northwest and northern China.

As a result of Sun Yat-sen's United Front with the Bolsheviks, China's revolutionary movement also changed dramatically. After the Leninist definition of nationalism was introduced and accepted by Chinese revolutionaries, Sun's revised *Three People's Principles* could be used not only to support the USSR's expansionist policies, but also to ensure that China's revolution would continue to be based on the struggle between socialism and capitalism. Although Moscow's hopes of sponsoring a socialist revolution in China during the 1920s were soon dashed, the Chinese communists' continued promotion of Leninist nationalism helps explain their enormously successful revolutionary program during the 1940s. The Chinese communists' primary strongholds after World War II were also strategically located in northwest and northern China, adjoining Outer Mongolia.

Thus, the long-range geopolitical impact of losing control over both Outer Mongolia and the CER proved to be far-reaching, and in both cases Sun's pro-Soviet policies played a crucial role. Seen in this light, Sun's decision to make such enormous concessions to the Bolsheviks was clearly a mistake. Mao Tse-tung, who took full advantage of the USSR's assistance even while personally opposing the loss of Outer Mongolia and the CER, was perhaps referring to this mistake on November 12, 1956, at a public commemoration of the 90th anniversary of Sun's birth, when he pointed out that "Dr. Sun, too, had his shortcomings. We must explain this in the light of historical circumstances so that people may understand it. We must not be too exacting with regard to our predecessors."[118]

Without a doubt, the Soviet-sponsored myth that Sun Yat-sen was China's greatest "nationalist" leader was one of the most enduring and important Soviet contributions to twentieth century Chinese history: this myth has been almost universally supported by Soviet, PRC, Taiwanese, and Western historians alike. It gained such widespread acceptance because calling Sun Yat-sen a "nationalist" meant different things to different people. For Taiwanese and Western scholars it meant Wilsonian nationalism, whereas for PRC and Soviet authors it meant Leninist nationalism. In fact, Sun Yat-sen fits both descriptions equally well, depending on whether one looks at his published works from before or after 1923. This simple fact helps explain why, to this day, the myth of Sun's nationalism continues to possess such potency.

Notes

1. The first United Front ended in 1927, while the second United Front was formed in the mid-1930s.

2. Stephen Uhalley dates the United Front policy from the second Comintern congress, which met during July 1920 (*A History of the Chinese Communist Party*, 18-19); Tony Saich concludes that this Comintern congress "heralded a change in relations between the Bolsheviks in Moscow and the eastern borderlands. Before this time, civil war and the expectation of revolution in the West had meant that little attention was paid to the East" (*The Origins of the First United Front in China: The Role of Sneevliet [Alias Maring]*, Vol. 1, 13); Hans J. van de Ven also concludes about the United Front Policy: "This issue can probably be traced to Maring" (*From Friend to Comrade, The Founding of the Chinese Communist Party, 1920-1927*, 88).

3. Hsiang Ch'ing's (向青)view that the alliance with Sun Yat-sen was adopted only in 1922 is characteristic of the Chinese Communist Party's historiography (共产国际和中国革命关系的历史概述 [*A Historical Summary of Relations Between the Communist International and the Chinese Revolution*], 22-26). Among Soviet historians, L. P. Deliusin (Л. П. Делюсин) and A. S. Kostiaeva (А. С. Костяева) are representative of the same viewpoint (*Революция 1925-1927 гг. в Китае: проблемы и оценки* [*Revolution of 1925-1927 in China: Problems and Appraisals*], 19). Most recently, a Russian collection of documents on the Comintern's policy in China has also supported this interpretation, since it not only did not reprint Chicherin's 1918 letter to Sun Yat-sen, but also included documents on the Comintern's China policy dating only from June 1920 and later (*ВКП(Б), Коминтерн и национально-революционное движение в Китае. Документы.* (*VKP(b), the Comintern and the National-Revolutionary Movement in China. Documents.*], Vol. 1 [1920-1925], 155-242).

4. Ch'en Tu-hsiu (陳獨秀), "社会主义批评" ("A Critique of Socialism"), January 19, 1921, 广东群报 (*Kuangtung Masses Paper*); reprinted in 陳獨秀选集 (*Collection of Ch'en Tu-hsiu's Works*), 132-147.

5. *Красный Архив* (Red Archive), Секретная телеграмма посланники в Пекине. Пекин. 2 (15) ноября 1911 г. No. 767, (Secret telegram from the envoy in Peking, Peking 2 [15] November 1911, No. 767), 18 (1926), No. 23.

6. *Great Soviet Encyclopedia*, 1973.

7. C. Martin Wilbur and Julie Lien-Ying How, *Documents on Communism, Nationalism, and Soviet Advisers in China, 1918-1927*, 138, 138 n.2; North, *Moscow and Chinese Communists*, 69.

8. *Советско-китайские отношения 1917-1957 Документы внешней политики СССР* (*Soviet-Chinese Relations, 1917-1957: Documents on the Foreign Policy of the USSR*), 40-41; Jane Degras, *Soviet Documents on Foreign Policy*, Vol. 1, 92-93.

9. Maurice Meisner, *Li Ta-chao and the Origins of Chinese Marxism*, 67, 72.

10. *Советско-китайские отношения 1917-1957 Документы внешней политики СССР* (*Soviet-Chinese Relations, 1917-1957: Documents on the Foreign Policy of the USSR*), 42-43.

11. According to C. Martin Wilbur and Julie Lien-ying How, while the KMT claimed 238,000 members in 1922, by late 1923, an enrollment drive turned up only 23,360 members in all of China, and 4,600 members overseas (*Missionaries of Revolution: Soviet Advisers and Nationalist China, 1920-1927*, 93-94). But a captured 1924 *KMT*

report lists 43,966 members abroad (see *Archives Nationales Section d'Outre-Mer [Aix-en-Provence], Service de Liaison avec des Originaires des Territories de la France Outre-Mer* V, 48). My thanks to Marilyn Levine for providing me with a copy of this document.

12. Lao Hsiu-ch'ao, "Представитель Китая о III Интернационале" ("The Chinese Representative About the Third International"), *Izvestiia,* March 6, 1919.

13. Xenia Joukoff Eudin and Robert C. North, *Soviet Russia and the East, 1920-1927,* 45-46.

14. Vladimir Dmitrievich Vilenskii-Sibiriakov (Владимир Дмитриевиц Виленский-Сибиряков), *Китай и Советская Россия* (*China and Soviet Russia*), 12.

15. Trotsky, Leon, Copy of a Military Report to the Central Committee of the Bolshevik Party, marked "Copy. Secret." (5 August 1919). Harvard University, Houghton Library, Trotsky Archives No. 2956, 4.

16. The importance of the USSR's foreign policy in Asia was acknowledged by the Comintern in 1929, when it divided the decade 1919-29 into two five-year periods: the first characterized "primarily by open battles of the proletariat in the European capitalist countries," and the second by "the development of waves of revolutionary insurrections and battles of the colonial peoples," "Коминтерн на Востоке" ("The Comintern in the East"), *Коммунистический Интернационал* (*Communist International*), No. 9-10 (1929), 20.

17. In addition to Sun Yat-sen, in 1920 and 1921 the Comintern also sounded out Wu P'ei-fu, the leader of the Chili clique; not only did Comintern propaganda refer to Wu as an "enlightened warlord," but Li Ta-chao was sent to talk to him about an alliance with Soviet Russia. At about the same time, Maring reportedly went with two Chinese communists, Tan Ping-shan and Ch'en Kung-po, to visit the Canton warlord Ch'en Chiung-ming on three different occasions to discuss forming an alliance with him. See the handwritten manuscript by Chou Fuo-hai, *A Report of a Flight from the Red Capital Wuhan,* (1927), 1, 7-8, in the Historical Commission of the Central Committee of the Kuomintang, Taipei, Taiwan.

18. The Chinese-language copy of this telegram writes Voitinskii's name phonetically as "Weiliansiji" [March 26, 1920, WCTA, 03-32, 462(3)].

19. Ch'en Kung-po, *The Communist Movement in China,* 6.

20. Hung-Yok Ip, "The Origins of Chinese Communism." *Modern China* 20, 1 (January 1994): 34-63.

21. Lee Feigon, *Chen Duxiu Founder of the Chinese Communist Party,* 143.

22. Ch'en Tu-hsiu (陳獨秀), "實行民治的基礎" ("The Basis of Putting Democracy into Practice"). 新青年 (*New Youth*), 7, 1. 1920.

23. Ch'en Tu-hsiu (陳獨秀), "新文化運動是什麼?" ("What is the New Culture Movement?"). 新青年 (*New Youth*), 7, 5. 1920.

24. Ch'en Tu-hsiu (陳獨秀), "勞動者底覺悟" ("Workers' Consciousness"). 新青年 (*New Youth*), 7, 6. 1920.

25. Ch'en Tu-hsiu (陳獨秀), "談政治" ("A Discussion of Politics"). 新青年 (*New Youth*), 8, 1. 1920.

26. James E. Sheridan, *China in Disintegration: The Republican Era in Chinese History, 1912-1949,* 143.

27. Voitinskii described this 1920 meeting with Sun Yat-sen in a March 15, 1925 *Pravda* article, written immediately after Sun's death.

28. Ch'en Tu-hsiu (陳獨秀), "社会主义批评" ("A Critique of Socialism"), 132-147.

29. *Сунъ Ятсен Избранные произведения, (Selected Works of Sun Yat-sen)*, (Moscow, 1964), 342-343.

30. E. Varga (Варга), "Проэкт теоретихческой программы Коминтерна" ("The Plan of the Theoretical Program of the Comintern") *Коммунистический Интернационал (Communist International)*, No. 23, November-December 1922, 6141-6150. Evgenii Samuilovich Varga was a Hungarian communist who fled to Soviet Russia in 1919 after the defeat of the Hungarian revolution; he was a prominant member of the Communist International and was a delegate to the Fourth, Fifth, and Sixth Comintern congresses. *Great Soviet Encyclopedia*, Vol. 4, 509.

31. V. Vilenskii (В. Виленский), "Политические группировки и партии в Китае" ("Political Groups and Parties in China"), *Коммунистический Интернационал (Communist International)*, No. 23, November-December 1922, 6077-6104.

32. Saich, Vol. 1, 352-353.

33. *Ibid.*, 356-359.

34. Sun To (孫鐸)(Maring), "俄國革命五週紀念" ("Honoring the Fifth Anniversary of the Russian Revolution"), 嚮導週報 (*The Guide Weekly*), 1922: 8, 66-67.

35. Joan Judge, "Public Opinion and the New Politics of Contestation in the Late Qing, 1904-1911." *Modern China* 20, 1 (January 1994): 64-91: 84-85.

36. Deliusin and Kostiaeva, 153.

37. 中国革命 (*History of the Chinese Revolution*), 181.

38. Chiang Kai-shek, *China's Destiny*, 15.

39. Immanuel C. Y. Hsu, *The Rise of Modern China*, 11, 518.

40. Harold Z. Schiffrin, *Sun Yat-sen and the Origins of the Chinese Revolution*, 212; Harold Z. Schiffrin, *Sun Yat-sen Reluctant Revolutionary*, 5.

41. C. Martin Wilbur, *Sun Yat-sen: Frustrated Patriot*, 288.

42. Donald A. Jordan, *The Northern Expedition China's National Revolution of 1926-1928*, 6.

43. Julie Lee Wei, Ramon H. Myers, and Donald G. Gillin, *Prescriptions for Saving China, Selected Writings of Sun Yat-sen*, xxi.

44. Paul Dukes, *The Last Great Game: USA Versus USSR, Events, Conjectures, Structures*, 63-88.

45. Arno J. Mayer, *Political Origins of the New Diplomacy, 1917-1918*, 358.

46. Louis L. Snyder, ed., *The Dynamics of Nationalism: Readings in its Meaning and Development*, 13; quoting Lenin's "Critical Remarks on the National Question, 1913."

47. Isaac Deutscher, *The Prophet Unarmed*, 215.

48. Mayer, 382, quoting *Le Temps*, January 9, 1919.

49. Richard Pipes, *The Formation of the Soviet Union: Communism and Nationalism 1917-1923*, 45.

50. J. Y. Wong, *The Origins of an Heroic Image: Sun Yatsen in London, 1896-1897*, 217.

51. Wei, Myers, and Gillin, 55-59.

52. Sun Yat-sen, *Memoirs of a Chinese Revolutionary*, 180-182.

53. *Ibid.*

54. *Ibid.*

55. Wei, Myers, and Gillin, 222-236.

56. Lyon Sharman, *Sun Yat-sen: His Life and Its Meaning*, 286-289.

57. *The Oxford English Dictionary*, 2nd ed., Vol. 10, 234; Webster's definition is similar: "Loyalty and devotion to a nation, *esp*: a sense of national consciousness exalting one nation above all others and placing primary emphasis on promotion of its culture and interests as opposed to those of other nations or supranational groups," (*Webster's Seventh New Collegiate Dictionary*, 563).

58. "Резолюция Президиума ИККИ по вопросу о национально-освободительном движении в Китае и о партии гоминьдан" ("Resolutions of the Presidium of the Comintern on the Question of the National-revolutionary Movement in China and about the Kuomintang Party"). *Коммунистический Интернационал и китайская революция Документы и материалы* (*The Communist International and the Chinese Revolution*), 41-44.

59. Martin Malia's work on the Soviet Union dates the beginning of this struggle from 1914: "And so, by 1914, a dual process of amalgamation had occurred: On the Right were aligned capitalism, unbridled individualism, nationalism, militarism, and social hierarchy; and on the Left were arrayed socialism, economical rationality, internationalism, peace, and equality. The stage was thus set for the great *Auseinandersetzung*, the world-historical clash, between capitalism and socialism that would dominate our short twentieth century" (*The Soviet Tragedy: A History of Socialism in Russia, 1917-1991*, 50).

60. *Webster's Seventh New Collegiate Dictionary*, 592; opportunism: "the art, policy, or practice of taking advantage of opportunities or circumstances esp. with little regard for principles or consequences."

61. Hoover Archives, Stanley K. Hornbeck Collection, Box 92.

62. Hoover Archives, Stanley K. Hornbeck Collection, Box 435; during the summer of 1921, almost two years before Sun allied with the Soviet Union, Stanley Hornbeck, an East Asian expert in the State Department's Far Eastern Department, wrote a memo criticizing Sun Yat-sen for being an "egotist, full of grandiose ideas," and stating that the "United States, of course, cannot recognize Sun Yat-sen or his Government or anyone professing to speak for them." But Hornbeck accurately warned that Sun Yat-sen himself embodied a political "idea, an idea which grips the minds of the more progressive and intellectually virile of the Chinese political public."

63. L. P. Deliusin (Л. П. Делюсин), *Аграрно-крестьянский Вопрос в Политике КПК 1921-1928* (*Agrarian and Peasant Questions in the Policies of the CCP 1921-1928*), 56.

64. Sergei Dalin (Сергей Далин), *В Рядах Китайской Революция* (*In the Ranks of the Chinese Revolution*), 68.

65. Letter from Joffe to Maring, November 17, 1922, Saich, Vol. 1, 356-359.

66. English-language note from Joffe to the Peking government, January 15, 1923, WCTA, 03-32, 462 (2).

67. *Советско-китайские Отношения 1917-1957 сборник документов* (*Soviet-Chinese Relations, 1917-1957, Collection of Documents*), 64-65; Chinese version, Archives of the Historical Commission of the Central Committee of the Kuomintang Party, No. 047/2; English version: "Joint Statement by Sun Yat-sen and Joffe on Soviet-Chinese Relations," Degras, Vol. 1, 370-371.

68. Anatolii Kallinikov (Анатолий Каллиников), *Революционная Монголия* (*Revolutionary Mongolia*), (Moskva, 1926), 92.

69. In a letter from Joffe to Maring, dated November 7, 1922, Joffe stated quite clearly: "I have reported to Moscow . . . that as long as Dr. Sun is not an official figure of

the Central Chinese state, we cannot, even by appealing to him, attempt an occupation in China." This reference to an "occupation" was then clarified in a report written by Maring of his conversation with P. A. Kobozev, former Chairman of the Far Eastern Republic Council of Ministers, in Chita during February 1923: "Three months ago it would have been possible to occupy the railway but now the good opportunity has already been lost." Although no military occupation of the Chinese Eastern Railway took place, it is important to clarify that a Soviet military campaign into Manchuria was seriously considered during the fall of 1922 (Saich, Vol. 1, 351-353; 400-401).

70. Degras, Vol. 1, 370-371.

71. Secret report from Maring to "Comrades Karakhan and Joffe, Copy for Members of the Politburo," entitled "Report Concerning My Trip to Mukden and My Discussions with Marshall Chang Tso-lin," February 15, 1923, Saich, Vol. 1, 407-408.

72. Letter from Maring to "Comrades Joffe, Davtian, and Zinoviev," May 31, 1923, Saich, Vol. 2, 545; also see telegram from Maring to Joffe, April 30, 1923, Saich, Vol. 1, 414.

73. Telegram from Joffe to Maring, May 1, 1923, Saich, Vol. 2, 527; that Moscow understood that its foreign aid to Sun could be interpreted as undermining China's sovereignty is best shown by its warning to Maring to be sure that this aid to Sun would "remain strictly secret."

74. Wilbur and How, *Missionaries,* 56.

75. David Lee Wilson, "The Attitudes of American Consular and Foreign Service Officers Toward Bolshevism in China, 1920-1927," 41.

76. Thomas William Ganschow, "A Study of Sun Yat-sen's Contacts with the United States Prior to 1922," 212.

77. Martin Mun-Loong Loh, "American Officials in China, 1923-1927: Their Use of Bolshevism to Explain the Rise of the Kuomintang and Chinese Anti-Foreignism," 48.

78. Ganschow, 205; Gilbert Chan and Thomas Etzold have commented that the American minister in China, Jacob Gould Schurman, even reported on June 25, 1922 that Sun was "the one outstanding obstacle to [the] reunification" of China (*China in the 1920s,* 22-25).

79. Saich, Vol. 1, 352.

80. Liu Cheng-yu (劉成禺), "先總理舊德錄" ("The Moral Teachings of the Late President [Sun Yat-sen]"), 國史館 館刊 No. 1 (December 1947), 44-56; my thanks to Eugene Wu for this citation.

81. Deliusin, 1972: 55.

82. Sun Yat-sen, *Memoirs,* 179-183.

83. 中国国民党第一，二次全国代表大会会议史料 (*Historical Materials from the Chinese Kuomintang's First and Second Party Congress*), Vol. 1, 85-88.

84. "Резолюция . . ." ("Resolutions..."). *Коммунистический Интернационал и . . .* (*The Communist International and...*), 41-44.

85. Sun Yat-sen, *Memoirs,* 182-185.

86. "Резолюция . . ." ("Resolutions..."). *Коммунистический Интернационал и . . .* (*The Communist International and...*), 41-44.

87. *Ibid.*

88. 中国国民党第一，二次全国代表大会会议史料 (*Historical Materials from the Chinese Kuomintang's First and Second Party Congress*), Vol. 1, 85-88.

89. Sun Yat-sen, *Memoirs ,* 184-190.

90. "Резолюция . . ." ("Resolutions..."). *Коммунистический Интернационал и . . .*

(*The Communist International and...*), 41-44.

91. 中国国民党第一，二次全国代表大会会议史料 (*Historical Materials from the Chinese Kuomintang's First and Second Party Congress*), Vol. 1, 85-88.

92. *Ibid*, Vol. 1, 88-90; also see Archives of the Historical Commission of the Central Committee of the Kuomintang Party, Document No. 445-8.

93. Sharman, 286-289.

94. One work did point out that "Sun's concept of Nationalism was equated with anti-imperialism," but did not clarify where this new definition of nationalism came from or how it was later used to oppose China's own central government in Peking (Robert C. North, *Chinese Communism*, 58).

95. Sharman, 291; Because this book was first published in 1934, the author was not overly influenced by Soviet propaganda claiming that Sun Yat-sen was a nationalist. ·

96. *Советско-китайские Отношения 1917-1957 сборник документов* (*Soviet-Chinese Relations, 1917-1957: Collection of Documents*), 66.

97. Lydia Holubnychy, *Borodin and the Chinese Revolution, 1923-1925*, 250-251.

98. Gaining visas to China was so difficult that the Soviet Union's first five military advisers to Canton had to be officially listed as "students" when they arrived in Peking during August 1922. Chinese and English lists, August 23, 1922, August 31, 1922, WCTA, 03-32, 462 (2).

99. An example of the constant communications between the Comintern representative in Canton and the Soviet diplomats in Peking was reported by a Canton government's unofficial representative in Peking, who recalled that Karakhan knew more about Canton then he did, since once when they were in a meeting together, Karakhan told him "Kuangtung will be recalling you soon," which is precisely what happened immediately thereafter. Archives of the Historical Commission of the Central Committee of the Kuomintang, Document No. 467-7.

100. Saich, Vol. 2: 555-64.

101. 中国国民党第一，二次全国代表大会会议史料 (*Historical Materials from the Chinese Kuomintang's First and Second Party Congress*), Vol. 1, 88-90;

102. *Black's Law Dictionary*, 1643.

103. The KMT archives still have these signed booklets, pledging to uphold the *KMT*'s 1924 foreign policy platform. When the author looked through a sample of about one hundred of these booklets, it appeared that as many *KMT* members identified themselves as "doctors," and "teachers," as they did "workers." This would suggest that support for the USSR was predominantly middle class. Archives of the Historical Commission of the Central Committee of the Kuomintang Party, Document No. 435-69.

104. Russian-language original of Karakhan's signed three-day ultimatum, March 16, 1924; WCTA, 03-32, 483(2), letter No. 1011.

105. Chu, 113.

106. Chinese-language letter from forty-seven professors at Peking University, including Li Ta-chao, calling for Peking to open relations with the USSR, March 13, 1924, WCTA, 03-32, 461(3).

107. Wilbur, *Sun Yat-sen*, 230.

108. Brian Thomas George, "The Open Door and the Rise of Chinese Nationalism: American Policy and China, 1917-1928," 227.

109. In 1953, the Kuomintang published an English-language abridged and edited version of Sun Yat-sen's speeches during 1924 under the title *San Min Chu I, The Three Principles of the People*, which eliminated Sun's negative references to capitalism and

capitalist countries. For an unabridged copy of these speeches, the author has relied on a 1946 Chinese-language version published in Japan: Sun Yat-sen, 三民主義 (*The Three People's Principles*), Tokyo: 龍文書店, 昭和二十一年, 1946, 11, 57.

110. Ku Hung-ting, "Urban Mass Politics in Southern China, 1923-1927: Some Case Studies," 74-82.

111. Wei, Myers, and Gillin, 279.

112. Chang Hsu-Hsin, "The Kuomintang's Foreign Policy 1925-1928," 118.

113. Sharman, 308; according to at least one report, Wang Ching-wei was actually responsible for writing this will, and Sun merely approved it prior to his death. Wilbur, *Sun Yat-sen*, 277.

114. "第三國際致國民黨之唁電" ("Telegram from the Third International to the Kuomintang"), 嚮導週報 (*The Guide Weekly*), March 21, 1925, No.107, 900; G. Zinoviev, "孫逸仙之死"("The Death of Sun Yat-sen"), 嚮導週報 (*The Guide Weekly*), April 12, 1925, No. 110, 1007-1008; in order to make Sun Yat-sen even more like Lenin, the Soviet government reportedly offered to send a special glass casket from Moscow so that Sun Yat-sen's body could be preserved and displayed. This plan was never actually carried into practice because the glass casket proved to be defective. Dan N. Jacobs, *Borodin, Stalin's Man in China*, 170.

115. Karl Radek (Карл Радек), "Вождь китайского народа" ("Leader of the Chinese People"), *Pravda*, March 14, 1925.

116. "俄國共產黨致國民黨之唁電" ("Russian Communist Party Telegram to the Kuomintang"), 嚮導週報 (*The Guide Weekly*), March 21, 1925, No. 107, 900.

117. Sun Yat-sen, *The Vital Problem of China*, 13-14.

118. Mao Tse-tung, "In Commemoration of Dr. Sun Yat-sen," *Dr. Sun Yat-sen Commemorative Articles and Speeches by Mao Tse-tung, Soong Ching Ling, Chou En-lai and Others*, 9-11.

84

Outer Mongolia, c. 1924

3
Outer Mongolia Enters the Communist Bloc

On May 31, 1924, Moscow and Peking signed a Sino-Soviet treaty that stated: "The Government of the Union of Soviet Socialist Republics recognizes that Outer Mongolia is an integral part of the Republic of China and respects China's sovereignty therein." In addition, the Soviet government promised to withdraw its troops from Outer Mongolia once a timetable had been decided at an official Sino-Soviet conference to convene one month later.[1] But by November 1924, the Soviet Union had completely dominated Outer Mongolia and sponsored the formation of the Mongolian People's Republic. From 1925 through the late 1980s, the Mongolian People's Republic was, in fact, more a part of the USSR than of China.

Previously, the secret Sino-Soviet negotiations that allowed Soviet diplomats to draw Outer Mongolia into the USSR's sphere of influence were largely unavailable to scholars. With the new accessibility of archival materials on Sino-Soviet diplomatic history, however, it is now possible for the first time to write a history explaining how Moscow diplomatically separated Outer Mongolia from China. This history is especially important since Outer Mongolia was arguably the first case in which the Soviet government used secret diplomacy to spread its influence and power beyond the traditional borders of the tsarist Russian empire. For this reason, the incorporation of Outer Mongolia into the Soviet sphere of influence can be seen as the beginning of the Soviet-led Communist bloc, one of the most important elements of the cold war.

Soviet Russia's negotiations with China can be divided into four periods. The first was characterized by the Bolsheviks' repeated promises from 1918 to 1920 to abolish all tsarist unequal treaties and its sphere of influence in Outer Mongolia. In the second period, from 1921 to 1922, Aleksandr Paikes, the head of the first official Soviet mission to Peking, tried unsuccessfully to convince China to recognize the 1915 tsarist tripartite treaty on Outer Mongolia, which had greatly expanded Russian influence. During the third period, 1923-24, the USSR's new envoy to China, Lev Karakhan, once again promised to abolish the tsarist unequal treaties but in fact resorted to secret diplomacy to retain them; Karakhan signed a secret protocol with the Peking government in which China tacitly recognized the 1915 tripartite treaty. Finally, during the fourth period, 1924-25, the USSR made use of this secret protocol to consolidate its control over Outer Mongolia and to draw Outer Mongolia into the Soviet-led Communist bloc. Each of the periods will be treated in greater detail below.

The October Revolution and Outer Mongolia

The tsarist Russian government took advantage of the turmoil surrounding the 1911 Chinese revolution to expand its influence in Outer Mongolia, that part of Mongolia north of the Gobi Desert.[2] Formerly, even Russian diplomats had admitted that Outer Mongolia was part of China, but with China's new republican government in disarray, tsarist Russia negotiated an advantageous treaty with Outer Mongolia in 1912 that enhanced its trading privileges.[3] Tsarist Russia then convinced China to sign a declaration in 1913 that limited China's rights in Outer Mongolia. Finally, in 1915, tsarist Russia pressured China to sign a tripartite treaty with both Russia and Outer Mongolia that recognized China's *suzerainty* over Outer Mongolia in exchange for China's recognition of Outer Mongolia's *autonomy*.

According to the generally accepted definition of *suzerainty*, China should have retained full control over Outer Mongolia's foreign policy, while recognizing Outer Mongolia's independent control of domestic policy. But China actually lost both rights, since these treaties specified that in all foreign negotiations concerning "commercial" or "industrial" rights, Outer Mongolia had full authority to negotiate with Russia without Chinese interference. It was only on political and territorial questions that "the Chinese Government shall come to an agreement with the Russian Government through negotiations in which the authorities of Outer Mongolia shall take part." Finally, the Russians could garrison troops in Outer Mongolia, although the treaties limited this to no more than "one hundred and fifty men as consular guards for its representatives at Urga," a number that China was allowed to match.[4]

The immediate effect of these treaties was that Outer Mongolia became almost completely cut off from Chinese political control. Gradually, it fell under the sway of the stronger Russian government, an action that was largely ignored by the United States and the European nations because of World War I. Following the October Revolution, the Soviet government renounced tsarist Russia's so-called unequal treaties with China as a first step in opening diplomatic relations with Peking. People's Commissar of Foreign Affairs Chicherin appeared before the Fifth Congress of the Soviets in July 1918, and presented a proposal tailored to satisfy China's desire to abolish all of the former Sino-Russian treaties: "We renounce the conquests of the tsarist government in Manchuria and we restore the sovereign rights of China in this territory. . . . We agree to renounce all land-rights of our citizens in China, Mongolia."[5]

Although Chicherin's promises were apparently never transmitted to China, they were repeated during the following year in the Karakhan Manifesto, which specifically promised to annul "all annexations of foreign lands, any subjugation of other nations, and indemnities whatever." In addition, it promised to abolish Russia's secret treaties with Japan from 1907 to 1916 that had divided Manchuria and Mongolia into Russian and Japanese spheres of influence.[6] On October 2, 1920, Karakhan's second manifesto repeated that all former Sino-Russian unequal treaties were now "null and void."[7] Finally, on April 24, 1921, the *Bulletins of the Far Eastern Secretariat of the Comintern* listed the Soviet government's promises to China as follows: "The Soviet Government renounces everything seized by the tsarist government in China, Manchuria and in other places."[8]

Although China had lost Outer Mongolia to Russia in 1915, during 1919 Outer Mongolia was beset by economic problems when the ruble collapsed, and by domestic problems when the competing factions in the Russian Civil War began to fight over its territory. This prompted the Outer Mongolian government to petition China to take it back on November 17, 1919, which the Peking government formally agreed to do on November 22, 1919. In their petition, Outer Mongolia's leaders renounced the 1915 tripartite agreement with China and Russia, as well as the agreements signed by Outer Mongolia and Russia in 1912 and 1913.[9]

Meanwhile, China still recognized the legitimacy of the former Kerensky Provisional government, whose representative, Prince Kudachev, reassured Peking that the 1915 tripartite treaty was void. Finally, Karakhan's two manifestos from 1919 and 1920 also seemed to confirm the complete abolition of this treaty. By 1920, not only had the two opposing Russian governments rejected the 1915 tripartite treaty, but Outer Mongolia and China had done the same. It appeared that this treaty was now abolished for good.

Although China was confident that tsarist Russia's imperialist policies in Outer Mongolia had been reversed, Baron Ungern von Sternberg's October 1920 advance into Outer Mongolia provided a pretext for the Red Army to intervene. On November 11, 1920, Chicherin sent Peking a note explaining that Soviet troops entering Chinese territory were merely "friendly troops who would consider their task fulfilled after the final destruction of White Guard bands in Mongolia, and the restoration of Chinese sovereignty, and would then immediately leave Chinese territory."[10] Although Ungern was repulsed, his troops then returned to conquer Urga in early February 1921, whereupon he declared an independent Mongolian government under his leadership.

Since 1918, the Bolsheviks had proclaimed on numerous occasions that all former unequal treaties with China had been abolished. But on May 4, 1921, the Soviet consulate in London presented an official letter to China's envoy to Great Britain, Wellington Koo, which indicated that the Red Army would soon be undertaking a military campaign in Outer Mongolia. Warning Koo that Japan was trying to transform Outer Mongolia into a buffer state between Russia and China, the Soviet letter explained that a "popular revolutionary party" was trying to oppose this plan by creating "an autonomous Mongolia, independent of Japan, but forming part of the Chinese Republic and remaining under the sovereignty of China." The Soviet letter then acknowledged that Moscow's "sympathies" were with this revolutionary party, and suggested: "If the Government of China wishes to prevent the eventual loss of Mongolia, it ought at once to enter into contact with the above-mentioned popular revolutionary party of Mongolia and concert its actions with the struggle carried on by this party."[11]

Peking quickly turned down Moscow's suggestion that it join forces, warning that a Soviet campaign into Outer Mongolia would involve the "territorial rights of China," and that "it should be mutually understood as a principle that China's territorial sovereignty is to be respected."[12] But this response probably reached Moscow after the Red Army entered Outer Mongolia in June and defeated Sternberg in a military campaign that ended with the occupation of Urga on July 6, 1921. This Soviet victory led to the formation of the Mongolian People's Revolutionary Government during July 1921, which then requested Moscow to continue the Red Army's presence in Outer Mongolia.

In the meantime, however, Moscow continued the fiction that Outer Mongolia was still a part of China. Early in July 1921, a Soviet note delivered to the Chinese consulate in London declared that the Soviet government "has no intention of claiming the restoration of any rights and privileges that the tsarist government has in the past acquired in Mongolia and that it renounces categorically all such rights and claims," as well as expressing its intention to "uphold the prerogatives of the Chinese Government" within Outer Mongolia.[13] But on August 10, 1921, Chicherin sent a telegram to the People's Government of Mongolia promising that Soviet troops would continue to be stationed in Outer Mongolia, and would remain there until the threat to Outer Mongolia and Russia was removed, and "that time has not yet come."[14]

The Bolsheviks also offered to act as an intermediary between Outer Mongolia and China. But once Mongolia's leaders agreed to this suggestion, the Soviet diplomats later implied that it was the Mongols who had requested that they act as the intermediary, not the other way around.[15] By the fall of 1921, therefore, the Soviet government had actually renewed tsarist Russia's imperialist strategy of negotiating Outer Mongolia's diplomatic relations with China.

The Soviet-Mongolian Treaty of November 5, 1921

In addition to regaining tsarist Russia's diplomatic stewardship over Outer Mongolia, Moscow signed a treaty with the Soviet-backed Urga government on November 5, 1921. This action is notable because while the Bolsheviks repeatedly denied that they were imperialistic, claiming that imperialism only applied to capitalist nations, their actions in Outer Mongolia contradicted their words. In fact, by 1921, the Soviet government's foreign policy was clearly imperialist.

One definition of *imperialism* is of "a nation whose foreign policy aims at acquiring more power than it actually has through expansion of its power beyond its frontiers, whose foreign policy, in other words, seeks a favorable change in power status, pursues a policy of imperialism."[16] A second definition states that *imperialism* means "simply the rule or control, political or economic, direct or indirect, of one state, nation or people over other similar groups."[17] A third definition of *imperialism* is of a government that tries to secure "strategic outposts," and achieves its ends through military, economic, or political means, often as a result of "treaties included with indigenous rulers."[18] In this regard, a fourth author has pointed to the importance of diplomacy: "Imperialism was the reality, diplomacy its superficial expression."[19]

Even though the Soviet government repeatedly stated that it was opposed to imperialism, Moscow's diplomacy proved that it had already adopted an imperialist foreign policy in Outer Mongolia by 1921.[20] On November 5, 1921, for example, it signed a treaty with Outer Mongolia that directly undermined Chinese sovereignty, since it gave the Soviet government many of the special rights and privileges that the tsarist government had formerly held. In the thirteen-article treaty, Moscow and Urga exchanged mutual recognition of each other's governments, agreed to open consulates in each other's capitals, and arranged for a joint committee to determine the boundary. But it also granted most-favored-nation status, as well as special privileges to own and lease property, and in matters of taxation. Since this treaty also specified that the anti-Soviet White Russian armies could not operate within Mongolian territory, Moscow had a perfect excuse to continue deploying the Red Army in Outer Mongolia.[21]

By recognizing Outer Mongolia's independent status, this treaty contradicted the two Karakhan Manifestos, as well as Chicherin's promise from the previous year that the Soviet government would respect China's sovereignty in Outer Mongolia. In fact, this treaty implicitly recognized that Outer Mongolia was not part of China. Furthermore, Moscow had negotiated this treaty without consulting China. Only in early January 1922, some two months later, did the Peking government even begin to hear rumors concerning the contents of the Soviet-Mongolian treaty. On February 2, 1922, for example, Peking published a translated copy of an article from the January 4, 1922 New York magazine *The Nation*, which claimed to be quoting a November 11, 1921 *Izvestiia* article announcing this treaty. While *The Nation* article inaccurately reported that it was only the Far Eastern Republic that had signed a treaty with Outer Mongolia, other sources soon clarified that Moscow had also signed this treaty.[22]

On March 5, 1922, the Soviet government's adoption of imperialist policies was once again revealed in the declaration of independence by the People's Government of the Urianghai region, better known as Tannu Tuva. This region was formerly part of Outer Mongolia, but from Urianghai's declaration of independence in 1922 until its formal annexation by the USSR in 1944, it was completely cut off from Outer Mongolia.[23] Although Tannu Tuva's population was small, it included much of the northwestern territory of Outer Mongolia, an area that was as large as Great Britain.[24]

Moscow's decision to separate and absorb Urianghai from Outer Mongolia not only represented a huge territorial gain, but was detrimental both to China's and Outer Mongol's interests. Documents from the Japanese Foreign Ministry archives in Tokyo further reveal that a councilor to the German Foreign Office visited Outer Mongolia during 1922 and afterward stated that Outer Mongolia "is practically on the way to be[coming] a Russian province," a development that showed that "the Russian face has turned eastwards again, and the Russians will take up the old [ts]arist imperialist policy against China."[25]

The most important difference between the Bolsheviks' imperialism and that of their tsarist predecessors was Lenin's 1913 division of the world into socialist and capitalist camps.[26] On February 22, 1919, Stalin divided the world into "the camp of imperialism and the camp of socialism." In the imperialist camp was the "United States and Britain, France, and Japan," while the socialist camp contained "Soviet Russia with the young soviet republics, and the growing proletariat revolution in the European countries."[27] The Soviet Union's new constitution of December 30, 1922 once again repeated Lenin's formula when it formally announced: "The world has been divided into two camps—the capitalist and the socialist." The importance in forming a socialist camp was to oppose "capitalist encirclement," as the soviet republics formed a "common front" to unify the workers of the whole World into a "World Socialist Soviet Republic."[28]

A Soviet declaration dated July 13, 1923 further specified that "all Soviet Socialist Republics which may be founded in the future," would have the option of "voluntarily joining the Union."[29] This declaration helps explain the Soviet government's 1921 treaty with Outer Mongolia, as well as its virtual annexation of Tannu Tuva in 1922, by clarifying that these actions were intended to create a military and political alliance with new Soviet republics in Tannu Tuva and Outer Mongolia. In other words, Moscow was in the process of creating a Soviet-led Communist bloc, with Mongolia as its first new member.

Aleksandr Paikes's Mission to Peking

To consolidate its territorial gains in Outer Mongolia, the Soviet government needed to obtain China's acquiescence to this new arrangement. Moscow sent an official representative to China to convince Peking to renew the former Sino-Russian unequal treaties concerning Outer Mongolia. To mask their intentions, however, Lenin and Chicherin signed official credentials on October 18, 1921 for Aleksandr K. Paikes, specifying that his duties as Plenipotentiary Extraordinary for the Russian Socialist Federal Soviet Republic to the Republic of China only included carrying out negotiations on the Chinese Eastern Railway.[30] Although the Chinese Eastern Railway was also a point of friction between Moscow and Peking, it soon became clear that Paikes's duties in China revolved primarily around negotiating the status of Outer Mongolia.

After Paikes arrived in Peking on December 14, 1921, he immediately denied that any Soviet treaty with Outer Mongolia had been signed. Later, he tried to explain this untruth by claiming that, because he had left Moscow before the treaty was concluded, he did not know about it. Since Paikes's official credentials specified that he was only empowered to negotiate on the CER, this technically made his negotiations on the Outer Mongolian problem unofficial, even though his instructions came directly from Moscow.

This tactic gave Paikes complete deniability and later allowed him to claim that he was not responsible for Moscow's treaty with Outer Mongolia. Moscow could likewise distance itself from Paikes, since his powers did not include conducting negotiations on Outer Mongolia. By arranging matters in such a fashion, the Soviet government successfully shielded itself from being held accountable for Paikes's statements on Outer Mongolia. This ploy helps explain why so little is known about this early chapter of Sino-Soviet diplomatic relations, since it was useless for Peking to release details of the failed negotiations.

It is important to note, therefore, that during the very first meeting between Aleksandr Paikes and Li Yuan, the Chinese attaché, Paikes suggested that a conference be convened among representatives from China, Russia, and Outer Mongolia during which the three governments would resolve all outstanding problems. But since the Chinese officials considered the Mongols to be citizens of China, they regarded according Outer Mongolia's government equal status at the negotiations to be a breach of Chinese sovereignty. In fact, Paikes's suggestion exactly followed the format of the 1915 tsarist-imposed tripartite treaty. For this reason, Li immediately rejected this plan as an attempt to interfere in a strictly Chinese internal matter.[31]

When Paikes met with attache Li for a second time, however, he modified his position. To Li's question: "And has the Soviet government finally decided on what day it will withdraw the Russian troops from Mongolian territory?" Paikes responded: "As soon as the Chinese government's and the Mongolian government's negotiations have been successful, then my country's troops will withdraw." In response to Paikes's veiled military threat, Li reminded him that Mongolia was an integral part of China and accused the Soviet government of "infringing on China's sovereignty," when it sent troops into Mongolia without first obtaining the permission of the Chinese government.[32]

Paikes then tried to put himself in the role of an unofficial intermediary between Urga and Peking, by assuring Li that he could act as a "Soviet mediator" if the Peking government wanted to carry on negotiations with the Mongolian government. To this suggestion Li responded that the Chinese government could not tolerate a "second party" interfering in China's affairs, and especially "could not tolerate an ambitious country carrying out an aggressive policy," a direct reference to tsarist Russia's earlier involvement on Outer Mongolia. Li's use of the word "ambitious" (野心) was especially interesting, since it was a word usually reserved for describing imperialist encroachments on China during the nineteenth century, an indication that Peking saw little difference between Soviet imperialism and earlier, Russian, imperialism.[33]

When Peking first began to hear rumors of the Soviet-Mongolian treaty, it asked Paikes to comment on these reports. On February 7, 1922, Paikes announced that Soviet troops were in Outer Mongolia at the request of the Mongolian government and he once again denied that Moscow had any designs on Mongolia.[34] Only during March did the Chinese consul in Chita telegraph a complete copy of the thirteen-article treaty between Soviet Russia and Outer Mongolia, and it became impossible for Paikes to deny its existence any longer.[35]

Li presented this information to Paikes on April 26, 1922, when he asked point-blank whether Paikes had or had not earlier denied that the Soviet government signed a treaty with Outer Mongolia. Paikes admitted that he had denied its existence, but excused himself by saying that he had left Moscow on October 18, 1921, while the treaty had been signed on November 5, 1921. According to Paikes, the first time he had known about the treaty was when he received a telegram from Moscow in the middle of February 1922, almost a full month after the Peking government had learned of the treaty from *The Nation* magazine. Paikes's denial was therefore met with skepticism.

Li then asked when Moscow planned to withdraw its troops from Outer Mongolia, to which Paikes answered: "If I telegram my government I am afraid that they will want me to demand a formal guarantee of Outer Mongolia's government and security." Li next tried to determine what exactly the Soviet government hoped to accomplish in Mongolia[36]:

> **Li:** Does the Soviet government think that its troops will stay in Mongolia forever?
>
> **Paikes:** My government doesn't think that.
>
> **Li:** Did the Soviet government send troops into Outer Mongolia to guard against Whites or really to invade Mongolia, and isn't it now repeatedly breaking its word when it says that it doesn't want to develop communism in Mongolia?
>
> **Paikes:** That's also not what it thinks.
>
> **Li :** Then why won't your government withdraw its troops?
>
> **Paikes:** My government formerly announced that all of the prior tsarist treaties were abolished, it did not say that the basis for these treaties was abolished. These matters have to be studied. But your government mistakenly thought that the 1919 [Karakhan] manifesto unconditionally canceled the 1915 treaty; at the same time it never said that Outer Mongolia's autonomy was abolished and that the Chinese Eastern Railway was already returned to China's control. On these matters your government is mistaken. Your Excellency has repeatedly asked when Soviet troops will be withdrawn, which is something I really am not in a position to decide quickly.

Paikes's statement was the first clarification Peking had received from a Soviet diplomat on the true meaning of the Karakhan Manifestos, i.e. the tsarist treaties may have been abolished but the basis for these treaties remained (see Document 9). In practical terms this meant that Moscow planned to renew all of tsarist Russia's treaties, including reaffirming the autonomy of Outer Mongolia.

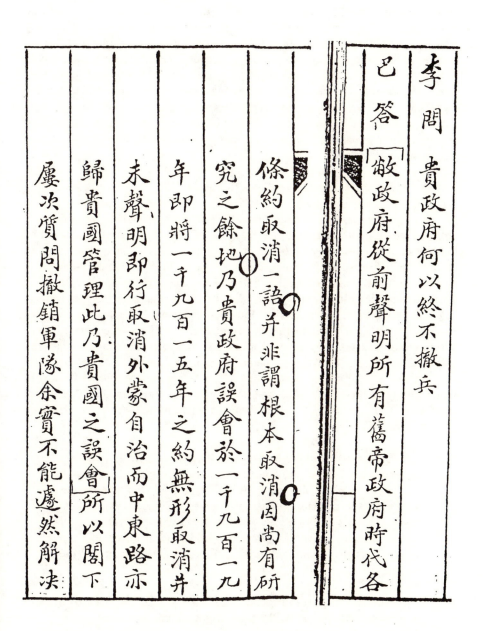

李問　貴政府何以終不撤兵

已答　敬政府從前聲明所有舊帝政府時代各

條約取消一語并非謂根本取消因尚有所

究之餘地乃貴政府誤會於一千九百一九

年即將一千九百一五年之約無形取消并

未聲明即行取消外蒙自治而中東路亦

歸貴國管理此乃貴國之誤會所以閣下

屢次質問撤銷軍隊余實不能遽然解決

Document 9
Paikes's April 26, 1922 Explanation of the Karakhan Manifestos

Paikes's explanation is important for several reasons. First, it shows that the Bolsheviks' repeated promises to annul all the tsarist treaties clearly had no meaning so long as they could renew the old terms, as they had already accomplished in Outer Mongolia. Second, Paikes had given the first hint that not only was Moscow no longer willing to agree to abolish Outer Mongolia's autonomy, but that all previous indications to the contrary were to be blamed on China's "misunderstanding" of the two Karakhan Manifestos. Third, it clarified that the Karakhan Manifestos' and Chicherin's repeated promises not to interfere with China's sovereignty in Outer Mongolia had been made merely to prompt Peking into opening negotiations with Moscow, not because the Soviet government was serious about its offers.

Paikes Claims the Unequal Treaties Are Valid

Li continued to press Paikes to discuss a timetable for a Soviet troop withdrawal from Outer Mongolia, but Paikes once again insisted that a conference first be held among Mongolian, Chinese, and Soviet delegates, a suggestion that Li firmly rejected because of Moscow's unwelcome participation in the conference. But the two finally reached a compromise in which Li agreed to talk alone with the Mongolian delegate but then gave Paikes the right to talk with him separately–in effect allowing Paikes to coach the Mongolian delegate. Once this decision was reached, Paikes ended the meeting by promising: "I will telegraph a message to Moscow and ask them to transmit a message to Outer Mongolia, requesting them quickly to dispatch a representative to Peking to attend the conference."[37]

The Peking government made a public protest against Moscow's actions in Outer Mongolia on May 1, 1922, as Foreign Minister Yen reminded Paikes that the Soviet government had repeatedly broken its promise not to encroach on Chinese territory[38]:

> The Soviet government has repeatedly declared to the Chinese government: That all previous treaties made between the Russian government and China shall be null and void: that the Soviet government renounces all encroachments of Chinese territory and all concessions within China, and that the Soviet government will unconditionally and forever return what has been forcibly seized from China by the former Imperial Russian government and the bourgeois.
>
> Now the Soviet government has suddenly gone back on its own word and, secretly and without any right, concluded a treaty with Mongolia. Such action on the part of the Soviet government is similar to the policy the former Imperialist Russian government assumed toward China.

It must be observed that Mongolia is a part of Chinese territory and, as such, has long been recognized by all countries. In secretly concluding a treaty with Mongolia, the Soviet government has not only broke faith with its previous declarations but also violates all principles of justice.

But even though Peking publicly criticized Paikes, it had little choice but to continue negotiations with him since it had no direct communications with the Outer Mongolian government. On May 15, the Peking Cabinet circulated an official letter to this effect which mentioned that Paikes was arranging for a Mongolian delegate to come to Peking in exchange for a promise that the Mongolian delegate would be in "absolutely no danger."[39]

When Paikes met with Yen on May 23, Yen bluntly asked Paikes why the Soviet government had invaded Chinese sovereign territory. Paikes repeated his previous argument that just because Moscow had abolished all previous tsarist treaties, it did not mean that the 1915 treaty by which China recognized Outer Mongolia's autonomy was void. This treaty could now be amended, however, which was why the Soviet government "had taken the responsibility upon itself to mediate Chinese-Mongolian relations." In response, Foreign Minister Yen berated Paikes for interfering in a Chinese internal government matter, just as if an outsider were interfering in a family dispute between an "older and a younger brother," and he told Paikes that the Soviet government had to terminate its role as the "unofficial mediator" of the Sino-Mongolian problem.[40]

While Paikes was trying to insert himself as the middleman between Peking and Urga, the Soviet government signed a second agreement with the Outer Mongolian government on May 31, 1922, which stated that all "buildings and property on the territory of Outer Mongolia, which previously belonged to the former Russian Government . . . are recognized . . . as the property of the RSFSR [Soviet government]." This protocol then went on to state that buildings and property owned by "former Russian public local governments" would also be returned to Soviet control.[41]

It is important to recall that less than a year before, Moscow had delivered a note to the Chinese consulate in London declaring that the Soviet government had no intention of claiming the restoration of any of the tsarist government's former "rights and privileges" in Outer Mongolia.[42] This new agreement provides further evidence that Moscow did not intend to return Outer Mongolia to China.

In a meeting between Paikes and Li on June 29, Li asked why it had been over a month since Paikes had telegraphed Mongolia to send a representative to Peking, and yet no one had yet arrived. In Paikes's role as go-between between China and Outer Mongolia, he now applied direct pressure on Li by stating that the first step was to arrange a "three-way treaty," and that if Peking did not willingly agree, then it would be necessary for Paikes to make a "formal and official request" to this effect. The negotiations quickly became more acrimonious as Li accused Paikes of being insincere in his earlier claims of wanting friendly border relations and in his announcements that Moscow would unconditionally retreat from Outer Mongolia: "The three-way agreement was signed in the tsarist period. The Soviet government has repeatedly announced that it has abolished all treaties and aggressions of the tsarist period, and yet aren't you once again following the tsarist government's methods?" Finally, Li also reminded Paikes that the latter's letter from February 7, 1922 had renounced any Soviet ambitions in Mongolia and yet Paikes was now demanding the re-creation of the 1915 tripartite treaty.[43]

None of these criticisms apparently had any effect, as Paikes announced that in order to change the previous treaty it was first necessary to hold a conference, and that this would be impossible without the participation of a Mongolian representative. Li then asked yet again the question that had started off the day's discussion: "When will the Outer Mongolian representative arrive in Peking?" Paikes's response to this question was undoubtedly another shock to Li, as Paikes insisted that the tripartite conference not be held in Peking, as they had earlier agreed, but in the Inner Mongolian city of Kalgan. If Li had agreed to this suggestion he would have sent a clear signal that Peking recognized the *de facto* autonomy of the Outer Mongolian government, since Kalgan was located halfway between Peking to Urga, and so implied that the two governments were equals. This was an action that Li refused to consider, and he informed Paikes that he would have to consult higher officials for instructions.[44]

A final meeting between Paikes and Foreign Minister Yen took place on July 6, 1922. Peking had accompanied its official protest on May 1, with demands sent directly to Moscow that Paikes be recalled and replaced with another diplomat with full negotiating powers. Telegrams received from the Chinese Consul in Moscow confirmed that Paikes was going to be recalled and replaced by Adolf Joffe.[45]

Perhaps for this reason the foreign minister took a much firmer position with Paikes, stating: "China and Mongolia ought to make their own decisions, the Soviet government must not interfere." Yen then described Soviet troops on Chinese territory as a "pistol pointed at China's head," and further declared that no decision could be reached if the Red Army was not first withdrawn from Outer Mongolia. When Paikes began to repeat that these troops were only there to protect against White Russians, Yen interrupted him, and asked Paikes to write a letter explaining what political and military treaties had been signed between the Soviet government and Outer Mongolia.[46]

Paikes's letter of August 3, 1922, was a revealing statement of the Soviet government's true intentions in Outer Mongolia (see Document 10): "Replying to the protest of His Excellency, the Minister, against the conclusion of a trade agreement between the Soviet Government and Mongolia, I explained that [it] was by no means in conflict with the triple agreement entered in 1915, which has not yet been revised, and that the revision of the agreement could take place by the participation of the contracting parties."[47]

No. 533.   Peking, 3rd August, 1922.

TO THE MINISTRY OF FOREIGN AFFAIRS OF THE REPUBLIC OF CHINA

M E M O R A N D U M

Acknowledging the receipt of the Memorandum No. 100 of 22d July, I am constrained to express my surprise about it, for I do not understand to what concession does it refer. Replying to the protest of His Excellency, the Minister, against the conclusion of a trade agreement between the Soviet Government and Mongolia, I explained that that was by no means in conflict with the triple agreement entered in 1915, which has not yet been revised, and that the revision of the agreement could take place by the participation of the contracting parties. Since my arrival in Peking I have repeatedly insisted in my conversations with His Excellency, the Minister, upon the commencement of negotiations in general, and upon the convocation of a Conference for the discussion of the Mongolian matter in particular, but I have been given systematic assurances that the negotiations would start within a few days. It *Is* is therefore the fault of the Soviet Government, if the Chinese Ministry of Foreign Affairs does not adhere to its promises, and prefers to write Memoranda and formulate questions which can only be settled at a formal Conference. I wish to express the hope that the Ministry has already realized the inexpediency of such a policy, and will, in order to settle the problems with which the friendly nations of China and Russia are now confronted, commence official negotiations immediately.

(signed) A. Paikess
PLENIPOTENTIARY EXTRAORDINARY
of the Socialist Federal Soviet Republic.

Copied/RSY

Document 10
Paikes's August 3, 1922 Letter Claiming the Unequal Treaties Were Valid

With this statement, Soviet diplomacy had gone full circle: from supporting the total abolition of all of its unequal treaties with China only three years before, Paikes now stated that the Soviet government considered the 1915 treaty on Outer Mongolia still to be in effect. Furthermore, the only way to revise this treaty would be for all of the contracting parties–including Outer Mongolia–to jointly participate in the negotiations, which *ipso facto* would have meant that China recognized Outer Mongolia's autonomy, which was exactly the part of the 1915 unequal treaty that China disputed. These first Sino-Soviet negotiations on Outer Mongolia broke down over this very issue.

Lev Karakhan's Mission to China

With Paikes's failure to convince Peking to renew the former unequal Sino-Russian treaties, Moscow was forced to adopt new tactics. While continuing to announce in public that the USSR had abolished the former 1915 tripartite treaty, therefore, Moscow sought to adopt in secret the terms of this former treaty. The USSR's efforts were rewarded in 1924, when its envoy to China, Lev Karakhan, convinced Peking to recognize the existence of the 1915 treaty, even though both sides agreed that it was no longer to be enforced. But Peking's recognition meant that Moscow could continue to adhere to the terms of the 1915 treaty until a new treaty was negotiated, an eventuality that was further delayed by Moscow when it refused to convene a promised Sino-Soviet conference on time.

Karakhan's arrival in Peking was celebrated at an official banquet on September 4, 1923, where he was greeted with applause for emphasizing that his two manifestos of 1919 and 1920 were still in force and were "the basis for his future work in China."[48] In talks with C. T. Wang, the Chinese official in charge of negotiations with the USSR, Karakhan further clarified that the Red Army was in Outer Mongolia only to deter attacks from the White Russian troops.[49] But when Wang asked why Soviet troops were in Outer Mongolia since there were no longer any organized White Russian soldiers, Karakhan replied: "If the Chinese government could clearly guarantee that the Whites won't return then the issue of withdrawing troops from Outer Mongolia would not be a problem."[50]

The Peking government could not very well prevent White Russian interference if it could not garrison troops in Outer Mongolia. For this reason, China first wanted all unequal treaties abolished and all Soviet troops pulled out of Outer Mongolia, listing these three goals in a draft of what it hoped would be the upcoming Sino-Soviet agreement[51]:

> 1) The Government of the Republic of China and the Government of the Union of Russian Socialist Soviet Republics declare that all treaties, conventions, agreements, protocols, etc., concluded between China and the former tsarist regime are null and void. The Governments of the two Contracting Parties shall conclude[d] new arrangements based on the principles of justice and equality.

2) The Soviet Government agrees to withdraw all the troops at present stationed by it in Outer Mongolia and to complete such withdrawal not later than six months after the signing of this agreement. China shall independently despatch troops to garrison Outer Mongolia.

3) The Soviet Government agrees to consider as null and void all its treaties and agreements concluded with Outer Mongolia.

A second proposed draft specified that Soviet troops should be withdrawn within a month of signing an official Sino-Soviet Treaty, instead of six months.[52]

In a radical change from Paikes's repeated attempts to renew the 1915 unequal treaty, Karakhan agreed in early 1924 that Moscow was willing to recognize that Outer Mongolia was Chinese territory and was subject to Chinese control. The only outstanding problem was to determine the schedule for withdrawing the Red Army from Outer Mongolia. Karakhan proposed that this issue be decided at the official conference that was scheduled to follow the opening of diplomatic relations.[53]

A rough draft of these basic resolutions was quickly hammered out and Wang communicated the results of the negotiations to Foreign Minister Koo on March 3, 1924. On March 7, Koo telegraphed the Chinese consul in Moscow and ordered him to talk to Chicherin about several outstanding disputes: 1) China wanted to abolish all prior Sino-Russian and Sino-Soviet treaties immediately, while Karakhan insisted that they be abolished at the conference following the opening of official diplomatic relations; 2) China wanted the Red Army troops in Outer Mongolia to be withdrawn immediately and the Soviet government's treaties with Outer Mongolia to be abolished, while Karakhan wanted to decide these issues at the conference and refused to allow specific mention of the abolition of the 1921 Soviet-Mongolian treaty in the Sino-Soviet agreement.[54]

The Peking government's cabinet met on March 13, and agreed with the basic points of this March 1 draft, although it suggested that all Sino-Russian treaties be abolished immediately and that the status of the White Russians in China be defined more clearly as jointly under Sino-Soviet responsibility.[55] Meanwhile, the Chinese Ministry of Foreign Affairs had circulated "top secret" copies of the March 1 draft Sino-Soviet agreement to the different ministries in the Peking government. Responses were returned from several ministries that cautioned Wang that he should eliminate an oft-repeated clause stating that all new Sino-Soviet treaties should "be decided at the conference," since by simply delaying the upcoming Sino-Soviet conference, Moscow could avoid abolishing all of the old unequal treaties. The Ministry of Education and the Ministry of Finance then both warned that all former treaties should be abolished immediately, and the Ministry of Education further recommended that an additional clause be added: "Prior to the convening of the conference, all treaties, agreements, protocols, contracts, will no longer be in effect."[56]

The problem with these suggestions was that the draft treaty clearly stated that annulling the old treaties and replacing them with new treaties should happen simultaneously, ensuring that treaty relations would continue unbroken. The Chinese officials were worried, however, that if the old treaties were not abolished prior to recognition, then the USSR might try to retain the former treaties at the upcoming conference. Thus, the Ministry of Education's suggestion to agree that all of the old treaties were no longer in effect from the signing of the Sino-Soviet agreement to the convening of the conference actually left a one-month gap, during which time China and the Soviet Union would have no operative treaties. But, this undoubtedly appeared to be a minor problem at the time, and following what seemed to be almost total support within the Peking government, Karakhan and Wang met again on March 14, to finalize the draft Sino-Soviet treaty.

The March 14, 1924 Secret Protocol

When Karakhan and Wang met on March 14, it is unknown whether Wang tried to take out the phrase "to be decided at the conference," but, in any case, it remained unchanged in later versions of the treaty. Although Wang was unsuccessful in making this change, he did convince Karakhan to agree to add a new clause stating that all former agreements would not be enforced. It was decided not to make this change in the text, but to sign a separate secret protocol.

This protocol was very simple, but had far-reaching consequences for China (see Document 11). It stated that all former conventions, treaties, agreements, protocols, contracts, etc., would be annulled at the upcoming Sino-Soviet Conference, at which time new treaties would also be adopted, but then added: "It is agreed that pending the conclusion of such new Treaties, Agreements, etcetera, all the old Conventions, Treaties, Agreements, Protocols, Contracts, etcetera, will not be enforced." This protocol was then signed by Karakhan and Wang, but it was not dated, and did not have a seal, which meant that this protocol would take effect only if ratified by the Peking government.[57]

This secret protocol was never previously published, but the original signed copy is included with the other treaty provisions. Although there is no way to know for sure, it might have been decided to make this protocol secret so that outsiders could not take advantage of the one month during which none of the Sino-Russian treaties would be valid; apparently Wang never seriously considered that the Soviet government might try to take advantage of this suspension.

By including only one of the Ministry of Education's two suggested amendments, however, Wang altered the whole intent of these suggestions. Now, the draft agreement clearly stated that all former Sino-Russian agreements would not be enforced until after the official Sino-Soviet conference convened and concluded new treaties, thus making the revision of China's and the USSR's commercial, consular, and border relations all dependent on the convening of the conference. The wording of this secret protocol was all-important, since the previous agreements were not abolished, they were simply not enforced.

/Secret/

PROTOCOL

Upon the signing of the Agreement of General Principles for the Settlement of the Questions between the Republic of China and the Union of Soviet Socialist Republics of March , 1924, the Government of the Union of Soviet Socialist Republics declares as follos:

Whereas Article III of the aforementioned Agreement provides as follows:

"The Governments of the two Contracting Parties agree to annul at the Conference, as provided in the preceding Article, all Conventions, Treaties, Agreements, Protocols, Contracts, etcetera, concluded between the Government of China and the Tsarist Government, and to replace them with new Treaties, Agreements, etc., on the basis of equality, reciprocity and justice, as well as the spirit of the Declarations of the Soviet Government of the years 1919 and 1920":

It is agreed that pending the conclusion of such new Treaties, Agreements etcetera, all the old Conventions, Treaties, Agreements, Protocols, Contracts, etcetera, will not be enforced.

In witness whereof, the respective Plenipotentiaries of the Governments of the two Contracting Parties have signed the present Protocol in duplicate in the English language and have affixed thereto their seals.

Done at the City of Peking this day of March One Thousand Nine Hundred and Twenty-Four.

Document 11
Text of the March 14, 1924 Karakhan-Wang Secret Protocol

Agreeing not to enforce the former agreements proved to be an important distinction, since the Peking government had now recognized the legitimacy of these earlier agreements, even though both sides agreed that they were suspended. If the Soviet Union violated the old agreements, as later happened, the Peking government could not publicly protest, because a public announcement would immediately expose Peking's complicity in signing a secret protocol that had actually reaffirmed the validity of these former Sino-Russian agreements.

While the Peking government literally made dozens of protests to the Soviet government during the following years about its numerous treaty infractions, these protests were all confidential. Copies of China's private remonstrances against Soviet mistreatment are located in the Foreign Ministry Archives in Taiwan. The most important include the October 14, 1924 protest against Moscow's signing of the September 20, 1924 supplemental agreement with Chang Tso-lin,[58] as well as two separate protests against the Soviet Union's January 20, 1925 Convention with Japan, dated February 11, 1925 and February 21, 1925.[59] The Soviet Union could and did ignore China's secret objections with impunity, however, since it could not very well break a treaty that both sides had agreed not to enforce.

By signing this secret protocol, while failing to eliminate the clause that specified that all new agreements could only be made at the upcoming Sino-Soviet conference, Wang unintentionally placed enormous power in the Soviet government's hands. Since China was too weak to oppose the USSR on its own, it could not back up its protests with actions: if China had later turned to other countries for help, such as Great Britain, the United States, or Japan, it would have had to confess that it had signed a secret agreement with the Soviet Union. But admitting the existence of a secret protocol with Moscow would have called the legitimacy of the Peking government into question, and would have undermined the very support that Peking hoped to gain from these other countries.

This fact helps explain why the Peking government never acknowledged the existence of its secret protocol with Moscow, a protocol that allowed the Soviet Union to expand its influence in China enormously from 1924 through 1927, when the Peking government broke off diplomatic relations with Moscow. During this three-year period, however, the Soviet government was completely unfettered by the myriad of treaty restrictions that applied to other countries.

Karakhan understood quite well the power that this secret protocol gave to the Soviet government and was willing to take many risks to make sure that the draft treaty was ratified without changes. When it looked as if the Peking government might not accept this draft agreement, Karakhan sent an ultimatum to C. T. Wang on March 16, insisting that the Peking government recognize the draft treaty unchanged within three days or else all further negotiations would end. As discussed above, on the same day Sun Yat-sen signed directive twenty-four supporting the USSR's foreign policy goals in China.

Karakhan publicly blamed the Peking government's hesitation to ratify the agreement on foreign intervention, pointing to a March 13, 1924 French protest that the proposed Sino-Soviet joint control over the CER interfered with the Russo-Asiatic Bank's legal rights over the railway. But, in fact, the Peking government had ignored the French protest when Wang signed the draft treaty on March 14, and several Chinese internal foreign ministry letters denied that foreign interference had any effect on the ongoing negotiations.

Karakhan next arranged to have the contents of the March 14 draft treaty published in the local Chinese press–minus the crucial secret protocol, of course. Karakhan's accusation against foreign interference was then picked up by the Kuomintang and the Chinese Communist Party, which led the way in condemning the Peking government for caving into foreign pressure not to ratify the draft Sino-Soviet treaty. As a result, the Peking government was subjected to enormous public pressure; according to one source, Wu P'ei-fu sent a total of six telegrams urging ratification between March 18 and March 26; nine public groups in Shanghai alone made similar demands; and students at Peking's Teachers University, Engineering University, Teachers Colleges for Girls, and the College of Fine Arts organized a pro-treaty demonstration.[60]

Although Karakhan's three-day ultimatum harkened back to similar ultimatums forced upon China by tsarist Russian diplomats, as well as to the pressure tactics that Japan had used to coerce China into accepting the Twenty-one Demands, the Soviet government added a new twist by marshalling Chinese public opinion against the Peking government. Since the secret protocol was never published along with the other parts of the draft Sino-Soviet treaty, it is ironic that Chinese public support for the Soviet position proved to be so important in securing Peking's ratification of the secret protocol.

After two months of fruitless negotiations, Peking finally relented to persistent Chinese public pressure, sponsored mainly by the Soviet-backed KMT/CCP United Front, which came out in favor of the draft agreement. On May 31, 1924, the final version of the Sino-Soviet Treaty was signed by Lev Karakhan, ambassador extraordinary of the USSR, and Wellington Koo, the minister of foreign affairs, Republic of China. While this treaty agreed that Outer Mongolia was "an integral part of the Republic of China" and the Soviet government promised to respect "China's sovereignty therein," it further specified that the timetable for withdrawing Soviet troops from Outer Mongolia was to be determined at an official Sino-Soviet conference to convene one month later.[61]

Moscow refused, however, to abolish its treaties with Outer Mongolia. In a separate declaration, Peking stated that it "will not and does not recognize as valid any treaty, agreement, etcetera, concluded between Russia since the tsarist regime and any third party or parties, affecting the sovereign rights and interests of the Republic of China."[62] Although this declaration reaffirmed Peking's disapproval of the 1921 and 1922 Soviet-Mongolian treaties, and thus proved to the Chinese public that it was standing up for China's interests, it had no practical effect on the status of these agreements.

On the day before this Sino-Soviet Treaty was signed, the president of the Republic of China, Ts'ao K'un, issued Wellington Koo complete powers to sign the agreement in China's name. Koo's powers included the signing of a fifteen-article "Agreement on General Principles" and an eleven-article "Agreement for the Provisional Management of the Chinese Eastern Railway," as well as "one Protocol, seven Declarations, and one exchange of Notes" (see Document 12).[63] The "one Protocol" was the secret agreement signed by Karakhan and Koo. This protocol was never published along with the rest of the treaty.

Karakhan Delays the Sino-Soviet Conference

Peking had originally suggested that the secret protocol be signed in order to guarantee that Moscow did not try to retain the tsarist treaties once the Sino-Soviet conference met. With the inclusion of the secret protocol, however, both China and the Soviet Union formally agreed that the 1915 tripartite treaty on Outer Mongolia would not be enforced after May 31, 1924. Although this solution seemed to satisfy China's desires to abolish the unequal Sino-Russian treaties, agreeing not to enforce the 1915 treaty was not the same as abolishing it. Until a new agreement was negotiated to replace the 1915 treaty, the secret protocol actually recognized that the treaty existed, even though unenforced.

Although this distinction may seem slight, all Moscow had to do was delay the convening of the Sino-Soviet conference in order to continue occupying Outer Mongolia under the pretext that the 1915 treaty still existed. Moreover, the timetable for withdrawing the Red Army could also not be determined without the Sino-Soviet conference. So as long as a new treaty concerning Outer Mongolia was never negotiated, and the timetable for the Red Army's withdrawal was not set, the Soviet troops could technically remain in Outer Mongolia indefinitely.

In order to delay the convening of the Sino-Soviet conference, Karakhan insisted on June 28, 1924 that the official Sino-Soviet conference be postponed because his "experts and secretaries" had not yet arrived from Moscow.[64] At the end of his letter to Koo, Karakhan threatened further delays: he stated that he would reach an understanding with Koo for scheduling the conference only "upon the receipt of instructions from my Government."[65]

Foreign Minister Koo reminded Karakhan that under the terms of the May 31, 1924 agreement, June 30 was the last date on which the official conference could be convened. Fearful of exposing Peking's secret diplomacy with Moscow, however, Koo did not protest Karakhan's letter as a violation of the treaty, and instead merely commented: "I shall therefore be pleased to learn that you have received the necessary instructions from your Government and that you are authorized to proceed with the Conference forthwith."[66] That Karakhan's delaying tactics were countenanced at the highest levels of the Soviet government was shown by Foreign Minister Chicherin's reply to the Chinese consul in Moscow, who had requested that the Sino-Soviet conference convene according to the treaty: "The benefits to Russia are too small. Until now we have not received anything. Let's wait a few days, and then we can discuss it again."[67]

CERTIFICATE OF FULL POWER GIVEN
TO VI KYUIN WELLINGTON KOO PLENIPOTENTIARY.

Vi Kyuin wellington Koo, Minister of Foreign
Affairs, reports that he has concluded with the
Soviet Envoy L. M. Karakhan an Agreement on General
Principles for the Settlement of the Questions
between the Republic of China and the Union of Soviet
Socialist Republics (15 articles), an Agreement for the
Provisional Management of the Chinese Eastern Railway
(11 articles), one Protocol, seven Declarations, and
one exchange of Notes, and requests to be given Ins-
tructions thereanent.

I. The President, have personally perused and
examined the same and deem them worthy of being
approved.

Therefore Vi Kyuin Wellington Koo is hereby
specially appointed Plenipotentiary and invested
with full powers to sign the aforementioned Agreements and supplementary Documents.

In faith whereof, I, the president, have
hereunto set my hand and caused the seal of the
Republic of China to be affixed.

Given in Peking this Thirtieth Day of the
Fifth Month of the Thirteenth Year of the Republic
of China.

(Signed) Tsao Kun

Seal

(Countersigned) Vi Kyuin Wellington Koo

Minister for Foreign Affairs.

Document 12
Wellington Koo's May 30, 1924 Powers

China had come to a diplomatic impasse: on the one hand, there was no easy way for Peking to force Moscow to begin the Sino-Soviet conference, while on the other hand, Peking could not make a public protest or involve the other foreign powers to oppose Moscow's delaying tactics, since this would have been tantamount to a public admission of Peking's weakness. In addition, turning to outsiders for help might expose the secret agreement with the USSR. Finally, once the original June 30 deadline for the Sino-Soviet conference passed without China's making a formal protest, then a protest against any additional delays might simply raise the question of why Peking had waited so long.

Moscow could continue its military occupation of Outer Mongolia simply by delaying the Sino-Soviet conference. Now that an official agreement that recognized the 1915 tripartite treaty had been signed, the Soviet government could also undertake the task of consolidating its control over Outer Mongolia. During the next fourteen months, therefore, Moscow's intelligence services supported a coup in Outer Mongolia that drew it completely into the Communist bloc, presenting the Peking government with a *fait accompli* when the official Sino-Soviet conference finally convened during August 1925.

Outer Mongolia Joins the Communist Bloc

Although the Soviet Union acknowledged that Outer Mongolia remained an integral part of China, without the Sino-Soviet conference a deadline could not be set for withdrawing the Red Army from Outer Mongolia. Furthermore, the secret protocol signed on May 31, 1924 tacitly reaffirmed the legitimacy of all former Sino-Russian treaties by agreeing that these treaties would not be enforced. This protocol actually recognized the legal existence of these unequal treaties, therefore, since they were never renounced, simply suspended. This meant that the USSR's legal hold over Outer Mongolia had now received *de facto* recognition from China. As long as the Sino-Soviet conference did not meet, or if once it did meet, it failed to negotiate new terms, the Soviet Union could retain its special position in Outer Mongolia.

Although the specific strategy that Moscow used to retain Outer Mongolia remained a mystery to outsiders, the outcome did not surprise American foreign service officials working in China. During May 1924, for example, the American vice-consul in Kalgan, Edwin F. Stanton, had even warned Washington that the USSR was not planning to return Outer Mongolia to China, reporting that "the present Soviet Government, acting in an advisory capacity to the Mongolian Government, but actually dictating its policies and its administration, does not intend to relinquish either political or economic control of Outer Mongolia."[68]

The Soviet Union tightened its hold over Outer Mongolia during September 1924, when a purge organized by the Revolutionary Youth League, an organization "entirely dominated by Soviet Advisers and more particularly the head of the Secret Police," orchestrated the execution of the commander-in-chief of the Outer Mongolian Army as well the execution of five other prominent Mongol leaders.[69] In early September 1924, the USSR exerted economic pressure on the last remaining American, European, and Japanese businessmen in Outer Mongolia, and they were all eventually arrested and expelled from the country. Meanwhile, Moscow attempted to end China's strong ties with Outer Mongolia, as all remaining Chinese merchants were also forced to leave.

By late September 1924, almost all non-Soviet foreign activities in Outer Mongolia ended, as the USSR absorbed Outer Mongolia's political, economic, and cultural life into its own. The political purge allowed the Mongolian secret police to pave "the way for the complete Sovietization of Outer Mongolia."[70] The Mongolian People's Republic was duly founded on November 25, 1924 a new constitution was promulgated and the name of Outer Mongolia's capital was changed from Urga to Ulan Bator. Links between the Soviet government and Outer Mongolia became so close that, beginning in 1925, "Stalinist restrictions, controls, and political radicalization unfolded in Mongolia with seeming inevitability, just at they were developing in the Soviet Union itself."[71]

It was China's secret protocol with the USSR agreeing not to enforce all prior Sino-Russian treaties, coupled with repeated Soviet delays in convening the conference to decide the deadline for withdrawing the Red Army, that gave the Soviet Union so much leeway in its policies toward Outer Mongolia. Although he was unaware of the existence of this secret protocol, one historian accurately observed that China's power in Outer Mongolia had been greatly diminished: "The absence of a tripartite treaty similar to that of 1915, or a direct Sino-Mongol convention, was particularly disadvantageous to China, since it permitted Mongolia to interpret her autonomy as widely as she wished, and permitted Russia, while admitting Chinese sovereignty, to turn this wider interpretation to account."[72]

Foreign Minister Chicherin confirmed this wider interpretation of Outer Mongolia's autonomy at the end of 1924 when he explained: "We recognize the Mongolian People's Republic as part of the Chinese Republic, but we recognize also its autonomy in so far-reaching a sense that we regard it not only as independent of China in its internal affairs, but also as capable of pursuing its foreign policy independently."[73] Chicherin's interpretation of Outer Mongolia's rights far exceeded that of the tsarist government, which had only recognized Outer Mongolia's right to determine its foreign relations regarding commercial and industrial matters, not in matters relating to government, economy, and society.

Once the Soviet Union had fully asserted its political, military, and economic authority over Outer Mongolia, Karakhan announced on March 6, 1925 that Moscow had decided to withdraw its troops and that the Red Army had already left Outer Mongolia.[74] But American officials in Kalgan reported that about 500 Soviet troops had actually remained in Outer Mongolia, and that these troops had helped train an estimated 40,000 to 50,000 Mongolian troops.[75] That the Soviet Union had no intention of returning Outer Mongolia to China's control was confirmed in a May 7, 1925 meeting between Chicherin and the Chinese consul in Moscow. In response to the consul's comment that Peking planned to garrison troops in Outer Mongolia to replace the Red Army, Chicherin immediately warned that if Chinese troops were sent into Outer Mongolia, the "Mongolian people would certainly resist and the Soviet Union would not just sit by and watch but would immediately support them."[76] Chicherin was clearly threatening to use force if China interfered in Outer Mongolia, which casts doubt on Outer Mongolia's "independent" status.

Meanwhile, the fiction of Outer Mongolia's independence was maintained by insisting that all Red Army troops had already been withdrawn from Outer Mongolia. In fact, these troops remained, but China could not force the USSR to discuss a timetable for withdrawal, since Moscow now claimed that such a timetable was no longer necessary. Although negotiations for withdrawing the Red Army from Outer Mongolia were of the greatest importance to China, when the official Sino-Soviet conference finally convened after a fourteen-month delay, this question was never even raised.[77] Not only was the deadline for withdrawing Soviet troops from Outer Mongolia not discussed, therefore, but the 1915 tripartite treaty was never renegotiated. This meant that, theoretically at least, the 1915 tripartite treaty continued to be the basis for the Soviet Union's and China's relations with Outer Mongolia.

Moscow outmaneuvered Peking by convincing it to recognize the 1915 tripartite treaty at the same time that both countries agreed not to enforce it. When the USSR then refused to renegotiate a new treaty, China had little choice–short of war–but to accept that Outer Mongolia had now become a part of the Soviet-led Communist bloc. In 1945, Stalin defended the Soviet government's actions, citing Outer Mongolia's strategic importance: "It was necessary that Outer Mongolia be independent because of its strategic position, highly important for the Soviet Union; if a military power were to attack through Mongolia and cut the Trans-Siberian Railway, the USSR would be finished."[78] But the imperialistic nature of the USSR's foreign policy in Outer Mongolia was made especially clear after the success of the Chinese communist revolution in 1949, when the Soviet government refused to open negotiations with the People's Republic of China on the status of Outer Mongolia, and continued the active occupation of Outer Mongolia until the late 1980s.

The reality of the Soviet occupation of Outer Mongolia was a far cry from the anti-imperialist propaganda employed throughout Soviet history. Archival documents show that within five years after the October Revolution, the Bolsheviks were already resorting to secret diplomacy to support their imperialist expansion. Furthermore, Moscow directed these techniques against a weaker, undeveloped country–China–whose interests it publicly claimed to represent. The USSR's duplicity represents one of the first documented cases of how the Bolsheviks carried out their expansionist policies in an underdeveloped country. Although Soviet propaganda claimed that the USSR was fighting for China's economic and political rights, no amount of ideology could mask the Soviet leaders' desire to expand their control within China's traditional borders. In this regard, Robert C. Tucker's description of Stalin's desire for *control* as being the USSR's "operative aim" after World War II appears to have had its roots in the 1920s.[79]

Conclusions

Outer Mongolia remained an integral part of the Soviet-led Communist bloc from 1924 through the late 1980s, longer than any other region, except Tannu Tuva, which had not previously been claimed as part of the tsarist Russian empire. Although the Soviet government regained its hold over Outer Mongolia through the intervention of the Red Army in 1921, it consolidated its position through its secret diplomacy with China from 1921 through 1925. This secret diplomacy remained undiscovered for most of the history of the Soviet Union. That Moscow even signed a secret protocol with Peking to promote its imperialist policies in Outer Mongolia provides important insight into the methods that the USSR was willing to resort to in order to expand its power and influence.

Following the October Revolution, Bolshevik propaganda harshly denounced imperialism in the Far East. Soviet protestations were particularly notable in China during the 1920s, as well as during the post-World War II confrontations in Korea and Vietnam. But, the USSR itself engaged in imperialistic policies in the Far East at an early date. Indeed, the absorption of Tannu Tuva and Outer Mongolia in the 1920s preceded Vietnam and Korea by over a quarter of a century. This suggests that the USSR's decision to promote anti-imperialist propaganda during the early 1920s merely disguised its own imperialist ambitions.

Most importantly, the USSR's secret diplomacy with China took place more than twenty years prior to the generally-accepted beginning of the cold war, which most scholars have posited only after the end of World War II. This necessarily raises the question of whether this post–World War II date is appropriate, or whether the following interpretation expressed by David Dallin in 1949 is actually more accurate: "The methods of Soviet penetration of Outer Mongolia and the technique applied are the more remarkable in that they represent the first instance of extension of Soviet control over a neighboring non-Russian area. All the slogans and devices employed two decades later in other parts of the Eurasian continent were present in this first experiment: propaganda about 'friendly government,' 'higher type' of democracy, 'struggle against world imperialism,' and actually rule by a small minority, political alliance with Moscow, and military and economic control of the resources of the distant state by the Soviet Government."[80] Barrington Moore Jr. later agreed with Dallin, when he stated that the Soviet government's tactics in China during the 1920s "foreshadowed their policy in Europe after World War II, nearly a quarter of a century later."[81]

The simple fact that the methods that the USSR used to draw Outer Mongolia into the Soviet-led Communist bloc preceded similar methods used throughout Eastern Europe after World War II is convincing evidence that some, if not all, of the diplomatic characteristics that later became associated with the cold war were already in play during the 1920s. Certainly, the evidence presented above is consistent with one commonly accepted Western definition of the cold war as a worldwide "struggle for power and prestige . . . between the Western powers and the Communist bloc."[82]

Perhaps more surprisingly, it conforms almost exactly to the USSR's own definition of the cold war, as published in the *Great Soviet Encyclopedia*: "The various forms of the cold war and its arsenal of methods include the formation of a system of military and political alliances . . . the establishment of an extensive network of military bases . . . the use of force, the threat of force . . . the application of economic pressure . . . increased subversive activity on the part of the intelligence services . . . the encouragement of putsches and coups d'etat . . . propaganda and ideologically diversionary activities . . . and the attempt to obstruct the establishment and implementation of political, economic, and cultural ties among states."[83] An evaluation of the USSR's own 'arsenal of methods' for adding Outer Mongolia to the Communist bloc suggests that the cold war was not a phenomenon that first appeared in Europe, but was a Soviet creation that was systematically developed in the Far East during the 1920s.

Notes

1. "Agreement of the General Principles for the Settlement of the Questions Between the Republic of China and the Union of Soviet Socialist Republics," May 31, 1924, WCTA, 03-32, 495(1).

2. Peter S. H. Tang, *Russian and Soviet Policy in Manchuria and Outer Mongolia, 1911-1931*, 279-292.

3. George Alexander Lensen, ed., *Russia's Eastward Expansion*, 137; Abrikossow, a tsarist diplomat, admitted that Russia considered Outer Mongolia to be part of China.

4. "Tripartite Agreement in regard to Outer Mongolia–Russia, Mongolia, and China," June 7, 1915; John V. A. MacMurray, *Treaties and Agreements with and Concerning China*, 1240.

5. Allen S. Whiting, *Soviet Policies in China, 1917-1924*, 29; quoting *Izvestiia*, no. 138 (402) July 5, 1918.

6. Original French-language telegram sent from Moscow to Peking via Irkutsk, March 26, 1920, WCTA, 03-32, 463(1).

7. Chinese-language copy of Karakhan's second manifesto, October 2, 1920, original dated September 27, 1920, WCTA, 03-32, 479(1).

8. *Бюллетени Дальне-восточного Секретариата Коминтерна* (*Bulletins of the Far Eastern Secretariat of the Comintern*), No. 5, Irkutsk, April 24, 1921, 3.

9. S. C. M. Paine, *Imperial Rivals: China, Russia, and Their Disputed Frontier*, 318.

10. David J. Dallin, *The Rise of Russia in Asia*, 191; citing *The China Yearbook, 1924-25*, 860.

11. English-language letter from a Mr. Klishko to Wellington Koo, May 4, 1921, WCTA, 03-32, 197(1); according to Thomas E. Ewing, if China had taken the Soviet Union up on this offer of cooperation, then "it is probable that the Soviets would have honored that promise" (*Between the Hammer and the Anvil? Chinese and Russian Policies in Outer Mongolia 1911-1921*, 264). The archival documents suggest otherwise.

12. English-language note from Peking handed to Russian Trade Commission for transfer to Moscow, June 20, 1921, WCTA, 03-32, 198(3).

13. English-language note from the Soviet official in London, Krassin, to Wellington

Koo, concerning Outer Mongolia, July 1921, WCTA, 03-32, 175(1).

14. "Reply by Chicherin to the Request of the Provisional Government of Outer Mongolia for the Assistance of Russian Troops," August 10, 1921; Jane Degras, *Soviet Documents on Foreign Policy*, Vol. 1, 252-253.

15. Paine, 322.

16. Hans J. Morgenthau, *Politics Among Nation: The Struggle for Power and Peace*, 21; a similar definition is: "An imperial policy is one that enables a metropolis to create and maintain an external system of effective control. The control may be exerted by political, economic, strategic, cultural, religious, or ideological means, or by a combination of some or all of these" (A. P. Thornton, *Imperialism in the Twentieth Century*, 3).

17. William L. Langer, *The Diplomacy of Imperialism 1890-1902*, 67.

18. Richard Koebner and Helmut Dan Schmidt, *Imperialism: The Story and Significance of a Political Word, 1840-1960*, xviii.

19. Parker Thomas Moon, *Imperialism and World Politics*, viii.

20. Martin Sicker commented on the continuity of Russian expansion: "For some 400 years, first under the [ts]ars and later under its commissars, Russia has pursued an unrelenting policy of imperialism" (*The Strategy of Soviet Imperialism: Expansion in Eurasia*, 3).

21. Russian copy of the Soviet treaty with Outer Mongolia, November 5, 1921, WCTA, 03-32, 475(1).

22. *Ibid.*

23. Dallin, 191.

24. Tang, 428.

25. This was reported by a German journalist, von Salzmann, who interviewed Assmis and sent a secret report to Tokyo, November 9, 1922. Gaimushō, 2.5.1.106-1, 437.

26. Louis L. Snyder, ed., *The Dynamics of Nationalism: Readings in its Meaning and Development*, 13; quoting Lenin's "Critical Remarks on the National Question, 1913."

27. Xenia Joukoff Eudin and Robert C. North, *Soviet Russia and the East, 1920-1927: A Documentary Survey*, 45-46; quoting *Izvestiia*, February 22, 1919.

28. English-language copy of the Soviet Union's "Fundamental Law," dated December 30, 1922 but not ratified until July 6, 1923, and presented by Karakhan on September 5, 1923, WCTA, 03-32, 461(3),

29. English-language copy of the official "Declaration of the Union of Soviet Socialist Republics," July 13, 1923, and presented by Karakhan on September 5, 1923, WCTA, 03-32, 461(3).

30. French-language credentials for "Alexandre Constantinowitch Paikes," October 18, 1921. This document also specified that any agreement Paikes signed had to be ratified by the Soviet government, October 18, 1921, WCTA, 03-32, 474(2).

31. Chinese-language minutes of three meetings with Paikes, January 16, 1922, WCTA, 03-32, 204(1).

32. *Ibid.*

33. *Ibid.*

34. Chinese-language translation of Paikes's letter 235, February 7, 1922, WCTA, 03-32, 204(1). [The hand-written Russian-language letter is at 03-32, 200(3)].

35. Chinese-language telegram from the Peking government consul in Chita, March 11, 1922, WCTA, 03-32, 475(1).

36. Chinese-language minutes of Paikes's meeting with Chinese Ministry of Foreign Affairs Officials, April 26, 1922, WCTA, 03-32, 200(3); also see Paine, 323.

37. *Ibid.*

38. *The China Yearbook*, 1923, Vol. 2, 680.

39. Official Cabinet Official Letter 1035, May 15, 1922, WCTA, 03-32, 475(1).

40. Chinese-language minutes of a meeting between Foreign Minister Yen and Paikes, May 23, 1922, WCTA, 03-32, 163(3).

41. "Soviet-Mongolian Protocol Concerning the Ownership of Various Property," May 31, 1922, Degras, Vol. 1, 489-491.

42. English-language note from the Soviet official in London, Krassin, to Wellington Koo, concerning Outer Mongolia, July 1921, WCTA, 03-32, 175 (1).

43. Chinese-language minutes of Paikes's meeting with Chinese Ministry of Foreign Affairs Officials, June 29, 1922, WCTA, 03-32, 200(3).

44. *Ibid.*

45. Chinese-language telegram from Moscow, June 29, 1922, WCTA, 03-32, 462(2); Joffe spent six months in Peking, but his demand that China first recognize the Soviet government stymied talks, since Peking wanted to negotiate agreements prior to recognition.

46. Chinese-language minutes of a meeting between Foreign Minister Yen and Paikes, July 6, 1922, WCTA, 03-32, 204(1).

47. English-language memorandum No. 533 from Paikes to the Ministry of Foreign Affairs of the Republic of China, August 3, 1922, WCTA, 03-32, 207(1).

48. Russian-language text of Karakhan's speech at the luncheon given by Wang, September 4, 1923, WCTA, 03-32, 467(1).

49. Chinese-language minutes of the conversation between Karakhan and C. T. Wang, Director of the Sino-Soviet negotiations, September 14, 1923, WCTA, 03-32, 483(5).

50. *Ibid.*

51. The official English-language translation of the Chinese-language original, entitled "Draft Agreement for the Resumption of Relations Between China and Russia." This draft had fourteen points, October 13, 1923, WCTA, 03-32, 481(5).

52. English-language "Draft Agreement for the Resumption of Relations Between China and Russia," including eleven points, October 26, 1923, WCTA, 03-32, 481(5).

53. Chinese-language minutes of Chu Ho-hsiang's meeting with Karakhan," February 27, 1924, WCTA, 03-32, 487(1).

54. Secret Chinese-language telegram from Wellington Koo to Li Chia-ao in Moscow, March 7, 1924, WCTA, 03-32, 487(1).

55. Chu Pao-chin, *V. K. Wellington Koo: A Case Study of China's Diplomat and Diplomacy of Nationalism, 1912-1966*, 107-108.

56. Multiple Chinese-language copies of the draft Sino-Soviet treaty, including suggested changes written on the copies. The most important came from the Ministry of Finance and the Ministry of Education, March 1, 1924, WCTA, 03-32, 488(1).

57. English-language original copy of the draft treaty, including the secret protocol. This draft was signed by Karakhan and Wang, but the document is not dated and there are no official seals, which supports Peking's later claim that this draft was initialed merely to show agreement between the parties, March 14, 1924, WCTA, 03-32, 506(5); Sow-Theng Leong, *Sino-Soviet Diplomatic Relations, 1917-1926*, 264-265.

58. Russian-language letter No. 575 to Foreign Minister Chicherin from Li Chia-ao, October 14, 1924, WCTA, 03-32, 494(3).

59. Chinese-language minutes of a meeting between Li Chia-ao and Chicherin, February 21, 1925, WCTA, 03-32, 498(1).

60. Chu, 113.

61. Chinese-language copy of the final Sino-Soviet agreement; this version includes

the Secret Protocol with the Instructions "Secret Protocol, Do Not Publish," May 31, 1924, WCTA, 03-32, 454(1); a published English-language copy without the secret protocol is at WCTA, 03-32, 495(1); this treaty was subsequently published in 1959 without the secret protocol in: *Советско-китайские Отношения 1917-1957 сборник документов* (*Soviet-Chinese Relations, 1917-1957: Collection of Documents*), 81-90.

62. *Ibid.*

63. English-language copy of the "Certificate of Full Power Given to VI Kyuin Wellington Koo Plenipotentiary," signed by President "Ts'ao K'un" and countersigned by Foreign Minister Wellington Koo, May 30, 1924, WCTA, 03-32, 495(2).

64. English-language minutes of the meeting between Karakhan and Koo, at the Ministry of Foreign Affairs, starting at 12:45 p.m., June 28, 1924, WCTA, 03-32, 489(1).

65. English-language letter No. 2524/26 to Foreign Minister Koo, signed by Karakhan, delaying the official Sino-Soviet conference, June 28, 1924, WCTA, 03-32, 499(4).

66. English-language letter to Karakhan from Wellington Koo, in which he stressed that June 30 was the last day to convene the Sino-Soviet conference, as stipulated by the May 31, 1924 Agreement on General Principles, June 30, 1924, WCTA, 03-32, 499(4).

67. Chinese-language minutes of Li Chia-ao's meetings with Soviet Foreign Minister officials on June 27 and 29, to request that the Sino-Soviet conference be convened on time, June 27, 1924, WCTA, 03-32, 488(2).

68. Alecia J. Campi, "The Political Relationship Between the United States and Outer Mongolia, 1915-1927: The Kalgan Consular Records," 202-203.

69. *Ibid.*, 206.

70. Tang, 388-389.

71. Robert Rupen, *How Mongolia Is Really Ruled: A Political History of the Mongolian People's Republic, 1900-1978*, 44.

72. Michael N. Pavlovsky, *Chinese and Russian Relations*, 90.

73. Tang, 382.

74. English-language letter No. 35002/26 to Foreign Minister Shen Jui-lin from Karakhan, announcing that Red Army troops had withdrawn from Outer Mongolia, March 6, 1925, WCTA, 03-32, 497(3).

75. Campi, 218.

76. Chinese-language transcripts of Li Chia-ao's meeting with Foreign Minister Chicherin, during which Outer Mongolia was discussed, May 7, 1925, WCTA, 03-32, 204(3); also see Paine, 326.

77. English-language minutes of the opening day of the Sino-Soviet conference, entitled: "Minutes of the First Meeting of the Sino-Soviet Conference," August 26, 1925, WCTA, 03-32, 503(3).

78. Rupen, 45.

79. "The Psychology of Soviet Foreign Policy," Alexander Dallin, ed., *Soviet Conduct in World Affairs*), 231.

80. Dallin, 189.

81. Barrington Moore Jr., *Soviet Politics–The Dilemma of Power*, 211.

82. *The Columbia Encyclopedia*, 447.

83. *Great Soviet Encyclopedia*, Vol. 28, 203.

114

Chinese Eastern Railway, c. 1917

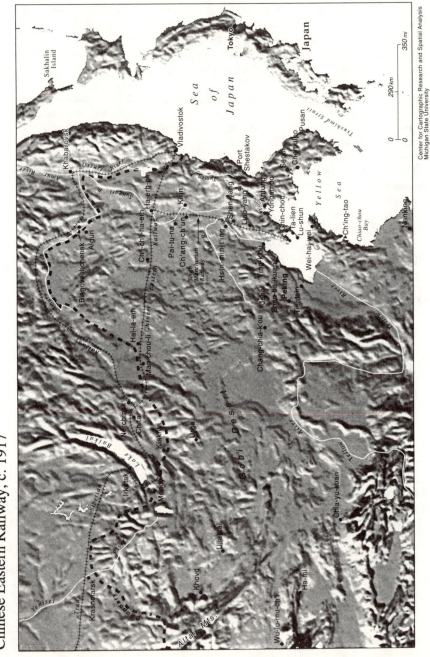

Center for Cartographic Research and Spatial Analysis
Michigan State University

4

Assertion of Soviet Control over the Chinese Eastern Railway

The Soviet Union regained majority control over the strategically located Chinese Eastern Railway that ran through Manchuria by signing two previously unpublished secret protocols: the first with the Peking government on May 31, 1924, and the second with Chang Tso-lin's Manchurian government on September 20, 1924. These secret agreements were signed despite the Bolsheviks' repeated promises that they would never resort to secret diplomacy. In order to consolidate Soviet power over this railway, the USSR then signed the January 20, 1925 convention with Japan that recognized Japan's authority over the South Manchuria Railway in return for Japan's acquiescence to full Soviet authority over the Chinese Eastern Railway.

These events flew in the face of the Soviet Union's propaganda, which had repeatedly called on the other great powers to follow the USSR's lead and give up their concessions in China; for example, the CER was valued at over half a billion gold rubles and was the single largest foreign railway concession in China, encompassing 250,000 acres of territory stretched out over 1073 miles of railway track running through the heart of northern Manchuria.[1] But from the time that the Soviet government first promised to return the railway in July 1919 to the signing of its agreement with Japan in January 1925, less than six years passed. During this time the Soviet government gradually reneged on its former promises to treat China as an equal.

The final step in the Soviet rejection of its earlier promises of equality was reached on February 26, 1925, when the Soviet Union's first ambassador to China, Lev Karakhan, recognized the validity of Japan's Twenty-one Demands, considered by many Chinese to be the most humiliating example of China's mistreatment by the capitalist countries. Moscow's actions were kept secret from the Chinese public, however, and in the mass anti-imperialist movements in China during May 1925, the focus of the Chinese people's anger was directed largely at Great Britain, Japan, and the United States, not at the Soviet Union.

The long-range effects of the Soviet Union's secret diplomacy in China were enormous. The popularity of the Chinese Communist Party was largely based on the widely held belief that the Soviet government treated China better than the other great powers. To a large degree, it was this claim that prompted Chinese intellectuals to form the Chinese Communist Party during the 1920s, and this pro-Soviet propaganda continued to bolster the Chinese communist movement through the 1949 revolution and well into the 1950s. The Soviet Union's secret diplomacy with China was completely at odds with its propaganda. Had the existence of these secret Sino-Soviet agreements been known at the time, the legitimacy of the communist movement in China would have been seriously undermined.

Early Sino-Soviet Diplomacy over the CER

The Bolsheviks' first problem during 1920 was to renew diplomatic relations with the Peking government. Peking was especially interested in Karakhan's promise to return the CER to China. China's preeminent railway expert, Wang Chin-chun, wrote a letter to Foreign Minister Yen on May 3, 1921, advocating that China take advantage of the current situation to solve the sticky ownership disputes that revolved around the CER (see Document 13). Wang said: "Today presents the only and most unexpected opportunity for some solution of the problem, for it is the first time for many years that Russia and Japan are really at logger heads, while other Powers are in no position to interfere as they used to do." In addition, Wang warned that further conflict over the CER might arise: "Manchuria has twice been the battle field in recent years, and will be the bone of contention for more international conflicts, unless the statesmen of today can arrange matters in such a way as will ameliorate the situation. The Chinese Eastern [Railway] plays a most important part and constitutes a most important factor in the Manchuria question."[2]

On October 2, 1920, Karakhan presented his second Karakhan Manifesto in which he stated that Soviet Russia wanted to maintain some control over the railway by signing a "special treaty on the way of working the Chinese Eastern Railway with regard to the needs of the Russian Socialist Federative Soviet Republic."[3] These proposals were officially dated September 27, 1920, but seem to have been publicly announced in Moscow on October 27, 1920, which caused a certain amount of confusion about the dating of this second Karakhan Manifesto, not dissimilar to the dating problems associated with the two versions of the first Karakhan Manifesto, but for entirely different reasons. It is even possible that this second dating problem was used to help cover up the intentional use of two versions of the first Karakhan Manifesto the year earlier.

Although Karakhan's new proposal concerning the CER was not nearly as advantageous to China as the offer made in his original manifesto, it did not seem to contradict the intent of his former promise. Only after the Soviet government's first official diplomat, Aleksandr Paikes, arrived in Peking in December 1921, did the Soviet government's true intentions start to become clear. According to Paikes's interpretation, the Soviet government's former declaration that it would annul all of the tsarist unequal treaties meant nothing so long as China could be convinced to agree to the old terms. Considering that Vladimir Vilenskii, the author of the propaganda pamphlet that had first printed the promise to return the CER to China without compensation, had also been sent to Peking as Paikes's counselor, it cannot be doubted that Paikes knew of the contents of the original Karakhan Manifesto.[4]

𝕴nter-𝕬llied 𝕿echnical 𝕭oard.

HARBIN, _____ May _____ 3rd, _____ 192 1.

H. E. Dr. W. W. Yen,
Minister of Foreign Affairs,
Peking,

My Dear Dr. Yen:-

With reference to our recent conversation in
Peking concerning the Chinese Eastern Railway, I beg to enclose
herein a memorandum which I have prepared concering the question and beg to ask you to give it due consideration. Manchuria
has twice been the battle field in recent years, and will be
the bone of contention for more international conflicts, unless the statesmen of to-day can arrange matters in such a way
as will ameliorate the situation. The Chinese Eastern plays a
most important part and constitutes a most important factor in
the Manchuria question. The main difficulty in the past has
been, as you well know, the combined intrigues of Russia and
Japan against all efforts towards improvement. So endeavors of
Knox etc., all failed. To-day presents the only and most unexpected opportunity for some solution of the problem, for it
is the first time for many years that Russia and Japan are
really at logger heads, while other Powers are in no position
to interfere as they used to do. What John Hay and Knox failed,
our statesmen may be able to accomplish, provided they seize
and take proper advantage of the opportunity. To my opionion
the fundamental solution of the Chinese Eastern problem is
monumental. I earnestly and heartly wish your success in all
your patriotic efforts.

With kind regards and best wishes,

I beg to remain,

Yours very respectfully,

[signature]

Document 13
Wang Chin-chun's May 3, 1921 Letter to Foreign Minister Yen

When Adolf Joffe replaced Paikes later in 1922 as the Soviet Union's official envoy, he tried unsuccessfully to convince the Peking government to agree to the joint management of the CER. Joffe now swore that the Soviet government had never promised to return the CER to China, denying that this promise was "contained either in the authentic text of the Declaration of 25th July, 1919, which the Plenipotentiary Mission has in its possession, or in the text of the same published at the time in the official collection of the People's Commissariat of Nationalities."[5]

Moscow's use of two versions of the Karakhan Manifesto to convince Peking to open negotiations was now complete: Joffe's denial was the final step in the three-year process of using Karakhan's promise to get Sino-Soviet negotiations started, and then gradually disclaiming the original July 25, 1919 Karakhan Manifesto and putting the published August 26, 1919 version–which did not include the promise to return the CER–in its place. But, in the meantime, Karakhan's original manifesto had served another purpose: it helped the Soviet-supported Comintern sponsor the creation of a communist party in China during 1921, and then promoted its rapid growth in the following years.

The USSR's generous promise to return the CER to China was a mainstay of the Comintern's propaganda: for example, as late as April 24, 1921, the Comintern's Siberian journal repeated this promise, and in August 1922, Vilenskii published an article in *Izvestiia* stating that the CER was being returned "to China without redemption."[6] Meanwhile, in China, Ts'ai Ho-sen, a member of the Chinese Communist Party, wrote in the party's journal, *The Guide Weekly*, during the fall of 1922, that the Soviets had offered to return to China all of the tsarist holdings in Manchuria, including, "land, mines, and the Chinese Eastern Railway."[7]

Karakhan's promise also paved the way for an alliance between the Soviet Union and Sun Yat-sen, the leader of the Kuomintang, and the head of the opposition Canton government. When Peking was unwilling to negotiate, the Soviet government turned to Sun Yat-sen, who quickly signed away China's rights to all of the CER in exchange for promises of Soviet military and financial support. According to one recently published history of China, it was Karakhan's generous promises, therefore, that made the Chinese people think that the Soviet Union was now "China's truest friend."[8]

The 1921-22 Washington Conference

To strengthen the Open Door Policy's protection for China's and Russia's territorial integrity, Washington announced during the summer of 1921 that it would be convening a conference to discuss issues of importance to the Far East. On July 19, 1921, Foreign Minister Chicherin protested that Soviet Russia had not been invited to attend.[9] But, characteristically, the Soviet government newspaper *Izvestiia* had called on Asian nations to oppose capitalism only two days earlier: "Just as we are the hopeful bulwark for oriental peoples in their struggle for independence, they in turn are our allies in one common struggle against world imperialism."[10] The Comintern also denounced the Washington Conference as an international effort to assume control over China's markets, calling on the Chinese people to join with Soviet Russia to oppose capitalism.[11]

On February 6, 1922, the Washington Conference, including Wellington Koo at the head of China's delegation, established the Open Door Policy into "formal treaty form for the first time," by adopting the Nine Power Treaty's four principles[12]:

1) to respect the sovereignty, independence, and territorial and administrative inviolability of China;

2) to grant China completely and without constraint the opportunity to develop and to support its capable and stable government;

3) to utilize their influence for the purpose of truly establishing and supporting the principle of equal opportunity for trade and industry of all nations in all the territory of China;

4) to abstain, at the present time in the Chinese theater, from striving for special rights and advantages, detrimental to the rights of the subjects or citizens of friendly nations, or the support of activities hostile to the security of these nations.

The signatories also promised not to sign agreements to establish "superior rights in relation to mercantile or economic development in any particular region of China," "monopolies or preferences," or "spheres of influence."[13]

The Washington Conference also raised China's international tariff rates and set up two commissions, the first to study ways of revising China's tariff system to make it autonomous of foreign control, and the second to find a way to help China adopt legislation and judicial reforms that would allow for the relinquishing of extraterritoriality rights.[14] All of these efforts were intended to draw China gradually into the international community as an equal, not as a subservient, as Comintern propaganda claimed.

In a sweeping analysis of the Washington Conference, Hans Morgenthau has concluded: "The Nine Power Treaty transformed the American policy of the 'open door' in China into a multilateral policy which the nations mostly interested in trade with China, as well as China itself, pledged themselves to uphold. Its main purpose was to stabilize the distribution of power which existed at the time between the contracting nations with regard to China."[15] But Washington also hoped that by supporting gradual reforms—as opposed to a Bolshevik-style revolution—China could gradually be integrated into the new world order.

An unintended diplomatic outcome of the Nine Power Treaty was the destruction of the Anglo-Japanese alliance, which had been in effect since 1902. This alliance was at the heart of Great Britain's policies in Asia, since it guaranteed Britain's holdings in South China and Japan's position in North China. Great Britain's decision to embrace the principle of mutual security was made during October and November 1920, when the British Foreign Office was confronted with a choice between the United States and Japan, and felt compelled to side with America: "If the cardinal feature of our foreign policy in the future is to cultivate closer relations with the United States . . . the renewal of the alliance [with Japan] in anything like its present shape may prove a formidable obstacle to the realization of that aim."[16]

Although the Washington Conference did create a new "Four Power Treaty" among Great Britain, France, Japan, and the United States to replace the former Anglo-Japanese alliance, this agreement only allowed for consultations among the four members, and made no provisions to work jointly together on military matters.[17] This problem was further exacerbated when the Washington Conference prohibited active interference in China's internal affairs, a decision that actually removed one of the last restraints to Soviet expansionism.

Events would soon show that mutual security would not work if even one country—in this case, the Soviet Union—refused to adhere to the basic principles of the Open Door Policy. In fact, the Washington Conference's structure for supporting the Open Door Policy unintentionally worked to the advantage of the USSR, since the capitalist governments tied their hands by promising not to interfere in China's internal affairs. Furthermore, the checks and balances by which the Anglo-Japanese alliance had formerly opposed Russian expansionism in China disappeared altogether, and were not replaced by a similar system to control renewed Soviet expansion. For these reasons, Moscow's opportunity to increase its sphere of influence in China was greatly enhanced.

A final decision of the Washington Conference was to refuse to agree to China's claim that the CER should be recognized as Chinese property. Instead, it determined that Peking could continue as trustee of the CER until an international settlement was achieved that took all interested parties into account. Peking was unwilling to wait, however, and so once again turned to negotiate directly with the Soviet government over the ownership and management of the CER.

Karakhan Proposes Joint Management of the CER

Since Adolf Joffe had failed to convince Peking to manage the CER jointly, Moscow decided to appoint Lev Karakhan as the USSR's plenipotentiary extraordinary to China, charged with strengthening "friendly bonds" between the two countries.[18] After arriving in Peking, Karakhan gave a speech in which he repeated that the Soviet Union hoped to maintain relations with China on the basis of "complete and absolute equality."[19] But, on December 2, 1923, when Karakhan sent the Ministry of Foreign Affairs an English-language copy of his 1919 manifesto, it turned out to be the text published in *Izvestiia* on August 26, 1919, which did not include the promise to return the CER to China. This document was marked "True to the original," however, and was stamped with the official Soviet seal and signed by the first secretary of the mission.[20]

In a note to Karakhan dated January 9, 1924, C. T. Wang pointed out the discrepancy between the copy that the Soviet mission had given to him and the original telegram the Peking government had received on March 26, 1920, which was also "signed certifying that there were no mistakes in the copy." Since Wang now had two different copies of the 1919 Karakhan Manifesto, both of which claimed to be true to the original, he suggested that Karakhan might want to clear this problem up before the Chinese people began to doubt the "sincerity" of the Soviet offers.[21] In reply, on January 17, 1924, Karakhan expressed his "deep amazement" that Wang would want to discuss the 1919 declaration, since he had just "handed over authentic texts of the 1919 and 1920 declarations." Karakhan then called the original March 26, 1920 telegram that Peking had received a "false version of the 1919 declaration." Karakhan further insisted that it did not "give any kind of rights to China."[22]

In an attempt to break the resulting stalemate, Li Chia-ao, the Chinese consul to Moscow, informed Koo on January 18, 1924 of an off-the-record talk he had with Karakhan, in which Karakhan listed four reasons why Moscow did not want to return the CER to China: 1) the Russian people would lose their capital investment in the CER; 2) the continued existence of the Kuomintang government in Canton showed that China was not yet united and so could not manage the railway herself; 3) the CER was still in the hands of White Russian factions that opposed the Soviet government; and 4) after the CER was returned to China it might fall prey to Japan's attempts to gain control over it.[23]

The first reason was not really valid since a great deal of the capital to build the CER had come from foreign investors and so the Soviet citizens actually had very little capital at stake; furthermore, even though Moscow had earlier renounced all tsarist debts, it now apparently wanted to take credit for the tsarist CER expenditures.[24] As for point 2, the Soviet government and the Comintern were actively supporting and funding the KMT government in Canton, and so using the existence of Sun Yat-sen's government as an excuse for why the CER should stay under Soviet control was hardly convincing. Third, although the White Russians did have some influence over the CER, Karakhan greatly exaggerated their military power and knew that they were no match for the Red Army. Finally, Karakhan's fear that the Japanese would take over the CER actually worked better in reverse, since if the Soviet Union regained full control over the CER, Japan's economic interests in southern Manchuria would be directly threatened and Japan might feel compelled to respond.

Although these four reasons do not stand up under close scrutiny, the Peking government had no way of forcing Karakhan to live up to his earlier promise to return the CER to China without compensation. On February 2, 1924, Karakhan indicated a sudden willingness to exchange mutual recognition simultaneously with a general agreement resolving Sino-Soviet problems. Retreating from his former proposal that China and the USSR jointly manage the CER, Karakhan now agreed that, after a short period of joint management, China could acquire full authority over the CER as well as over the territory along the railway line.[25]

Specifically, Karakhan stated that China could buy back the railway from the Soviet government in exchange for continued Soviet use of the CER to transport goods from Manchouli to Vladivostok. Until the terms of its return were decided, however, Karakhan suggested temporary joint management of the railway with China, with a managing board composed of five Russians and five Chinese members. Karakhan further proposed that the price and the terms of the sale and return of the CER to China should be decided at a Sino-Soviet conference that would follow one month after official relations were opened.[26]

Li once again supported Karakhan in a long letter from Moscow: "If China tried to pay for the complete return of the Railway then it would create a whole range of difficult problems which would not exist if China and the Soviet Union jointly managed the Railway." Li also praised Karakhan's plan as "comparatively secure," "very fair," and "comparatively easy."[27] Since Moscow had already convinced Sun Yat-sen to support joint Sino-Soviet management of the CER, Koo was left with few viable alternatives and so accepted Karakhan's proposal.

Although China's decision to agree to joint management over the CER seemed to promise the railway's eventual return to China, it in fact merely proved the efficacy of using two versions of the 1919 Karakhan Manifesto, since the Soviet government had pulled off a propaganda coup by promising to return the same railway that it was now being allowed to manage jointly. Once the Peking government agreed to this solution, Karakhan and Wang quickly hammered out a draft agreement by March 1, 1924. Koo telegraphed an order to Li in Moscow on March 7, telling him to talk to Foreign Minister Chicherin about several outstanding problems, including China's desire to fix the price and immediately determine new management regulations for the CER.[28] As ordered, Li met with Chicherin for a three-hour discussion on March 9, 1924. He requested that Chicherin encourage Karakhan to be more "amiable" and willing to make concessions, so that "the future of our two countries' friendship will really be close."[29] But Chicherin also wanted to decide these important problems only at the Sino-Soviet conference after official relations were opened.

On May 3, 1924, Jacob Schurman, the U.S. minister to China, sent a letter to Koo protesting the draft terms of the Sino-Soviet treaty (see Document 14). He reminded Koo that while the Washington Conference's thirteenth resolution had made China the trustee of the CER, the powers had reserved the "right to insist hereafter upon the responsibility of China for performance or non-performance of the obligations towards the foreign stockholders, bondholders and creditors of the Chinese Eastern Railway Company."[30] Although Schurman reassured Koo that Washington did not oppose the Sino-Soviet negotiations and "has no desire to prevent the conclusion of a Sino-Russian agreement," he did want "to prevent future embarrassments, especially for Your Excellency's Government." Schurman warned Koo: "The Government of the United States of America stands for the protection of all interests in the Railway, including Russian, and could not approve a change of any kind in the *status quo* by whomsoever initiated unless the rights of all creditors and other parties in interest were adequately protected."[31]

No. 810   Peking, May 3, 1924.

Your Excellency:

With regard to the negotiations which I understand are taking place between the Government of
the Republic of China and the Soviet Government, I
am directed by my Government to recall to Your
Excellency's attention the Thirteenth Resolution
adopted by the Conference on the Limitation of
Armament at Washington at its Sixth Plenary Session;
and to remind Your Excellency's Government that China's
responsibility as Trustee for the Chinese Eastern Railway is an obligation that is not to be ignored or unilaterally invalidated by China in the course of any
negotiations with other parties regarding the Railway.

The Government of the United States of America
stands for the protection of all interests in the Railway, including Russian, and could not approve a change
of any kind in the status quo by whomsoever initiated
unless the rights of all creditors and other parties
in interest were adequately protected.

I take the opportunity afforded by the communication of the foregoing declaration and reminder to repeat to Your Excellency, what Your Excellency already
knows from my earlier oral assurances, that the Government of the United States has no desire to prevent the
conclusion of a Sino-Russian Agreement. The object
of my Government is to prevent future embarrassments,
specially for Your Excellency's Government, by calling
timely attention to the rights and interests as well
as to the obligations which China is bound respectively
to safeguard and to fulfill in performance of the
duties she has undertaken in respect of the Chinese
Eastern Railway, as set forth in the Resolution quoted above.

I avail myself of this opportunity to extend
to Your Excellency the renewed assurances of my
highest consideration.

Jacob Gould Schurman

Document 14
Excerpts from Schurman's May 3, 1924 Letter to Wellington Koo

Other Washington Conference participants–including, most important, Japan–also wrote to Koo protesting the terms of the Sino-Soviet treaty. After almost two months of delay and sporadic secret negotiations, however, the final version of the Sino-Soviet treaty was signed on May 31, 1924. Included in this treaty was an eleven-article "Agreement for the Provisional Management of the Chinese Eastern Railway."[32] The intent of this agreement was to make the CER an exclusive Sino-Soviet joint venture. As a result, the interests of all of the other "stockholders, bondholders and creditors of the Chinese Eastern Railway Company" were completely ignored.

Several articles in this May 31, 1924 treaty later proved to be the key to Karakhan's success in reclaiming majority control over the CER: for example, Article I stated that all former Russian consulates and government property should be turned over to the Soviet government, while Article IX specified that the CER would be jointly managed by the Soviet Union and China until its status was determined at the upcoming Sino-Soviet conference.[33] In Karakhan's opinion, the wording of the agreement showed that all Russian property had to be returned and the joint management of the CER had to be in effect prior to the convening of the Sino-Soviet conference. He used this interpretation to justify delaying the conference. Meanwhile, Karakhan publicly blamed the Peking government for all of these delays, citing its inability to carry through on its obligations.

But, so long as the conference did not convene, then the Soviet government's obligations under the May 31, 1924 treaty to sell the CER to China was blocked and the secret protocol allowed Karakhan to claim that the terms of all former Sino-Russian treaties were still valid. The Peking government's only recourse, therefore, was to try to satisfy Karakhan's numerous preconditions so that he would finally agree to begin the conference. Using these tactics, Karakhan delayed the convening of the official Sino-Soviet conference for fourteen months after the official treaty was signed on May 31, 1924. Even when the conference finally met in August 1925, new treaties and conventions concerning the CER were never completed, thus leaving the secret protocol in effect.

Karakhan's Pressure Tactics

With the complete suspension of all prior Sino-Russian agreements on May 31, 1924, the USSR was in a strong position to force China to put the CER under joint control. Simply by delaying the Sino-Soviet conference it continued to suspend all of the benefits that this treaty guaranteed Peking, such as the sale and return of the CER to China. Karakhan used his new leverage to force the Peking government into accepting three preconditions during June and July, 1924: 1) return all Russian consulates to the Soviet government, 2) make Karakhan China's first full ambassador, and 3) start joint management of the CER.[34] Karakhan's pressure tactics were not temporary measures; after Peking fulfilled these three points, Karakhan presented others.[35]

It was at a June 6, 1924 meeting with Koo that Karakhan first demanded that the CER immediately be put under joint management. Karakhan proposed that the new joint board of directors be determined and he asked Koo to provide him with the names of the Chinese nominees, so that "the control of the Railway might pass into Russian and Chinese hands."[36] The main obstacle to this plan was Chang Tso-lin, the strongest warlord in Manchuria, who appeared to be opposing Peking's participation in the joint management of the CER.

On June 13, Karakhan proposed two possible countermeasures against Chang: 1) to use "armed force against Manchuria" or 2) to negotiate a separate agreement between the USSR and Chang Tso-lin's government in Mukden that would cover the CER and "one or two other minor matters." As for declaring war on Chang, Karakhan suggested that it was politically less desirable and would require consultations with the Soviet government officials in Moscow. The second proposal, however, would be a low risk way of gaining Manchuria's compliance.[37]

Karakhan reassured Koo that should he be "obliged" to sign a separate agreement with Chang Tso-lin, the agreement with Peking would still be considered valid. But negotiations with Chang were clearly already under way, since Karakhan then informed Koo that in this new agreement the original lease on the CER would be reduced from eighty years to sixty years, and the cost of purchasing the railway from the Soviet Union would be determined as the "original cost" of building the railway, or some 200 to 300 million rubles, instead of the current appraised value of 700 million rubles.[38]

The fact that Karakhan was already able to quote the exact terms of the upcoming agreement with Chang Tso-lin is highly suspicious. When one recalls that it took Karakhan almost nine full months of negotiations with Peking to come to terms, it hardly seems reasonable to expect that a separate agreement with Chang could get so far in only thirteen days. A more logical interpretation is that Karakhan had been carrying on negotiations secretly with Chang for some time prior to the signing of the May 31, 1924 Sino-Soviet agreement; as shown above, Sun Yat-sen had tried to convince Chang to agree to a 7-3 division of the CER during the spring of 1923. What Karakhan now wanted was to pressure Foreign Minister Koo into giving his permission in advance for a separate agreement to be signed between the Soviet government and Chang's government in Mukden. This was a suggestion that Koo refused to consider, since any new agreement might undermine the Peking government's rights over the CER.[39]

It was Karakhan's strategy of pressuring Peking to enforce the joint administration of the CER prior to the convening of the Sino-Soviet conference that gave him leverage over Koo. As the official deadline for opening the Sino-Soviet conference neared—one month after the signing of the May 31, 1924 agreement—it became an open question whether the conference would convene on time. In a conversation with Karakhan on June 28, 1924, Koo gave three reasons why the conference should convene as scheduled: 1) the May 31 agreement specifically stated that the conference should convene within one month's time; 2) the conference would resolve issues "of equal interest to Moscow and Peking";

and 3) a delay in opening the conference would hurt Koo's position within the Peking government since he had personally supported the signing of the treaty.[40] Based on these three reasons, Koo stated that he wanted the Sino-Soviet conference to convene as scheduled on June 30, 1924.

But Karakhan disagreed, insisting that the opening of the conference was "a mere formality, not substance," since discussions could not begin in earnest until the autumn anyway and, furthermore, the Soviet government could not be convinced to open the conference as long as joint management of the "Chinese Eastern Railway had not yet been carried out." Karakhan even went so far as to predict that "people might laugh at them if they should sit at a Conference when the old obligations had not been fulfilled."[41]

Karakhan further suggested that a good excuse for the Chinese public to explain the delay in opening the conference would be to say that Soviet officials had not yet arrived from Moscow, while "between themselves they knew the cause for the delay," i.e., the joint management of the CER had not yet begun. When Koo stated that he would not be a party to the "undoing of the Agreement," Karakhan countered by accusing the Chinese government of not carrying through on its obligations.[42] Karakhan left the door open for even further delays when he informed Koo that the conference could be convened only "upon the receipt of instructions from my Government."[43]

Koo's open admission that a delay in opening the conference would hurt his personal position as foreign minister shows how complete Karakhan's power really was. Although Koo protested Karakhan's delays in secret, he was unwilling to lodge a strong public protest against the postponement of the conference. This gave Karakhan the opportunity he needed to delay it again and again. On July 7, for example, Koo complained that delays in convening the planned Sino-Soviet conference merely encouraged Chang Tso-lin, and that "instead of helping the Chinese Government to execute the Agreement was rendering it more difficult of execution."[44] On August 12, Koo again suggested that the long-delayed conference begin in a few days time, but Karakhan disagreed, proposing that they wait "a few days more until a settlement has been reached." Karakhan further suggested that if Peking approved the separate agreement between Moscow and Mukden, it would make matters easier, requesting that "the sanction of Peking be put in writing and be published after the agreement had been signed and put into execution."[45]

Koo now argued that "the Chinese Government had ever so many obligations under the Agreement while the Soviet Government had only one principal obligation, namely, the Conference." Koo also asked Karakhan not to interfere in Chinese internal matters, pointing out that Karakhan had placed them all in a dilemma, since all three parties were working at cross purposes: "Mr. Karakhan held that the CER question must be settled first before the Conference. Mukden held so long as the Conference was not opened then there was hope of a separate agreement, to which the Central Government would object. Never would they reach anywhere. On the other hand, if the Conference was started Mukden's hope of a separate agreement would be dashed to the ground. He wished to break up this vicious circle." Karakhan countered by stating that the Soviet government had given up much in the May 31, 1924 treaty and the "only question on which the Soviet Government wished to keep its rights was the CER."[46]

In fact, while Karakhan had promised to give up much, in reality all of his promises could be acted on only when the Sino-Soviet conference met. From the beginning of June until September 1924, Foreign Minister Koo repeatedly warned Karakhan not to interfere with Peking's efforts to convince Chang Tso-lin to accept the May 31, 1924 agreement on the CER. But Karakhan's separate negotiations with Chang effectively sabotaged Peking's attempts to carry out its obligations under the agreement, as well as put pressure on Koo to recognize in advance a separate Soviet agreement with the Mukden government, which would have given the USSR a *carte blanche* in its negotiations with Chang Tso-lin, something Koo was unwilling to do.

Even though Karakhan repeatedly stated that any separate treaty with Mukden would not conflict with the agreement previously made with the Peking government, and swore that he would submit any such treaty to Peking for its approval, this did not happen. When Wellington Koo was removed from his post as foreign minister in the middle of September 1924, no doubt partly because of his failure to convince Karakhan to convene the long-overdue conference, the Soviet government used the resulting confusion in the Peking government to further consolidate its control over the CER, only this time by signing a secret agreement with Chang Tso-lin's government in Manchuria.

The September 20, 1924 Secret Agreement

After the Peking government failed to initiate joint management over the CER, the Soviet Union signed a supplemental agreement with the Manchurian "Autonomous Three Eastern Provinces" on September 20, 1924. Although this new agreement was written to sound as if it were an addition to the former May 31, 1924 agreement with Peking, the inclusion of a secret protocol actually meant that Moscow's agreement with Chang superseded its agreement with Peking. To call this new treaty a supplemental agreement was really a misnomer, therefore, since it in fact transferred full control of the Chinese share of the CER to Chang Tso-lin. Because the supplemental agreement's secret protocol was not previously published, however, scholars have falsely concluded that this supplemental agreement did not depart "in principle from the terms of the earlier Peking agreement."[47] Two signed copies of this secret protocol are now available, one copy in the PRC and the other in Taiwan.[48]

The real meaning of the September 20, 1924 supplemental agreement was explained in the secret protocol. This protocol stated that whenever the term "China" appeared in clauses six and seven of the agreement's first section, its actual meaning was the "Government of the Autonomous Three Eastern Provinces of the Republic of China," the official name of Chang Tso-lin's government (see

Document 15).[49] This gave Chang the power to choose which Chinese officials would represent China in the joint commission running the railway, thus giving him absolute control over the Chinese half of the CER.

In addition, while the original agreement signed by Karakhan and Koo said that joint management would continue only until the Sino-Soviet conference met, at which time terms for purchasing the railway from the USSR would be determined, the supplemental agreement only admitted that China had the "right" to buy back the railway. This statement was much weaker than the former clause stating it would be sold back, effectively negating Karakhan's numerous promises that the Soviet government would give or sell the railway back to China. Even when the Sino-Soviet conference was finally convened, therefore, the USSR no longer felt obliged to discuss terms for selling the CER to China. But, once again, this state of affairs was not presented to the Chinese public, which continued to believe that the Soviet Union was treating China as an equal.

To make matters worse, Peking not only lost control over the CER it had to take the blame for defrauding foreign investors of their share of the railway as well. On October 3, 1924, the French legation sent a protest to the Peking government warning it of the "serious consequences" ensuing from this "arbitrary action" which ignored the rights of the Russo-Asiatic Bank.[50] Previously, Peking had consistently ignored the Russo-Asiatic Bank's claim over the CER because it appeared that at least half control of the CER would remain in its hands. Now, even though Peking lost all authority over the CER, it was caught in the middle and took the brunt of the criticism as the Russo-Asiatic Bank disputed both the May 31 and the September 20 agreements. For Peking to admit that it had lost its share in the CER to outsiders would have destroyed the last vestige of its credibility, so it never publicly protested the signing of the new supplemental agreement. Peking was forced to accept full blame for defrauding the Russo-Asiatic Bank, therefore, while the Soviet government secretly took the spoils.

In exchange for helping the USSR regain control over the railway, Moscow rewarded Chang by changing the terms of the 1896 railway contract to reduce the original eighty-year lease to sixty years. At the end of sixty years the Autonomous Three Eastern Provinces of the Republic of China would receive the railway and the surrounding railway property free of charge. Other changes included a provision stating that all profits from the management of the CER would be divided equally between the USSR and Chang Tso-lin.

The joint management of the railway was patterned on the May 31, 1924 agreement: a committee composed of five Russians and five Chinese, with the executive manager being selected by the Chinese and the assistant manager selected by the Soviets, would manage the railway. All management details pertaining to the railway were to be decided by special commissions that were to meet within a month after the agreement was signed, and would finish their work within six months.[51] The similarity in these terms with the May agreement with Peking is striking, since delays in the convening of these special commissions would have given the Soviet government similar leverage over Chang Tso-lin.

密件

聲明書

中華民國東三省自治省政府與蘇維亞社會聯邦政
府聲明經東三省政府要求對於一千九百二十四年九月二十
日締約雙方政府在奉天所簽訂之協定第一條第六七
兩項內所載「中國」之字樣應加以中華民國東三省自治省
政府之解釋此項解釋一俟中華民國東三省自治省
政府正式承認北京政府時即行無效
為此雙方全權代表將本協定華俄英三國之文各兩份各簽
字蓋印遇有疑義應以英文為準

于奉天

中華民國十三年九月二十日即西曆一千九百二十四年九月二十日訂

鄭謙 印

呂榮寰 印

印

鍾世銘 印

H. Kyzueeyob

Document 15
Text of the September 20, 1924 Secret Protocol

On October 18, 1924, Foreign Minister Chicherin made a speech in Moscow in which he praised the Soviet government for its enormous diplomatic victory in regaining control over a railway line that was valued in excess of half a billion gold rubles. He portrayed this success as "one of the most remarkable instances of return of Soviet property that was seized by its enemies who hoped to use it against the workers and peasants of the USSR." Turning a blind eye to the Soviet government's secret diplomacy in China, Chicherin then predicted that "the aggressive policy of imperialism towards Eastern peoples and its attacks on them strengthen their friendly links with us." This was especially true in China, and Chicherin optimistically stated that the "Soviet-Chinese friendship has already become a weighty factor in international politics."[52]

The vast chasm between Chicherin's public statements and his private actions was merely emphasized by the fact that Li Chia-ao had already presented an official, although secret, protest from Peking only four days before, condemning Moscow's decision to sign the supplemental agreement with Chang Tso-lin. In particular, Li denounced a statement made by Chicherin on September 27, 1924, that the supplemental agreement had been negotiated with the "previous approval of the Minister of Foreign Affairs Mr. Koo."[53] To date, no evidence that Koo agreed to the supplemental agreement in advance has appeared, while there is much evidence that he opposed it from June all the way through September.

Although this second secret agreement made it appear that Chang Tso-lin would retain half control over the management of the CER, Moscow used two techniques to take majority control away from Chang. In the May 31, 1924 CER agreement with Peking, Article V stated that: "The employment of persons in the various departments of the railway shall be in accordance with the principle of equal representation between the nationals of the Union of Soviet Socialist Republics and those of the Republic of China." In order to circumvent this provision, in the separate agreement with Chang the following note was added: "In carrying out the principle of equal representation the normal course of life and activities of the Railway shall in no case be interrupted or injured, that is to say the employment of the people of both nationalities shall be based in accordance with experience, personal qualifications and fitness of the applicants."[54]

Since Russians had traditionally run the railway, it was a foregone conclusion that they would take the majority of the positions on the railway, claiming that any other solution would interrupt or injure the railway. In the months following the signing of this supplemental agreement, therefore, the Soviet government rapidly reorganized the administration of the railway so as to increase the number of Russian employees of the CER from 10,833 to 11,251, while the number of Chinese employees fell from 5,912 to 5,556.[55]

A second method of taking full control of the CER was simply to make use of the May 31, 1924 secret protocol with the Peking government, which specified that all former contracts between China and Russia would not be enforced. Chang Tso-lin clearly did not know about this secret protocol, because the September 20, 1924 supplemental agreement specified that the 1896 CER contract would continue to be valid during the first four months of operation. Since only the Soviet diplomats knew that the secret protocol had suspended this 1896 contract, Soviet officials immediately began to fill the majority of the administrative posts on the CER.

Although the president of the railway was Chinese, he was evidently little better than a figurehead, and it was reported that he never even went to the railway headquarters in Harbin. The real control of the CER resided in its eight main committees and eighteen subcommittees. Soviet officials eventually took charge of twenty-four of these twenty-six committees, and they also greatly outnumbered their Chinese counterparts; there were a total of 120 Soviet officials to 80 Chinese officials in the railway administration.[56]

By using these two techniques–the agreement not to fire skilled workers and the May 31, 1924 secret protocol–not only did Moscow soon control the most important positions within the railway management, but its officials outnumbered the Chinese officials by a ratio of three to two. This was hardly the equal joint management that had been promised in the May 31, 1924 Sino-Soviet Treaty, since the USSR controlled approximately 67 percent of all positions on the railway, which almost exactly fulfilled its 1923 goal of gaining seven of the ten seats on the CER's board of directors. Thus, by playing the two secret protocols off each other, the Soviet Union regained majority control of the CER.

The January 20, 1925 Soviet-Japanese Convention

Previously, Moscow had transferred authority over the CER away from Peking by making use of a separate agreement with Chang Tso-lin. Now, it used almost the exact same tactic with Tokyo to ensure that Chang Tso-lin could not interfere with the USSR's management of the railway. Earlier Soviet attempts to open official diplomatic relations with Japan had all failed, but, with the CER back in Soviet hands, Japan had to come to adapt to the new situation in Manchuria.

Tokyo had suspected all along that the Soviet government was attempting to regain full control over the CER. In May 1924, the Japanese government had offered its help to China in managing the Chinese share of the CER, but Peking turned Tokyo down. Although this Japanese offer was intended to counterbalance the Soviet Union, instead of seeing this as insurance against the USSR the Peking government merely saw it as one more attempt to interfere in China's domestic affairs and so immediately refused. When the Peking government realized its mistake in August 1925, and asked Japan to help force the Soviet Union to return the CER to China, it was already too late and it was now Tokyo's turn to refuse.[57]

As recently as July 1, 1924, the Shidehara cabinet in Japan had reaffirmed its support for Washington's Open Door Policy in China, and had promoted its relations with China on the basis of "coexistence" and "mutual prosperity." The Japanese foreign minister had even announced: "We think that if the nations of the world altogether observe these basic principles, solutions will be found to all the world's problems."[58] But the September 20, 1924 protocol that led to the CER's return to majority Soviet control was crucial in pushing the Japanese minister to Peking, Kenkichi Yoshizawa, into talks with Karakhan that eventually resulted in the Soviet-Japanese convention, signed in Peking in early 1925. Faced with a renewed threat from Russia, Japanese diplomats agreed to return to the *status quo ante* in existence prior to World War I.

There can be little doubt that Karakhan carefully orchestrated the timing of this whole affair so that the Peking government could not interfere: this is perhaps best shown by the fact that on January 19, 1925, Chang Tso-lin sent a copy of the September 20, 1924 supplemental agreement's secret protocol to Peking to make sure that it realized that it had lost all power over the CER and that it could not make a public protest.[59] This would seem to indicate that the Peking government's Ministry of Foreign Affairs did not know about, or did not have a copy of, the second secret protocol before January 19, 1925, but this cannot be known for sure. Although Peking did not make a public protest, it did made several secret protests to the Soviet government on February 11, and on February 21.

On January 20, 1925, the USSR and Japan successfully renewed political and economic relations. While this convention agreed that all treaties signed before November 7, 1917, had to be reviewed by a special joint conference, it reaffirmed the validity of the Portsmouth Peace Treaty of September 5, 1905.[60] By renewing the Portsmouth Peace Treaty, the Soviet Union and Japan once more adopted the diplomatic relationship formerly maintained by tsarist Russia and Japan, as Tokyo tacitly acknowledged the USSR's control over the CER, while Moscow likewise reaffirmed Japan's control of the South Manchurian Railway. Following in the tradition of these two imperial governments, the USSR and Japan also concluded a secret protocol (see Appendix A).

As a result of the Soviet-Japanese convention, the USSR's near-total control over the CER was now guaranteed. Karakhan later admitted that "without the resumption of normal relations with Japan," it would have been "impossible to hope for the full resumption of our rights on the Chinese Eastern Railway."[61] Even more dangerous to China was the fact that the Portsmouth Treaty had been part of the turn-of-the-century process of dividing Manchuria into Russian and Japanese spheres of influence, with Russia predominant in northern Manchuria and Japan predominant in southern Manchuria. The Soviet-Japanese convention, therefore, tacitly redivided Manchuria into Japanese and Soviet spheres of influence, and in the process completely undermined the Washington Conference's 1922 goal of enforcing the Open Door Policy in China.

As shown above, Moscow made full use of the Open Door Policy to protect its territorial interests in Siberia, but opposed it whenever the Open Door blocked Soviet expansion into China. Rapid shifts between secretly supporting and publicly denouncing the Open Door Policy proved to be a constant theme in the Bolsheviks' foreign policy in the Far East. In fact, the Soviet leaders' decision to make use of the Open Door Policy for their own territorial protection against Japanese aggression in Siberia shows that they did not really think that the Open Door Policy only supported "economic imperialism." If this were true, it seems highly unlikely that the Bolsheviks would have so readily and repeatedly turned to the Open Door Policy for assistance. A more reasonable interpretation is that while this policy helped protect Soviet territorial interests, it stood in the way of Soviet territorial expansion.

Although this dual policy might at first appear contradictory, both aspects in fact promoted the same goal–the preservation and expansion of the Soviet sphere of influence in the Far East. By January 1925, therefore, the USSR had succeeded in undermining the very protective structure that had formerly helped preserve China's territorial integrity. The goal of this policy was to eliminate foreign territorial competition in China, but with the resurgence of competition between the Soviet Union and Japan in Manchuria, the Open Door Policy was given a blow from which it could not recover. Akira Iriye has previously hypothesized that the Washington Conference's resolutions failed to work in China because of the active interference of "Russian officials and Comintern agitators," and this new archival evidence fully substantiates his view.[62]

Furthermore, the Soviet convention with Japan was also a total renunciation–albeit a secret renunciation–of the Bolshevik propaganda that opposed foreign imperialism in China. When China's new foreign minister, Shen Jui-lin, secretly protested the new Soviet-Japanese convention as a violation of the sovereign rights of China on February 11, 1925, Karakhan answered, on February 26, by accusing Shen of "fully ignoring those acts that the Chinese Government has itself concluded with Japan," and pointed to Chinese agreements with Japan signed in 1905 and 1915 that reaffirmed the Portsmouth agreement.[63] In Moscow, Li protested directly to Foreign Minister Chicherin that references to a 1915 treaty with Japan was none other than the notorious Twenty-one Demands, which China had not only never willingly agreed to, but had protested against as recently as the 1921-22 Washington Conference.[64]

Although this would have been the proper time for Peking to publicize Moscow's secret diplomacy in China, it chose not to do so, perhaps because it was waiting for the long-delayed Sino-Soviet conference to convene. Only at the conference could China finally determine whether Moscow would abide by its promises to treat China as an equal. When this conference met in August 1925, however, the Soviet diplomats quickly demanded that China reaffirm the former Sino-Russian unequal treaties, and all negotiations subsequently deadlocked.[65]

Soviet Imperialism and the May Thirtieth Movement

On July 25, 1919, Karakhan began his first manifesto to China by annulling all of tsarist Russia's former treaties with Japan, China, and the other great powers, treaties through which the tsarist Russian government had "enslaved" the people of China. Karakhan had further warned China that the Versailles powers were working "to transform it into a second Korea or a second India," a fate that could be avoided only by joining with the Soviet Union.[66] By February 26, 1925, however, Karakhan had not only helped to negotiate two secret agreements between the USSR and China; he had also secretly defended the legitimacy of his agreement with Japan by upholding the infamous Twenty-one Demands, demands that the United States had repeatedly condemned as a violation of "the political and territorial integrity of the Republic of China."[67]

The 1919 May Fourth Movement in China was motivated, in part at least, as a protest against Japan's Twenty-one Demands, which encroached on Chinese territory. In the aftermath of the May Fourth Movement, many Chinese intellectuals, students, and workers turned to the Soviet Union as a model for China's political, social, and economic development. The Chinese Communist Party was then organized with the help of the Soviet-sponsored Comintern and by 1925 the Chinese communists were active leaders in the anti-imperialist movement that was trying to free China from all foreign interference. However, when Lev Karakhan, now the USSR's official ambassador to China, secretly reaffirmed the validity of Japan's Twenty-one Demands, he directly contradicted the goals of this anti-imperialist movement. This action merely emphasizes the vast difference between the USSR's propaganda and diplomacy in China.

Furthermore, with the outbreak of the antiforeign May Thirtieth Movement during 1925, the Soviet Union was able to make even further gains (see Document 16). On May 21, 1925, Karakhan sent a confidential letter to Foreign Minister Shen in which he reiterated that the concession lands belonging to the Chinese Eastern Railway had to remain under the control of that organization.[68] During the following weeks, the May Thirtieth Movement demanded that foreigners give up their concessions in China, and the British concession in Canton was at the eye of the storm. But while the British concession on Shameen island was only 300,000 square yards in size, or about 60 acres, the CER concession area was over 250,000 acres in size, or more than 4,000 times larger.[69]

The Comintern worked closely with the KMT and the CCP to channel the Chinese peoples' anti-imperialist feelings against Great Britain, Japan, and the United States, countries that had agreed to support China's equality at the 1922 Washington Conference, once China unified and reformed her internal tariffs and judicial system.[70] Following the beginning of an anti-foreign movement in China, Zinoviev confidently stated on June 7, 1925 that the revolutionary movement in China "stood as the advanced post in the world proletarian struggle."[71]

Moscow's very success in directing the Chinese anti-imperialist movement against the British concession in Canton, and in the meantime ignoring the much larger Soviet concession in Manchuria, shows that only six years after Karakhan had promised to treat China as an equal, the Soviet Union had reestablished itself as one of the strongest imperialist powers in China. In January 1926, the Bolsheviks' carefully laid plans began to unravel, however, as Chang Tso-lin's army seized control of the CER and arrested its Soviet director.

█████ OF THE
███ SOCIALIST REPUBLICS
PEKING

35002/52.

May, 21th, 1925.

Monsieur le Ministre,

The Chinese Eastern Railway, built as it
was with the money of the Russian people, is actually an enterprise under joint Soviet-Chinese management. This latter circumstance should have served
for a guarantee that all measures would be taken both
on the Soviet and the Chinese side to consolidate
and further an enterprise in which there are involved
the interests of both states. And yet, the last few
months' practice has shown, unfortunately, that far
from doing anything to promote its further development
and prosperity, the Chinese local authorities have
been systematically encroaching upon the existing property of the Railway, their actions causing the latter
to suffer direct heavy losses.

Bringing the foregoing to Your Excellency's notice, I
must protest in the most energetic manner against the unlawful
acts of violence which are committed by Chinese authorities
counter to the existing Agreements, and insist on all attempts
at an arbitrary solution of the question be stopped pending
its settlement by decision of the commission mentioned above.
I shall much appreciate if Your Excellency were good enough to
let me know of the measures adopted in this reference and, in
particular, in prevention of illegal acts of the Headquarters
of the Railway Guard Troops at Harbin.

I avail myself of this opportunity to renew to you,
Monsieur le Ministre, the assurances of my highest consideration

L Karakhan.

His Excellency
Shen Jui-lin,
Minister of Foreign Affairs
of the Republic of China.

Document 16
Excerpts from Karakhan's May 21, 1925 Letter to Shen Jui-lin

War appeared imminent, as Foreign Minister Chicherin requested, on January 22, that Peking give "permission" for the Red Army to enter Manchuria if the incident was not resolved in three days. This ultimatum further specified that China reestablish the railway's Soviet administration, adhere to the 1924 treaty, and release the Soviet director.[72] Moscow's so-called red imperialism also seriously undermined the United Front Policy.[73] But when Ch'en Tu-hsiu proposed that the CCP withdraw from the United Front, he was censured by Nikolai Bukharin and Voitinskii was sent to China to reprimand him.[74]

In Moscow, a special Politburo commission headed by Trotsky warned that Moscow must try to minimize friction between the USSR and China. Trotsky recommended that the CER railway administration had to be more responsive to its Chinese partners, for example, by undertaking to conduct secretarial work both in Russian and Chinese, instead of only in Russian. The USSR should also try to determine points of friction between the Russian and Chinese workers and find ways to ensure that this friction did not escalate into open conflict.[75]

Although the KMT's Soviet advisers in Canton warned against supporting Chiang Kai-shek's 1926 Northern Expedition to unify China, Chiang pushed his plans through despite over their opposition. Fearful that the unification of China might lead to conflict with the USSR, Trotsky opposed the Northern Expedition. Trotsky also became the first Bolshevik leader to advocate that Moscow dissolve the United Front Policy.[76] Trotsky and Zinoviev, two of the oldest and most well-known Bolshevik leaders, later joined forces in the so-called United Opposition to oppose Stalin's and Bukharin's China policy.

The main demands of the United Opposition included "recalling Comrade Karakhan, relinquishing control over the Chinese Eastern Railroad, and withdrawing from the Kuomintang."[77] In fact, Trotsky's and Zinoviev's primary criticism was that Stalin's and Bukharin's contradictory policy of supporting the KMT's national revolution against "foreign imperialism," while simultaneously retaining the USSR's imperialist concessions—such as the Chinese Eastern Railway—was bound to increase tensions with China. Stalin and Bukharin, on the other hand, refused to consider giving up the CER and supported Karakhan's continued efforts to consolidate Soviet control over tsarist Russia's concessions, special rights, and privileges in China. Although Trotsky and Zinoviev further warned that this policy threatened to engender future Sino-Soviet conflicts, their concerns were dismissed; this warning was later borne out, however, in the 1929 Sino-Soviet war over the CER.

Conclusions

By far the greatest irony was that, after May 31, 1924, the Peking Ministry of Foreign Affairs had indisputable proof that Moscow's propaganda in China was being used merely to expand Soviet power, not to support a new era of equality with China. But the Chinese officials did not release this proof: fearing, in part, that Peking would be blamed for letting itself be cheated by Moscow, while undoubtedly even more concerned that the USSR might respond by taking greater advantage of the secret protocols' suspension of all Sino-Russian agreements. Since Washington and London did not know how Moscow was exerting such enormous influence over Peking, they could not act to oppose it. This gave the USSR the time it needed to consolidate its control over the territorial concessions taken from China, including the CER.

But there is another, more important, reason why the Peking government decided not to reveal the truth about its diplomatic relations with the Soviet Union. By actively promoting the myth of Sino-Soviet equality, Peking exerted enormous pressure on the capitalist countries to eliminate their own unequal treaties with China. In the midst of the anti-imperialist demonstrations during 1925, for example, the Peking government sent a note on June 24, 1925, to the nations that had signed the Washington Conference's *Nine Power Treaty*. This note requested that these governments immediately renegotiate all unequal treaties with China, declaring that the foreigners' "rights and interests can be better protected and more effectively advanced without, rather than with, the enjoyment of extraordinary privileges and immunities."[78]

Since it was widely believed that the Soviet Union really had abolished its unequal treaties with China, public opinion in the United States firmly supported Peking: the general secretary of the YMCA, American missionaries in China, and even Senator William Borah, the chairman of the Congressional Foreign Relations Committee, joined together in condemning the recent events in China, with a missionary journal *Christian Century* even explaining that the anti-imperialist demonstrations in China were a direct result of a "mounting exasperation" on the part of China's youth about their country's exploitation "both politically and economically by other states."[79]

Faced with overwhelming public support for China, on June 30, 1925, Secretary of State Frank Kellogg promised the Chinese minister that the United States would not only support returning to China full tariff autonomy but also eliminating all extraterritorial rights. With the U. S. government's backing, the nine foreign powers that had earlier attended the Washington Conference reconvened and recognized, on November 19, 1925, that China should be given the right to set its own tariffs: "The contracting powers other than China hereby recognize China's right to enjoy tariff autonomy, agree to remove the tariff restrictions which are contained in existing treaties between themselves respectively and China, and consent to the going into effect of the Chinese national tariff law on January 1st, 1929."[80]

Eliminating a century of treaties with China was an action that these governments had earlier refused to consider because of China's social and political instability. This decision was forced upon them by Peking's successful policy of playing the USSR off the capitalist powers. Secretary of State Kellogg would probably have been far less receptive to China's request, however, if he had realized that the USSR had signed secret agreements with China allowing it to regain and strengthen its own special privileges in China, including majority control over the CER.

By successfully playing the socialist and capitalist "camps" off each other, Peking scored other significant victories, including eliminating the Boxer Indemnity, retaking control over many of the foreign territorial concessions, and abolishing extraterritoriality, topics that will be discussed further below. In the process of reducing the capitalist countries' special rights and privileges, however, the USSR's power–as determined by its secret diplomacy–correspondingly increased. In league with its Chinese communist allies, Moscow continued to consolidate its position in Outer Mongolia and throughout northern Manchuria. It was this aspect of Moscow's and Peking's deceptive diplomacy that would prove so dangerous to China after the end of World War II.

Notes

1. The exact amount of land was 105,661.98 "dessiatins," with one dessiatin being equal to two and a half acres. See the report "The Lands and Land Administration of the Chinese Eastern Railway Company, and the Incident of August 1, 1923." WCTA, 03-32, 263(4). As for the length of the CER, it represented approximately 40 percent of all of China's railways; Japan's South Manchurian Railway represented 30 percent, while Japan's control of Germany's former railway in Shantung accounted for 12 percent. Meanwhile, France's 289-mile railway in Yunnan province accounted for just over 12 percent, while Great Britain's Canton-to-Kowloon railway equaled only 1 percent of the foreign-run railways in China. Chi-ming Hou, *Foreign Investment and Economic Development in China, 1840-1937*, 65.

2. Commonly called C. C. Wang, he had received his education through the doctorate level at Peking University, Yale University, and the University of Illinois, and in January, 1920, had been appointed director-general of the Chinese Eastern Railway. English-language letter from C. C. Wang to W. W. Yen, May 3, 1921, WCTA, 03-32, 242(2).

3. Chinese-language copy of Karakhan's second manifesto, October 2, 1920, originally dated September 27, 1920, WCTA, 03-32, 479(1).

4. English-language memorandum 311 signed by Paikes, listing the members of the RSFSR Mission as follows: "1. Aleksandr K. Paikes–Plenipotentiary Extraordinary. 2. Vladimir D. Vilenskii–Counselor. 3. David E. Sandler–Collaborator. 4. Boris Ph. Bernson–Collaborator. 5. Joseph M. Mussin–Collaborator. 6. Valentine B. Ezierskaia–Collaborator. 7. Charles A. Michelson–Collaborator. 8. Lidia A. Michelson–Collaborator," March 27, 1922, WCTA, 03-32, 470(2).

5. *New Russia*, Vol. 1, No. 10, January 6, 1923, 305.

6. Allen S. Whiting, *Soviet Policies in China, 1917-1924*, 210.

7. Ts'ai Ho-sen (和森), "中國國際地位與承認蘇維埃俄羅斯" ("China's International Position and the Recognition of Soviet Russia"), 嚮導週報 (*The Guide Weekly*), No. 3, September 27, 1922, 17-19.

8. Jonathan Spence, *The Search for Modern China*, 307.

9. "Protest from Chicherin to Britain, France, the United States, China, and Japan, Against the Exclusion of the RSFSR," July 19, 1921, Jane Degras, *Soviet Documents on Foreign Policy*, Vol. 1, 249-251.

10. Alfred L. P. Dennis, *The Foreign Policies of Soviet Russia*, 305-306, 295.

11. Xenia Joukoff Eudin and Robert C. North, *Soviet Russia and the East, 1920-1927:*

A Documentary Survey, 137.

12. Thomas H. Buckley, "The Icarus Factor: the American Pursuit of Myth in Naval Arms Control, 1921-36," in Erik Goldstein and John Maurer, *The Washington Conference, 1921-22: Naval Rivalry, East Asian Stability and the Road to Pearl Harbor*, 132.

13. Grimm, E. D. (Е. Д. Гримм). *Сборник договоров и других документов по истории международных отношений на Дальнем Востоке (1842-1925)* (*Collection of Treaties and Other Documents on the History of International Relations in the Far East [1842-1925]*), 204-209.

14. Akira Iriye, *After Imperialism: The Search for a New Order in the Far East, 1921-1931*, 21.

15. Hans J. Morgenthau, *Politics Among Nations: The Struggle for Power and Peace*, 21-23.

16. Richard Stremski, "Britain's China Policy 1920-1928," 21-22.

17. Iriye, 18.

18. French-language copy of Karakhan's credentials, signed by the head of the Central Executive Committee, N. Narimanov, and the Foreign Minister, G. Chicherin, August 1, 1923, WCTA, 03-32, 470(3).

19. Russian-language text of Karakhan's speech at the luncheon given by Wang, September 4, 1923, WCTA, 03-32, 467(1).

20. English-language copies of the 1919 and 1920 Karakhan manifestos, provided by the Soviet Mission in Peking and marked "True to the original," December 2, 1923, WCTA, 03-32, 481(3).

21. Chinese-language letter from Wang to Karakhan, January 9, 1924, WCTA, 03-32, 483(1).

22. Russian-language signed letter from Karakhan to Wang, January 17, 1924, WCTA, 03-32, 483(2).

23. Chinese Foreign Ministry report written by Li Chia-ao, the Chinese Consul in Moscow, to Foreign Minister Koo, entitled: "Opinion Paper from the Foreign Ministry Official in Moscow," January 18, 1924, WCTA 03-32, 461(3).

24. *The China Yearbook*, 1923, 613; the dispute over who owned the Chinese Eastern Railway was complicated by the fact that while French investors owned 60 percent of the shares of the Russo-Asiatic Bank, which actually owned the railway, the tsarist government had invested much money to build and guard the railway line.

25. Chinese-language minutes of Chu Ho-hsiang's meeting with Karakhan, February 2, 1924, WCTA, 03-32, 487(1).

26. *Ibid.*

27. Chinese Foreign Ministry report written by Li Chia-ao, the Chinese Consul in Moscow, to Foreign Minister Koo, February 24, 1924, WCTA 03-32, 461(3).

28. Secret Chinese-language telegram from Wellington Koo to Li Chia-ao in Moscow, March 7, 1924, WCTA, 03-32, 487(1).

29. Chinese-language minutes of a conversation between Li Chia-ao and Chicherin, March 9, 1924, WCTA, 03-32, 483(1); also see March 11, 1924 telegram 732, WCTA, 03-32, 477(1).

30. Letter from Jacob Gould Schurman, the American minister to China, to Foreign Minister Wellington Koo, May 3, 1924, WCTA, 03-32, 268(1).

31. *Ibid.*

32. Published English-language copy of the final Sino-Soviet agreement, May 31, 1924, WCTA, 03-32, 495(1).

33. *Ibid.*

34. *Ibid.*

35. Chinese-language minutes of a conversation between Karakhan and Wang Cheng-t'ing, the new acting foreign minister, during which Karakhan presented three new preconditions that Peking had to meet prior to opening the Sino-Soviet conference, November 6, 1924, WCTA, 03-32, 489(1).

36. English-language minutes of the meeting between Karakhan and Koo, at Koo's residence, starting at 5:00 p.m., June 6, 1924, WCTA, 03-32, 494(1).

37. English-language minutes of the meeting between Karakhan and Koo, at Koo's residence, starting at 9:00 p.m., June 13, 1924, WCTA, 03-32, 494(1).

38. *Ibid.*

39. *Ibid.*

40. English-language minutes of the meeting between Karakhan and Koo, at the Ministry of Foreign Affairs, starting at 12:45 p.m., June 28, 1924, WCTA, 03-32, 489(1).

41. *Ibid.*

42. *Ibid.*

43. English-language letter No. 2524/26 to Foreign Minister Koo, signed by Karakhan, delaying the opening of the official Sino-Soviet conference, June 28, 1924, WCTA, 03-32, 499(4).

44. English-language minutes of the meeting between Karakhan and Koo, at the Ministry of Foreign Affairs, starting at 11:00 a.m., July 7, 1924, WCTA, 03-32, 494(1).

45. English-language minutes of the meeting between Karakhan and Koo, at Koo's private residence, starting at 6:00 p.m., August 12, 1924, WCTA, 03-32, 494(1).

46. *Ibid.*

47. Gavan McCormack, *Chang Tso-lin in Northeast China, 1911-1928*, 114 - 115.

48. Supplemental Agreements Between the USSR and Chang Tso-lin, September 20, 1924, Number Two Historical Archives, Nanking, File 1039, No. 99, see 9, section 6, secret appendix; a signed copy of this treaty is also located at WCTA, 03-32, 491(2).

49. Sow-Theng Leong, *Sino-Soviet Diplomatic Relation, 1917-1926*, 274-275.

50. French legation in China protest to the Waichiaopu, warning them of the "serious consequences" that would ensue from its "arbitrary action" on the CER which ignored the rights of the Russo-Asiatic Bank, October 3, 1924, Number Two Historical Archives, Nanking, File 1039, No. 437, Vol. 3, 249.

51. Nanking, File 1039, No. 99.

52. Degras, Vol. 1, 459-469.

53. Russian-language letter No. 575 to Foreign Minister Chicherin from Li Chia-ao, October 14, 1924, WCTA, 03-32, 494(3).

54. Nanking, File 1039, No. 99.

55. McCormack, 115; these numbers were first printed in the *North-China Daily News,* May 2, 1925, and were cited originally by George Sokolsky, *The Story of the Chinese Eastern Railway.*

56. The administrative breakdown of the Chinese Eastern Railway was explained by a volume entitled 中俄關於中東路之交涉事略 (*A History of Sino-Russian Negotiations on the Chinese Eastern Railway*), 20-21; a copy of this rare volume is located in the Kuomintang archives in Taipei, Taiwan.

57. WCTA, 03-32, 491(3)

58. Daniel Bailey Ramsdell, "Japan's China Policy, 1929-1931, A Fateful Failure," 64; According to Chinliang Lawrence Huang, before 1925 Japan had not only signed the

Washington Conference's agreements, it had also largely given up its sphere of influence in China, such as in Shantung. The Shidehara cabinet in Japan based its relations with China on respect for her sovereignty and territorial integrity; further called for "economic cooperation" and promotion of "mutual well-being and prosperity;" and even promised to respect the "national aspirations of the Chinese people." These resolutions were all in line with President Wilson's fourteen points and the formula developed at the Washington Conference to enforce the Open Door Policy in China. In return, the Washington Conference offered Japan protection of its economic interests in China through mutual security; all the nations present at the Washington Conference agreed not to build spheres of influence in China which would compete with other nations. But with respect to mutual security, the Japanese government made it quite clear that if the current chaos in China directly threatened Japan's economic interests, then the Shidehara cabinet was prepared to "protect to the utmost her legitimate and important rights and interests in China through reasonable means" ("Japan's China Policy Under the Premier Tanaka, 1927-1929" [Ph.D. diss., New York University, 1968], 31).

59. WCTA 03-32, 491(2).

60. Grimm, 213-218.

61. Degras, Vol. 2, 8-9.

62. Iriye, 55.

63. English-language letter No. 35002/21 to Shen Jui-lin, signed by Karakhan, reminding him of China's own agreements with Japan, February 26, 1925, WCTA, 03-32, 497(2).

64. Chinese-language minutes of a meeting between Li Chia-ao and Chicherin, February 21, 1925, WCTA, 03-32, 498(1).

65. When the Sino-Soviet conference finally opened on August 26, 1925, negotiations were divided into the following six subcommittees: 1) commercial relations; 2) damage claims; 3) the Chinese Eastern Railway; 4) boundaries; 5) navigation; and 6) legal matters, such as consular relations. Talks quickly deadlocked, however, when Soviet diplomats tried to reassert the terms of the tsarist unequal treaties.

66. Original French-language telegram of the July 25, 1919, Karakhan Manifesto, as sent from Irkutsk to the Ministry of Foreign Affairs in Peking, March 26, 1920, WCTA, 03-32, 463(1).

67. Richard C. DeAngelis, "Jacob Gould Schurman and American Policy Towards China, 1921-1925," 83-84.

68. English-language letter No. 35002/52 to the Waichiaopu from Lev Karakhan, claiming that all of the CER property must remain under Soviet control, May 21, 1925, WCTA, 03-32, 265(1).

69. *The China Yearbook*, 1926-27, Vol. 1, 608.

70. Iriye, 21-22.

71. G. Zinoviev (Г. Зиновъев), "Всемирно—историческое значение шанхайских событий" ("The Worldwide Historical Significance of the Shanghai Events"), *Pravda*, June 7, 1925.

72. Telegram from Chicherin to Karakhan, January 22, 1926; Degras, Vol. 2, 82.

73. Edmund S. K. Fung, "Anti-Imperialism and the Left Guomindang." *Modern China*, 11, 1 (January 1985), 71.

74. C. Martin Wilbur and Julie Lien-ying How, *Documents on Communism, Nationalism, and Soviet Advisers in China 1918-1927*, 226.

75. Leon Trotsky, "Вопросы нашей политики в отношении Китая и Японии"

("Questions in Our Policies in Relations with China and Japan"), March 25, 1926, Harvard University, Houghton Library, Trotsky Archives, No. 870, 2.

76. This date was confirmed by Stalin himself, who later accused the United Opposition of "demanding the immediate 'withdrawal' of the communists from the Kuomintang" in April 1926. *Коммунистический Интернационал* (*Communist International*), October 14, 1927, 41, 18.

77. Les Evans and Russell Block, eds., *Leon Trotsky on China,* 256.

78. *The China Yearbook,* 1926, 932-933.

79. Roberta Allbert Dayer, *Bankers and Diplomats in China, 1917-1925: The Anglo-American Relationship*, 220-221.

80. Iriye, 75.

5
China's Revocation of the Boxer Indemnity

Although the Peking government has frequently been criticized for failing to secure equal treatment for China at the 1919 Paris Peace Conference, what has often been overlooked is that between 1917 and 1927, Peking officials succeeded in redirecting the majority of the 1901 Boxer Indemnity payments into supporting educational institutions and other infrastructure projects in China. This was no mean feat, since it meant that tens of millions of dollars remained within China, instead of being sent overseas. As a result, the Boxer Indemnity directly contributed to China's enormous educational, commercial, and industrial development during the 1920s and 1930s.

One important tactic that Peking used to pressure foreign governments into revoking their shares of the Boxer Indemnity was to sponsor friendly diplomatic relations with the Soviet Union. Following the 1917 October Revolution, the Bolsheviks gained enormous prestige in China by promising to abolish unilaterally their participation in the 1901 and 1904 Boxer Protocols. Based on the Soviet Union's public statements, one well-known historian of Sino-Soviet relations, concluded that Moscow actually "renounced . . . the Russian share of the Boxer Indemnity."[1] Other Sino-Soviet historians agreed.[2]

New archival documents have since revealed, however, that the Soviet Union never carried through on its promises: by 1924, the Soviet government not only renewed its participation in the 1901 and 1904 Boxer Protocols, which granted autonomy to the diplomatic quarter in Peking, but it also retained the right to determine how Russia's share of the Boxer Indemnity was to be allocated. Instead of representing better treatment for China, in fact, the Soviet Union followed exactly in the footsteps of the United States, which in 1908 was the first country to use its share of the Boxer Indemnity to support Chinese educational institutions such as Ch'inghua University.

By keeping all negotiations with the Soviet government secret, however, the Peking government used the Bolsheviks' magnanimous public promise to renounce unconditionally Russia's share of the Boxer Indemnity in order to push the other foreign countries into following suit. As Harold Isaacs accurately observed, good relations with the Soviet Union were used by China as a "lever for extracting concessions from the Western Powers."[3] Although the Soviet Union never actually carried through on its generous offer, the Peking government constantly referred to the Bolsheviks' oft-repeated promise to convince the United States, Great Britain, France, Italy, Japan, Holland, and Belgium to revoke their own shares of the Boxer Indemnity.

Traditionally, the Chinese employed a foreign policy strategy of playing one foreigner off another (以夷制夷), or literally "to use barbarians to govern barbarians."[4] This chapter will show that the Peking government's goal in opening diplomatic relations with Moscow was based in part on this strategy. By maintaining outwardly friendly relations with the USSR, the Peking government successfully pressured other foreign powers to revoke their own special rights and privileges. Peking's successful use of this policy is best shown by examining the Boxer Indemnity, since between 1917 and 1927 it succeeded in redirecting over 98 percent of the Boxer Indemnity for use within China. In the process, however, Peking gave even greater legitimacy to the potent myth that the USSR really had renounced its unequal treaties with China.

The Boxer Indemnity Through 1922

Historians have been critical of the Peking government for not gaining equal treatment for China at the 1919 Paris Peace Conference. But Peking achieved an enormous success by revoking Germany and Austria's 20.91 percent share of the Boxer Indemnity, as well as its agreements with most of the other Boxer Indemnity recipients to postpone payment of their shares through 1922. By 1922, therefore, China's Ministry of Finance could report that the "per capita debt of China is the smallest of all the nations in the world, and . . . can be paid off without considerable difficulty."[5] This optimistic financial report was largely due to the Peking government's successful diplomacy before, during, and after the Paris Peace Conference.

An estimated 231 foreigners, as well as thousands of Chinese Christians, were killed during the antiforeign movement in 1900 known as the Boxer Uprising.[6] After foreign troops quelled the disturbances, China agreed to pay an indemnity, as outlined in the 1901 Boxer Protocol. This indemnity was set at 450 million taels, to be paid from the revenues of the Maritime Customs and the Salt Gabelle. Including 4 percent annual interest over 39 years, the total came to 980 million taels, or approximately $700 million.[7] One historian has referred to the size of the Boxer Indemnity as "staggering."[8] Another has characterized the effect of the Boxer Indemnity on China as "humiliating and crippling."[9]

Because of damage to the CER in Manchuria, the tsarist Russian portion of the indemnity was the largest, at 28.97 percent; Germany was second–20.02 percent; then France–15.75 percent; England–11.25 percent; Japan–7.73 percent; the United States–7.32 percent; Italy–5.91 percent; Belgium–1.88 percent; Austria-Hungary–0.89 percent; Holland–0.17 percent; Spain–0.03 percent; Portugal–0.02 percent; and then Norway and Sweden–a combined 0.01 percent.[10] On December 28, 1908, the United States was the first country to remit $11,961,121.76 of its share of the Boxer Indemnity to finance Chinese students in America, as well as to support the construction of Ch'inghua University in Peking. Although America's actions were well received by the Chinese people, this remittance actually accounted for less than 2 percent of the entire Boxer Indemnity.

After the overthrow of the Ch'ing government in 1911, Boxer Indemnity payments came directly from the Maritime Customs. The Peking government agreed during November 1911 that a foreign official, the Inspector-General of Customs, would take charge of paying the indemnity from customs revenue.[11] When China declared war on Germany and Austria in 1917, their combined 20.91 percent share of the Boxer Indemnity was suspended.

In addition, Belgium, France, Great Britain, Italy, Japan, and Portugal allowed China to defer their payments for five years, beginning on December 1, 1917. The United States joined soon afterward. The main exception was Russia. On September 8, 1917, the Kerensky Provisional government decided that it would defer only one-third of its share, or 10 percent of the total indemnity. Significantly, this agreement was signed by Prince Kudachev, Kerensky's Minister in Peking, on November 30, 1917, three weeks after the Bolsheviks had seized power in Russia.[12]

Once news of the Bolsheviks' success reached China, the Peking government attempted to stop payment of the Boxer Indemnity to the officials of the Kerensky Provisional government residing and working in China. Minutes of meetings between Peking officials and their British, French, and Japanese counterparts show that the Peking government initially protested that since the Russian "radical government has already signified that it does not recognize its foreign debts, so [China] no longer has to pay" the indemnity.[13] In June 1918, the Peking government actually stopped payment of the Russian share of the Boxer Indemnity, citing the ongoing Civil War in Russia. But, the Japanese and French Ministers wrote letters on behalf of the Russian officials in Peking, and the British Minister presented a verbal note of support for the White Russians, forcing the Peking government to back down and continue making indemnity payments to Prince Kudachev.

At the Paris Peace Conference the Peking government succeeded in completely revoking the German and Austrian shares of the Boxer Indemnity.[14] By the summer of 1919, therefore, the Peking government had succeeded in not only eliminating over one-fifth of the Boxer Indemnity outright, but it could continue to defer payment on the majority of the remaining indemnity shares for another three years, until December 1, 1922. These diplomatic victories represented a significant step toward achieving China's long-range goal of completely revoking the Boxer Indemnity.

The Bolsheviks and the Boxer Indemnity

Following the 1917 Bolshevik Revolution, it appeared that Russia's 28.97 percent share of the Boxer Indemnity might soon be canceled outright. During July 1918, for example, the People's Commissar of Foreign Affairs, Georgii Chicherin, presented a proposal to the Fifth Congress of the Soviets announcing that the Soviet government was ready to "renounce all indemnities. . . . We only desire that these millions of the people's money go toward the cultural development of the mass of the people and toward the matter of drawing together Eastern democracy with Russia."[15] On December 2, 1918, the Bolsheviks appeared to carry through on this promise when they issued an official decree abolishing Russia's share of the Boxer Indemnity.[16]

At the Paris Peace Conference, Chinese diplomats were disappointed that the participating nations planned to reform their relations with China gradually, instead of all at once. The Chinese officials attempted to make use of the Bolsheviks' lofty ideals, widely circulated after 1917, to pry concessions more quickly out the capitalist nations. On April 11, 1919, for example, a Peking communique suggested that China was confident: "That the Republic of Russia, once internal peace has been re-established, will not fail to satisfy the legitimate aspirations of her neighbor."[17]

Three months later the Bolsheviks responded to China's entreaty in the Karakhan Manifesto. This document promised to respect China's territorial integrity by abolishing all unequal treaties with China, and in particular, Russia's participation in the 1901 and 1904 Boxer Protocols. In addition, Karakhan stated yet again that the Soviet government would no longer collect its share of the Boxer Indemnity.[18] On April 24, 1921, the Comintern's Siberian journal published this promise as follows: "The Soviet government renounces the receipt of the Boxer Indemnity from China."[19]

The Karakhan Manifesto's timing raises grave doubts about one historian's conclusion that the Soviet government's generous promises were "unsolicited."[20] In fact, China's own April 1919 communique shows that Peking hoped the Bolsheviks' public renunciation of the Boxer Protocols would push the Western nations and Japan into following suit. It is this tactic that helps explain Chinese diplomats' insistence during the following decades that the USSR had really given up its portion of the Boxer Indemnity, despite the series of agreements that secretly renewed tsarist Russia's special rights and privileges.

During 1919 and 1920, the Peking government was forced by Great Britain, France, and Japan to continue paying two-thirds of the Russian share of the Boxer Indemnity to the Kerensky officials. On September 23, 1920, however, the Peking government withdrew its recognition of Prince Kudachev and all other Russian officials appointed by the Kerensky government. Prince Kudachev immediately sent letters of protest to the diplomatic corps, denouncing Peking for violating "the position of the Russian citizens and their property, based on the provisions of all of the Russo-Chinese treaties signed in 1689, 1727, 1851, 1858, 1860, and 1881."[21] All of Kudachev's protests proved futile.

Peking's decision to suspend payment of the Russian share of the Boxer Indemnity and sever diplomatic relations with representatives of the former Kerensky Provisional government has been portrayed as China's first step in forcibly abolishing foreigners' special rights and privileges in China, a goal it failed to achieve diplomatically. Following Peking's decision to break diplomatic relations with the Kerensky officials, Karakhan presented China with a second manifesto on October 2, 1920 that repeated his promise to abolish the indemnity.

It was the Soviet promises of immediate and unconditional equality for China that made the more gradual reforms sponsored by the Western nations and Japan appear to be inadequate. Karakhan's promise to cancel unconditionally Russia's share of the Boxer Indemnity bested the United States' decision to use its share of the Boxer Indemnity to fund education in China. It was this apparent disparity that provided the Peking government with diplomatic leverage to pressure the other foreign powers into matching the Bolsheviks' more generous offer. It also increased the Chinese public's interest in the Bolshevik revolution and in socialism in general.

Russia's Boxer Indemnity Is Renewed

Prior to Lev Karakhan's arrival in Peking during the fall of 1923, Sino-Soviet negotiators had not yet clarified what would happen to the Russian share of the Boxer Indemnity. Although numerous Soviet promises to renounce this indemnity unconditionally had been made, Karakhan soon informed Peking officials that the Soviet Union expected to retain control over how this money was to be spent. This meant that the Bolsheviks' position actually differed very little from that taken by the United States in 1908, when America's share of the Boxer Indemnity was used to fund education in China.

Upon Karakhan's arrival in China, Wang expressed his hope that Karakhan would fulfill promises to renounce Russia's indemnity. In particular, Wang pointed to Washington's decision to return a portion of its indemnity in 1908: "We have no doubt that in its relations, Soviet Russia will not be inferior to America"; in response, Karakhan insisted that "America is not an example for Russia."[22] Karakhan also reminded Wang that the Soviet Union was the first country to announce its total renunciation of its share of the Boxer Indemnity.

Nevertheless, Karakhan soon afterward insisted in private that the Russian share had to be used to promote education in China. Karakhan was assisted in his efforts by the official resolutions of the Kuomintang's First Congress, held during January 1924, which called on all foreign countries to return the Boxer Indemnity to be fully used to support education in China. This KMT resolution perhaps unintentionally supported Karakhan's efforts not to carry through on his earlier, more generous promise to renounce unconditionally the Russian share of the Boxer Indemnity.

During February 1924 Karakhan presented Wang with a proposal stating that "the Soviet portion of the Boxer Indemnity would be allocated to Chinese educational institutions."[23] Although Karakhan continued to insist in private that the Russian indemnity had to be used to support Chinese education, in public Karakhan and Wang completed a draft Sino-Soviet agreement on March 14, 1924, that stated: "The government of the Union of Soviet Socialist Republics agrees to renounce the Russian portion of the Boxer Indemnity."[24]

Copies of these terms were published in the Chinese press, where they were received enthusiastically throughout China. This positive public reaction pushed other countries into matching the USSR. For example, on May 21, 1924, the U.S. Congress agreed to remit to China the final $6,137,552.90 of the American portion of the Boxer Indemnity. That this decision might have been made to compete with the Soviet Union's generous-sounding offers is suggested by the fact that the remission was dated from October 1, 1917, several weeks prior to the Bolshevik's October Revolution.[25] In addition, soon after this plan was announced, Minister Schurman apparently tried to match the USSR's positive press by proclaiming that the United States government's decision was an important "sign of friendship" between America and China.[26]

Only on May 31, 1924, when the Sino-Soviet "friendship" agreement was signed, did it become apparent that the USSR did not intend to carry through on its earlier promises (see Document 17). In the meantime a separate declaration had been added to the March 14 draft, stating: "The Russian share of the Boxer Indemnity which the government of the Union of Soviet Socialist Republic renounces, will, after the satisfaction of all prior obligations secured thereon, be entirely appropriated to create a fund for the promotion of education among the Chinese people."[27] Furthermore, this declaration stipulated that the Soviet Union would retain some control over how this money was to be spent, since a three-man committee, composed of two Chinese and one Soviet representatives, would allocate Russia's share of the Boxer Indemnity.

News of this change only appeared after the United States had already revoked its final share of the Boxer Indemnity. On September 16, 1924, Peking and Washington announced the formation of "The China Foundation for the Promotion of Education and Culture." A mixed Sino-American board of directors decided on June 3, 1925, that these funds would be "devoted to the development of scientific knowledge and to the application of such knowledge to the conditions in China through the promotion of technical training of scientific research, experimentation, and demonstration, and training in science teaching, and the advancement of cultural enterprises of a permanent character such as libraries and the like." On July 16, 1925, President Calvin Coolidge signed Presidential Order No. 4268, releasing America's remaining Boxer Indemnity to the China Foundation.[28]

Although it is difficult to know for sure, the timing of these events suggests that the Peking government used Moscow's March 14, 1924 promise to exert diplomatic pressure on Washington to revoke its indemnity on May 21, 1924. Thereafter, when the final May 31, 1924 Sino-Soviet agreement was announced, it specified that Russia's share of the Boxer Indemnity would be used to promote education in China and that the Soviet government would retain control over how this money was to be spent. While the Bolsheviks' public renunciation of the Boxer Indemnity initially made the USSR appear superior to the U.S., in the end the Sino-Soviet agreement exactly conformed to the American model.

DECLARATION (V)

The Government of the Republic of China and the Government of the Union of Soviet Socialist Republics jointly declare that it is understood that with reference to Article XI of the Agreement on General Principles between the Republic of China and the Union of Soviet Socialist Republics 31,1924:

1. The Russian share of the Boxer Indemnity which the Government of the Union of Soviet Socialist Republics renounces, will after the satisfaction of all prior obligations secured thereon be entirely appropriated to create a fund for the promotion of education among the Chinese people.

2. A special Commission will be established to administer and allocate the said fund. This Commission will consist of three persons, two of whom will be appointed by the Government of the Republic of China and one by the Government of the Union of Soviet Socialist Republics. Decisions of the said Commission will be taken by unanimous vote.

3. The said fund will be deposited as it accrues from time to time in a Bank to be designated by the said Commission.

It is further understood that this expression of understanding has the same force and validity as a general declaration embodied in the said Agreement on General Principles.

In faith whereof, the respective Plenipotentiaries of the Governments of the two Contracting Parties have signed the present Declaration in duplicate in the English language and have affixed thereto their seals.

Done at the City of Peking this Thirty-First Day of the Fifth Month of the Thirteenth Year of the Republic of China, which is, the Thirty-First Day of May One Thousand Nine Hundred and Twenty-Four.

(Seal) V. K. Wellington Koo
(Seal) L. M. Karakhan

Document 17
The May 31, 1924 Boxer Indemnity Declaration

Karakhan Adopts the 1901 and 1904 Boxer Protocols

From 1919 through 1924, Lev Karakhan repeatedly renounced the Boxer Protocols. In early June 1924, however, Karakhan sent a note to Foreign Minister Koo demanding that the Soviet mission be given permission to retake control over the Russian consulate buildings in Peking's diplomatic quarter.[29] When the foreign diplomatic corps insisted that the Soviet Union must first recognize the conditions of the 1901 and 1904 Boxer Protocols, Karakhan agreed. As a result, the Soviet government automatically regained all the special rights and privileges that the tsarist Russian government had formerly enjoyed in China.

On June 9, Koo requested that the foreign diplomatic corps allow Karakhan to move into the former Russian consulate in Peking's diplomatic quarter, which had been autonomous of the Peking government since 1901. In his letter to the Dutch Minister and the *doyen* of the diplomatic corps, W. J. Oudendijk, Koo acknowledged that this decision could only be made by the "interested Resident Ministers at Peking."[30] On July 12, however, Oudendijk informed Koo that according to the 1901 Boxer Protocol, Peking had no authority to act on behalf of the USSR. He requested that Karakhan get in touch directly with the diplomatic corps.[31] Koo immediately began working to bring about a meeting between Karakhan and Oudendijk's successor, Jacob Schurman.

During this meeting, which took place on July 24, Schurman told Karakhan that before the USSR could take control of the Russian consulate, the Soviet government must first acknowledge that the Soviet Union still considered itself to be a co-signatory of the 1901 Boxer Protocol. Karakhan agreed to this precondition. On July 26, Karakhan wrote a letter to Schurman acknowledging that the former Russian consulate was under the "guardianship of Eight Ministers of the Powers co-signatory to the 1901 Protocol."[32]

When the foreign diplomatic corps next insisted that the USSR recognize not only the 1901 Boxer Protocol but also the additional Boxer Protocol of 1904 as well, Karakhan also agreed to this new condition (see Document 18). Specifically, when Japan's Minister Yoshizawa wrote to Karakhan on August 18, he repeated that Karakhan had acknowledged on July 24 that the "Soviet government enjoys all the rights and is impressed with all the obligations of that [1901] Protocol and of the Protocol of 1904 and all subsequent arrangements which bind all the co-signatories to the maintenance of the conventional status of the Diplomatic Quarter."[33]

By recognizing the 1901 and 1904 Boxer Protocols in return for regaining control over the Russian consulate, Karakhan broke promises he had made on at least three separate occasions to renounce the USSR's participation in the "unequal" Boxer Protocols. As a result, Karakhan's actions directly contradicted his own anti-imperialist propaganda in China, as expressed in a June 9, 1924 speech at Peking University: "Long live the brotherhood of the peoples of China and the Soviet Union. Long live China, independent and free from imperialism."[34]

August 18, 1924.

Mr. Ambassador:

On August 1st the Senior Representative of the Powers Signatory to the Protocol of 1901 laid the communication you addressed to him on July 26, 1924, before his Colleagues, the Diplomatic Representatives of the said Powers, and also informed them that in his conversation with you of July 24 you informed him that the Soviet Government considered itself still to be a cosignatory of the aforesaid Protocol.

I am now requested by my Colleagues to inform you that in view of the above circumstance and the consequence thereof, namely, that the Soviet Government enjoys all the rights and is impressed with all the obligations of that Protocol and of the Protocol of 1904 and all subsequent arrangements which bind all the co-signatories to the maintenance of the conventional status of the Diplomatic Quarter, the Diplomatic Representatives of the Signatory Powers have decided to hand over to

Your Excellency the Russian Legation and the keys thereof and have appointed the Netherlands Charge d'Affaires, the Jonkheer W. F. Roell, to represent them in this business.

As to the intimation given by Your Excellency in the conversation above referred to that the Soviet Government might in the future renounce its interest in the Protocol of 1901, which was also reported to my Colleagues, I am requested to say that the Representatives of the other Powers Signatory to the 1901 and 1904 Protocols must reserve full liberty of action for their Governments in respect to the effect of such renunciation upon the rights, privileges and mutual obligations which accrue to and devolve upon all the signatories of these collective agreements.

If Your Excellency will acquaint me with the name of the person you may delegate to take over the Russian Legation and the keys I will communicate the information to the Netherlands Charge d'Affaires.

I avail myself of this opportunity to extend to Your Excellency the assurance of my highest consideration.

(Sd.) K. Yoshizawa.

Document 18
Kenkichi Yoshizawa's August 18, 1924 Letter to Karakhan

Karakhan's negotiations with the foreign diplomatic corps led to Moscow's renewal of the 1901 and 1904 Boxer Protocols; these agreements had set the terms and amounts of the Boxer Indemnity payments. Although the USSR's actions clearly contradicted numerous promises to eliminate all unequal Russo-Chinese treaties, the terms under which Karakhan regained control over the Russian consulate in Peking were not widely publicized. As a result, the Chinese people continued to live under the illusion that the USSR was the only country to renounce completely its participation in the Boxer Protocols.

"To Use Barbarians to Govern Barbarians"

By the summer of 1924, Peking had not only convinced the United States to revoke the final portion of its indemnity, but it had also signed a treaty with the USSR specifying that the Russian share would likewise support education in China. When added to the former German and Austrian shares, Peking had now ensured that almost 60 percent of the Boxer Indemnity would remain within China's borders, instead of being sent overseas. In order to apply pressure on the other recipients of the Boxer Indemnity to follow suit, Peking continued to use its relations with the Soviet Union as leverage. This tactic eventually allowed Peking to redirect over 98 percent of the Boxer Indemnity for use within China.

Once the Russian consulate was returned to the USSR under the terms of the 1901 and 1904 Boxer Protocols, Karakhan approached Peking's new foreign minister, C. T. Wang, with three new preconditions, although Karakhan later referred to these demands as only "certain preliminary technical points.[35] These three demands included: 1) organize a commission to determined how to use the Russian portion of the Boxer Indemnity to support Chinese education, 2) return all Russian church property in China to Soviet control, and 3) return three impounded Russian ships in Shanghai to the Soviet Union (see Document 19).[36]

According to Karakhan, Peking must immediately nominate two candidates for the three-person commission to decide how the Russian portion of the Boxer Indemnity was to be spent. He further specified that the Boxer Indemnity commission should include one representative from the Soviet government, one from the KMT government in Canton, and one from the Peking government. Since the Canton government was financially dependent on Moscow, this virtually guaranteed that the commission would back any Soviet decision.

Although this mixed Sino-Soviet commission met at the Soviet consulate in Peking on November 24, 1924, its work was stymied and quickly deadlocked because the Russian portion of the Boxer Indemnity was already committed for other purposes. In fact, there were no funds to distribute. On April 12, 1924, the Inspector-General of Customs, Sir Francis Aglen, had written to Foreign Minister Koo informing him that the entire portion of the Russian share of the Boxer Indemnity had "been allocated as security for obligations of various kinds," and that Russia's portion of the indemnity would only become available in 1927.[37]

嗾使表示希冀解決下列三項問題

館問答第　號民國　年　月　日　政務司錢存

（一）俄庚款委員会之華委員人選

（二）移交俄東正教教堂産業事宜

（三）停泊之俄艦三艘移交事宜

總長允飭主管司即時研究辦法辦理

Document 19
Lev Karakhan's November 6, 1924 Preconditions

According to Aglen, Russia's indemnity was divided into two groups known as the Deferred Portion and the Retained Portion. The first was being used as security for: 1) the eleventh-year loan, 2) the Peking government's account to pay for China's legations abroad. Meanwhile, the second group was being used as security for: 1) third- and fourth-year loans, and thereafter for 2) the consolidated loan service. Aglen threatened to resign and go public with this information unless Koo rewrote the March 14, 1924 Sino-Soviet draft agreement to take this situation into account.[38]

As a result of this threat, Koo convinced Karakhan to include a clause in the May 31, 1924 Sino-Soviet agreement specifying that the Russian portion of the Boxer Indemnity would be spent on education in China only "after the satisfaction of all prior obligations secured thereon."[39] What Koo apparently never told Karakhan, however, was that the Russian funds would not become available for educational use until almost three years after the Sino-Soviet agreement was signed. Conveniently, Peking later broke relations with Moscow immediately prior to when these funds again became available.

Documents from the Kuomintang archives also suggest that through the spring of 1927, Russia's share of the Boxer Indemnity was never actually used to support Chinese education.[40] Thereafter, the thirty-nine-year term of the Boxer Indemnity expired in 1940, immediately before the formal renewal of Sino-Soviet relations. As a result of these diplomatic maneuvers, and by careful timing, Koo succeeded in appropriating the Russian share of the Boxer Indemnity to pay not for Chinese education, but for Peking's overseas legations, among other things. This Chinese maneuver could not have pleased Karakhan.

In addition, although the Russian share of the Boxer Indemnity was fully committed until 1927, Peking could make immediate use of the USSR's formal renunciation of Russia's share of the Boxer Indemnity—as stated in the May 31, 1924 Sino-Soviet agreement—to exert pressure on the other foreign countries to renounce their own shares. The Canton government perhaps inadvertently played an important role in this diplomatic strategy when Sun Yat-sen marked the anniversary of the 1901 Boxer Protocol in a September 7, 1924 speech that praised the Soviet Union, but denounced the capitalist countries.[41] During 1925, the KMT also helped lead the May Thirtieth Movement, issuing manifestos demanding that foreign countries abrogate all of their unequal treaties.[42]

Faced with the combined efforts of both the Peking and the Canton governments, Great Britain quickly backed down and completed arrangements on March 3, 1925, to use its share of the Boxer Indemnity to support railway construction in China. France followed suit on April 12, asking that its indemnity be used to reopen a defunct Sino-French Bank. Italy signed an agreement with the Peking government on October 1, to spend its share on the construction of steel bridges. Holland's funds paid for harbor and land reclamation, while the Belgian funds were earmarked to be "spent on railway material in Belgium."[43] Finally, Japan's indemnity was also transferred to China during October 1925, to develop aviation in China under Japan's auspices.[44]

Once these countries' approximately 40 percent of the Boxer Indemnity was added to Germany's and Austria's combined 20.91 percent, the United States' 7.32 percent, and the Soviet Union's 28.97 percent share, the Peking government had accounted for over 98 percent of the entire Boxer Indemnity. By 1927, therefore, the Peking government had almost completely revoked Boxer Indemnity payments abroad.

The USSR's generous-sounding public promise to renounce unconditionally Russia's share of the Boxer Indemnity proved to be the most important lever for pressuring the other foreign countries to follow suit. But Sino-Soviet relations were anything but friendly: on the one hand, the Soviet government reneged on its promise and once again recognized the 1901 and 1904 Boxer Protocols, while on the other hand, Peking retained the use of Russia's portion of the Boxer Indemnity through 1927, at which time China broke diplomatic relations with the USSR. In the end, therefore, Peking retained absolute control over how the Russian share of the Boxer Indemnity was allocated.

Conclusions

As a result of the 1900 Boxer Uprising, the Ch'ing government was forced to pay an enormous indemnity. In the face of the united efforts of Russia, Germany, France, Great Britain, Japan, the United States, Italy, Belgium, Austria-Hungary, Holland, Spain, Portugal, Norway, and Sweden, the Peking government continued to pay the Boxer Indemnity after it came to power in 1911. Following the 1917 October Revolution, however, the Peking government was able to wield enormous leverage over the capitalist powers by criticizing their failure to match the Soviet government's generous promise to renounce unconditionally Russia's almost 30 percent share of the Boxer Indemnity.

The foreign policy strategy of playing one foreigner against another was a time-honored diplomatic tactic in China.[45] But this tactic often backfired during the nineteenth and early twentieth centuries whenever the foreign powers cooperated closely with each other against China. After the Bolsheviks seized power in Russia, however, the sharp bipolar divisions between the socialist and the capitalist camps appear to have given Peking an opportunity to exert much greater leverage over the foreign powers than China's comparatively weak economic, military, and political strength would normally have allowed. For this reason, the traditional Chinese tactic of "barbarian management" met with greater success. Peking's revocation of over 98 percent of the Boxer Indemnity between 1917 and 1927 is perhaps the most conspicuous example of this policy in action.

Although the Peking government used the Soviet government's promises of equality to goad the capitalist countries into renouncing their own special rights and privileges, archival documents now prove that the USSR never lived up to its generous-sounding declarations. In fact, the Soviet government ultimately renewed the 1901 and 1904 Boxer Protocols and retained the right to determine how Russia's share of the Boxer Indemnity would be spent within China. Both of these actions suggest that Karakhan's frequent promises to abolish the Boxer Protocol and to renounce Russia's share of the Boxer Indemnity were used merely to initiate diplomatic negotiations between Moscow and Peking; once negotiations were underway, Karakhan's position changed dramatically.

Archival documents furthermore prove that the Soviet government's method for remitting Russia's share of the Boxer Indemnity exactly followed the American model, which undermines the widespread belief that the Soviet Union treated China better than the United States. By keeping the capitalist countries largely ignorant of the true nature of Sino-Soviet affairs, however, the Peking government was able to exert enormous pressure on these countries to match the Bolsheviks' apparent generosity. In the process of using its outwardly friendly diplomatic relations with Moscow as leverage, however, Peking also inadvertently gave added legitimacy to the myth that the USSR really had treated China equally.

Notes

1. Robert C. North, *Moscow and Chinese Communists,* 51.

2. Allen Whiting, *Soviet Policies in China, 1917-1924.* 251; Sow-Theng Leong, *Sino-Soviet Diplomatic Relation, 1917-1926,* 276.

3. Harold R. Isaacs, *The Tragedy of the Chinese Revolution,* 60.

4. One scholar has concluded that this policy can be traced back to the Han dynasty. Yang Lien-shang, "Historical Notes on the Chinese World Order," John King Fairbank, ed., *On The Chinese World Order,* 33.

5. "China's Financial Situation in 1922. Dr. Lo Wen Kan's Report," *The China Yearbook,* 1924, 742-743.

6. Immanuel C. Y. Hsu, *The Rise of Modern China,* 398.

7. Joseph W. Esherick, *The Origins of the Boxer Uprising,* 311.

8. Jonathan Spence, *The Search for Modern China,* 235.

9. Victor Purcell, *The Boxer Uprising: A Background Study,* 261.

10. *The China Yearbook,* 1924, 742-743.

11. *The China Yearbook,* 1919-20, 348-349.

12. Собрание Документов, каскющихся деятельности Российской Миссий в Китай 1 Ноября 1917 г. по 31 Декабря 1920 г. (*Collection of Documents. Relating to the Activities of the Russian Mission in China from November 1, 1917 to December 31, 1920*), 58.

13. Chinese-language minutes of meeting between the Chinese Foreign Minister and the British Consul, March 30, 1918, WCTA, 03-08, 11(20).

14. Roy Watson Curry, *Woodrow Wilson and Far Eastern Policy 1913-1921,* 282-283.

15. Whiting, 29; Quoting *Izvestiia,* No. 138, July 5, 1918.

16. Советско-китайские отношения 1917-1957 Сборник Документов (*Soviet-Chinese Relations 1917-1957, Collection of Documents*),40-41.

17. Peking Government's Official Communique, "China's Reply to Japan," April 11, 1919; Reprinted from the *North-China Herald,* April 19, 1919, Hoover Institution Archives,

Stanley Hornbeck Collection, Box 328, 144.

18. Original French-language telegram received in Peking on March 26, 1920; WCTA; 03-32, 463(1).

19. Бюллетени Дальне-восточного Секретариата Коминтерна (*Bulletins of the Far Eastern Secretariat of the Comintern*), No. 5, Irkutsk, April 24, 1921, 3.

20. Hsu, 515.

21. French-language letter from Prince Kudachev to the Chinese Ministry of Foreign Affairs, Number Two Historical Archives, Nanking, September 29, 1920, File 1039, No. 153.

22. English-language transcript of C. T. Wang's speech which is a translation of the Chinese-language version, September 4, 1923, WCTA, 03-32, 467 (1).

23. Chinese-language minutes of the conversation between Lev Karakhan and Chu Ho-hsiang, February 2, 1924, WCTA, 03-32, 461(3).

24. Draft Sino-Soviet Treaty, March 14, 1924, WCTA, 03-32, 506(5).

25. Memorandum on the Boxer Indemnity from George Atcheson, Jr., to Stanley Hornbeck, April 6, 1943, Hoover Institution Archives, Stanley Hornbeck collection, Box 34.

26. Terence Eldon Brockhausen, "The Boxer Indemnity: Five Decades of Sino-American Dissension," 224.

27. "Agreement of General Principles for the Settlement of the Questions Between the Republic of China and the Union of Soviet Socialist Republics," May 31, 1924, WCTA, 03-32, 495(1).

28. Memorandum on the Boxer Indemnity from George Atcheson, Jr., to Stanley Hornbeck, April 6, 1943, Hoover Institution Archives, Stanley Hornbeck collection, Box 34.

29. English-language letter to V. K. Wellington Koo, signed by Lev Karakhan, June 7, 1924, WCTA, 03-32, 455(1).

30. English-language letter to W. J. Oudendijk, signed by V. K. Wellington Koo, June 9, 1924, WCTA, 03-32, 454(1).

31. French-language letter to V. K. Wellington Koo, signed by W. J. Oudendijk, July 12, 1924, WCTA, 03-32, 454(1).

32. English-language letter to Jacob Gould Schurman, signed by Lev Karakhan, July 26, 1924, WCTA, 03-32, 454(1).

33. English-language letter to Lev Karakhan, signed by the Japanese Minister to China, Kenichi Yoshizawa, August 18, 1924, WCTA, 03-32, 454(1).

34. Louis Fischer, *The Soviets in World Affairs,* Vol. 1, 550.

35. English-language letter to Foreign Minister Shen Rui-lin, signed by Lev Karakhan, 26 February 1925, WCTA, 03-32, 497(2).

36. Chinese-language minutes of meeting between Lev Karakhan and C. T. Wang, November 6, 1924, WCTA, 03-32, 489(1).

37. English-language letter from the Inspector-General of Customs, Sir Francis Algen, to V. K. Wellington Koo, April 12, 1924, WCTA, 03-32, 537(1).

38. *Ibid.*

39. "Agreement of General Principles for the Settlement of the Questions Between the Republic of China and the Union of Soviet Socialist Republics," May 31, 1924, WCTA, 03-32, 495 (1).

40. Archives of the Historical Commission of the Central Committee of the Kuomintang Party, Hankow Files, Documents No. 5004, 7963.

41. Michael Vincent Metallo, "The United States and Sun Yat-sen, 1911-1925," 258.

42. C. Martin Wilbur and Julie Lien-ying How, *Missionaries of Revolution: Soviet Advisers and Nationalist China, 1920-1927*, 150.

43. Memorandum called "The Boxer Indemnity," June 6, 1931, Hoover Institution Archives, Stanley Hornbeck collection, Box 34.

44. During March 1923, Japan had initially put its share of the Boxer Indemnity into a special fund to finance "education, medical assistance, research, and scholarly exchange" in China. Douglas R. Reynolds, "Training Young China Hands: Tōa Dōbun Shoin and Its Precursors, 1886-1945," in Peter Duus, Ramon H. Myers, and Mark R. Peattie, eds., *The Japanese Informal Empire in China, 1895-1937,* 210-271.

45. According to Yang Lien-shang, the Chinese policy of playing one foreigner off another "has continued to be resorted to by strategists from time to time in reality if not in name" (Fairbank, 33).

6
The Restoration of Russian Territorial Concessions

It was previously assumed that the Bolsheviks renounced all Russian territorial concessions in China. Perhaps the earliest historian to make this claim was Victor Yakhontoff, who in 1931 stated: "Russia actually renounced all special rights, privileges and concessions."[1] Other scholars later agreed, with Morris Rossabi concluding: "The Sino-Soviet treaty of May 1924 . . . ended the Soviet Union's special privileges in China."[2] Soviet scholars, not surprisingly, also supported this view, with Georgi Arbatov writing: "We changed our relations with Asian countries, too. Among other things, we renounced all the tsarist governments' colonial claims in Asia."[3]

Archival documents now show that by means of secret diplomacy the Bolsheviks regained control of most of the former tsarist Russian territorial concessions.[4] Following the opening of diplomatic relations with China in 1924, Moscow not only reopened consulates in sixteen cities throughout China, but in the process it retook possession of numerous consulate buildings, houses, and barracks. Soviet officials also regained control of all Russian Orthodox churches in China, as well as of tsarist military property, such as the former Russian military parade ground in Tientsin.

This chapter will show that by the spring and summer of 1925 the USSR once again controlled virtually the same territorial concessions in China as the tsarist Russian government before it. But because it was commonly accepted that the USSR renounced its territorial concessions in China, the Chinese people demanded that other foreign powers follow suit. This demand was leveled most frequently at Great Britain, since the retention of Hong Kong, Kowloon, the New Territories, and Shameen Island in Canton continued long after the USSR had supposedly returned all of its own concessions to China. During the May Thirtieth Movement, Chinese demonstrators in Canton tried to storm Shameen Island and the resulting massacre sparked anti-British boycotts.

The Soviet claim that Russian territorial concessions were returned to China was a myth. The outward appearance of friendly Sino-Soviet relations was actively promoted by Peking, however, since only the widely accepted belief that the USSR had already given up its concessions legitimated China's condemnation of the other countries for not doing the same. Although Chinese attempts from 1925 to 1927 to retake British concessions by force largely failed, this myth was destined to play an important role in the Bolsheviks' later propaganda, which helped fuel decades of controversy over continued British control of Hong Kong, Kowloon, and the New Territories.

The Tsarist Territorial Concessions in China

Following the 1917 October Revolution, the Bolsheviks quickly promised to open a new era of equal diplomatic relations with China: during July 1918, for example, the Soviet government publicly declared that it intended to "renounce all land-rights of our citizens in China."[5] Although their ulterior motive was to undermine the anti-Soviet White Russians based in China, these Bolshevik promises provided the Peking government with a long-awaited opportunity to demand the return of all foreign concessions. When the Paris Peace Conference refused to act on this proposal, additional Bolshevik declarations advocating equal Sino-Soviet relations supported China's position.

China's list of territorial demands going into the 1919 Paris Peace Conference was long: the Chinese delegation advocated the abolition of all foreign concessions plus the cancellation of special foreign rights and privileges. In particular, all foreign leased territories that had been fortified during World War I would have to be handed over to China immediately, since: "Removal of Germany from the Far East makes the retention of these territories unnecessary."[6] According to one account, this included the return of the leased territories of "Kiaochow (Chiao-chou) Wan, Port Arthur (Lü-shun), Talien Wan, Kwangchow (Kuangchou) Wan, and Kowloon."[7]

China's delegation clearly hoped that the major powers would support its proposals for eliminating foreign concessions. Once Peking failed, it turned to the Bolsheviks, who promised: "The Soviet Government renounces everything seized by the tsarist government in China, Manchuria and in other places."[8] Peking also decided to make use of the generous Soviet offers to help rid China of all foreign rights and privileges: on September 23, 1920, it ended formal recognition of all officials appointed by the Russian Provisional government and confiscated Russian property. The amount of privately held Russian property was actually quite small, however, since much of it had already been sold to non-Russians. For example, the American minister informed Peking that in Tientsin, "the bulk of the property in the Russian Concession is owned not by Russians but by Americans and subjects of other nations."[9]

As for Russia's government property, after Peking withdrew recognition from the White Russians the foreign diplomatic corps entrusted the Russian legation and its holdings in Peking to M. J. Oudendijk, the Minister of the Netherlands. During the spring of 1921, Iurin informed Peking that Soviet promises to eliminate their concessions did not include either the Russian legation in Peking or the many Russian consulates located all over China. He suggested two alternatives: 1) the Russian legation should be turned over to the FER Mission—Iurin assured Peking that the "Russian Soviet Government will approve the said proposal"—or 2) the Peking government should set up a committee with the FER in order to "safeguard this property which belongs to Russia."[10]

Neither of these suggestions suited Peking, however, since to act on either one of them would have interfered with the diplomatic corps' right to administer the foreign diplomatic quarter in Peking, as guaranteed by the 1901 Boxer protocol. Foreign Minister Yen side-stepped this difficulty on April 15, 1921, therefore, when he informed the diplomatic corps that "the Chinese Government will not be responsible to any party whatsoever for the safe-guarding of the buildings, furnitures, archive, and other appurtenances of the legation."[11]

With this decision, Peking pushed the problem off onto the foreign diplomatic corps, which continued to safeguard the Russian legation through 1924. Although this action temporarily protected Peking, this matter later resurfaced at a most inopportune time, since by renouncing responsibility over the Russian legation in 1921, Peking found that it could not so easily regain control in 1924, when it opened diplomatic relations with the USSR. This mistake would later give the Soviet diplomats enormous leverage over Peking officials.

The USSR Reclaims Tsarist Concessions

Although the Soviet government repeatedly promised that it would renounce all Russian territorial concessions in China, Karakhan actually gained Peking's pledge that once official diplomatic relations were opened, the Russian legation in Peking, as well as the other consulates and official property throughout China, would all be returned to Soviet control. Karakhan's success can be attributed mainly to the wording of Article I in the May 31, 1924 Sino-Soviet Treaty, whereby Peking agreed to turn over to Moscow control over the tsarist legation, as well as over numerous consulate buildings all over China.

To prepare for the fall 1923 arrival of the USSR's new envoy, Peking officials compiled a fourteen-point draft of what they hoped would be the future Sino-Soviet treaty. This draft was based closely on Karakhan's declarations of 1919 and 1920, so the Peking officials did not consider their negotiating goals to be unreasonable. In particular, this October 13, 1923 draft stated: "The Soviet Government agrees to renounce the concessions, military barracks, and parade grounds, leased as well as established by the former Russian Government in China."[12] Karakhan thereafter appeared to agree with this stipulation when he promised during February 1924 that the Soviet government would agree to "the complete abolition of Russian concessions."[13]

But on May 31, 1924, Article I of the Sino-Soviet treaty actually included the following line: "The Government of the Republic of China agrees to take the necessary steps to transfer to the Government of the Union of Soviet Socialist Republics the Legation and Consular buildings formerly belonging to the Tsarist Government." In a declaration that was added at the end of this treaty, Peking and Moscow also agreed that each government would "hand over to each other all the real estate and movable property owned by China and the former Tsarist Government and found in their respective territories." Finally, a third declaration agreed that China would return the Russian Orthodox church properties in Peking and Patachu, a town right outside of Peking, and that the question of "transfer or other suitable disposal" of all other Russian Orthodox churches would be discussed at the upcoming Sino-Soviet conference, scheduled to meet one month later (see Document 20).[14]

Taken together, these four categories of property–legations, consulates, real estate, and churches–included a large proportion of the buildings and lands that had formerly made up Russia's territorial concessions in China. Koo agreed to these conditions in return for Karakhan's official recognition that Outer Mongolia remained an integral part of China, for the promise that the CER would be sold to China, and for his additional assurances that all former unequal treaties would be abolished. Details of how to carry out these promises were postponed until the official Sino-Soviet conference, scheduled to meet at the end of June, which meant that Karakhan had one month to use these three resolutions to consolidate the USSR's new territorial gains throughout China.

Karakhan began this task on June 6, 1924, when he emphasized to Koo the necessity of quickly transferring all Russian consulates to the USSR. Karakhan was particularly interested in regaining the Peking legation, which was located in the diplomatic quarter and was therefore under the authority of the foreign diplomatic corps. After urging Koo to send a note demanding that this legation be turned over to the Soviet delegation, Karakhan went so far as to suggest that Koo "send a detachment of soldiers" to forcibly take control of the premises.[15]

Such an act not only would have violated the 1901 treaty that put the diplomatic quarter outside of Peking's control, but it would have undoubtedly also caused an international uproar, so Koo declined to follow Karakhan's advice. It is important to note, however, that Karakhan was attempting to push Koo into open conflict with the other foreign powers in Peking. As will be shown in greater detail below, after Koo refused to join Karakhan against the foreign diplomatic corps, Karakhan changed tactics and instead joined the diplomatic corps against Koo.

On June 7, 1924, Karakhan followed up the previous day's meeting by sending a letter to Koo requesting him to issue instructions to the "local Commissioners of the Ministry of Foreign Affairs" to transfer the Shanghai, Chefoo, Tientsin, and Hankow consulates, as well as their property and archives, to Soviet officials in those cities.[16] Koo complied and issued orders to wire the respective diplomatic commissioners to transfer the "grounds, buildings, archives, and belongings of the Consulates."[17] In addition, Koo also requested that the diplomatic corps transfer the Russian legation in Peking to Karakhan, asking the *doyen*, Netherlands's minister Oudendijk, to bring the matter to the attention of the other foreign diplomats.[18]

Oudendijk answered two days later, quoting W. W. Yen's 1921 letter that renounced responsibility over the tsarist Russian legation. He concluded that "the Foreign Representatives concerned can under the existing circumstances only consider the question of handing over the premises of the former Russian Legation if a request thereanent should be addressed to them by a Diplomatic Representative duly accredited to the Chinese Government by the Russian Government."[19] Koo had unknowingly backed himself into a corner by promising to return a legation that he did not control.

DECLARATION (II)

The Government of the Republic China and the Government of the Union of Soviet Socialist Republics hereby declare that it is understood that with regard to the buildings and landed property of the Russian Orthodox Mission belonging as it does to the Government of the Union of Soviet Socialist Republics the question of the transfer or other suitable disposal of the same will be jointly determined at the Conference provided in Article II of the Agreement on General Principles between the Republic of China and the Union of Soviet Socialist Republics of May 31, 1924, in accordance with the internal laws and regulations existing in China regarding property-holding in the inland. As regards the buildings and property of the Russian Orthodox Mission belonging as it does to the Government of the Union of Soviet Socialist Republics at Peking and Patachu, the Chinese Government will take steps to immediately transfer same as soon as the Government of the Union of Soviet Socialist Republics will designate a Chinese person or organization, in accordance with the laws and regulations existing in China regarding property-holding in the inland.

Meanwhile the Government of the Republic of China will at once take measures with a view to guarding all the said buildings and property and clearing them from all the persons now living there.

It is further understood that this expression of understanding has the same force and validity as a general declaration embodied in the said Agreement on General Principles.

In faith whereof, the respective Plenipotentiaries of the Governments of the two Contracting Parties have signed the present Declaration in duplicate in the English language and have affixed thereto their seals.

Done in the City of Peking this Thirty-First Day of the Fifth Month of the Thirteenth Year of the Republic of China, which is, the Thirty-First Day of May One Thousand Nine Hundred and Twenty-Four.

(Seal) V. K. Wellington Koo

(Seal) L. M. Karakhan

Document 20
May 31, 1924 Declaration on Russian Church Property

On June 21, Karakhan sent a bitter complaint to Koo, pointing out that the Shanghai consulate was still hoisting the tsarist tricolor flag: "In view of the foregoing, I must protest in the most energetic manner against the actions of the Chinese authorities at Shanghai and insist on the flag being immediately brought down, all the persons now living in the buildings of the Consulates being removed therefrom, and the transfer being immediately effected to the authorized representatives of the Extraordinary Plenipotentiary Mission of all the buildings, archives, belongings, etc." Karakhan further complained: "Twenty days have now passed since the Agreement was signed, and yet the Consulates of the Union of Soviet Socialist Republics are still, as before, in the hands of the White Guards, who do not wish to move from the buildings belonging to the Government of the Union of Soviet Socialist Republics."[20]

It became clear that Karakhan attached special importance to the fact that Peking had promised to hand over the former Russian consulates. In fact, five days later Karakhan sent a note demanding: "In virtue of Article I of the Agreement signed between the Union of Soviet Socialist Republics and the Republic of China on May 31, 1924, the Russian Legation at Peking must be handed over to the Soviet Government."[21] Furthermore, even though the May 31, 1924 treaty had stated that the official Sino-Soviet conference should begin within a month's time, Karakhan now made it clear that he would delay this conference until Koo carried through on Article I.

Reinstating the Boxer Protocols

Koo found himself in a difficult position because of Karakhan's interpretation that Peking had to return the Russian legation and consulates (Article I) prior to the planned Sino-Soviet conference (Article II). In fact, the May 31, 1924 treaty said nothing about a timetable for the consulates' return, while it did state that the Sino-Soviet conference had to convene within a month. Delaying the conference threatened to postpone talks on the timetable for withdrawing the Red Army from Outer Mongolia, arrangements for transferring ownership of the CER to Peking, and the negotiation of new Sino-Soviet treaties, which put tremendous pressure on Koo to carry out Karakhan's preliminary demands.

It was the ambiguity in the wording of the May 31, 1924 Sino-Soviet Treaty that gave Karakhan so much leverage over Koo. On June 27, therefore, Koo wrote Oudendijk once again, pleading with the foreign diplomatic corps to honor the USSR's claim to the Russian legation. Koo warned that its refusal to hand over this property would not only "embarrass" the Peking government, it would also interfere with China's ability to "discharge an obligation which they have undertaken vis-à-vis the Soviet Government in the Sino-Russian Agreement of May 31, 1924."[22]

Koo took further steps during early July, when the Hankow and Tientsin consulates were handed over to Soviet representatives. But, in a meeting on July 7, followed by a series of letters dated July 7, 8, 11, and 12, Karakhan protested that Soviet officials were encountering problems in Shanghai, Chefoo, and in Peking. In particular, on July 7, he accused the Chinese diplomatic commissar in Shanghai of admitting "several tens of armed men," described as "remnants of White bands" under the leadership of former White Russian General Glebov. By allowing these White Russians to occupy the Shanghai consulate, Karakhan accused Peking of violating two articles of the May 31, 1924 agreement: Article I because the consulates had not yet been handed over to the USSR, and Article VI because the representatives of the Peking government were continuing to render "criminal assistance" to White bands.[23]

Koo replied that instructions had been sent to Shanghai to turn the Russian consulate over to the Soviets officials and that on July 1, the bureau of Russian affairs had been closed, as ordered. Since the consulate building was located in Shanghai's international settlement, however, it was under the control of Shanghai's municipal council, so Koo's hands were tied.[24] Koo received another setback on July 12, when Oudendijk refused to hand over the Russian legation and requested that Karakhan get in touch directly with the *doyen* of the diplomatic corps.[25] As a result of these meetings, Karakhan agreed to adhere to the terms of the Boxer protocols, which formally reestablished tsarist Russia's concession in Peking.

It is important to recall that, according to Article VII of the 1901 Boxer Protocol: "The Chinese government has agreed that the quarter occupied by the legations shall be considered as one specially reserved for their use and placed under their exclusive control, in which Chinese shall not have the right to reside and which may be made defensible."[26] Thereafter, the 1904 Boxer Protocol stated that, not only would the diplomatic quarter have its own autonomous police force, but a separate governing body would be organized to collect taxes, pass laws, and maintain roads and public areas in the diplomatic quarter.[27]

In effect, the Peking diplomatic quarter operated almost like a separate, sovereign state within China. When Karakhan agreed to abide by the 1901 and 1904 Boxer Protocols, therefore, he not only ignored his 1919 manifesto promising to annul the Bolsheviks' participation in the Boxer Protocols, but he also contradicted his 1920 manifesto promising to void all unequal treaties concluded by the tsarist Russian government with China. Most important, Karakhan's action directly violated Article III of the recently concluded May 31, 1924 Sino-Soviet agreement, which stated that all former Russo-Chinese treaties would be renegotiated on the basis of "equality, reciprocity, and justice."[28]

Although Soviet propaganda continued to claim that the Bolsheviks had abolished all agreements that infringed on China's sovereignty and territorial integrity, the diplomatic record proves that the USSR renewed the tsarist concessions. Because these diplomatic transactions took place in secret, however, the Chinese populace truly believed that the USSR was the only country to have renounced its concessions. Karakhan relied on this myth to consolidate control over the remaining tsarist concessions during the following months.

Soviet Territorial Concessions in China

By the fall of 1924, the Soviet Union had regained control of the Russian legation in Peking, as well as many consulates throughout China. Meanwhile, Karakhan continued to delay the Sino-Soviet conference in order to pressure Koo to permit Soviet consulates-generals and consulates to be opened all over China, as well as force Peking to return all buildings and land connected with the former Russian consulates in these locations. Finally, Karakhan even coerced Peking into handing back all Russian Orthodox churches prior to the conference, even though the May 31, 1924 treaty had specifically stated that this issue would be discussed only at the upcoming conference. By the spring of 1925, therefore, the Soviet government had actually regained control over most of the buildings and property that had formerly made up the Russian concessions in China.

Following the transfer of the Russian legation in Peking, Karakhan announced on August 23, 1924, that Moscow had decided to set up five consulates-general at "Peking, Mukden, Canton, Harbin, and Shanghai," and eleven consulates at "Manchouli, Pogranitchnaya, Sakhalian, Chefoo, Hankow, Tientsin, Hailar, Tsitsikar, Kalgan, Tsindao, and K'uanchentzu."[29] After the USSR regained the buildings and real estate in these cities that had formerly belonged to the tsarist Russian government, its position in China was strengthened, since it gained working consulates in Manchuria, Sinkiang, and Inner Mongolia, not to mention China's major cities in north, central, and south China.

Of even greater importance was that Karakhan ignored his signed declaration of May 31, 1924, which promised that the status of the Russian Orthodox churches in China would be discussed at the Sino-Soviet conference. Instead, on November 6, 1924, he unilaterally demanded that all Russian church property be turned over to Soviet control immediately, prior to the beginning of the conference.[30] This proposal was a clear violation of the May 31, 1924 treaty, but Peking was powerless to refuse, since to ignore Karakhan's demand would simply lead to further delays in convening the long-overdue conference.

Karakhan's interest in acquiring control of the Russian Orthodox churches in China is especially noteworthy because of the Bolsheviks' avowed opposition to religion. This would suggest that Moscow planned to use these buildings for nonreligious purposes. This supposition is supported by the fact that the Soviet government quickly evicted the Orthodox Russian monks, who had continued their religious duties in China throughout the Russian civil war, as well as those White Russians who had fled war-torn Russia to take refuge in these churches.

The Soviet Union's territorial holdings throughout China were already quite extensive, but on April 10, 1925, Karakhan sent China's new foreign minister, Shen Jui-lin, an additional list of houses, barracks, and land in sixteen Chinese cities that had to be returned prior to the Sino-Soviet conference. The property in Manchuria was most numerous, with the Manchouli list alone including: "11 houses, 2 ice-houses, 1 water-station, 1 mortuary," as well as a church, house, school, 2 wooden barracks, and a post office (see Document 21).[31]

Annex I.

LIST OF PROPERTY

TO BE TAKEN OVER FROM

THE CHINESE AUTHORITIES

MANCHOULI.

1) Property of the Immigration Department
(11 houses, 2 ice-houses, 1 water-station, 1
mortuary.)

2) Conventual church and house and school.

3) Property of the Post Office at Manchouli:

a) 2 wooden barracks erected in the area
of the Railway Station.

b) Valuables: sums of money and securit-
ies; various stamps, undelivered money
letters and parcels.

c) Furniture and articles of special
equipment.

d) Books and documents

4) Property of Railway Post Office of the
Manchouli Station:

a) Post stamps and sums of money.

b) Movable property of the said Office
and Post Cars, consisting of furniture and special equipment: stamps, seals
etc.

c) Books, files and documents.

5) Telergaph and telephone property,
taken away by the White Guards from the Transbaikal Region. Part of such property to be found-
at the disposal of the Headquarters of the
Defence Corps at Harbin, while another part is
kept at the Chinese Custom-House at the Manchouli
Station.

Document 21
Excerpt from Karakhan's April 10, 1925 Letter to Foreign Minister Shen

In Hailar, the list included the: "Building, furniture, and archives of the Tribunal." In Tsitsikar, it was the: "Grounds and building of the Consulate; Secretary's house; office; doctor's house; house of chief of convoy; soldier's barracks; stable; servants' house and cellar." Meanwhile, in Harbin, a separate two page list included two post offices, a bank, a "tinned store-house," five wooden barracks, and stables. This list further specified that a "Ground lot in Post Street, New City," had to be turned over to Soviet officials, which is important insofar as this land was undeveloped real estate. Finally, even Russian charitable organizations found themselves on the list: "Building and equipment of the Community of the Sisters of Charity of the Russian Red Cross Society: grounds with houses and buildings and hospital equipment."[32]

The story was much the same throughout the rest of China. In particular, tsarist Russian territorial holdings in China's major port cities were extensive. In Tsingtao, Karakhan's list included: "Lot of ground belonging to the Consulate with appurtenant property." In Tsingwangtao: "Villa on the beach with esplanade: dependencies; barracks." In Shanghai: "Church property:–lot of ground; 2 two-storied houses; 2 churches; 1 three-storied house; 1 small wooden house; 1 stone dining hall; 1 wooden barrack; 1 dormitory."[33]

Even more important, Karakhan's list included former Russian military property, such as barracks, and he also expected 1,500 mow of property and ground lots of the former "Russian War Department" in Tientsin to be handed over.[34] This property was, in fact, tsarist Russia's military parade ground. At 733.5 square yards per mow, or a total of 227 acres, this parade ground alone was almost four times larger than the entire British concession area in Canton, which was only 300,000 square yards in size, or about 60 acres.[35] It should be recalled that it was territorial concessions exactly like these that Peking had formerly wanted Moscow to abolish, even including this request in its 1923 draft treaty, which had called on the USSR "to renounce the concessions, military barracks, and parade grounds."[36]

As a result of its secret diplomacy, the Soviet Union had once again acquired control over military properties that not only far exceeded in size the British consulates throughout China, but also dwarfed Britain's Shameen Island concession in Canton. In addition, during 1924-25, the Soviet diplomats consolidated their control over Outer Mongolia. If Outer Mongolia's 600,000 square miles are treated as if they constituted a Soviet territorial concession–China's inability even to send officials into Outer Mongolia, an area that Karakhan publicly acknowledged was an "integral part of China," is strong evidence that this was the case–then this Soviet-controlled territory alone was more than 1,500 times larger than the New Territories, estimated to be only slightly greater than 350 square miles.[37]

Since Moscow's negotiations with Peking were carried out in complete secrecy, the Chinese public was not aware of the large transfers of property to the Soviet Union. These transactions remained completely hidden from public view, allowing the Soviet diplomats to play successfully an elaborate "shell game" in which

Comintern-sponsored propaganda accused Great Britain of refusing to give up its territorial concessions in southern China at virtually the same time that the Soviet Union was reconsolidating its control over much larger Russian concessions in northern China.

Soviet Concessions and the May Thirtieth Movement

By the spring of 1925, it was taken for granted by the vast majority of Chinese that the Soviet Union had renounced its territorial concessions throughout China. This misconception makes the events surrounding the 1925 May Thirtieth Movement easier to understand, since at the heart of this movement was Moscow's goal of forcing Great Britain to give up its territorial concessions while the Soviet Union retained its own, thereby shifting the balance of power in its favor. This goal is not at all surprising when seen in the context of the traditional Anglo-Russian rivalry, which one diplomatic historian of the nineteenth century concluded formed the "constant theme of the century."[38]

The origins of the May Thirtieth Movement can be traced to the middle of May 1925, when a Shanghai rioter was killed at a Japanese cotton mill. This action prompted Chinese students in Shanghai to meet on May 27, to plan a demonstration. On May 30, these students rallied outside the Louza police station in the Shanghai foreign settlement. When they refused to disperse, three of them were arrested. Several of the participants tried to take away the firearms of two constables, who then fought back using batons. When the crowd started shouting "Kill the foreigners!" and began converging on the door of the police station, the British police inspector gave the order to fire. As a result of the ensuring fighting, Sikh and Chinese constables killed four students and wounded several others.[39]

These details are important since they show that the original incident took place in a Japanese cotton factory and the Chinese worker was killed by a Japanese guard. But the student demonstration was directed at the British-run police station in the Shanghai international settlement. According to the police investigation, many of the students who participated in the demonstration were from Shanghai University, which was reported to have a large pro-Bolshevik student following. Although this does not prove any direct involvement, certainly the selection of a British target for the fatal demonstration, instead of a Japanese target, fit exactly with the Soviet-sponsored anti-British propaganda circulating in south and central China.

The demonstrations in Shanghai ignited antiforeign agitation throughout China. This movement quickly spread to Canton, where a strike at the British concession on Shameen Island began on June 20, 1925. The Chinese Communist Party and the Kuomintang organized a mass march composed of thousands of Chinese students, workers, and ordinary citizens, who converged on Shameen Island on June 23, 1925. This demonstration ended in tragedy, however, when shooting erupted, killing a small number of British guards and a much larger number of Chinese citizens. This incident became know as the Shakee Bridge Massacre.

There are two versions of what really caused the Shakee massacre: the British version was that the Chinese demonstrators were trying forcibly to take over the British concession and that when they reached the Shakee bridge, firing began, killing two British citizens and an unspecified number of Chinese. One account later estimated that fifty Chinese were killed and one hundred wounded.[40] The Chinese version of these events was quite different, claiming that the demonstrators were merely marching by peacefully when they were fired on without provocation.[41]

It may never be known what actually prompted this incident, but it soon became the major focal point for the Chinese revolutionaries' anti-British agitation. Unbeknownst to the Chinese, however, after consolidating control over Outer Mongolia, the Chinese Eastern Railway, the Peking legation, and numerous Russian consulates, property, and churches all over China, Karakhan finally agreed to convene the long-overdue Sino-Soviet conference. When it opened during August 1925, however, at the height of the May Thirtieth Movement, four of the eleven proposed articles in the USSR's "Draft of Trade and Navigation" included requests that the USSR be accorded most-favored-nation status along with the other foreign powers.

On January 10, 1926, Peking officials protested the Soviet draft (see Document 22). If accepted, their protest argued, the Soviet proposals would not only "operate automatically in the direction of the renewal of the 'unequal treaties' so severely attacked by the representative of the Soviet Government," but would also restore to Russia "many of the unjust rights and privileges formerly secured during the tsarist regime but now renounced by Soviet Russia." Therefore, this protest concluded, the Soviet delegation should be cognizant of the "fact that any proposal or suggestion which might give rise to misgivings on the part of the Chinese people would not only hurt their awakened national pride but also, it is feared, alienate their cordial and sympathetic feelings towards Russians."[42]

Details of the formerly secret Sino-Soviet conference prove that after the USSR retook control over tsarist Russia's territorial concessions in China, it tried to once again renew the terms of tsarist Russia's unequal treaties. Although the Sino-Soviet negotiations quickly deadlocked, Soviet diplomats effectively retained all of these special rights and privileges by claiming that the terms of the old treaties continued to apply until revised. In other words, the Bolsheviks reneged on their public offers to abolish the unequal treaties.

Due to the Soviet diplomats' unparalleled skill at secret diplomacy the myth that the Soviet Union treated China as an equal remained intact. This misunderstanding was sponsored in large part by China's own government officials. As a result, one early historian of Sino-Soviet relations reached the following misguided conclusion: "No wonder that this growing sympathy of the New China for the New Russia was not welcomed by other Powers, who did not renounce their rights and continued to keep their concessions in the Orient."[43]

GENERAL OBSERVATION ON
THE PRELIMINARY SOVIET DRAFT OF TRADE
AND NAVIGATION.

-+++++++++++++++++++-

Upon examination of the draft treaty presented by the Soviet Delegation, the Chinese Delegation to its great regret is obliged to observe that this document, while apparently purporting to give expression to the principle of reciprocity, embodies in fact a veiled attempt at the restoration to Russia of many of the unjust rights and privileges formerly secured during the Tsarist regime but now renounced by Soviet Russia. The proposed treaty not only betrays a marked deviation from the spirit of the Declarations of the Soviet Government of 1919 and 1920, but also represents a retrogression from the agreement of May 31st, 1924.

Nothing is perhaps more objectionable than the most favoured nation clause found in four out of the proposed eleven articles. The Soviet Delegation is certainly aware of the fact that it is this clause which would operate automatically in the direction of the renewal of the "unequal treaties" so severely attacked by the representative of the Soviet Government. For Soviet Russia to propose to incorporate this clause into the new treaty would be tantamount to voluntary association with the group of Powers whose treaty relations with China are out of date. China is now seeking to readjust her relations with them. A stipulation for the extension of all facilities, privileges or immunities "at once, gratis, unconditionally and without any restriction" would perhaps be deprived of its objectionable feature, had a new regime of international intercourse been inaugurated and established in China.

In conclusion, the Chinese Delegation ventures to call the attention of the Soviet Delegation to the fact that any proposal or suggestion which might give rise to misgivings on the part of the Chinese people would not only hurt their awakened national pride but also, it is feared, alienate their cordial and sympathetic feelings towards Russians which form the keystone of the friendly relations happily subsisting between the two peoples.

Peking, January 10th, 1926.

Document 22
Excerpt from Peking's January 10, 1926 Protest to the Soviet Delegation

The Anglo-Russian Proxy War in China

From 1925 through until the spring of 1927, the Soviet-funded Comintern worked closely with Chinese revolutionaries to undermine British, American, French, and Japanese commercial interests in China. Great Britain's position in southern China was especially vulnerable because of its close proximity to the Kuomintang and the Chinese communist government in Canton. Soviet attempts to oust Britain from southern China almost succeeded, but fell apart during the spring of 1927, when both the Peking government and Chiang Kai-shek simultaneously turned on their Soviet backers after they succeeded in pushing the foreign powers into renouncing important territorial concessions.

The absolute secrecy with which the Soviet Union carried out its expansionist policies in China meant that it continued to enjoy great prestige among the Chinese people, while the Shakee massacre completely undermined Great Britain's standing: "Through these acts of violence, the foreigners–representatives of Western democracies–were playing directly into the hands of Communist specialists in force, maneuver, and deceit. The May 30 and Shakee-Shameen shootings made truth out of Soviet propaganda against the "foreign imperialists," and, by inflaming latent Nationalist militancy, strengthened the Communist position within the Kuomintang."[44] As a result of the massacre in Canton, a boycott of all British goods was organized, an action that the British merchants living in Hong Kong interpreted as almost an act of war.

The Hong Kong boycott continued throughout the rest of 1925, leaving 100,000 Chinese workers in Canton unemployed. Fifty thousand of these were reportedly sent by the Kuomintang to rural areas to help distribute revolutionary propaganda, while another fifty thousand stayed in Canton and took courses from Soviet advisers on "political theory and revolutionary tactics."[45] According to one Soviet estimate, Hong Kong's imports and exports fell by 60 percent, making British mercantile losses equal to 250,000 pounds sterling per day. The USSR took advantage of this boycott to bring its own goods directly to Canton, with the Soviet ships, *Simferopol, Astrakhan, Tomsk, Yeravan, Pamyat Lenina,* and the *Mengkuhai* (Mongolian Revolution) carrying "oil, weapons, and even disassembled airplanes" from Vladivostok.[46]

As a result of the May Thirtieth Movement, friction between Great Britain and the Soviet Union quickly intensified. During 1926, the Comintern's official journal, *The Communist International*, published an editorial entitled "Prepare for the Imperialist Attack," which blamed Great Britain for fomenting war against the USSR. Beginning with the words "There is a new danger of war!" this editorial warned that: "English imperialism would lead the rabid attack on the country of the dictatorship of the proletariat." Accordingly, the Soviet press concluded: "The English pirates are leading, in such a way, a direct war against the Chinese people and they are preparing with incredible speed a war against the USSR."[47]

Articles printed by the British press in early 1927 also agreed that a state of undeclared international war existed in China. Entitled "Soviet Influence in China," an editorial in the January 15, 1927 edition of the *North China Herald* retorted: "All Soviet Russia's activities have been spent on an attack on Great Britain in China. It has been and is a war between Soviet Russia and the British Empire. Unfortunately, the weapons used are the Chinese people; the scene of the conflict is China; the retaliation, the reprisal must be against China."[48] With these words, Great Britain prepared to intervene in China to oppose the Soviet Union.

Early in 1927, the KMT-led Northern Expedition forced the evacuation of the Hankow and Kiukiang concessions. Great Britain opened negotiations with the Kuomintang soon afterwards to discuss their permanent return to China. The British government was now willing to discuss the status of its other concessions in China as well, and negotiations with the KMT eventually led to British promises to place many of its concessions under Chinese authorities, as well as to prohibit British missionaries from buying land in China.[49]

During these early months of 1927, there was great concern in Hong Kong that it, Kowloon, and the New Territories would have to be returned to China. In opposition, Sir Cecil Clementi, the governor of Hong Kong from 1925 until 1930, suggested that Great Britain annex the New Territories outright. But the British government was determined to stand by its official treaties with China, announcing[50]:

> His Majesty's Government will give the fullest protection to Hong Kong and its mainland territories during the civil war now unhappily raging in China, and they have no intention whatever of surrendering Hong Kong or of abandoning or diminishing in any way its rights or authority in any part of the adjacent mainland territories under British administration, to the maintenance of which His Majesty's Government attach the highest importance.

To a large degree, this 1927 policy statement remained applicable during the almost seventy years of British rule in Hong Kong that followed.

During early March 1927, the Soviet press interpreted Great Britain's decision to back down in its negotiations as not only the zenith of China's revolution, but also as the beginning of the long-awaited world revolution: "The Chinese revolution is growing more and more into an object of struggle between the European proletariat and the European bourgeoisie. The collapse of British influence in China, in turn, appears to be one of the most important reasons for the new strained relations between England and the Soviet Union."[51]

On March 24, 1927, British, American, French, Italian, and Japanese warships bombarded Nanking in retaliation for the KMT army's massacre of defenseless foreigners. Sated by the success of the Sino-British negotiations and by the return of the foreign concessions in Hankow, Kiukiang, and Nanking, the Peking government decided that the time was ripe to turn on its former ally, the Soviet Union. On April 6, 1927, the Dutch minister, Oudendijk, acting on behalf of the foreign diplomatic corps, gave the Peking municipal police permission to raid the Soviet legation; secret dispatches and propaganda were discovered that Peking claimed were proof that the Soviet Union was trying to undermine China's sovereignty. Although Peking already had sufficient evidence against the USSR, it used the raid as an excuse to break diplomatic relations with Moscow. Soon afterward, and perhaps in part as a result of the documents discovered during the raid, Chiang Kai-shek also turned against his Soviet advisers on April 12, 1927.

Conclusions

Formerly, historians took it for granted that during 1917-27 the Soviet government actually returned all tsarist territorial concessions to China. In fact, Moscow secretly regained control over the Russian legations and consulates, as well as over houses, barracks, and parade grounds that had formerly belonged to the tsarist Russian government. Furthermore, the Bolsheviks–avowed atheists notwithstanding–took back all of the Russian Orthodox churches in China. About the only Russian lands actually returned to China were those owned by the Bolsheviks' enemies, the White Russians. Even this relatively small gain is questionable, since many of the White Russians sold their property to other foreigners prior to the opening of Sino-Soviet negotiations in 1920.

In truth, China gained little from the Bolsheviks' many promises to renounce Russia's concessions. The only substantive advantage for China was the use of the Soviet threat to push other foreigners from their leased concessions in China, which it did with some success during 1925-27. After forcing Britain to come to terms in 1927, however, the Peking government and Chiang Kai-shek then turned on their former ally, quickly occupying the Soviet legation in Peking, as well as other Soviet consulates throughout central China.

Although the Soviet government lost its foothold in central China, it retained its hold over Outer Mongolia and the CER, not to mention numerous consulates throughout Manchuria, Inner Mongolia, and Sinkiang.[52] By retaining control over these territorial concessions along China's borderlands, the USSR could continue to threaten central China. After World War II, other important areas once again fell under Soviet control. Detailed information about what really happened in China during the 1920s is particularly important, therefore, because it foreshadowed the similarly intricate conflicts during the 1940s, when the Soviet Union used all of these strategically located concessions to renew its earlier expansion into China.

Notes

1. Victor A. Yakhontoff, *Russia and the Soviet Union in the Far East*, 137.
2.. Morris Rossabi, *China and Inner Asia: From 1368 to the Present Day*, 254.
3. Georgi A. Arbatov, *The Soviet Viewpoint*, 49.
4. The legal definitions of "concession" and "settlements" differ. *Concessions* were "leased in perpetuity by the Chinese government to certain foreign powers," while *leases*

"were directly issued by the Chinese local authorities." William L. Tung, *China and the Foreign Powers: The Impact of an Reaction to Unequal Treaties*, 73.

5. Allen S. Whiting, *Soviet Policies in China, 1917-1924*, 28.

6. "China Before the Peace Conference, Preamble," marked "Confidential," Hoover Institution Archives, Stanley Hornbeck collection, Box 328.

7. Chu Pao-chin, *V. K. Wellington Koo: A Case Study of China's Diplomat and Diplomacy of Nationalism, 1912-1966*, 15-17.

8. Бюллетени Дальне-восточного Секретариата Коминтерна (*Bulletins of the Far Eastern Secretariat of the Comintern*), No. 5, Irkutsk, April 24, 1921, 3.

9. English-language letter from American Minister Crane to Dr. W. W. Yen, October 5, 1920, WCTA, 03-32, 438(1).

10. English-language memorandum from the FER Mission in Peking, April 6, 1921, WCTA, 03-32, 434(1).

11. English-language translation of letter from W. W. Yen to Doyen Batalha de Freitas, April 15, 1921, WCTA, 03-32, 434(1).

12. Official English translation of the Chinese-language original fourteen-point plan, October 13, 1923, WCTA, 03-32, 481(5).

13. Chinese-language minutes of the conversation between Lev Karakhan and Chu Ho-hsiang, February 2, 1924, WCTA, 03-32, 487(1).

14. Official Chinese-language copy of the Sino-Soviet Treaty, May 31, 1924, WCTA, 03-32, 454(1).

15. English-language minutes of the meeting between Lev Karakhan and V. K. Wellington Koo, June 6, 1924, WCTA, 03-32, 494(1).

16. English-language letter signed by Lev Karakhan, June 7, 1924, WCTA, 03-32, 455(1).

17. English-language letter signed by Lev Karakhan, June 21, 1924, WCTA, 03-32, 455(4).

18. English-language letter signed by V. K. Wellington Koo, June 9, 1924, WCTA, 03-32, 454(1).

19. English-language letter signed by W. J. Oudendijk, June 11, 1924, WCTA, 03-32, 454(1).

20. English-language letter signed by Lev Karakhan, June 21, 1924, WCTA, 03-32, 455(4).

21. English-language letter signed by Lev Karakhan, June 26, 1924, WCTA, 03-32, 455(4).

22. Copy of V. K. Wellington Koo's note included with the French-language letter signed by W. J. Oudendijk, July 12, 1924, WCTA, 03-32, 454(1).

23. English-language letter signed by Lev Karakhan, July 7, 1924, WCTA, 03-32, 455(4).

24. English-language minutes of the meeting between V. K. Wellington Koo and Lev Karakhan, July 7, 1924, WCTA, 03-32, 494(1).

25. French-language letter signed by W. J. Oudendijk, July 12, 1924, WCTA, 03-32, 454(1).

26. "Final Protocol for the Settlement of the Disturbances of 1900–September 7, 1901," John V. A. MacMurray, *Treaties and Agreements with and Concerning China*, Vol. 1, 282.

27. "Protocol Regarding Legation Quarter at Peking–June 13, 1904," *Ibid.*, 315-316.

28. "Agreement of General Principles for the Settlement of the Questions Between the Republic of China and the Union of Soviet Socialist Republics," May 31, 1924, WCTA, 03-32, 495 (1).

29. English-language letter to V. K. Wellington Koo, signed by Lev Karakhan, August 23, 1924, WCTA, 03-32, 456(1); place names as spelled in original document.

30. Chinese-language minutes of meeting between Lev Karakhan and C. T. Wang, November 6, 1924, WCTA, 03-32, 489(1).

31. English-language letter from Lev Karakhan to Shen Jui-lin, April 10, 1925, WCTA, 03-32, 265(1).

32. *Ibid.*

33. *Ibid.*

34. *Ibid.*

35. On Britain's Canton concession, see *The China Yearbook*, 1926-27, Vol. 1, 608.

36. Official English translation of the Chinese-language original fourteen-point plan, October 13, 1923, WCTA, 03-32, 481(5).

37. *The New Encyclopedia Britannica*, 15th ed., Vol. 12, 362.

38. Barbara Jelavich, *A Century of Russian Foreign Policy 1814-1914*, 293.

39. *The China Yearbook*, 1926-27, Vol. 1, 608; quoting from the "Shanghai Municipal Council's Police Report."

40. Robert C. North, *Moscow and Chinese Communists,* 82.

41. The French author, André Malraux, was in China at this time, and his book, *The Conquerors*, explains how the Comintern hoped to create an anti-British incident in Canton. He also described the larger Soviet-British conflict as a "tremendous struggle initiated by the very empire of chaos, suddenly organized, against the one nation that stands more than any other for will, tenacity, strength" (*The Conquerors*, 4).

42. English-language Protest from Chinese Delegation to Soviet Delegation, January 10, 1926, WCTA, 03-32, 536(4).

43. Yakhontoff, 40.

44. North, 82.

45. Louis Fischer, *The Soviets in World Affairs,* Vol. 2, 645.

46. Vera Vladimirovna Vishnyakova-Akimova, *Two Years in Revolutionary China 1925-1927*, 177.

47. "Подготовка Империалистской Атаки" ("Prepare for the Imperialist Attack"), *Коммунистический Интернационал* (*The Communist International*), September 24, 1926, No. 2, 3-5.

48. *North China Herald,* January 15, 1927.

49. *North China Herald,* February 12, 1927.

50. Peter Wesley-Smith, *Unequal Treaty, 1898-1997: China, Great Britain and Hong Kong's New Territories*, 156-157.

51. "Эссенс" ("Essence"), *Коммунистический Интернационал* (*The Communist International*), March 11, 1927, No. 10, 4.

52. The extent of the USSR's involvement in Sinkiang is still unclear. Arthur Christos Hasiotis, Jr., "A Study of Secret Political, Economic, and Military Involvement in Sinkiang from 1928-1949" (Ph.D. diss., New York University, 1981); Gennady Nicholas Jakimetz "An Interpretation of Czarist-Communist Economic-Political Policy in Sinkiang: With Emphasis on the Years 1851-1955" (M.A. Thesis, University of Nevada, Reno, 1981).

7
The Resumption of Russian Extraterritoriality

The history of China's efforts to end extraterritoriality requires fundamental reanalysis.[1] It was formerly thought that Moscow abolished extraterritoriality on May 31, 1924, when it signed the Sino-Soviet agreement stating: "The Government of the Union of Soviet Socialist Republics agrees to relinquish the rights of extraterritoriality and consular jurisdiction."[2] Legal scholars such as Wesley Fishel concluded that China completely abolished extraterritoriality on January 11, 1943, when the United States and Great Britain followed the USSR and signed treaties with China eliminating their final extraterritorial rights.[3]

In fact, the archival documents presented below reveal that the Soviet Union retained the special legal rights of extraterritoriality and consular jurisdiction, first by refusing to negotiate new agreements with China, and later by signing a series of secret agreements with the KMT's Nationalist government in Nanking in 1929 and 1939 that renewed these rights. As a result of the USSR's secret diplomacy, Soviet officials, troops, and advisers living and working in China continued to enjoy special legal protection long after 1943.

As with the Boxer Indemnity and tsarist Russia's territorial concessions, Moscow's public statements that it had abolished extraterritoriality proved useful to Chinese officials as leverage over the other foreign powers. But this strategy was inherently dangerous, since it was difficult to use the foreign powers to regulate the USSR's behavior. Chinese diplomats like Wellington Koo and C. T. Wang were prepared to take this risk, however, adopting a dual policy whereby the Chinese government actively sponsored the myth of friendly Sino-Soviet relations, while simultaneously adopting harsh legal measures to undermine and destroy Bolshevik sympathizers in China, such as the CCP.

This dual policy helps explain what appeared to outsiders to be rapid shifts between Sino-Soviet friendship and animosity. Although China's "Russia card" proved quite effective from the mid-1920s through the mid-1940s, this policy proved disastrous immediately after World War II, when China's escalating domestic unrest gave the Soviet-sponsored CCP an unforeseen opportunity to expand its power throughout mainland China. It was during this period that the USSR's special rights and privileges were to play an especially important role.

Only the widely held belief that the USSR actually abolished extraterritoriality in 1924 enabled Chinese diplomats to pressure American and British officials to do the same in 1943. This chapter will show, however, that the USSR, quite far from being the first major power to abolish extraterritoriality in China, was actually the last one to do so, retaining tsarist Russia's special legal rights and privileges in China longer than both the United States and Great Britain.

Peking Eliminates the White Russians' Extraterritoriality

After almost a century of extraterritoriality for foreigners residing in China, the Peking government's delegation to the 1919 Paris Peace Conference demanded that China be allowed to safeguard her "sovereign rights," by abolishing "extraterritoriality."[4] The nations participating at Paris, while not absolutely refusing these requests, first wanted China to complete Western-style legal and administrative reforms: only after China adopted a modern legal system could extraterritoriality be eliminated. Therefore, this complex problem was referred to the newly created League of Nations for further discussion.

On July 25, 1919, the Karakhan Manifesto promised to abolish all of Russia's special rights and privileges in China, including extraterritoriality. On September 27, 1920, Karakhan confirmed these promises in a second manifesto.[5] Finally, on April 24, 1921, the Comintern's Siberian journal stated: "The Soviet Government renounces all privileges, which were used by the tsarist government, such as extraterritoriality of Russian officials, priests, and others."[6]

During the fall of 1920, the Peking government used the Karakhan manifesto to abolish all extraterritorial rights for White Russians living in China. After receiving protests from the diplomatic corps, however, Foreign Minister Yen explained on October 22, 1920, that Russian citizens residing in China would continue to enjoy their former treaty rights. But, on December 10, 1920, the senior consul in Peking reported that all Russians would actually be treated like other nontreaty residents. This decision led one legal scholar to conclude: "The action of the Chinese Government in suspending the functions of the Russian diplomatic representation in China did not abolish the existing Treaties between China and Russia, though it placed Russians enjoying the privileges of extraterritorial rights under the jurisdiction of the native authorities."[7]

As a result, Russians were actually tried in a special Shanghai mixed court under the supervision of N. A. Ivanov, the former tsarist Russian vice consul-general and consular judge. From February 18, 1921 until October 15, 1924, when the practice was abolished, Russians continued to be tried under Russian law. But it is important to note that whenever Russian law conflicted with the Chinese provisional criminal code or "contravened the lawful interests of the Chinese population," then Chinese law and customs were followed.[8]

Peking's unilateral action against the White Russians threatened the extraterritorial rights of all other foreigners living in China. This led to protests accusing Peking of taking advantage of the Karakhan Manifesto to open relations with Moscow, a charge that Peking officials denied.[9] Although China's delegation to the 1921-22 Washington Conference once again demanded that all extraterritorial rights be eliminated immediately, the Washington Conference determined that extraterritoriality should remain until China completed comprehensive legal reforms.

On February 6, 1922, the nine nations signing the *Nine Power Treaty* agreed "to respect the sovereignty, independence, and territorial and administrative inviolability of China," and also to "abstain, at the present time in the Chinese theater, from striving for special rights and advantages."[10] The Washington Conference's ultimate goal was to give Peking time to carry out Western-style legislative and judicial reforms, after which China would obtain international recognition as an equal.[11] To help achieve this goal, the Washington Conference powers set up a commission "to assist and further the efforts of the Chinese Government to effect such legislation and judicial reforms as would warrant the several Powers in relinquishing either progressively or otherwise their respective rights of extraterritoriality."[12]

The Washington Conference's gradual approach toward eliminating extraterritoriality in China attempted to copy Japan's experience. From the 1850s until 1899 Japan had also been subjected to so-called unequal treaty relations with Western nations, but instead of protesting these inequalities, the Meiji government had quickly developed a Western legal system. Its efforts culminated in the 1896 adoption of a legal code based on the German model.[13] Once Japan adopted a modern legal code and court system, then all foreign extraterritorial rights were abolished in 1899. Meanwhile, Japanese citizens soon obtained extraterritorial rights in China like the other foreigners.[14]

Extraterritoriality was not a legal system that only benefited European nations. Not only did Japan fully participate in it, but China also demanded, and received, extraterritorial rights in areas that were even more backward. For example, in its 1915 tripartite treaty with Outer Mongolia, China inserted a clause stating that Han Chinese in Outer Mongolia were not subject to Mongolian law but should be tried under Chinese law instead.[15] China's very success in gaining extraterritoriality in Outer Mongolia shows that the legal structure that Bolshevik-supported propaganda denounced as being merely "unequal" actually helped developing countries adopt Western legal customs and procedures gradually.

During the spring of 1923, however, domestic developments in China derailed Washington's goal of eliminating extraterritorial rights soon. On May 6, 1923, Chinese bandits hijacked a train near Lincheng, Shantung, killing one British citizen and kidnapping twenty foreign tourists. The "Lincheng incident" threatened to delay the convening of an international conference to discuss the elimination of extraterritoriality in China by highlighting Peking's apparent inability to quell rampant social unrest.

On June 7, 1923, as a direct result of the Lincheng incident, Secretary of State Hughes met with Sao-Ke Alfred Sze, the Chinese minister to the United States, and warned: "It was idle for China to disclaim, as she had at the Washington Conference with respect to her sovereignty and her political integrity and her rights as a nation while, at the same time, she failed to provide a Government which could exercise a competent authority throughout her national territory, discharge her international obligations, and afford a basis for the development that all friends of China desired to see."[16]

Hughes's criticism suggests that Peking's inability to protect foreigners' security was the major obstacle to Washington's goal of eliminating extraterritoriality.

During December 1925, the American Chamber of Commerce in Tientsin also complained that it was "not so much the state of the promulgated laws as the manner in which in practice the laws of China are administered." As a result, this organization cautioned: "It is submitted that until such time as China's control of all of China is absolute, until such time as its Judicial System is capable of free and independent action and its order and judgments operative and effective within the area of its jurisdiction and over military and administrative officials any question of relinquishing extraterritoriality or even of fixing a definite time in the future when such relinquishment should take place is entirely premature irrespective of the condition of the Chinese law or the manner in which it is administered."[17]

During 1922, the nations participating in the Washington Conference agreed to work with Peking to eliminate extraterritoriality, but only after China had adopted judicial reforms and practices that would make her legal system conform to international norms, as Japan had done a quarter of a century earlier. Although the Washington Conference clearly hoped that China would complete those reforms that were necessary to eliminate her unequal status, this goal was undermined by Soviet-backed propaganda claiming that China's domestic problems were a *result* of the "unequal" treaties, not a *symptom* of China's preexisting backwardness. Moscow's propaganda was bolstered by its apparent fulfillment of promises to eliminate extraterritoriality, as outlined in the May 31, 1924 Sino-Soviet Treaty.

The May 31, 1924 Sino-Soviet Treaty

In sharp contrast to the Washington Conference's support for the gradual relinquishment of extraterritoriality, Karakhan's 1919 and 1920 manifestos promised the immediate abolition of tsarist Russia's extraterritorial rights. Once these generous-sounding Soviet offers were confirmed by treaty, as they apparently were during 1924, then Peking officials could use this treaty as diplomatic leverage to demand that the other foreigners also give up their own extraterritorial rights prior to China's completion of comprehensive legal reforms. This demand ultimately stymied China's gradual transition toward a Western-style legal system.

On September 4, 1923, when Lev Karakhan arrived in Peking as the ambassador extraordinary of the USSR, he repeated that the USSR had already promised to maintain relations with China on the basis of "complete and absolute equality."[18] Later, Karakhan recommended that after China extended full diplomatic recognition to the USSR, the Sino-Soviet conference should discuss how Soviet citizens living in China would be treated once extraterritoriality had been abolished.[19] As a result of these negotiations, it was agreed that Russia's extraterritorial rights would actually remain in effect until an official conference was convened one month after the signing of the Sino-Soviet treaty.

In public, however, Karakhan repeatedly promised that the Soviet Union intended to abolish extraterritoriality. This promise was included both in a draft

Sino-Soviet treaty, dated March 14, 1924, and also in the final version of the Sino-Soviet treaty, signed on May 31, 1924, by Lev Karakhan and Wellington Koo, the foreign minister of China. According to Article XII in the section entitled "An Agreement on the General Principles for the Settlement of Problems Between the USSR and the Chinese Republic," the USSR "agrees to relinquish the rights of extraterritoriality and consular jurisdiction."[20]

Although it appeared that Moscow had bested the Washington Conference powers by renouncing extraterritoriality prior to China's adoption of a Western-style legal system, in reality, by specifying that Russia's extraterritorial rights would be abolished only at the upcoming Sino-Soviet conference, simply by postponing this conference Soviet citizens continued to enjoy extraterritorial rights. Meanwhile, Soviet-funded propaganda continued to proclaim that all of China's problems were due to the "unequal" treaties. For example, Karakhan explained in a 1925 speech: "Chinese people indeed suffer much from the disgraceful policy of imperialism and from not less disgraceful unequal treaties which bound by chains the living body of China."[21]

Although the USSR actually retained its extraterritorial rights, eight well-known Chinese intellectuals–including Wellington Koo–sent an open letter to the foreign legations demanding that they follow the Soviet government's lead in renouncing extraterritoriality: "[I]t would be well for the foreign nations or their agents in China, who still exercise special rights of a political character nowhere enjoyed by foreigners in other civilized lands, to seek to understand the viewpoint of the Chinese people."[22]

Chinese diplomats like Koo certainly knew the truth behind the outwardly friendly Sino-Soviet relations, but they were prepared to take the risk of allowing the USSR to retain temporarily its special rights and privileges so that they could continue to use the Soviet promises to exert pressure on the other foreign powers. The Peking government, and later the Kuomintang government in Nanking, thus adopted a dual policy whereby they actively sponsored the myth that the USSR had already abolished extraterritoriality, while simultaneously adopting harsh legal measures to undermine and destroy the threat posed by the Bolsheviks and their sympathizers in China.

The USSR's Nationalization of Foreign Trade

Soviet citizens living and working in China effectively retained extraterritorial rights after May 31, 1924. One important method that Moscow used to accomplish this task was its 1923 decision to nationalize foreign trade, since this meant that all Soviet citizens engaged in trade with China had to be government officials. According to the USSR's legal interpretation, this made all Soviet merchants eligible for "diplomatic immunity," which was a privilege that the other major powers reserved only for diplomats.[23]

During September 1923, the Soviet mission to Peking announced that the Russian Socialist Federative Soviet Republic had joined with the Ukraine,

Belorussia, Azerbaijan, Georgia, and Armenia to form the Union of Soviet Socialist Republics. In accordance with the USSR's new constitution, which came into force on July 6, 1923, all diplomatic and commercial relations between the USSR and China would be carried out by the People's Commissariat for Foreign Affairs and the People's Commissariat for Foreign Trade.[24]

Thereafter, a separate declaration dated July 13, 1923, specified that all foreign trade was now a "state monopoly" under the direct control of the Soviet central government (see Document 23). What this really meant was that all Soviet citizens involved in foreign trade with China had to be Soviet government officials.[25] By means of this document, the Soviet government attempted to legitimize its decision to grant all Soviet businessmen in China the special legal protection of "diplomatic immunity." Thus, although in 1924 the Soviet government forfeited–in theory at least–the legal protection provided to Soviet businessmen under extraterritoriality, during 1923 it had already secured the equally effective right of diplomatic immunity for its commercial agents living and working in China.

Since about the only Russians able to travel to China during the 1920s were diplomats or merchants, the nationalization of foreign trade provided virtually all Soviet citizens with effective extraterritorial rights; one scholar has even concluded that "it is important to note that there were no Russians in China other than [those in] official capacities."[26] In sharp contrast to the USSR, however, the Western nations and Japan had large numbers of private businessmen, educators, missionaries, and tourists visiting China every year. These visitors could only receive special legal protection under extraterritoriality, since they were not eligible for diplomatic immunity.

While the Bolsheviks' public offers to abolish extraterritoriality resulted in an enormous outpouring of sympathy for the USSR throughout China, the nationalization of foreign trade granted virtually all Soviet citizens the equally effective legal protection of diplomatic immunity. By resorting to this sleight of hand, Soviet propaganda in China could publicly denounce the Western countries and Japan for not giving up extraterritoriality, while secretly retaining equivalent rights for its own citizens.

Although the May 31, 1924 Sino-Soviet treaty had promised to abolish extraterritoriality and consular jurisdiction at a future conference, Karakhan time and time again delayed negotiations to revise the terms of tsarist Russia's former treaties with China. As a result, the official Sino-Soviet conference was postponed until August 1925. But, once it convened, Soviet diplomats immediately attempted to confirm by treaty that Soviet businessmen would enjoy both extraterritoriality and the right of consular jurisdiction. This meant that the USSR attempted not only to regain Russia's former special rights and privileges, but also to extend their scope beyond that accorded to other foreigners.

Translated from the
Authentic Russian Text

DECLARATION OF THE UNION OF SOVIET SOCIALIST REPUBLICS

To all Nations and Governments of the World

On July 6 the Declaration and the Covenant, adopted by the Soviet Republics which entered into the Union, were approved by the Central Executive Committee of the Union and came into force.

In view of the necessity for Soviet Republics to join their forces for the defence against outside attacks, a united People's Commissariat of the Union for War and Navy was created.

In view of the fact that the Soviet Republics have common tasks and interests in the face of capitalist States, there was organized a United People's Commissariat of the Union for Foreign Affairs.

The necessity of full centralization in the conduct of foreign trade on the basis of State monopoly, in order to protect the Soviet Republics from any attempt of capitalist States to enslave them, has compelled them to create a united People's Commissariat of the Union for Foreign Trade.

Chairmen of the Central Executive Committee of the Union of Soviet Socialist Republics:

(Signed) M. I. Kalinin

G. I. Petrowsky

N. N. Narimanov

A. G. Cherviakov

Members of the Presidium of the Central Executive Committee of the Union of Soviet Socialist Republics:

(Signed) Enukidze, Kamenev, Kon, Kursky,

Manuilsky, Miasnikian, Rakowsky,

Rudzetak, Rykov, Sapronov,

Smidowitch, Stalin, Tomsky,

Zhakaya, Hibir-Aliev.

Secretary of the Central Executive Committee of the Union of Soviet Socialist Republics:

(Signed) A. Enukidze.

Moscow, Kremlin, July 13th, 1923.

Document 23
July 13, 1923 Soviet Letter Stating All Foreign Trade Was a State Monopoly

Due to the absolute secrecy surrounding the 1925 Sino-Soviet conference, it was never formerly reported that Moscow attempted to reinstate extraterritoriality. But the Soviet draft demanded this right (see Document 24): "The Trade Representative of the USSR and the members of the Council of the Trade Mission shall, independently of their actual domicile, constitute an indivisible part of the Diplomatic Representation of the U.S.S.R. in China and shall enjoy besides the extraterritorial status of their offices and warehouses, the privilege and immunities to the members of the Diplomatic Missions."[27]

If Peking had accepted this proposal, then all Soviet offices and warehouses would have once again enjoyed extraterritoriality, while all Soviet citizens engaged in trade with China would have officially been granted diplomatic immunity. On January 10, 1926, Peking criticized the Soviet proposal to grant extraterritoriality to members of their trade mission. The Peking protest criticized Moscow for its blatant attempt "to invest the so-called Russian Trade Mission in China with a diplomatic character," and concluded that if the Soviet proposal were accepted: "Apart from the juridical question of the recognition of the Russian State monopoly of foreign trade in China, the stipulation . . . would tend to produce practical consequences not altogether desirable."[28]

Although Peking protested Moscow's proposal, the Soviet diplomats continued to retain Russia's former special rights and privileges in China simply by stonewalling negotiations, which they did through 1929. Since Peking could not easily prevent Moscow from granting diplomatic immunity to those citizens that it chose, Soviet businessmen continued to claim this right. This claim put Soviet citizens in China in a rather unique legal position, since at the same time that they could publicly state that they had given up extraterritoriality, they could privately claim equivalent rights under consular jurisdiction.

Two Case Studies of Soviet Extraterritoriality

Soviet diplomats' attempts to secure both extraterritoriality and consular jurisdiction meant that Soviet citizens in China lived in a legal "limbo," where their true rights remained open to a wide range of juridical interpretations. As a result, Soviet diplomats attempted to turn these legal ambiguities to their advantage by alternately claiming and disclaiming extraterritoriality as suited their purposes. Two case studies provide pertinent details about how the USSR used these apparently conflicting legal positions to its advantage.

On June 30, 1925, British authorities in Hong Kong arrested Z. N. Dosser, a Soviet citizen who said he represented the All-Union Oil Syndicate of the Far East. The British claimed instead that he was a Soviet agent and charged him with organizing anti-British strike committees in Hong Kong and Canton. Dosser's case was subsequently transferred to the mixed courts in Shanghai for trial. But on July 6, Foreign Minister Chicherin, sent an official protest to Minister Li, challenging the legal jurisdiction of the Shanghai mixed courts over Dosser.

A R T I C L E III.

The State Monopoly of Foreign Trade having been established in the U. S. S. R. and the Commercial relations between the U. S. S. R. and China having to be pursued from the Soviet side through the organs of this monopoly the Trade Mission of the U. S. S. R. in China and its offices in all important commercial centres on the Chinese territory, the Government of the Chinese Republic agrees to affort to the said organisations most fabourable possibilities and conditons for the attaining of their purpose of developing, facilitating and regulating the commercial relations between the U. S. S. R. and China. To that purpose and taking into account the Governmental character of these organizations, the Chinese Government confirms that the Trade Representative of the U. S. S. R. and the members of the Council of theTrade Mission shall, independently of their actual domicile, constitute an indivisible part of the the Diplomatic Representation of the U. S. S. R. in China and shall enjoy besides the extraterritorial status of their offices and warehouses, the privileges andimmunities accorded to the members of diplomatic Missions.

Document 24
The Soviet Union's Fall 1925 Draft on Trade and Navigation

In this protest, Foreign Minister Chicherin pointedly reminded Minister Li that on July 25, 1919 and September 27, 1920 the Soviet government had renounced extraterritoriality in China. According to Chicherin's interpretation, therefore, by the terms of the Sino-Soviet treaty of May 31, 1924, Soviet citizens on Chinese territory were solely under the legal jurisdiction of the Chinese courts. As a result, Chicherin claimed that Dosser's arraignment in Shanghai's mixed courts was a "direct violation of the agreement between China and the USSR from May 31, 1924," and he demanded that Peking officials immediately intervene with the Shanghai mixed court to free Dosser: "On the basis of this exposition, on behalf of my government, I entreat you, Gentleman Minister to take urgent measures for the liberation of the Soviet citizen Dosser, seized on Chinese territory by foreign powers."[29]

As shown by this case, Moscow attempted to use its formal renunciation of extraterritoriality to free Dosser from the legal jurisdiction of the Shanghai mixed courts. By doing so, Soviet diplomats hoped to exempt Soviet citizens from crimes committed within foreign-administered territories throughout China, such as in Hong Kong. If successful, this strategy would have granted Soviet citizens special Chinese-guaranteed immunities within the foreign concessions, a kind of extraterritoriality from extraterritoriality.

But, in similar cases where it was the Peking government that accused Soviet citizens of crimes committed on Chinese territory, Soviet diplomats acted quite differently. For example, on February 28, 1927, Chinese authorities impounded the *Banner of Lenin*, a Soviet-registered ship accused of transporting communist propaganda to cities along the Yangtze River. If true, then the Soviet ship had indeed violated the May 31, 1924 Sino-Soviet treaty, which clearly prohibited the distribution of propaganda. In a note dated March 5, 1927, however, the USSR did not challenge the validity of China's accusation, but instead condemned China's seizure as a "clear violation of the principles of international law."[30]

Ignoring its earlier insistence that Soviet citizens were subject only to Chinese courts, on March 10, Moscow also protested the arrest of three Soviet diplomatic couriers, who were passengers on this ship: "It is even more clear, that without a doubt the [Chinese] Ministry of Foreign Affairs is working in close coordination with the same local authorities who are implicated in this monstrous crime." Thereafter, on March 17, a third Soviet protest reiterated that Peking's decision to impound the Soviet ship operating in Chinese waters represented a "violent action, directed against the USSR, which transgressed the elemental principles of international law."[31]

These two cases provide graphic examples of how the Soviet government tried to use to its advantage the amorphous legal standing of Soviet citizens in China. On the one hand, by insisting that the USSR had renounced extraterritoriality, Moscow tried to remove its citizens from the jurisdiction of the Shanghai mixed courts, and thus protect them from being held accountable to international law. But, on the other hand, when the Chinese government took legal action against Soviet citizens, the Soviet government tried to hold China accountable for violating international law. In effect, Moscow was now appealing for protection under the very same international legal system that it had so recently attempted to circumvent.

Soviet Diplomats Retain Extraterritoriality

Even after the Sino-Soviet break in 1927, Soviet citizens continued to enjoy quasi-extraterritorial rights throughout China by claiming diplomatic immunity in place of extraterritoriality and by insisting that the terms of tsarist Russia's unequal treaties with China continued to apply until revised by new treaties. Increasing Sino-Soviet tensions over control of the Chinese Eastern Railway in Manchuria, however, gave the USSR the opportunity to reconfirm its extraterritorial rights by treaty. This official treaty, signed by the Soviet government and the semiautonomous Mukden government on December 22, 1929, restored Sino-Soviet diplomatic relations based on the principles of "international law and customs," a catchword for extraterritoriality and consular jurisdiction. Thereafter, a 1939 Sino-Soviet trade treaty officially extended these special rights to Soviet trade representatives and their offices throughout China.

In May 1929, Sino-Soviet friction boiled over when Chinese police raided the Soviet consulate in Harbin, Manchuria, and arrested a number of Soviet citizens accused of spreading Bolshevik propaganda. In response, on May 21, the USSR declared that "since the Chinese Authorities have proved by all their actions their clear unwillingness and inability to reckon with the generally accepted principle of International law and customs, it on its part does not henceforth regard itself bound by these principles in relation to Chinese representatives in Moscow and Chinese Consulates in Soviet Territory and that this representation and these Consulates will no longer enjoy the extraterritoriality to which International Law entitles them."[32]

Although the USSR accused China of violating international law, a second Soviet statement from December 4, admitted that the USSR had officially renounced extraterritoriality and consular jurisdiction in 1924: "During last year, the Nanking Government, evading the usual methods for settlement of conflicts through diplomatic channels, carried towards the Soviet Union a provocative policy in violation of the usual international rules and treaties, notwithstanding the fact that these treaties were not imposed on China by force of arms or any other forcible method, but were concluded on a basis of full equality and free will, while the Soviet Union, as is known, voluntarily gave up in these treaties the privileges of consular jurisdiction and extraterritoriality and other privileges which the Chinese Government is still trying in vain to abolish in regard to the other Powers."[33]

According to the peculiar logic revealed by these statements, so long as China continued to respect the USSR's extraterritoriality and consular jurisdiction, then the pretense that they had been eliminated would be continued; when these rights were violated, however, the USSR felt justified in forcing China to reconfirm them by treaty. On December 22, 1929, Soviet diplomats signed a treaty with the Chinese government in Mukden, stating that "both parties intend to restore consular relations between them on a basis conforming with the principles of International Law and customs, the Mukden Government declares it undertakes to assure the Soviet Consulates on the territory of the Three Eastern Provinces full inviolability and all privileges to which international law and custom entitle them and will of course refrain from any actions violating this inviolability and these privileges."[34]

This little-known treaty once again guaranteed the USSR the full range of legal protection under extraterritoriality and consular jurisdiction. During the late 1930s, a confidential annex attached to the end of another official Sino-Soviet treaty confirmed that Soviet trade representatives would also enjoy this protection (see Document 25). Signed on June 16, 1939, the annex to the "Treaty of Commerce Between the Republic of China and the Union of Soviet Socialist Republics" stated: "The Trade Representative of the Union of Soviet Socialist Republics and his two deputies shall be regarded as a part of the diplomatic staff of the Embassy of the Union of Soviet Socialist Republics and shall be accorded all the diplomatic rights and privileges which are accorded to the members of diplomatic missions." In addition, the staff of the trade office "shall not be subjected to the jurisdiction of the Courts of China in respect to any question arising out of their official relations to the Trade Representation."[35]

It is important to emphasize that these special rights and privileges were the very same as those that Soviet diplomats had specifically renounced in the May 31, 1924 Sino-Soviet treaty. By signing these 1929 and 1939 treaties, therefore, the Bolsheviks contradicted their numerous public claims to have given up tsarist Russia's unequal treaties with China. But the wall of secrecy surrounding these agreements obscured the USSR's true intentions from the Chinese public. This is perhaps best reflected in Mao Tse-tung's December 20, 1939 birthday greeting to Stalin, in which he insisted: "No other country has renounced its privileges in China; the Soviet Union alone has done so."[36] The majority of Western observers also did not appear to understand the legal ramifications of these Sino-Soviet treaties, and so continued to believe that the USSR had abolished extraterritoriality in China.

Great Britain and the United States Abolish Extraterritoriality

Due to the secrecy with which the Soviet Union carried out its diplomacy with China, Western legal historians have generally concluded that Great Britain's and the United States' 1943 decision to abolish the last vestiges of their extraterritorial rights in China lagged behind the USSR by almost twenty years. Wesley Fishel, the author of *The End of Extraterritoriality in China* and widely acknowledged as one of the leading scholars on this topic, even criticized London and Washington as being the "two major Powers which thus far had escaped complete nullification of their legal rights."[37]

A N N E X

to the Treaty of Commerce between the Republic of China and
the Union of Soviet Socialist Republics
dated June 16, 1939

Concerning

TnE LEGAL STATUS OF THE TRADE REPRESENTATION OF THE UNION OF SOVIET SOCIALIST REPUBLICS IN THE REPUBLIC OF CHINA.

SECTION 1.

The Trade Representation of the Union of Soviet Socialist Republics in the Republic of China shall exercise the following functions:

a) to facilitate the development of economic relations between the Union of Soviet Socialist Republics and the Republic of China;

b) to represent the interests of the Union of Soviet Socialist Republics in all that pertains to foreign trade;

c) to regulate on behalf of the Union of Soviet Socialist Republics the trade between the Union of Soviet Socialist Republics and the Republic of China;

d) to carry on the trade between the Union of Soviet Socialist Republics and the Republic of China.

The Trade Representation of the Union of Soviet Socialist Republics in the Republic of China acting as an organ exercising the monopoly of foreign trade of the Union of Soviet Socialist Republics shall form an integral part of the Embassy of the Union of Soviet Socialist Republics.

The Trade Representation of the Union of Soviet Socialist Republics shall be in the capital of the Republic of China.

The Trade Representative of the Union of Soviet Socialist Republics and his two deputies shall be regarded as a part of the diplomatic staff of the Embassy of the Union of Soviet Socialist Republics and shall be accorded all the diplomatic rights and privileges which are accorded to the members of diplomatic missions.

The Trade Representation of the Union of Soviet Socialist Republics in China shall have their Branches in the following cities: Tientsin, Shanghai, Hankow, Canton and Lanchow.

New Branches of the Trade Representation in China shall be established by agreement between the above mentioned Trade Representation and the competent authorities of the National Government of the Republic of China.

Document 25

Annex Attached to the June 16, 1939 "Treaty of Commerce Between the Republic of China and the Union of Soviet Socialist Republics"

In fact, the archival documents discussed above show that Soviet diplomats effectively retained extraterritorial rights from 1924 to 1929, and that during 1929 and 1939 they reinstated these rights in official Sino-Soviet treaties. Only the absolute secrecy surrounding these diplomatic negotiations allowed China's Nationalist leaders to exert sufficient moral pressure on Great Britain and the United States to force them to eliminate extraterritoriality. As part of this campaign, on April 14, 1942, Madame Chiang Kai-shek published a *New York Times Magazine* article that castigated the West for creating "the vicious legal device known as extraterritoriality."[38]

The enormous wartime outpouring of Western goodwill toward China, coupled with ignorance of the USSR's actual retention of extraterritoriality, convinced American and British diplomats to abolish all of their remaining special rights and privileges in China on January 11, 1943. Simultaneously, all foreign attempts to uphold and enforce international law throughout China ended. For example, the Annex attached to the Sino-British treaty specifically stated: "His Majesty the King relinquishes all existing treaty rights relating to the special courts in the International Settlements at Shanghai and Amoy."[39]

The Chinese populace jubilantly greeted the signing of treaties that accorded China legal equality with Great Britain and the United States. Unheeded went the advice given in 1925 by the American Chamber of Commerce that extraterritoriality should be eliminated only when China's central government met three conditions: 1) its "control of all of China is absolute," 2) "its Judicial System is capable of free and independent action," and 3) "its order and judgments are operative and effective within the area of its jurisdiction and over military and administrative officials."[40] Needless to say, the Nationalist government did not come close to achieving these three conditions by 1943 or during the years that followed. Also, the Chinese public apparently did not realize that the very means by which Great Britain and the United States had formerly protected China from Soviet intervention, namely the adherence to international law in the foreign settlements, was being dismantled right when China was at its weakest.

To the Chinese public at large–a public that was blissfully ignorant of the Soviet Union's almost twenty years of secret diplomacy with China–the elimination of Great Britain's and the United States' final extraterritorial rights seemed to mark a new era for China. As described by Wesley Fishel: "Thus ended a century of legal inequality and semicolonialism for China. The readjustment of its political and economic relations with the countries of the West was not to be a simple matter, but China undertook that task in full possession of its sovereignty, at long last a legally equal member of the family of nations."[41] The Chinese public, completely unaware that the USSR had secretly retained its own special rights and privileges, greeted the British and American renunciation of extraterritoriality with renewed hope.

Conclusions

Previously, legal scholars of China have universally concluded that the Chinese government completely eliminated extraterritoriality by 1943. But archival documents suggest that the USSR actually retained extraterritorial rights well beyond 1943, thus allowing thousands of Soviet officials, Red Army troops, and military and scientific advisers stationed in China to continue to enjoy special legal rights and privileges both during and after World War II that had been eliminated for most other foreigners. By means of its secret diplomacy, the Soviet Union retained its "unequal" treaties many years longer than the American and British governments.

As discussed above, once the myth that the USSR treated China equally was created it became very difficult to disprove, since all of the Peking government's Foreign Ministry records showing that the reverse was actually the case remained confidential. Shortly after the KMT's 1927 split with the Soviet Union and its purge of the Chinese Communist Party, as well as after the reunification of China under the auspices of the Kuomintang in 1928, Wellington Koo and C. T. Wang took charge of renegotiating China's unequal treaties with the capitalist nations. But while the KMT-controlled Nanking government quickly signed new treaties with the United States, Great Britain, and Japan, a KMT source published in November 1929, acknowledged that Moscow had ignored thirty Chinese requests from 1924-29 to renegotiate the former Sino-Russian treaties.[42]

In fact, only after the United States and Great Britain completely eliminated all of their remaining extraterritorial rights and special privileges in China on January 11, 1943, did Chiang Kai-shek for the first time confirm that "the Sino-Soviet Agreement concluded on the basis of equality was not fully carried out."[43] Only then did the truly unfriendly nature of Sino-Soviet relations become apparent. China's repeated attempts to use the USSR as leverage prompted Hsu Shu-hsi, Director of the Kuomintang's Department of Russian Affairs, to warn Foreign Minister T. V. Soong on September 28, 1944, that: "she [Russia] would have to be angelic in nature, if she were not to harbor a grudge against us."[44]

Following World War II, the USSR once again began to encroach upon China. But, unlike in the 1920s, when China could depend on the capitalist powers to intercede if necessary to limit Soviet excesses–as they did in Nanking during March 1927–the KMT had virtually guaranteed that foreign intervention would not take place. For example, the Sino-American treaty abolishing extraterritoriality explicitly stated: "It is mutually understood that the Government of the United States of America relinquishes the special rights which naval vessels of the United States of America have been accorded in the waters of the Republic of China."[45] On February 20, 1948, Secretary of State George C. Marshall explained to the House Committee on Foreign Affairs what impact this clause had on America's China policy: "Strong Chinese sensibilities regarding infringement of China's sovereignty . . . argue strongly against attempting any such [military] solution."[46] Faced with renewed Soviet aggression in China, America stood aside.

Notes

1. Extraterritoriality, or the "removal of diplomatic premises from the control of the state in which they are situated," should not be confused with extraterritorial jurisdiction, defined as the "exercise of authority over activities or persons outside the boundaries of the territory in which the acting body sits" (*Dictionary of International and Comparative Law*, 147). For articles discussing extraterritorial jurisdiction, see: Alan Simon and Spencer Waller, "A Theory of Economic Sovereignty: An Alternative to Extraterritorial Jurisdictional Disputes," *Stanford Journal of International Law*, Vol. XXII; No. 2, 1986, 337-360; Abraham Abramovsky, "Extraterritorial Jurisdiction: The United States Unwarranted Attempt to Alter International Law in *United States v. Yunis*," *The Yale Journal of International Law*, Vol. 15; No. 121, 1990, 121-161.

2. Official Chinese-language copy of the Sino-Soviet Treaty, May 31, 1924, WCTA, 03-32, 454(1).

3. Wesley R. Fishel, *The End of Extraterritoriality in China*, 207.

4. Chu Pao-chin, *V. K. Wellington Koo: A Case Study of China's Diplomat and Diplomacy of Nationalism, 1912-1966*, 15-16.

5. Chinese-language Karakhan manifesto, October 2, 1920, WCTA, 03-32, 479(1).

6. *Бюллетени Дальне-восточного Секретариата Коминтерна* (*Bulletins of the Far Eastern Secretariat of the Comintern*), No. 5, Irkutsk, April 24, 1921, 3.

7. Anatol M. Kotenev, *Shanghai: Its Mixed Court and Council*, 227-230.

8. *Ibid.*, 227-230.

9. "China for Harmony," *The Washington Post*, October 2, 1920.

10. E. D. Grimm (Гримм Е. Д.), *Сборник договоров и других документов по истории международных отношений на Дальнем Востоке (1842-1925)* (*Collection of Treaties and Other Documents on the History of International Relations in the Far East [1842-1925]*), 204–209.

11. That American concerns about eliminating extraterritoriality in China were justified is best shown by referring to a 1924 letter from Li Chia-ao, Peking's minister to the USSR, where he proposed gradually exiling the White Russian leaders who were causing the USSR trouble back to the Soviet Union. Li then recommended that those Russians who were not exiled immediately could be arrested and imprisoned indefinitely in Chinese prisons simply by claiming that they were subject to Chinese law. It was exactly this kind of judicial abuse that concerned Washington. Chinese-language letter from China's Minister to the USSR Li Chia-ao to Foreign Minister Wellington Koo, January 18, 1924, WCTA, 03-32, 461(3).

12. *Memorandum of the American Chamber of Commerce of Tientsin Relative to Extraterritoriality in China*, 4.

13. As a result of Japan's comprehensive legal and social reforms, Carol Gluck has concluded: "Japan in 1865 bore small resemblance to the Japan of 1890" (*Japan's Modern Myths, Ideology in the Late Meiji Period*, 37).

14. Foreigners in China considered extraterritoriality to be an important legal protection, because public torture and executions were still common in China through the 1920s. For example, when stationed in China during the 1920s, Joseph Stilwell described the following public execution: "Executions were equally popular, watched by eager crowds as the victim with hands bound was kicked to his knees and his head severed by a stroke of the heavy sword to admiring shouts of *Hao!* When the blood spurted, women and children rushed forward to dip strings of copper coins in it which were then hung around the

children's necks to frighten away evil spirits" (Barbara W. Tuchman, *Stilwell and the American Experience in China, 1911-45*, 67).

15. S. C. M. Paine, *Imperial Rivals: China, Russia, and Their Disputed Frontier*, 287-305.

16. Paul Hibbert Clyde, ed., *United States Policy Toward China*, 284-285.

17. *Memorandum of the American . . .* , 4.

18. Russian-language minutes of Karakhan's speech, September 4, 1923, WCTA, 03-32, 467(1).

19. Chinese-language minutes of the conversation between Karakhan and Chu Ho-hsiang, February 2, 1924,WCTA, 03-32, 487(1).

20. Official Chinese-language copy of the Sino-Soviet Treaty, May 31, 1924, WCTA, 03-32, 454(1).

21. English-language transcript of Karakhan's speech, August 26, 1925, WCTA, 03-32, 503 (3).

22. *The China Yearbook*, 1926, 932-933.

23. Joan Donoghue has described the debate over foreign state immunity in terms of the Communist governments' support for an "absolute theory" of immunity, as opposed to the Western governments' "restrictive theory" which differentiated between "governmental" acts versus "commercial" or "private" acts. By advocating this view, the Soviet government tried to include Soviet trade representatives under consular jurisdiction ("Taking the 'Sovereign' Out of the Foreign Sovereign Immunities Act: A Functional Approach to the Commercial Activity Exception," *The Yale Journal of International Law*, Vol. 17, No.489, 1992, 489-538).

24. Russian-language letter, September 5, 1923,WCTA, 03-32, 461(3).

25. English-language declaration, July 13, 1923, WCTA, 03-32, 461(3).

26. Vera Vladimirovna Vishnyakova-Akimova. *Two Years in Revolutionary China, 1925-1927*, xiv.

27. Soviet Draft on Trade and Navigation, Fall 1925, WCTA, 03-32, 506(7).

28. English-language protest by the Peking government to the Soviet Union, January 10, 1926, WCTA, 03-32, 536(4).

29. Russian-language text of Foreign Minister Chicherin's Protest to Minister Li, July 6, 1925, WCTA, 03-32, 500(3).

30. F. S. Borodina (Ф. С. Бородина), *В Застенках Китайскых Сатрапов* (*In the Torture-chambers of the Chinese Satrapies*), 131-132.

31. *Ibid.*, 132-133, 135-139.

32. *The Japan Advertiser*, December 23, 1929.

33. *The Japan Advertiser*, December 5, 1929.

34. *The Japan Advertiser*, December 23, 1929.

35. "Treaty of Commerce Between the Republic of China and the Union of Soviet Socialist Republics." June 16, 1939, Hoover Institution Archives, T. V. Soong Collection, Schedule A, Box 23.

36. *Selected Works of Mao Tse-tung*, Vol. 2, 335-336.

37. Fishel, 207.

38. Madame Chiang Kai-shek, "First Lady of the East Speaks to the West," *New York Times Magazine*, April 14, 1942, 5; quoted in Julia Fukuda Cosgrove, *United States Foreign Economic Policy Toward China, 1943-1946*, 46.

39. William L. Tung, *China and the Foreign Powers: The Impact of and Reaction to Unequal Treaties*, 468.

40. *Memorandum of the American* . . . , 4.

41. Fishel, 215.

42. 中俄關於中東路之交涉事略 (*A History of Sino-Russian Negotiations on the Chinese Eastern Railway*), 36.

43. Chiang Kai-shek, *China's Destiny,* 143-144.

44. Memorandum from Hsu Shu-hsi to T. V. Soong, September 28, 1944, Hoover Institution Archives, T. V. Soong collection, Schedule A, Box No. 30.

45. "Treaty Between the United States and China for the Relinquishment of Extraterritorial Rights in China and the Regulation of Related Matters, Signed at Washington, January 11, 1943, With Accompanying Exchange of Notes," *The China White Paper, August 1949*, 514-519.

46. *Ibid.*, 380-384.

8
Soviet Foreign Policy and the Chinese Communist Party

From 1921 to 1927 the CCP championed Soviet efforts to renew the terms of the tsarist Russian unequal treaties. Previously, the close coordination between the Comintern's and the Soviet Commissariat of Foreign Affairs' (Narkomindel) policies in China during the 1920s was questioned, with one noted historian even comparing the USSR's "divergent policies" in China to "an acrobat juggling several balls in the air."[1] But the publication of the personal archives of perhaps the most important Comintern agent in China, Maring, has helped clarify that these two Soviet-funded organizations actually worked closely together.[2]

This cooperation was especially important during the 1924 Sino-Soviet negotiations, when the Comintern helped rally Chinese public opinion to support Soviet diplomats in Peking. Central to Moscow's success was the Comintern's decision to found the CCP during 1921, and then its order to enter into an alliance with the KMT during 1922 to augment the ability of Sun Yat-sen and the KMT to marshal Chinese public opinion in support of Soviet diplomacy. The Chinese communists then backed the Soviet diplomats both confidentially, in their party resolutions, and publicly, in their official journals like *Hsiang-tao Chou-bao* [嚮導週報] (*The Guide Weekly*) and *Ch'ien-feng* [前鋒] (*The Vanguard*).

The most dramatic example of this coordination was over Outer Mongolia. According to Moscow, the terms of the 1915 tsarist treaty would remain valid until renegotiated, which could only happen if representatives from China, Russia, and Outer Mongolia met. To include an Outer Mongolian representative in the negotiations, however, would have tacitly recognized Outer Mongolia's autonomy. For this reason, Peking refused, claiming that Moscow was attempting to renew the most onerous section of the 1915 unequal treaty, i.e., that Sino-Mongolian agreements could only be negotiated with Russia's participation and approval.

The USSR's victory in Outer Mongolia would not have been possible without the full cooperation of the Comintern and the CCP. Instead of siding with Peking in opposing all former Sino-Russian unequal treaties, the CCP supported Moscow. In addition to passing party resolutions supporting Outer Mongolia's autonomy, the CCP's official journals publicly called for the convening of a Sino-Soviet-Mongolian conference in which a representative from Outer Mongolia would be treated as an equal. By taking this stance, the CCP actively supported the USSR's attempts to renew the terms of the 1915 unequal treaty. But the CCP supported Soviet efforts to maintain Outer Mongolia as a Russian protectorate only in return for the Comintern's promise that Outer Mongolia would revert to China after the communist revolution succeeded. When Stalin dissolved the Comintern in 1943, however, he unilaterally canceled this promise.

The Formation of the Chinese Communist Party

Soon after Maring arrived in China during April 1921, he brought the United Front Policy to an important new stage by helping to establish the Chinese Communist Party and to form the United Front with the Kuomintang. Maring's support for the United Front was well known, since he backed Lenin at the second Comintern congress in 1920 by stating that it was not a matter of *whether* to work with the bourgeoisie, but of *how* to work with them.[3] Maring has since been given sole credit for having proposed greater cooperation between the KMT and the CCP. In fact, Maring's contribution was merely to persuade the CCP to adopt this preexisting policy over the opposition of its major leaders.

Following a 1935 interview with Maring, Harold Isaacs reported that when Maring arrived in China he had "no specific instructions" from the Comintern, and his "only prior preparation was the discussions and theses of the Second World Congress of the Comintern."[4] This comment was previously interpreted to mean that forming a KMT/CCP United Front did not originate directly with the Comintern, but with Maring himself.[5] But, if Ch'en Tu-hsiu's official position as head of Canton's Education Committee is considered as an early stage of the United Front, then Maring's task was simply to further this preexisting policy.[6]

Maring traveled to Shanghai during June 1921. According to one scholar, it was Maring who suggested that a party congress be held, a plan that was received "enthusiastically" by the members of the Marxist study groups.[7] During the first day of the CCP's founding congress, Maring took charge during a five-hour speech: "Deciding the program and furnishing funds was completely in the hands of Maring."[8] But, Maring's support for the United Front prompted an acrimonious debate, during which he took the unusual position of opposing the more "orthodox" Marxists.[9] As a result, the CCP's Executive Committee decided not to publish the party manifesto, since it was too critical of Sun; one delegate at the first congress reported that this manifesto stated that the "government of Dr. Sun Yat-sen was no better than the government of the northern militarist party."[10] Maring also tried to convince the Chinese communists to join the Comintern, which they did during 1922.[11]

During late 1921, Maring pressured the CCP to work with the KMT. On April 6, 1922, Ch'en protested in a letter to Voitinskii in Moscow that the CCP would be hurt by this alliance, since people thought the KMT was a political group "fighting for power and profit." In addition, Ch'en claimed comrades in Canton, "Peking, Shanghai, Changsha, [and] Wuchang" were "absolutely not in favor" of working with the KMT.[12] Ch'en's warning about CCP antipathy to the KMT was confirmed by Sergei Dalin. In meetings with CCP leaders in Canton, Dalin urged them to display three types of slogans during the 1922 May Day parade. Slogans pertaining to foreign affairs included "Down with the foreign imperialists" and "Long live Soviet Russia," while domestic slogans were aimed against the "Chinese reaction." Finally, a third set of slogans were in support of Sun and the KMT. On May Day, Dalin recalled that besides holding up copies of Marx and

Engels, Chinese workers carried rare items like Trotsky's newly published book *October Revolution*, but he did not see a single slogan supporting Sun Yat-sen.[13]

Articles debating the United Front appeared in a variety of journals in both China and Soviet Russia. In China, the CCP opposed the KMT's leadership of the United Front, accusing it of being just like other warlord groups, since it advocated forming a private army to reunite China under its control and had already formed alliances with warlords Ch'en Chiung-ming in Canton and Chang Tso-lin in Mukden. In addition, the CCP questioned whether the KMT was a party or merely a faction revolving around Sun and his clique. In 1913, it should be recalled, Ch'en refused to join Sun Yat-sen's earlier revolutionary party, because it required that all members take a blood oath directly to Sun.[14]

On May 23, 1922, Ch'en Tu-hsiu publicly voiced his opposition to the KMT's leadership of China's revolutionary movement, warning that in the near future the "Kuomintang's most important work would be its war with the feudalistic northern warlords." Ch'en further claimed that only the CCP could assume the two most important tasks in China's revolution: "[T]o be the first to stand up to benefit, struggle, and sacrifice for the working class," and "to supervise the other parties to make sure that they do not have the opportunity to use the worker's movement to gain bureaucratic power or wealth."[15]

But, during spring 1922, Maring argued that since workers' unions were most developed in Canton, the Comintern had no choice but "completely to support the national-revolutionary elements in the South." By unifying all "revolutionary-nationalist elements," and then by using the CCP to shift this movement to the left, Maring predicted that China's revolution could be pushed "into cooperating with Soviet Russia and with us–the communists–and opens the possibility of vastly productive work in union with the Chinese revolutionaries."[16]

The central Comintern leadership in Moscow ignored Ch'en's concerns, therefore, and supported the KMT's leadership of the United Front. But, the CCP's continued opposition threatened the Comintern's adoption of this plan: according to Dalin, many other CCP leaders joined Ch'en and "stubbornly did not agree to enter into a bloc with the petty bourgeoisie."[17] As a result of Dalin's constant prodding, however, the CCP published an invitation in the June 20, 1922 issue of *Hsien-ch'u* [先驅] (*The Pioneer*), to hold a conference to organize the United Front. Once again, the CCP's distrust resurfaced in its warning that if the KMT compromised with the "northern warlords," it would surely be defeated.[18]

Ignoring all opposition, the Comintern ordered the CCP to forge a "democratic United Front of workers, poor peasants, and petty bourgeoisie."[19] It also adopted the following order: "The Central Committee of the Communist Party of China, according to the decision of the Presidium of the Comintern 18 July, must remove its seat to Canton immediately after receiving this note and do all its work in close contact with Comrade [Maring]."[20] Since Canton was still under Sun's control in July 1922, this order clearly supported a KMT-led United Front.

While, in May 1922, the CCP called on "the oppressed masses, the workers, and peasants to rally under the party's own banner in the struggle for the democratic revolution,"[21] in June, the CCP admitted that "only the Kuomintang was a comparatively revolutionary democratic faction,"[22] and by July, the CCP was ordered to accept a KMT-led United Front. These rapid changes show that in May the CCP still thought it was the leader of China's revolution, but by July had been demoted to a secondary role once the Comintern decided that only the KMT could lead the United Front. This was nothing new, it was simply the final stage in the pro-KMT policy first proposed by Chicherin and Karakhan in 1918.

The Comintern Orders the CCP to Join the United Front

During August 1922, Maring ordered the Chinese communists to join the KMT as individuals. An August 1922 Comintern telegram supported Maring, proving that the United Front was sanctioned at the highest levels of the Comintern. Moscow clearly had high hopes for this policy, as shown in a *Pravda* article's claim that the KMT's organization of 50,000 Chinese workers during the Canton strikes proved that it was possible for a "thorough and serious attempt to unite the revolutionary movement and the communists."[23] An article by Maring also predicted: "The communist party, without a doubt, will grow on the soil of the revolutionary trade union movement in South China."[24]

Ironically, within days of the Comintern's decision, Sun's ongoing dispute with Ch'en Chiung-ming ended when the warlord bombarded the presidential palace, forcing Sun to flee to Shanghai. Even though Sun's flight greatly weakened him, he turned down Maring's proposal to form a closer alliance with the CCP. Sun maintained that the communists could join the KMT only as individuals. As a result, Maring called a special plenum of the CCP's Central Committee to order the CCP members to join the KMT. This special plenum opened at Hangchow's West Lake on August 22, 1922, only eight days after Sun arrived in Shanghai as a political refugee. Under these circumstances, it is not surprising that Maring met with stiff opposition when he tried to convince the CCP to join the KMT. In a 1935 interview, however, he claimed that there were only "one or two opponents, of whom the strongest, if I remember correctly, was Chang Kuo-tao." Maring also insisted that he had not received any orders from Moscow, claiming that having the CCP work within the KMT was his own idea.[25]

But, Ch'en Tu-hsiu later challenged this view, recounting that when he, Li Ta-chao, Chang Kuo-tao, Ts'ai Ho-sen, and Kao Chun-yu opposed the United Front, Maring asked whether they planned to disobey a Comintern decision, and thus, "the Central Committee of the CCP could not but accept the proposal of the International and agree to join the Kuomintang."[26] Ch'en's version of events has since been confirmed by the 1986 Soviet publication of an August 1922 Comintern telegram ordering the CCP to join the KMT (see Document 26). This telegram explained that the Comintern "considered the KMT as a revolutionary party, which upheld the Testament of the 1911 revolution and was striving to build an independent Chinese republic," and after joining the KMT the "communists must build groups of followers in the KMT and in the trade unions."[27]

№ 8

*Из инструкции Исполкома Коминтерна
представителю Коммунистического Интернационала
в Южном Китае*

Август 1922 г.

1. Вся деятельность представителя должна базироваться на резолюции II конгресса Коминтерна по колониальному вопросу.

2. ИККИ рассматривает гоминьдан как революционную партию, которая хранит заветы революции 1911 г. и стремится создать независимую китайскую республику.

3. С целью выполнения задач коммунисты должны создать группы приверженцев в самом гоминьдане и в профсоюзах

Из этих групп предлагалось сформировать пропагандистскую организацию, которая будет распространять идеи борьбы против иностранного империализма, за создание китайской народной республики, за организацию классовой борьбы против иностранных и китайских эксплуататоров.

4. Эта организация должна быть создана по возможности с согласия гоминьдана, хотя она и должна сохранить полную независимость; так как гоминьдан является ответственным за Южное правительство [1], пока он должен избегать столкновений с империалистическими державами.

Document 26
The Comintern's August 1922 Telegram Ordering the CCP to Join the KMT

Clearly, responsibility for the success or failure of the United Front Policy rested on the Comintern's central leadership in Moscow, not on a single Comintern operative in China. Formerly, Soviet commentators willingly granted Maring this dubious honor. For example, Pavel Mif, a member of the Far Eastern Bureau of the Comintern, seemed to support Maring's central role in forming the United Front by ignoring the August 1922 telegram. Mif claimed that the first instructions to coordinate the activities of the CCP with the KMT were contained in a special January 12, 1923 decision of the Comintern Executive Committee.[28]

Although the Comintern's central leadership in Moscow ordered the CCP members to join the KMT, all available evidence suggests that the CCP only grudgingly obeyed this resolution. From the Chinese communists' point of view, the United Front Policy really amounted to an alliance between the CCP and Sun's personal clique. A Soviet historian has reported that as late as the fall of 1924, the CCP continued to portray the KMT as merely Sun's faction, warning the Comintern of Sun's illness: "In China it is not said in vain that 'the Kuomintang is Sun Yat-sen,' and when he dies, the Chinese revolution will come to a stop."[29]

In the beginning, the Chinese communists did not even attempt to hide their dissatisfaction with the KMT-led United Front. For example, the October 4, 1922 edition of *The Guide Weekly* published a harsh critique, as well as a defense, of Ch'en Tu-hsiu's earlier article supporting the United Front; this joint editorial was the first, and last, time that such a critical view appeared in *The Guide Weekly*. The author of the critique, writing under the name Ssu Shun, rejected Ch'en's call for unity between the capitalist and proletarian classes, and denied that the KMT was revolutionary. He further warned that a "dictatorship of the capitalists" would result and the revolution would remain "incomplete."[30]

An editor of *The Guide Weekly*, Kao Chun-yu, criticized this editorial, but his response was almost as damning. He claimed that the Chinese capitalists and proletariat shared a common desire to "overthrow international imperialism and the feudal warlords," but China's "economic backwardness" had not allowed the proletariat class to develop; thus, allying with the capitalists was necessary. Kao acknowledged that the United Front was imperative since the Chinese proletariat was virtually nonexistent.[31]

Although this was the last direct criticism of the United Front to appear in the CCP press, as late as November 8, 1922, *The Guide Weekly* reprinted a speech by the Comintern delegate, G. Safarov, who had cautioned that workers would never be treated as equals under capitalism, so they should not "hope that a government made up of capitalists and landowners would be able to give the oppressed people sunshine, bread, air, and other equally important liberties."[32] Safarov especially distrusted the national-bourgeoisie in colonial and semicolonial countries. During 1921, he warned the Asian proletariat "to struggle with the bourgeois-democratic movements within their nations."[33]

Conflict over whether the CCP should join the KMT, or whether it should continue its fight alone, continued long after the Comintern had ordered the United Front. Editorials like those referred to above indicate that the United

Front Policy was not popular with the CCP leadership and that it was accepted only with great reluctance. This interpretation is confirmed by Karl Radek's November 22, 1922 condemnation of the Chinese communists for not carrying through on their duty to enter the KMT.[34]

Because the CCP continued to procrastinate, on January 12, 1923, the Comintern sent a telegram to China that outlined the fourth Comintern congress's resolutions on the United Front Policy. Although discussion had been heated and many delegates had still opposed the Chinese communists' close relations with Sun Yat-sen, the congress had finally agreed that the United Front should be implemented, conceding that the KMT was the "only serious national-revolutionary group in China." For this reason, the Comintern had decided that "under the present circumstances it is expedient for members of the CCP to remain within the Kuomintang . . . in the struggle against European, American, and Japanese imperialism."[35]

The Open Door Policy and Outer Mongolia

The Comintern condemned the Open Door in China because it supported China's sovereignty and territorial integrity, thereby actively interfering with the USSR's attempts to expand communism. Soon after the October Revolution, Lenin declared that a clash between Soviet Russia and the capitalist nations was unavoidable: "[I]t is inconceivable that the Soviet Republic should continue to exist for a long period side by side with imperial states . . . a number of terrible clashes between the Soviet Republic and bourgeois states is inevitable."[36] Beginning on February 22, 1918, the Bolsheviks released an appeal to the Far East to rise up against the capitalist countries.[37] The destruction of the Open Door Policy was considered to be an essential precondition for the spread of the Bolshevik revolution to China.

While the Bolsheviks secretly turned to the Open Door Policy to protect Siberia from Japanese invaders they publicly called for the destruction of the Open Door Policy in China. On March 6, 1919, one of the two Chinese delegates in attendance at the first Comintern congress published an article claiming that 500 million Chinese were being exploited by the capitalist powers of Europe, America, and Japan under the guise of the Open Door Policy.[38] On the same day, the Comintern accused the United States of contemplating "the exploitation of weak States and peoples by means of trade and capital investment."[39]

As early as March 1919, therefore, the Bolsheviks called for the destruction of the Open Door Policy. The Comintern assigned Maring the task of undermining the Open Door in China. Maring openly acknowledged the difficulties, however, since "the American open-door policy has the appearance of defending oppressed peoples."[40] But, in Chinese-language articles written under his Chinese pen name, Maring nevertheless warned the Chinese people not to trust the Open Door Policy, claiming that it would be used as an excuse to send "foreign ships, gunships, airships, and troops."[41] Elsewhere, Maring cautioned that the nature of capitalism would ensure that "China and Russia will be their victims."[42]

In one of the first anti–Open Door articles written by a leading Chinese communist, Ts'ai Ho-sen also described this policy as an imperialist tool to "dominate" China's industry and commerce, so that the capitalist powers could "forever make China a dumping ground for their goods." China would soon become just like the rest of the world's colonial countries, Ts'ai warned, and the Chinese people would forever remain capitalist "slaves" if the world proletarian revolution did not free them. Ts'ai then claimed that if China wanted to rid herself of the Open Door and escape from this fate, she should join the world revolution and "work hand in hand with Soviet Russia."[43]

These excerpts prove that while the Soviet government continued to rely on the Open Door Policy in Siberia for protection from Japanese aggression, it denounced this same policy as being harmful to China. In fact, the Bolsheviks were willing to work diplomatically with capitalist countries when it was to their advantage, while simultaneously supporting revolutionary propaganda advocating the destruction of these same governments. The USSR's contradictory attitude toward the capitalist nations did not go unnoticed; in early 1919, for example, the American chargé d'affaires at Archangel pointed out that the Bolsheviks' call to organize the Comintern did not conform to their apparent eagerness to participate in Allied-sponsored peace talks.[44]

The most pertinent example of the failure of the Open Door Policy is Outer Mongolia. Beginning in 1918, the Bolsheviks publicly proclaimed the abolition of all former unequal treaties with China, but in 1922, Aleksandr Paikes privately told Peking officials that the terms of the 1915 tripartite treaty were still in effect and that the only way to revise this treaty would be for all parties, including Outer Mongolia, to negotiate jointly new terms. Since allowing an Outer Mongolian representative at the negotiations would have meant that China recognized Outer Mongolia's autonomy, however, Sino-Soviet negotiations quickly deadlocked, forcing the Soviet diplomats in Peking to turn to the Comintern and the CCP for support.

Paikes was soon replaced by Adolf Joffe, who arrived in China during August 1922, with a diplomatic mission that quickly grew to include almost thirty Soviet officials. Only a handful of these actually participated in diplomatic negotiations with Peking, while most were involved with publishing pro-Soviet propaganda in China. For example, in an early attempt to influence Chinese public opinion, the Soviet mission temporarily supported the publication of a Russian-language journal, called *Shanghai Life*, and then published its own English-language journal, called *New Russia*.[45] The most influential, of course, were the CCP's own official journals, such as *The Guide Weekly* and *The Vanguard*, which were published in Chinese and so could reach a much larger audience.

The CCP second party congress met during summer 1922. At this time, the CCP formally joined the Comintern and passed resolutions supporting Outer Mongolia's autonomy from China. A CCP proposal proclaimed that China should not try to reunite with Outer Mongolia, Tibet, or Turkestan (Sinkiang), since each of these regions had different economic needs: "If these different races with their different economic phases be compulsorily united under the military control of those who even cannot unite China as it now exists, the result is only to expand the domain of this military control and interrupt the progress of these people towards self-determination and autonomy, with little profit to China proper."[46] In line with this resolution, therefore, the Chinese communists then decided: "To recognize Mongolia, Tibet, and Turkestan as autonomous states."[47]

The autonomy of these areas was intended to be merely temporary, however, as the CCP's resolutions further specified that once the Chinese people overthrew the militarists and were able to "establish the real republic by the union of the people themselves," then the next priority would be to "reunite China Proper, Mongolia, Tibet, and Turkestan, and to establish them as the United States of China, a Republic."[48] It is important to note that this resolution implied that the so-called "United States of China" would be the result of a successful communist revolution. This meant that the CCP actually agreed to support Moscow's occupation of Outer Mongolia only as an interim measure until the Chinese communists came to power in China.

This interpretation is supported by referring to one of the first of many public talks presented by Joffe after arriving in China. When hosting a dinner in Peking for the Chinese press on August 19, 1922, Joffe promised: "Although the Mongolian question cannot be taken out from many other questions, Russia will be most pleased to withdraw the few troops that are now there when the proper moment in the interest of the whole Chinese nation really comes. Accept my assurances that when all of us agree that the moment has come, Russia will not retain her Red Army in Mongolia even one second longer." Joffe furthermore assured his audience: "As regards Mongolia, it is only natural that Russia herself cannot have any imperialistic aims."[49]

In hindsight, it is easier to see that Joffe's assurances that the Red Army would be withdrawn when it was in the interests of the "whole Chinese nation" really meant that Moscow would take this action only after China had experienced its own communist revolution. In other words, the Soviet Union intended to hand back Outer Mongolia only to a Chinese government under the CCP. This interpretation is fully supported by the CCP's own resolutions, which had to be approved by the Comintern's central organization in Moscow. In effect, the CCP and the Comintern had concluded a secret agreement on Outer Mongolia.

It should be remembered, however, that China's outlying border territories had previously been the target of tsarist Russian expansion. Soviet Russia's efforts to create an autonomous Outer Mongolia actually followed in line with former tsarist practices. In fact, by 1922 an interview with a German envoy, identified simply as Assmis, who had just completed a lengthy visit to Outer Mongolia revealed that it was already becoming an integral part of Soviet Russia[50]:

> Outer Mongolia, said Mr. Assmis, is practically on the way to be[coming] a Russian province. Nearly every domestic Mongolian institution is in the hands of Russian experts. The Moscow

Government has sent the best men available for running the Mongolian affairs. All of these new type Russians do their work [with] no noise and no boasting, no alcoholism to be found on the Mongolian territory. The Foreign Office, the board of interior, posts, telegraphs, telephones, schools, etc. are in the hands of the Russian emissaries. . . . Mr. Assmis believes that the evacuation of Mongolia by Soviet troops will come rather soon, but that this means nothing in the general development. Outer Mongolia is practically a Russian colony today.

Soviet diplomats in Peking even admitted in private that Moscow's primary goal was to regain the former tsarist borders, which included Soviet control over Outer Mongolia: "Here in the Far East, Russia stands clear for the recovery of her historical rights which means recovery of her old boundaries."[51] Before Soviet Russia could consolidate full control over Outer Mongolia, however, it would be necessary to gain Peking's recognition of the 1915 unequal treaty. Upon arriving in China, Joffe publicly announced that he would forbear from the "aggressive imperialist policy of the tsar's government," and he expressed his hope that relations could be opened with China based on the "full political and economic equality of both parties."[52] But when Peking officials insisted that an estimated 1,200 Red Army troops had to first be withdrawn from Outer Mongolia prior to negotiations, Joffe refused.[53]

Joffe instead claimed that Outer Mongolia was governed by local Mongolian authorities, and that "Russian forces temporarily remain on Mongolian soil solely in order to prevent making Mongolia once again the staging area for White Guardist forces that are assembled in the Russian Far East and on the territory of China."[54] Even though the White Russians no longer represented a real military threat, Joffe announced that the Red Army would be withdrawn from Outer Mongolia only when it "would really serve the interests of the Russian and Chinese people. . . . Unfortunately, however, this moment has not yet arrived."[55]

To support Joffe's ongoing negotiations with Peking, the Comintern ordered the CCP to move its headquarters from Shanghai to Peking, a move that was completed by early September 1922. Under Maring's guidance, and with Comintern funding, the CCP's first issue of *The Guide Weekly* also appeared in early September 1922. This journal soon became a strong advocate for Moscow's position in its diplomatic negotiations with Peking, and according to one of Maring's Chinese assistants, it was Maring who held unchallenged authority over the contents of this journal: "I had to translate and explain every article to him, and at every incorrect place he would put forward his view and would demand that we make corrections."[56]

Comintern and Narkomindel cooperation in these propaganda efforts is best shown by referring to letters Maring received from Joffe. One in particular advised that in *New Russia* "all material must be systematically arranged so that each issue is devoted to an important set of information and that this predominates."[57] In addition to funding their own journals in Russian, English, and Chinese, a foreign adviser to the Peking government reported that Joffe was also attempting to influence independent organizations, by offering subsidies to "various newspapers published in the English and Chinese languages."[58] All of these different newspapers and journals were used by the Comintern to gain support among the Chinese public for an "autonomous" Outer Mongolia under Soviet Russia's aegis.

Moscow's tactics rapidly met with success, since at the same time Washington applied pressure on Tokyo not to annex Russian territory in Siberia, Maring helped organize opposition to the Open Door in China. The Bolsheviks' initial success in the Far East can even be partially attributed to the Open Door Policy, since it was only this policy's active protection of Russia's territorial integrity that gave the Bolsheviks sufficient time to organize a movement opposing the Open Door Policy in China.

The CCP Supports Outer Mongolian Autonomy

As part of Moscow's efforts to renew the terms of the 1915 treaty granting Outer Mongolia its autonomy, the CCP publicly supported tsarist Russia's unequal treaties in Chinese-language articles published in its official journals, such as *The Guide Weekly* and *The Vanguard*. The CCP agreed to help the Soviet diplomats in exchange for Comintern assurances that Outer Mongolia would be returned to China after the success of the communist revolution. It was this secret CCP-Comintern arrangement that the CCP considered broken when the Soviet Union later retained its hold over Outer Mongolia following the 1949 formation of the People's Republic of China.

The position taken by the CCP in its official journals supported the Soviet diplomats' ongoing attempts to renew the 1915 unequal treaty. For example, in an article by Kao Chun-yu, the CCP advocated that in the upcoming diplomatic talks between Moscow and Peking, Outer Mongolia should be allowed to have its own representative participating on the basis of "independence and equality."[59] If Peking agreed to allow an Outer Mongolian representative at the Sino-Soviet negotiations, however, it not only would have tacitly recognized Outer Mongolia's autonomy, but it also would have sanctioned Soviet attempts to return to tsarist Russia's strategy of mediating Outer Mongolia's relations with China.

In a similar article written by Ts'ai Ho-sen, the CCP recommended that only after Peking recognized the Soviet government could a Sino-Soviet conference be convened "to decide the problems between China and Russia."[60] Although this suggestion might sound reasonable enough, in fact, the Peking government's continued refusal to recognize the legitimacy of the Soviet Union put pressure on Moscow to withdraw the Red Army from Outer Mongolia prior to the opening of formal Sino-Soviet negotiations. The Peking officials were especially displeased that Moscow continued to station troops on territory that it had earlier acknowledged was subject to Chinese sovereignty.

The CCP press also resorted to economic arguments to convince the Chinese public to grant Outer Mongolia autonomy. For example, Ch'en Tu-hsiu argued that because China and Outer Mongolia represented "various stages of economic development," the Chinese people should recognize the "independence of Outer Mongolia."[61] In a similar vein, Kao Chun-yu reasoned that Outer Mongolia should be independent from China because its economy was more primitive: "We know that political organization is determined by the economic situation, so to expect to convince the backwards Mongolia into accepting the administration of the economically advanced Chinese government would not conform with the needs of the Mongolian people, since China would economically and politically exert a great deal of pressure on the Mongolian way of life."[62] The obvious fallacy of these economic arguments was that they applied equally well to the Soviet occupation of Outer Mongolia, in fact, more so, since the Bolsheviks claimed that Russia's economy was even more advanced than China's.

During subsequent negotiations between Moscow and Peking, the CCP journal *The Vanguard* published a long article during 1924 that supported Outer Mongolia's full independence from China.[63] Entitled "The *Status Quo* of Outer Mongolia's Independence," this article not only did not condemn the 1915 unequal treaty for making Outer Mongolia a Russian protectorate, but praised it for granting Outer Mongolia "complete independence," since afterward China and Mongolia "only had partial territorial relations."[64] To the Comintern and the CCP, therefore, *status quo* clearly meant retaining the terms of the 1915 tsarist treaty.

Moreover, when discussing Outer Mongolia's recent treaties with the Soviet Union, this article acknowledged that tsarist Russia's former right to garrison troops in Urga had been renewed, and that, as under the tsars, the Soviet "troops numbered two hundred people." But, while under the 1915 treaty China had also been allowed to garrison an equal number of troops in Outer Mongolia, this article confirmed that Peking had lost this right, making Sino-Soviet relations even more unequal. The article further warned that if Peking "succeeded in sending troops, the moment they crossed Outer Mongolia's border hostilities would be unavoidable."[65]

Finally, while completely ignoring the USSR's continued military occupation of territory claimed by China, Ch'en Tu-hsiu wrote an article immediately after the signing of the May 31, 1924 Sino-Soviet treaty in which he called those people who had consistently opposed Outer Mongolia's autonomy "shortsighted." Ch'en explained how every time the Chinese communists had advocated Outer Mongolia's autonomy, there had been people who feared that the USSR would not respect the new borders. The recent agreement between the Soviet Union and China, however, in which Moscow publicly acknowledged that Outer Mongolia was an integral part of China, showed that it had all been "a big uproar over nothing."[66] But Ch'en's public support for the Comintern's propaganda ignored Moscow's secret protocol with Peking recognizing Outer Mongolia's *de facto* autonomy. Following this diplomatic coup, Outer Mongolia was drawn completely into the Soviet-led communist bloc.

The CCP and the United Front Policy

Even after the Comintern ordered the CCP to join the KMT, there continued to be opposition within the CCP to the United Front Policy. The signing of the Joffe-Sun pact should not be seen as the end of this opposition, therefore, and it took some time before the Comintern's decision was fully enacted. What Moscow viewed as "expedient," the Chinese communists viewed as the end of their independence. But since the CCP was a member of the Comintern, it was duty-bound to follow the decisions of that organization, and the Chinese communists grudgingly joined the KMT as individuals. The CCP members also had to follow Mikhail Borodin's orders to infiltrate the KMT organization and make the KMT's policies conform more closely with the Comintern's.

Borodin's primary responsibility in Canton was to reorganize the KMT. Maring had started this assignment earlier during 1923, and two draft plans were found later in his personal files.[67] After Borodin convinced Sun Yat-sen to reorganize the KMT, he immediately presented an English-language draft of the KMT's new organization to Liao Chung-k'ai, who helped to translate the more than four hundred points into Chinese. Borodin's proposed party structure was based on the Bolshevik party's centralized organization and included party functionaries that extended the KMT's power all the way down to small cities and towns, which it had never had before. Orders from the central executive committee had to be exactly followed, and the chairman of this committee would be elected by the KMT congress. Although this post was supposedly retained for Sun Yat-sen, Borodin's draft did not specifically state this.[68]

The KMT's top leaders were concerned about these changes, since their own power within the organization was dependent on their personal relationship with Sun Yat-sen. On December 3, 1923, eleven KMT officials wrote to Sun Yat-sen protesting Borodin's influence. They particularly warned that the reforms would give Ch'en Tu-hsiu the opportunity to become the head of the KMT within five years, and that this was the Soviet government's real goal.[69] Sun backed Borodin, however, and reassured these officials that the communists would not achieve greater power as a result of the reorganization. Sun personally gave Borodin permission to go ahead with the reforms.

Previous KMT reorganizations were comparatively simple, and were never completely adopted. Now, the KMT's January 1924 first congress called for "strict party discipline, an intense propaganda offensive, extensive social legislation, the 'equalization' (but not the nationalization) of land, the state control of capital and of monopolistic industries, and the forging of an army to attack both domestic and foreign 'imperialism'." Ignoring Borodin's proposal to limit Sun's personal powers, it placed supreme power in the hands of a KMT national congress, made Sun the lifelong president of the party, and gave him the right to veto resolutions of the national congress and in the central executive committee.[70]

Although Sun's powers seemed absolute, the new structure of the KMT was so complex that it quickly grew beyond his immediate control. The veto powers given to Sun over the national congress and the central executive committee were effectively bypassed when a new committee was formed in July 1924–called the central political committee. This new committee became the real power in the KMT and continued in this important role until July 1926, at which time its name was changed to the central political conference and its responsibilities diminished.

The decision to give veto powers to Sun, as opposed to requiring that Sun agree to every decision, was also quite important. As Sun's work load increased, therefore, more and more party decisions took place at lower levels. Since Sun's acceptance was not required for most matters, only those decisions made at the highest levels of the KMT were actually presented to Sun for his approval. By creating a more complicated party organization, Borodin made it much easier for the CCP to bypass Sun Yat-sen and funnel his personal power to Chinese communists who had gained positions of authority within the KMT.

Even though Sun had promised otherwise, the convening of the KMT's first national congress clearly increased the communists' power, as Li Ta-chao and Mao Tse-tung were elected to the KMT's central committee. In his speech to the congress, Li Ta-chao further reminded the KMT members that it was only thanks to the Chinese communists that the KMT was able to form closer connections with the Comintern and the Soviet Union.[71] Ch'en Tu-hsiu also gave a speech at the congress and tried to reassure those KMT members who accused the Chinese communists of wanting to use the KMT for their own benefit: "A communist revolution is a struggle between the working class and the bourgeoisie, but the national revolution is a union of all of the classes fighting against the warlords and foreigners; therefore, while the Kuomintang can use the Communist party, the Communist party is definitely not able to use the Kuomintang party."[72]

But what Ch'en did not explain was that, like the two-stage Russian revolution in 1917, the Chinese revolution was supposed to be a two stage revolution. During the first stage–the national revolution–the bourgeoisie KMT would take the lead. But, after the success of this first revolution, the second stage would be the proletariat revolution under the leadership of the Chinese communists. Ch'en's reassuring words were true, therefore, but represented only half the truth, since he had conveniently not mentioned the second half of the story.

Borodin worked diligently to increase the power of the Chinese communists within the KMT. One former Chinese communist later recalled that in April 1924, Borodin was already proposing that the KMT be divided into right and left factions so that the communists could gradually assume full control over the party's administrative organs.[73] Soviet attempts to increase the communists' power almost immediately ran into opposition, however, and on June 25, 1924, Borodin held a conversation with Chang Chih, a member of the KMT's central control yuan, about this strategy[74]:

> **Borodin:** It is unavoidable that the party will split into factions, since the Kuomintang's central executive committee is really not able to act

as the party's center. Naturally small groups have appeared within the party, and there is a split between the left faction and the right faction. If we take as being the right faction people like Jui Lin, etc., who have publicly opposed the Sino-Russian treaty, then the Communist Party would be the left faction.

Control Yuan: But do you think that it is rational for the Communist Party to enter the Kuomintang and then carry out its group activities within that Party?

Borodin: The Kuomintang is already dead, it is no longer a united party. You can only say that there are Kuomintang members, you can not say that there is a Kuomintang. The new-entered members, like the Communist Party members, are organizing party groups which might lead the old party members to be more competitive, and would thus resurrect the party.

When Borodin claimed that the KMT was "dead," he meant that Sun's original faction was dead, as its former leaders were gradually being displaced. A struggle was under way over who would be the new leaders, and Borodin's description of a newly resurrected party really meant a party under the leadership of the Chinese communists and thus indirectly under the control of the Comintern. In June 1924, Voitinskii acknowledged the tensions that existed between the KMT's left and right factions, referring in particular to the right faction's opposition to the recently signed Sino-Soviet treaty, in which the Soviet Union officially recognized the legitimacy of the Peking government as China's sole government. Sun supported this treaty, however, making it clear that he "understood thoroughly the meaning of the treaty between the USSR and the Chinese government, as well as the significance of it for the Chinese people in general."[75]

In July, the KMT even issued a manifesto stating that this Sino-Soviet treaty was decided on the principle of equality and mutual respect for sovereignty, which was in sharp contrast to the other powers "whose treaties over the past several decades were all invasions of China's sovereignty."[76] Meanwhile, Voitinskii explained how the Chinese communists should further undermine the right faction to shift the KMT's policies to oppose the foreign capitalist countries: "The historical problem of the Chinese communists working together with the Kuomintang, appears to be the organization of workers, peasants, and the young Chinese intelligentsia, and by working from day to day through all of these organizations, as well as by means of propaganda and declarations, to force the Kuomintang to change the direction of their policies to oppose the big merchants and the feudal landowners and to support the working masses of China and the Soviet Republic against world imperialism."[77]

The attempt to shift the KMT to the left produced friction between the Chinese communists and the KMT. Soviet scholars have acknowledged that the KMT/CCP

United Front was in turmoil: "By the summer or fall of 1924, relations between the nationalists and the communists little by little became strained and heated up to the breaking point. The leaders of the CCP even raised the question of breaking with the Kuomintang and withdrawing all of the communists from it."[78]

But Borodin was not willing to give up the power the communists already had within the KMT, and so all CCP proposals to leave the United Front were denied. This conflict between the Chinese communists and the KMT's old guard was settled temporarily in August 1924, as the newly founded central political committee proposed that the communists' special job was to be responsible for the proletariat within the KMT. It also proposed that a new three-man committee be organized, with one KMT member, one Chinese communist member, and one Comintern member, to resolve all such conflicts. The KMT's central executive committee endorsed this plan, but evidently only after Sun Yat-sen came out in support of it.[79] This decision merely strengthened the CCP's position within the KMT, and especially among the workers' movement, since the CCP and Comintern members could easily outvote the lone KMT representative.

The CCP and the Workers' Movement

The important role that the workers movement played in Asia was early recognized by the Bolsheviks. This was best shown by Lenin, when he began discussing Asian nationalist revolutions in 1919. For example, while giving a talk to a group of Asian communists living in Russia during December 1919, Lenin emphasized that although China did not have a European-type proletariat it did have a growing nationalist movement. Lenin's decision to widen the Bolsheviks' base of support from only the more advanced countries to incorporate workers in all stages of their development meant that he hoped China's nationalist revolution could now be joined with proletariat revolutions in Europe.

Lenin advised the Bolsheviks to rely on "bourgeois nationalism, which is awakening these peoples and cannot help awakening them," and then added: "We see that they [the British, French, German proletariat] cannot win without the help of the working mass of the oppressed colonial peoples, especially the people of the East. We must report that a single vanguard cannot realize the transition to communism. The task lies in awakening revolutionary activity, independence, and an organized mass of workers, regardless of what stage they are in, in translating original Communist studies, intended for Communists of more advanced countries, into the language of each people, and in accomplishing the practical problems which must be solved immediately and joining in the general struggle with the proletariat of other countries."[80]

By redefining the meaning of "worker," Lenin was really proposing that the Bolsheviks try to tap into the large pool of largely unfulfilled nationalist hopes that had been awakened by World War I and by President Wilson's promises of national self-determination. Lenin's solution was to channel this latent bourgeois nationalism into an anti-imperialist revolution that would eventually undermine the capitalist countries' colonial base. Lenin's eventual goal was to destroy capitalism by joining national-bourgeois revolutions in colonial countries with proletarian revolution in Europe. To accomplish this task it was a necessary prerequisite, however, to pull the oppressed colonial peoples into the larger revolutionary movement led by Soviet Russia.

In the spring of 1922, Maring first proposed that since the Chinese proletariat was still in the "beginning stages of its development" and since the workers' unions in South China were the most developed, the Comintern had no choice but "completely to support the national-revolutionary elements in the South." By unifying all of the "revolutionary-nationalist elements" and then using the Chinese communists to push the whole movement to the left, Maring calculated that the nationalist movement could be used to oppose the capitalists since China was the "arena in which the great powers were struggling to achieve hegemony in the Pacific Ocean." The desire of the capitalists to treat China as their "spoils" would thus work in favor of the Bolsheviks, as the leaders of the Chinese revolutionary movement would be pushed "into cooperating with Soviet Russia and with us–the communists–and opens the possibility of vastly productive work in union with the Chinese revolutionaries."[81]

But, in Maring's speech before the Comintern's Executive Committee on July 11, 1922, he described progress with the organization of labor unions in Shanghai during 1921, concluding that it had been "very troublesome." Although Shanghai was China's largest industrial center, as well as the center of American commercial interests in China, Maring warned that it did not have an active workers' movement, in part because the number of industrial workers was still so small. Instead, Maring was much more impressed by his observations of the anti-British strikes which he had seen during his travels in southern China between December 1921, and April 1922. Maring reported that "this journey to the South was the most important part of my stay in China," because it showed the greater potential of the Chinese workers' movement in South China.[82]

In later articles, Maring also discussed the worldwide struggle between socialism and capitalism. He warned that for China "to be victorious in the larger battle they must unite with Russia."[83] The October Revolution gave "new hope" to Asia's colonial and semicolonial nationalist movements.[84] Because of the crises in Europe following World War I, the power of the capitalists had been weakened and "the oppressed nationalities of the East now had an opportunity" to gain their independence.[85] The Bolshevik's 1917 October Revolution, therefore, was the first strike against the capitalists, while the peoples of Asia–the 300 million Indians, the 100 Moslems, and the 400 million Chinese–would deliver the next blow.[86]

But to carry this revolution out, the Chinese needed to organize a mass party composed of "merchants, intellectuals, peasants, workers, and soldiers," and they needed to leave behind the "old customs and old thinking and change the Kuomintang into a real people's party."[87] It was the working class that should take the lead, and Maring insisted that among the "creators of the new China" the workers held the "most important position."[88] The USSR was in a unique position to take advantage of this unrest since it was balanced between two worlds: the capitalist countries of the West and the enormously populated countries of the East. The USSR's revolutionary tactics linked proletariat revolutions in Europe with nationalist revolutions in Asia under the slogan: "The Victory of the Broad Masses of Workers in the West and the Oppressed Peoples of the East." These tactics represented a significant step away from the Bolsheviks' Europe-centered revolutionary philosophy, as the Comintern began to redeploy a larger share of its scarce manpower and financial resources from Europe to Asia.[89]

A Comintern telegram entitled "Directives of the Executive Committee of the Comintern to the Third Congress of the Chinese Communist Party" dated May 24, 1923, reflected these new tactics as it affirmed that the "basic demand with regards to the KMT national-democratic party should be the *unconditional support of the workers' movement* in China, both in the North and in the South."[90] To do this, the CCP had to increase its activities in this area: "The workers' movement in the center of China has developed without being connected with the Kuomintang party. Of course, nationalist ideals are now creeping into this movement, but the organizational work is being led mainly by radical elements from the ranks of the students, who have moved closer to communist ideals, thanks to the leadership of our young communist party in China."[91]

The CCP's third congress followed the Comintern's lead in warning that the KMT was depending too much on capitalists helping the national revolution, and that it was disregarding the mass movement in favor of centralizing military power under the party. Being overly dependent on a military solution was also a mistake, and the party manifesto warned the KMT not to lose its position as a political leader, and especially not to lose the sympathy of the common people, since they could "never succeed by simply depending on the military."[92]

At this congress Ch'en Tu-hsiu followed the Comintern's instructions and dutifully proposed that the CCP and the KMT jointly develop labor unions. But Chang Kuo-tao headed a group of Chinese communists who continued to insist on the "independence" of the trade unions and opposed allowing the KMT joint control of their operation.[93] This division threatened to disrupt the CCP even more, but by August 1923, the Comintern's central committee had reversed itself and resolved to keep organized labor "independent" of the KMT's control.[94]

China's socialist revolution, the Comintern claimed, would follow on the heels of the KMT's nationalist revolution, in a pattern that closely followed the Russian experience. With the reorganization of the KMT party, the Comintern immediately advised the KMT that the Chinese workers were the KMT's strongest ally against the foreign capitalists. Voitinskii, in particular, gave suggestions on how the KMT leadership could best make use of the workers' movement, "first, to organize their internal policies in such a way that the working masses would really see that the government wanted to help them, and second, if the . . . KMT Party in its own matters would promote the organization of the worker's masses into independent class and economic organizations."[95]

Since it was the Comintern's plan to follow the nationalist revolution with a socialist revolution, it was especially important to begin organizing the Chinese workers as quickly as possible. To direct the KMT's activities against the capitalist countries, the Chinese communists led the way in reorganizing the local chapters of the KMT. One of the most important of these was in Shanghai, since it was in Shanghai where the largest foreign firms were located.

The newly reorganized executive committee of the Shanghai branch of the KMT met for the first time on February 14, 1924. A minute book of this branch is now available and covers the period between February 14 and March 11, 1924, giving minute details of the decisions made and who made them.[96] One could easily confuse this record wth a CCP document, since two of the most prevalent names are Ch'u Ch'iu-pai, the leader of the CCP in the late 1920s, and then Mao Tse-tung, the leader of the CCP during the mid-1930s and afterward.

This first meeting was followed by others on February 20, 23, 24, and 25. On February 25, the executive committee decided to publish the KMT's decisions, which included the KMT's foreign policy resolutions, and it further decided to organize a committee to prepare for a Lenin memorial demonstration during March, to commemorate Lenin's recent death in January. On March 1, the Shanghai secretariat began operations, and on March 6, it had already decided to organize a special committee to promote education for the common people, and, in particular, it decided that every KMT section, and especially every factory and shop, had to have study sessions discussing the international situation, solutions to these international problems, and ways to carry out those solutions.[97]

During 1925, the Comintern continued to promote the workers' movement. At the CCP's fourth congress during January 1925, the Chinese communists even called for putting the Chinese proletariat at the center of the upcoming revolution. To increase contacts with the workers' movement, the congress decided to cooperate more with the left wing of the KMT. It was also forced by the Comintern to acknowledge that Sun Yat-sen was responsible for holding the United Front together, as the CCP admitted that it was only "thanks to the entry into the Kuomintang and to the utilization of Sun Yat-sen's authority, that they were able to take part in the active political life of the national-democratic movement."[98]

China's 1925-27 Revolution and the Cold War

The revolutionary intensification in China was part of a gradual shift in Soviet Russia's tactics from Europe to Asia, as the Soviet government began to realize that the site of the next world conflict might be in the Far East. Only later, after the USSR's policies in China met with defeat, was the importance of this early turn toward Asia deemphasized by Soviet historians.[99] Early in 1923, Nikolai Bukharin, in a meeting with the Comintern's executive committee, emphasized this revision as part of the Soviet government's report on the world situation. Bukharin pointed to the KMT's recent "common revolutionary bloc" with the CCP, and predicted that the KMT would lead the struggle for China's national liberation. Once China gained its independence, this would bring about a crisis in all of Asia that would ultimately disrupt the whole world economy.[100]

While Sun Yat-sen's unexpected death on March 12, 1925 threatened to destroy the KMT's alliance with the CCP, it also gave the Comintern its long-awaited opportunity to turn the KMT even more solidly against the foreign capitalists in China. Even before Sun's death, one of the leaders of the so-called left KMT, Wang Ching-wei, had taken nominal control into his own hands, when he expelled over three hundred anticommunists from the KMT's ranks.[101] Ch'en Tu-hsiu publicly supported this "weeding-out" process to eliminate those who were not "true" KMT members, and predicted that the prestige of the KMT within Chinese society would become even greater.[102] Meanwhile, the CCP's Central Committee emphasized the Leninist characteristics of China's nationalist movement by calling on it to oppose the "world capitalist-imperialist oppressors," which it described as China's main "obstacles on their path to liberty."[103]

In order to strengthen the United Front, the pro-Soviet members of the KMT then arranged to have Sun Yat-sen's will published. According to one report, Wang Ching-wei was actually responsible for writing this will, and Sun merely approved it prior to his death.[104] An examination of this document reemphasizes how important the Comintern's redefinition of nationalism really was, since the will stated that with the heritage of Lenin to help them, "the victims of imperialism will inevitably achieve emancipation from that international regime whose foundations have been rooted for ages in slavery, wars, and injustice." To achieve this goal, Sun then ordered the KMT to continue its close alliance with the Soviet government in "the historic work of the final liberation of China and other exploited countries from the yoke of imperialism."[105]

From 1925 until 1927 no colonial revolution outweighed China's in importance, since it was from China that the USSR hoped to launch a simultaneous attack on its most important capitalist enemies, the United States and Great Britain. Soviet government officials themselves talked of events in China in turns of a worldwide conflict between capitalism and socialism. For example, as early as September 4, 1923, Karakhan had acknowledged that China was at the heart of the international struggle between the socialist and capitalist camps: "China is still the theater of this struggle, although it is hidden from view."[106] On June 1, 1924, the day after the Soviet Union and China formally opened diplomatic relations, Chicherin also explained that an alliance with China was crucial, since the "political and economic interests of the world are more and more located on the Pacific ocean."[107]

During March 1925, Stalin called for "marshalling" the proletarian forces in the capitalist countries, the intensification of the struggle in the colonies for "liberation from imperialism," and for the "further development of industry" in the Soviet Union, so that the Soviet Union could act as the "bulwark of the revolutionary movement of all countries."[108] In a May 18, 1925 speech to the graduates of the University of the Toilers of the East, Stalin clarified that the first step in liberating the colonial countries would be to liberate China from the Chinese bourgeoisie and the foreign capitalists.[109]

Stalin also announced that the Bolshevik revolution had entered a new stage, the "overthrow of the bourgeoisie on a world scale." He defined the two opposing camps as "the camp of capitalism under the leadership of Anglo-American capital, and the camp of socialism under the leadership of the Soviet Union." Stalin set the terms of this conflict by announcing that "the international situation will in a greater and greater degree be determined by the relationship of forces between the two camps," and that if the capitalist countries tried to attack the USSR, it would once more become an "impregnable fortress" and would call on its allies, the "workers of the West and the oppressed peoples of the East," to "unleash the revolutionary lion in every country of the world."[110] Stalin also set the stage for this struggle when he emphasized that capitalism would be overthrown with the help of "the oppressed peoples of the East."[111]

After helping to organize, fund, and lead the KMT's revolutionary movement in China, Moscow had high hopes that it could draw China completely into the Soviet camp. It was especially important to promote the Chinese revolution because of the lengthy Sino-Soviet border; if China joined the socialist camp, it would increase the size of the Soviet bloc by four hundred million people. The Comintern supported temporarily the KMT's leading role in China's national revolution, but then clearly hoped to carry out a socialist revolution in China under the leadership of the workers movement.[112]

By May 1925, both the Comintern and the Narkomindel were prepared to bring the Chinese revolution to a new level of activity. In the middle of May, the death of a striking Chinese worker sparked the May Thirtieth Movement. The anticapitalist movement that started in Shanghai quickly spread to Canton, where a strike at the British concession on Shameen island began on June 20, 1925. A mass demonstration was organized by the CCP and the KMT, and thousands of Chinese students, workers, and ordinary citizens marched on Shameen island on June 23, 1925, precipitating conflict with the British. It was only after these incidents that the KMT's revolutionary movement became really prominent, and with the KMT's rise the CCP's status rose with it; from only about 1,000 members in January 1925, the membership of the CCP shot up to 30,000 in July 1926, and then doubled again to a high of 57,900 members in the spring of 1927, immediately before the KMT's purge of the communists.[113]

When word spread to Moscow of the May Thirtieth demonstrations in China, Zinoviev immediately published an article in *Pravda* on June 7, 1925, which listed China as being the most important of the colonial revolutionary movements. This represented a dramatic change from his analysis six months earlier when China was ranked third behind Persia and Turkey. The immediate target of the Chinese revolution were now clarified by Zinoviev to be England and Japan, with the United States being accused of supporting the other two. Zinoviev confidently stated that the situation in China had developed to the point that if the British and Japanese imperialists tried to repress it, it would be like adding "oil to the fire." Zinoviev also promised that the Shanghai workers' demand that the imperialists withdraw their warships from China would be met "with powerful echoes not only from Moscow and Leningrad, but in all the capitals of the world," as the world proletariat realized that the Chinese proletariat "stood as the advanced post in the world proletarian struggle."[114]

According to the Chinese communist, Ch'u Ch'iu-pai, the May Thirtieth Movement marked the real "beginning of the Chinese national revolution," and the Soviet press went so far as to predict: "Today China has woken up, tomorrow Indo-China and India will awaken. Today Shanghai, Hong Kong, Peking, and Canton have risen up, tomorrow Calcutta and Madras will rise up."[115] The rallying cry of the new worldwide revolution would be the May Thirtieth massacres: "With their volleys [of gunfire], the English and Japanese imperialists have stirred up and set in motion a wide section of the Chinese masses with much greater success, then could have been accomplished by even the most eloquent Comintern agitator. As a result, the movement, which began with a simple economic strike, has passed into the wider arena of political struggle, causing it to collide face to face with the most cruel oppressors of the Chinese people–the foreign imperialists."[116]

On June 17, the Comintern tried to expand the anticapitalist conflict in China to include proletariat in both Europe and the United States. In a telegram that it sent to the communist parties in France, Italy, the United States, and other countries, the Comintern ordered the local communists to organize protest meetings and to use the slogans: "1) Get the Imperialists out of China; 2) Abolish China's infamous unequal treaties; 3) Abolish extraterritoriality; 4) Satisfy the striking workers; 5) Immediately try those responsible for and guilty of shooting workers and students in Shanghai, Hankow, Tsingtao, and other places."[117] The slogans demanding the abolition of the capitalists' unequal treaties and extraterritoriality were especially important to the Comintern's strategy in China, as Zinoviev emphasized that the "main hope for the awakening East is the USSR."[118]

On July 6, the Comintern sent a letter to the Central Committee of the CCP instructing it to form local committees to organize workers and especially the peasantry, which they described as China's "decisive strength" and a group which "properly organized and armed would make the Chinese revolution invincible."[119] In a speech called "Eight Years of the Revolution," Zinoviev quoted a letter from a Comintern representative describing the revolution in China: "He reports that Canton reminds one of Leningrad or Moscow: the trade unions there are in the best homes, with red guards protecting the buildings of the trade unions, and parades in honor of visiting representatives of the Russian trade unions. Canton is a small Leningrad or a small Moscow."[120]

The Shameen incident further sparked off a boycott of all British goods in Canton, an action that was seen as almost an act of war by the British in Hong Kong. In the meantime, the workers' unrest spread to Hong Kong itself where a secret group called the Hong Kong Labor Commission helped organize the Hong Kong workers. This anti-British boycott was to last a whole year, and it became pivotal to the USSR's continued attempts to undermine and destroy the British economic position in China. It also turned the Bolsheviks' attention to the country that was now proclaimed to be the USSR's number one opponent, the United States. During the spring of 1925, the Bolshevik leader A. I. Rykov explained to the Central Executive Committee that all of the United States' attempts to isolate the Soviet Union had failed and that "it is the United States' policy towards the USSR which turns out to be isolated."[121]

Events in Asia were so important to Moscow that they were placed ahead of revolutionary events in Europe, as Zinoviev stated that Asia "appears now to be especially important, to its liking and with furious strength they are advancing like a torrent, undermining the stronghold of the world.[122] Now that Great Britain appeared immobilized by the Hong Kong strike, the United States grew in importance. Furthermore, during the fall of 1925, E. Varga, the Hungarian Comintern theoretician, even predicted for the first time that "the final struggle between the world bourgeoisie and proletariat will take place under the leadership of the United States and the Union of Socialist Republics."[123] The first battle of the cold war loomed on the horizon.

The Defeat of the United Front Policy

With the support of Stalin and Bukharin, and over the opposition of Trotsky and Zinoviev, the KMT/CCP's northern expedition began during the summer of 1926. By late fall it had moved north to the Yangtze river, had taken the important city of Wuhan, and was threatening to lay siege to Shanghai. Faced with the rapidly deteriorating position in China, the British Foreign Office issued a statement on September 30, 1926, warning that Great Britain was prepared to defend its interests in China "from pirates and robbers who, with their actions, pose a threat to the lives and property of British subjects."[124]

Great Britain tried to convince the United States to intervene in China, but its efforts failed.[125] Convinced of the moral correctness of China's claim for equal treatment, Secretary of State Kellogg telegraphed the following statement to the American consulate in Peking on November 29, 1926, in which he denied a request that American naval forces be used to protect the foreign customs house in Hankow from attack: "The Chinese Maritime Customs was brought into existence by the Government of China. It is a Chinese national service; it functions under the orders and protection of the Government of China, and the foreigners employed in it are servants of that Government. If that Government should desire the destruction of the Customs Administration, or if the desire of the Chinese people is to destroy the Government of China and the Customs Administration it has created, the basis of right upon which this Government may intervene in order to prevent either purpose from being accomplished is difficult to see. In consequence, I am unable to see my way clear, in regard to preventing the operation of the Customs house at Hankow from being paralyzed, to authorize landing an armed force in cooperation with other powers."[126]

Instead of fighting, the United States government backed down. In other words, the United States decided to dismantle voluntarily its Open Door Policy in

China, even though those policies had originally been intended to help China's development. Secretary of State Kellogg's decision not to intervene in China was based on his firm belief that the Chinese people were exercising their natural right to choose their own government. Kellogg, therefore, like many other foreigners, saw the events in China in terms of a Wilsonian nationalist revolution. He would probably not have come to this conclusion if not for the myth of Sino-Soviet equality, since it was that very myth that gave a veneer of moral legitimacy to the Soviet-supported revolutionary movement in China.

During 1926 and 1927 the Comintern declared that the revolution in China promised to expand the world revolution into Asia and would deliver the "fatal blow" to capitalism. Moscow's intense interest in China can best be seen by the sheer quantity of material that addressed the future of the Chinese revolution: for example, during 1927, thirty-one of the fifty-one editorials–over 60 percent–from the Comintern's editorial board and published in the *Communist International,* were about China.[127] As the Japanese Comintern member, Katayama Sen, enthusiastically declared: "China will stand–and this is inevitable–as the main center of the great collision between capitalism and communism. One of these is represented by the imperialist nations, while the other by the USSR."[128]

On December 10, 1926, the leading editorial of the *Communist International* called for the beginning of a "new phase" of the revolution in China in which "the struggle for hegemony between the proletariat and the bourgeoisie would determine the further direction of the revolution." This editorial stated that China was facing two paths: 1) the full independence of China by joining with the Soviet Union against imperialism with the final goal being socialism, 2) the semi-independence of China by making a compromise with the imperialist powers to take the path of capitalist development. Although the Chinese proletariat had played an important role in the Shanghai strikes of 1925, in the sixteen-month-long Hong Kong boycott, and in helping to make Canton its revolutionary base, the editorial admitted that the bourgeoisie were still in control and that the proletariat "have not yet played the role of the hegemony of the revolution."[129]

By late fall 1926, Chiang's Soviet-trained forces had moved north to the Yangtze river, had captured the city of Wuhan, and were threatening to lay siege to Shanghai. As the news of the British government decision to evacuate its Hankow concession spread to Moscow, the students at the Sun Yat-sen University reportedly cried with happiness and "embraced one another with joy and excitement."[130] The capture of Shanghai by the workers militia was also celebrated as a socialist victory, as Chinese students led thousands of Russian workers in a demonstration through the streets of Moscow to the Comintern building near Red Square. Radek addressed the crowd: "Shanghai is now in the hands of the Chinese, but when the revolutionary army marched into Shanghai they could still see the barbed wire set up by the British soldiers! The revolution in China is still in its embryonic stage; the counterrevolutionary forces have not been driven out. . . . Let the imperialists be aware that in case of necessity, the proletariat of Soviet Russia will not hesitate to support the Chinese Revolutionary Movement."[131]

This victory fed Comintern hopes of bringing China's anticapitalist revolution to fruition. But, the very success of the Northern Expedition also resulted in the foreign powers' long-awaited recognition of the KMT. With the start of diplomatic talks between British and KMT negotiators during 1926, and the KMT-British agreement that was reached in early 1927, the primary goal that had originally motivated Sun Yat-sen to join the United Front was achieved. From the KMT's perspective, the United Front Policy, and the CCP with it, were now expendable.

The March massacre of foreigners in Nanking also undermined the United States' earlier decision to remain aloof, and prompted American, British, French, Italian, and Japanese warships to bombard Nanking on March 24, 1927. The Bolsheviks responded by calling on worker's organizations around the world to prevent a new world war in China by recalling all foreign troops. Moscow also accused the foreigners of supporting Peking, calling the retaliation against Nanking, "intervention in the internal struggle in China and cannot be considered otherwise than active assistance for the Northerners with a view to giving them the possibility of forcing their way through the encircling Nationalist troops."[132]

At this crucial moment the Comintern once again called for intensifying the revolution in China: "On the one side, it will hasten the danger of intervention, which actually has already begun. At this threatening moment, by demanding great exertions of revolutionary energy, the Chinese proletariat ought to and will be able to win for themselves hegemony in the revolution. At this terrible moment, the international proletariat should collect all of its strength, so as to deliver a blow from the rear at rapacious imperialism."[133] According to an important CCP document captured during the KMT's anticommunist purges, and entitled *Essential Information About the Communist Party's Secret Work,* the CCP was actively training its members to infiltrate the KMT's party, government, and military organizations (see Appendix B).

The CCP's goal was to take over China's nationalist revolution and turn it into a socialist revolution. But on March 7, 1927, Chiang Kai-shek gave a speech in which he sent a clear warning to Moscow that they should not try to take control of the Chinese revolution. Referring to Sun's pro-Soviet policy, Chiang said: "Our President wanted freedom and equality, and as Soviet Russia was willing to treat us on equal footing, it is natural that we should make her our ally. So long as Russia deals with us in the same spirit, we shall not forsake the pro-Soviet policy."[134] Soon after Chiang made his speech denouncing the Soviet Union, the left KMT and the CCP consolidated control over the KMT's Central Committee. On March 13, the Central Committee stripped Chiang of his chairmanships of the Political Committee, the Standing Committee, and the Military Council. His only remaining official post was as Commander of the Expeditionary Forces.

This action appeared to be a complete victory for the Comintern, as many Chinese communist members were elected to top positions within the KMT party. Influential left KMT leaders, such as "George Hsu Chien, Sun Fo, Teng Yen-da, Eugene Chen, and T. V. Soong," also gained more power. But these actions brought about an immediate response, as the right KMT faction denounced the Central Committee's decisions and agitated for the "discharge of comrade Borodin."[135] When Chiang Kai-shek also demanded that the Comintern recall Borodin, the Political Committee in Wuhan responded by stripping him of his last official title as military commander.

Ignoring this decision, Chiang issued an order on April 5, to disarm all militia in Shanghai who were not members of the KMT nationalist army. This included many members of the Shanghai communist cells. Then, on April 6, Chiang ordered the Second and Sixth armies to march northwards toward Nanking in order to cut Wuhan off from the communists in Shanghai. In a meeting in Wuhan on April 7, Borodin recommended that the left KMT government move quickly to Nanking in order to beat Chiang there, but he was too late, as Chiang Kai-shek personally entered Nanking on April 9, and consolidated his control.[136]

On April 9, reports also began to circulate that Chiang's troops were taking action against communists in Shanghai, described as the "first definite attack on the Communist Party in the Shanghai area."[137] On April 12, the KMT repression increased into full-blown purge that lasted well into 1928, and eventually resulted in the demise of thousands of communists; one Soviet report later estimated that during the first eight months of 1928 alone, some 100,000 workers and peasants lost their lives–27,000 of them reportedly executed by the KMT.[138]

On April 18, Chiang Kai-shek established a new government in Nanking under the control of the right KMT. With the end of the United Front, Soviet military advisers were forced to withdraw to the USSR. One scholar has described this purge as "an expression of Chinese nationalism directed at Russian imperialism."[139] The news of Chiang's coup took several days to reach Moscow, however, and so in a speech to the Fourth Soviet Congress on April 18, Rykov continued to insist that China and the Soviet Union were the "chief nodal points in international affairs today." This was only in part because the two countries jointly accounted for "one-third of the world's population," but a more important reason was that the conflict in China was now the "focus of colonial policy" and the outcome of the Chinese revolution would decide the "future of imperialism, at least the future of imperialism in the forms in which it has developed over the last decades."[140]

Only one month earlier, Radek had warned the capitalist nations that "in case of necessity, the proletariat of Soviet Russia would not hesitate to support the Chinese Revolutionary Movement." On April 25, however, the Soviet military commander Kliment Voroshilov reported that the "Red Army is very weak in modern heavy technical equipment, that the Red Air Force is small and not independent of foreign technical resource."[141] In fact, the Soviet Union's military weakness meant that it could not afford to intervene in China. By refusing to come to the aid of its communist allies in China, however, the Soviet government condemned the CCP to a one-sided battle against the KMT, a battle that the Chinese communists' repeated opposition to the United Front Policy from 1921 through 1927 proves they had never wanted to undertake in the first place. As a result, China's socialist revolution ended with barely a whimper.[142]

Conclusions

Moscow created the KMT/CCP United Front to marshal Chinese public opinion behind Soviet diplomats in Peking. Thereafter, the United Front became the leader of China's nationalist revolution, the first stage in China's two-stage socialist revolution. Every time CCP leaders requested that they be allowed to withdraw from the United Front, Moscow refused. In addition, when a handful of Bolsheviks supported Ch'en's attempts to end the United Front, they too were roundly criticized by Stalin and Bukharin. Trotsky's vocal support for an independent CCP later played a role in his expulsion from the CPSU in 1927.

But, if the Soviet-supported Comintern formed the CCP and promoted its entry into the United Front to support Moscow's imperialistic diplomacy with Peking, then, by extension, the USSR would also be primarily responsible for the subsequent failure of that policy. Soviet historians have traditionally skirted this unsettling conclusion, tending to blame the United Front's failure on Ch'en Tu-hsiu's poor leadership instead. Soviet attempts to redirect blame for the defeat of the United Front onto Ch'en are undermined, however, by the wide range of sources that reveal this policy to have been highly unpopular within the CCP.[143] In addition, Borodin, arguably the most important Comintern adviser in China, admitted that the Comintern condemned Ch'en Tu-hsiu for his repeated attempts to withdraw from the KMT before it was too late.[144]

Chinese communists who survived the KMT purges could not have been blind to the Soviet government's imperialistic policies in Manchuria and Outer Mongolia, nor could they have been oblivious to the fact that they were made the scapegoat for Stalin's failed plans, nor unaware of their leaders' repeated attempts to withdraw from the United Front between 1924 to 1927. Yet, all of these painfully obvious facts were denied by the Comintern's central leadership in Moscow.

One can only speculate, therefore, about the bitterness engendered among Chinese communists who risked their lives to support the USSR's "red imperialism" in China. The most striking case of Soviet imperialism was Outer Mongolia, where Soviet diplomatic efforts to retain control over Outer Mongolia were actively supported by the CCP. To bring about this diplomatic victory, the Comintern worked closely with the Narkomindel to develop propaganda designed to sway Chinese public opinion in the Soviet Union's favor. Articles written by such notable communists as Kao Chun-yu, Ts'ai Ho-sen, and Ch'en Tu-hsiu, and then published in the CCP journals during 1922-24, were an important part of this plan. By supporting the Soviet diplomats against the Peking government, however, the CCP's publications became a public platform advocating the return to China's unequal treaties with Russia. In this regard, there can be little doubt that Comintern-funded CCP journals like *The Guide Weekly* and *The Vanguard* played an important role in supporting the Soviet foreign policy agenda in China.

A comparison of the USSR's propaganda and diplomacy in China shows that there were intimate links between the Comintern's and the Narkomindel's activities. While Comintern agents in China publicly supported Outer Mongolia's "autonomy," Soviet diplomats secretly worked to reassert tsarist Russia's unequal treaties and once again turn Outer Mongolia into a Russian protectorate. Maring's position as the *de facto* editor of the CCP's party journals made him one of the Comintern's most valued agents in China. As such, it is important to note that Maring even admitted in a 1924 letter to Moscow that there was a "close connection in many Eastern countries between Comintern and Narkomindel."[145]

Throughout the late 1920s and all of the 1930s, the Chinese communists continued to believe that the USSR's control over Outer Mongolia was merely temporary. Mao Tse-tung, a member of the CCP since its formation in 1921, even referred to this arrangement in a 1936 interview with Edgar Snow. In answer to Snow's question about the status Outer Mongolia, Mao repeated the 1922 resolutions almost word for word: "The relationship between Outer Mongolia and the Soviet Union, now and in the past, has always been based on the principle of complete equality. When the people's revolution has been victorious in China the Outer Mongolian republic will automatically become a part of the Chinese federation, at their own will. The Mohammedan and Tibetan peoples, likewise, will form autonomous republics attached to the China federation." In the meantime, however, Snow concluded that Outer Mongolia was already "definitely under the Red banner," even though China's suzerainty was still "nominally recognized, even by Russia."[146]

The Chinese communists' expectation that Outer Mongolia would be returned to their control was undermined on May 15, 1943, when the Comintern was officially dissolved by Stalin. Historians have generally interpreted Stalin's action as an attempt to deceive his Western allies into believing that Moscow no longer supported communist expansion.[147] But it can be argued that Moscow's secret pact with the CCP was also terminated with the Comintern's dissolution. Abolishing the Comintern's 1922 agreement with the CCP was the first step in Moscow's successful post–World War II policy of using secret diplomacy to consolidate permanent control over Outer Mongolia and to expand its influence into central China, actions that will be discussed in greater detail in the Conclusions.

Notes

1. Adam B. Ulam, *Expansion and Coexistence*, 172.

2. This cooperation is shown most clearly by the fact that many of Maring's progress reports were addressed both to the Comintern and to the Narkomindel; for example, on July 11, 1922, Maring reported: "The Consul [Paikes] sent my preliminary report for Narkomindel and the Comintern to Russia." Tony Saich, *The Origins of the First United Front in China: The Role of Sneevliet (Alias Maring)*, Vol. 1, 323.

3. Allen S. Whiting, *Soviet Policies in China, 1917-1924*, 53.

4. Harold Isaacs, "Documents on the Comintern and the Chinese Revolution." *China Quarterly* 45: 1971, 100-115: 102.

5. Dov Bing provided perhaps the best example of how the United Front was formerly attributed solely to Maring, even to the point where Maring is given credit for

convincing the Soviet government to adopt this policy: "It was, as we shall see, in the China of 1921-23 that Sneevliet initiated the formal establishment of the CCP, founded the Secretariat of the Chinese Labour Federation and almost singlehanded brought about the famous and controversial KMT/CCP alliance. In fact, he not only persuaded the leadership of the Comintern to adopt his policies, but also the KMT of Sun Yat-sen, the young CCP and the People's Commissariat of Foreign Affairs of Soviet Russia (Narkomindel)" (Dov Bing, "Sneevliet and the Early Days of the Chinese Communist Party," *The China Quarterly*, No. 48 [October-December 1971], 677-697; a reprint also appears in 马林在中国的关于资料 [*Documents on Maring in China*]).

6. According to Warren Lerner, only the deaths of Rosa Luxemburg and Karl Liebknecht, who had supported purely proletarian revolutions over Russia's mixed worker-peasant revolution, freed Lenin's hands and allowed him to adopt formally the United Front Policy during the Comintern's second congress in 1920. The ideological conflict between Lenin and Luxemburg might explain why the Bolsheviks *de facto* adopted the United Front Policy in China almost two years prior to its formal adoption (*Karl Radek: The Last Internationalist,* 93).

7. Bing, 677-697.

8. Bao Hui-seng (包惠僧), "回忆马林" ("Memories of Maring"), 马林在中国的关于资料 (*Documents on Maring in China*), 95.

9. Bing, 681.

10. Ch'en Kung-po. *The Communist Movement in China: As Essay Written in 1924.* Edited by C. Martin Wilbur, 84.

11. The CCP's 1922 resolution to join the Comintern meant that it had to adopt twenty-one organizational rules, the most important being that all members had to follow the orders sent to them by the Comintern's Executive Committee in Moscow. As a result, all CCP members were subordinate to the Comintern and could face disciplinary action if they failed to carry out Moscow's orders. Roy Medvedev observed that a "tight, almost military discipline was maintained within these sections" (*Let History Judge*, 378).

12. 中共中央文件选集 (*A Collection of Documents of the Chinese Communist Party's Central Committee*), Vol. 1, 31-32.

13. Sergei Dalin (Сергей Далин), *В Рядах Китайской Революция (In the Ranks of the Chinese Revolution*), 70-95.

14. Lee Feigon, *Chen Duxiu: Founder of the Chinese Communist Party,* 103.

15. Ch'en Tu-hsiu (陈独秀), 陈独秀文章选编 (*A Collection of Ch'en Tu-hsiu's Articles*), 182-183.

16. G. Maring (Г. Маринга), "Революционно-националистическое движение в южном Китае" (The Revolutionary-Nationalist Movement in Southern China"), *Коммунистический Интернационал (Communist International*), 1922, No. 21-22, 5815.

17. Dalin, 77.

18. 先驅 (*The Pioneer*), "中國共產黨對於時局的主張" ("The Chinese Communist Party's Proprosals with Regard to the Current Political Situation"), June 20, 1922, No. 9, 1-3.

19. "Manifesto of the Second National Congress of the CCP," Conrad Brandt, Benjamin Schwartz, and John K. Fairbank, eds., *A Documentary History of Chinese Communism,* 64-65.

20. V. I. Glunin (В. И. Глунин), *Коминтерн и Восток (The Comintern and the East*), 352.

21. Ch'en Kung-po, 83.

22. 先驅 (*The Pioneer*), "中國共產黨對於 . . ." ("The Chinese Communist Party's Proprosals . . . "). June 20, 1922, No. 9, 1-3.

23. "Состояние Коммунистического движения в Китае" ("The Situation of the Communist Movement in China"), *Pravda* , July 30, 1922.

24. G. Maring (Г. Маринга), "У революционеров Южн. Китая" ("With the Revolutionaries of Southern China"). *Pravda*, September 7, 1922.

25. Isaacs, 106.

26. Feigon,169-170.

27. *Коммунистический Интернационал и китайская революция Документы и материалы* (*The Communist International and the Chinese Revolution, Documents and Materials*), 25.

28. Pavel Mif, *Heroic China*, 21.

29. L. P. Deliusin (Л. П. Делюсин), *Аграрно-крестьянский Вопрос в Политике КПК 1921-1928* (Agrarian and Peasant Questions in the Policies of the CCP 1921-1928), 129.

30. Ssu Shun (思順) and Kao Chun-yu (君宇), "陳獨秀君造國論底疑問" ("Questions upon reading [Chen] Duxiu's 'Theory of Building the Country'"). 嚮導週報 (*The Guide Weekly*), October 4, 1922, No. 4, 34-35.

31. *Ibid.*

32. G. Safarov (薩發洛夫), "第三國際與遠東民族問題" ("The Third International and the Problem of Eastern Nationalities"). 嚮導週報 (*The Guide Weekly*), November 8, 1922, No. 9, 74-76.

33. G. Safarov (Г. Сафаров), "Восток и Революция" ("Revolution and the East"). *Коммунистический Интернационал* (*Communist International*), 1921, No. 15, 3127-3140.

34. Benjamin I. Schwartz, *Chinese Communism and the Rise of Mao*, 47.

35. *Коммунистический Интернационал. . .* (*The Communist International . . .*), 37.

36. E. H. Carr, *The Bolshevik Revolution*, Volume 3, 123.

37. *Советско-китайские Отношения 1917-1957 сборник документов*(*Soviet-Chinese Relations, 1917-1957: Collection of Documents*), 109-111.

38. Lao Hsiu-ch'ao, "Представитель Китая о III Интернационале" ("The Chinese Representative about the Third International "), *Izvestiia*, March 6, 1919.

39. "Extracts from the Thesis on the International Situation and the Policy of the Entente Adopted by the First Comintern Congress," March 6, 1919, Jane Degras, *The Communist International 1919-1943*, Vol. 1, 34.

40. Saich, Vol. 1, 370.

41. Sun To (孫鐸)(Maring), "墓中人語" ("An Epitaph of the Chinese People"), 嚮導週報 (*The Guide Weekly*), May 23, 1923, No. 26, 191-192.

42. Saich, Vol. 1, 230.

43. Ts'ai Ho-sen (和森), "中國國際地位與承認蘇維埃俄羅斯" ("China's International Position and the Recognition of Soviet Russia"), 嚮導週報 (*The Guide Weekly*), September 27, 1922, No. 3, 17-19.

44. Richard Ullman, *Anglo-Soviet Relations 1917-1921*, Vol. 2, 113, footnote 30.

45. In addition to the diplomats themselves, this Soviet mission included Joffe's private secretary, an attaché, a China expert, and then an Information Bureau chief, backed up by two interpreters, two cipher specialists, three typists, and two diplomatic couriers. At this time the mission included (spellings same as original): "A. A. Joffe,

Extraordinary Plenipotentiary Envoy; N. K. Kuznetsoff, Second Secretary; I. K. Levin, Private Secretary; A. A. Rigin, Attache; A. I. Ivanov, Expert; A. I. Gekker, Military Expert; I. N. Batrakoff, Head of the Financial Section; B. F. Lebedeff, Head of the Information Bureau; S. K. Schwartsalon, Interpreter; B. V. Zvonareff, Interpreter; G. A. Evlampieff, Head of the Cipher Section; A. J. Klimoff, Member of the Cipher Section; Mrs. Z. A. Rigin, Typist; Mrs. E. L. Lebedeff, Typist; Mrs. L. A. Michelson, Typist; L. J. Berkowsky, Diplomatic Courier; J. A. Joffe, Diplomatic Courier." On August 31, 1922, they added: "I. E. Leonidov, Commercial Attache at Shanghai; C. A. Michelson, Assistant Manager of the Economics Department; A. S. Gatsky, Chauffeur." On October 28, 1922, they added: "J. M. Blioch, The Diplomatic Courier; Miss Popkova, the official." On January 1, 1922, they added: "Davtian, Councillor." On February 27, 1923, they added: "Golzmann, the diplomatic Courier; Mrs. Tatyana, The Wife of one of the Commercial employees of the mission; Petrovna Bagdanova, with daugher Miss Tamara." On June 27, 1923, they added the names of five "students" who were later revealed to be military advisers to the Kuomintang: "Smolenzeff, Mrs. Smolenzeff, A. I. Terechatoff, Y. Y. Guerman, A. I. Tcherepanoff, V. E. Poliak." The members of Paikes's earlier mission might also have stayed on in China after Joffe's arrival, but this is not made clear by these documents. English- and Chinese-language lists, August 23, 1923, WCTA, 03-32, 462(2).

46. Ch'en Kung-po, 119.

47. *Ibid.*, 121.

48. *Ibid.*, 122.

49. "Russia and Weak Nations Must Unite to Block Imperialist," *North China Star,* August 20, 1922.

50. Erich von Salzmann's November 9, 1922 interview with the councillor of the German Foreign Office, identified simply as Dr. Assmis; Gaimushō, 2.5.1 106-1.

51. Erich von Salzmann's January 23, 1923 interview with Soviet diplomat J. Davtian, listed as the Soviet mission's "councillor," Gaimushō, 2.5.1 106-2 .

52. English-language memorandum from the "Extraordinary Plenipotentiary Mission of the Russian Socialist Federative Soviet Republic," August 25, 1922, WCTA, 03-32, 207(1).

53. These numbers appear in the Chinese-language minutes of a meeting between Wellington Koo and Jacob Schurman, the American minister in China, September 13, 1922, WCTA, 03-32, 199(1).

54. David Dallin, *The Rise of Russia in Asia,* 193.

55. *New Russia,* January 6, 1923, Vol. 1, No. 1, 31.

56. 马林在中国的关于资料 (*Documents on Maring in China*), 109.

57. Letter from Joffe to Maring, November 7, 1922, Saich, Vol. 1, 353.

58. John C. Ferguson's letter to the president of the Republic of China, with a copy to Wellington Koo, September 8, 1922, WCTA, 03-32, 472(3).

59. Kao Chun-yu (君宇), "國人對蒙古問題應持的態度," ("What Chinese People's Attitude Towards the Mongolian Problem Ought to Be"), 嚮導週報 (*The Guide Weekly*), September 27, 1922, No. 3, 19-20.

60. Ts'ai Ho-sen, (和森) "中國國際地位與. . ." ("China's International Position and. . . ."), 嚮導週報 (*The Guide Weekly*), September 27, 1922, No. 3, 17-19.

61. Ch'en Tu-hsiu, "The Immediate Tactics of the Communist Party of China," November 1922, Saich, Vol. 1, 364.

62. Kao Chun-yu (君宇), "國人對. . ." ("What Chinese People's. . . ."), 嚮導週報 (*The Guide Weekly*), September 27, 1922, No. 3, 19-20.

63. *The Vanguard* was initially published with money from the Comintern, as shown in a report from Maring that listed the monthly expenses during 1923 for political and propaganda work at 770 rubles. Saich, Vol. 1, 191. On July 3, 1923, Maring reported to the Communist International: "On the 15th, the first number of the new magazine *Vanguard* will appear and we expect that this monthly, with good administration, will pay for itself." Saich, Vol. 2, 668-670.

64. De Fu (德輔), "外蒙古獨立現狀" ("The *Status Quo* of Outer Mongolia's Independence"), 前鋒 (*The Vanguard*), 1924, No. 3, 49-59.

65. *Ibid.*

66. Ch'en Tu-hsiu (獨秀), "美國侵略與蒙古獨立" ("American Aggression and Mongolian Independence") 嚮導週報 (*The Guide Weekly*), July 23, 1924, No. 75, 597-598.

67. Two Draft Plans for the Reorganization of the Kuomintang, undated, Saich, Vol. 2, 555-564; of special interest is that Maring's budget for one year of operation was $420,000–a sizable sum in 1923.

68. C. Martin Wilbur, *Sun Yat-sen Frustrated Patriot,* 193.

69. Letter from eleven top Kuomintang leaders to Sun Yat-sen protesting Borodin's influence, December 3, 1923. Reprinted in September 1927, Archives of the Historical Commission of the Central Committee of the Kuomintang Party, Document No. 467-3.

70. Robert C. North, *Moscow and Chinese Communists,* 76.

71. Deliusin (Делюсин), *Аграрно-крестьянский Вопрос . . . (Agrarian and Peasant Questions. . . .*), 99.

72. Ch'en Tu-hsiu (獨秀), "利用國民黨" ("To Use the Kuomintang"), 嚮導週報 (*The Guide Weekly*), March 26, 1924, No. 58, 466.

73. Historical Commission of the Central Committee of the Kuomintang Party–Contemporary History Collection: 467-39, 15; Chou Fo-hai was an early CCP member who was present at the first party congress, but then later left the CCP. His manuscript, entitled *A Report of a Flight from the Red Capital Wuhan,* was written immediately after the 1927 split, and is his attempt to exonerate his early CCP activities (quite possiby to save himself from being arrested and executed by Chiang Kai-shek's forces).

74. This interview is included in a volume published by the Central Control Yuan of the Kuomintang Party during September 1927 (Archives of the Historical Commission of the Central Committee of the Kuomintang Party, Document 467-3). It was later reprinted in Vol. 9 of 革命文獻 (*Documents of the Revolution*) but with important omissions.

75. Wilbur, *Sun Yat-sen*, 231.

76. *Ibid.*

77. G. Voitinskii (Г. Войтинский), "Положение на юге Китая и правительство Сун Ят–Сена " ("The Situation in South China and the Government of Sun Yat-sen"), *Коммунистический Интернационал (Communist International*), 1924, No. 36, 202.

78. Deliusin (Делюсин), *Аграрно-крестьянский Вопрос . . . (Agrarian and Peasant Questions. . . .*), 122.

79. C. Martin Wilbur and Julie Lien-ying How, *Missionaries of Revolution: Soviet Advisers and Nationalist China, 1920-1927,* 105-106.

80. Whiting, 39.

81. G. Maring (Г. Маринга), "Революционно-националистическое движение в южном Китае," ("The Revolutionary-Nationalist Movement in Southern China"), *Коммунистический Интернационал (Communist International*), 1922, No 21-22, 5815.

82. 马林在中国的关于资料 (*Documents on Maring in China*), 11-15.

83. Sun To (孫鐸) (Maring), "中國改造之外國援助" ("China's Reconstruction and Foreign Aid"), 嚮導週報 (*The Guide Weekly*), June 13, 1923, No. 29, 214-215.

84. Sun To (孫鐸) (Maring), "中國國民運動之過去及將來" ("China's Nationalist Movement's Past and Future"), 前鋒 (*The Vanguard*), July 1923, No. 1, 2-9.

85. Sun To (孫鐸) (Maring), "他們的道路與我們的道路" ("Their Path and Our Path"), 嚮導週報 (*The Guide Weekly*), July 18, 1923, No. 33, 248-250.

86. Sun To (孫鐸) (Maring), "中國國民運動之 . . ." ("China's Nationalist Movement's. . . ."), 前鋒 (*The Vanguard*), July 1923, No. 1, 2-9.

87. Sun To (孫鐸) (Maring), "他們的道路與. . ." ("Their Path and. . . ."), 嚮導週報 (*The Guide Weekly*), July 18, 1923, No. 33, 248-250.

88. Sun To (孫鐸) (Maring), "北京政變與上海工會之主張" ("The Peking Government Restructuring and the Shanghai Workers Union's Position"), 嚮導週報 (*The Guide Weekly*), July 11, 1923, No. 31/32, 237-239.

89. N. Bukharin (Н. Бухарина), "Отчет Российского представителя в Исполкоме Коминтерна" ("Account of the Russian Representative of the Central Executive Committee of the Comintern"), *Pravda*, April 21, 1923.

90. *Коммунистический Интернационал* . . . (*The Communist International.* . . .), 42.

91. G. Maring (Г. Маринга), "Кровавый Эпизод в истории китайского рабочего движения" ("The Bloody Episode in the History of the Chinese Workers' Movement"), *Коммунистический Интернационал* (*Communist International*), Summer 1923, No. 26-27, 7457-7458.

92. "中國共產黨第三次全國大宣言" ("The Manifesto of the Chinese Communist Party's Third Congress"), 嚮導週報 (*The Guide Weekly*), June 20, 1923, No. 30, 228.

93. Sergei Dalin (Сергей Далин), *В Рядах Китайской Революция* (*In the Ranks of the Chinese Revolution*), 147.

94. Conrad Brandt, *Stalin's Failure in China*, 38.

95. G. Voitinskii (Г. Войтинский), "Положение на юге Китая и правительство Сун Ят–Сена " ("The Situation in South China and the Government of Sun Yat-sen"), *Коммунистический Интернационал* (*Communist International*), 1924, No. 36, 198.

96. A minute book of the executive committee of the Shanghai branch of the Kuomintang (Archives of the Historical Commission of the Central Committee of the Kuomintang Party, Document No. 435-79).

97. This Kuomintang branch was very busy, with an executive committee meeting every Thursday, while the secretariat met every day from 1:00 p.m. to 2:00 p.m. to carry out business. On February 28, 1924, Hu Han-min, Mao Tse-tung, and Ch'u Ch'iu-pai participated in forming sections, deciding how they would carry out business, and in making sure that the sections realized that they had to obey all of the decisions of the local executive committee. These decisions would be published during the monthly printing of 3,000 *China Daily* newspapers (Archives of the Historical Commission of the Central Committee of the Kuomintang Party, Document No. 435-79).

98. Deliusin (Делюсин), *Аграрно-крестьянский Вопрос* . . . (*Agrarian and Peasant Questions.* . . .), 125.

99. For example, L. P. Deliusin (Л. П. Делюсин), and A. S. Kostiaeva (А. С. Костяева) state that early Soviet historiography of the 1925-27 Chinese Revolution largely ignored the importance of the Chinese revolution to the Soviet Union. During the 1950s,

Soviet historiography was still not willing to approach this topic objectively and only later raised the question of Soviet responsibility (*Революция 1925-1927 гг. в Китае: проблемы и оценки* [*Revolution of 1925-1927 in China: Problems and Appraisals*], 3-11).

100. Sun To (孫鐸)(Maring), "北京政變與. . ." ("The Peking Government Restructuring and. . . ."), 嚮導週報 (*The Guide Weekly*), July 11, 1923, No. 31/32, 237-239.

101. Chang Hsu-hsin, "The Kuomintang's Foreign Policy, 1925-1928,"138.

102. Ch'en Tu-hsiu (獨秀), "悼孫中山先生!," ("Mourn Dr. Sun Yat-sen!"), 嚮導週報 (*The Guide Weekly*), March 14, 1925, No. 106, 881.

103. "中國共產黨為孫中山之死告中國民眾" ("The Chinese Communist Party Announces Sun Yat-sen's Death to the Chinese Masses"), 嚮導週報 (*The Guide Weekly*), March 21, 1925, No. 107, 889-890.

104. Wilbur, *Sun Yat-sen* , 277.

105. Lyon Sharman, *Sun Yat-sen: His Life and Its Meaning*, 308.

106. Russian-language minutes of Karakhan's speech, September 4, 1923; WCTA, 03-32, 467 (1).

107. Georgii Chicherin (Георгий Чичерин), "Соглащение СССР с Китаем" ("The USSR's Agreement with China"), *Pravda*, June 1, 1924.

108. "Article by Stalin on the International Situation and the Tasks of the Communist Parties," March 22, 1925, Degras, Vol. 2, 19-23.

109. William James Megginson III, "Britain's Response to Chinese Nationalism, 1925-1927: The Foreign Office Search for a New Policy," 65.

110. "Extracts from a Report by Stalin on the Work of the Fourteenth Conference of the Communist Party of the Soviet Union," May 9, 1925, Degras, Vol. 2, 25-28.

111. *Ibid.*

112. H. Lentsner (Н. Ленцнер), *Китайская Революция и Оппозиция* (*The Chinese Revolution and the Opposition*), 55.

113. According to Jordan, the Kuomintang figures listed the first figure as only 7,000 but agreed with the second figure, 226-227.

114. G. Zinoviev (Г. Зиновьев), "Всемирно—историческое значение шанхайских событий" ("The Worldwide Historical Significance of the Shanghai Events"), *Pravda*, June 7, 1925.

115. Deliusin (Делюсин), *Аграрно-крестьянский Вопрос* . . . (*Agrarian and Peasant Questions*. . . .), 150.

116. F. F. (Ф. Ф.) "Пробудившиися Китая" ("Awakening China"), *Коммунистический Интернационал* (Communist International), July 1925, No. 8, 3-21.

117. *Коммунистический Интернационал*... (*Communist International*. . . .), 53.

118. G. Zinoviev (Г. Зиновьев), "Наше международное положение" ("Our International Position"), *Коммунистический Интернационал* (*Communist International*), October 1, 1925, No. 10, 7.

119.*Коммунистический Интернационал* . . . (*Communist International*. . . .), 535.

120. G. Zinoviev (Г. Зиновьев), "8 лет революции" ("Eight Years of Revolution"), *Коммунистический Интернационал* (*Communist International*), November 1925, No. 11, 15.

121. "Extracts from a Speech by Rykov at the Central Executive Committee," March 3, 1925, Degras, Vol. 2, 12-15.

122. *Ibid.*

123. E. Varga (Е. Варга), "Пути и препятствия мировой революции" ("Paths and Obstacles of the World Revolution"), *Коммунистический Интернационал* (*Communist International*), December1925, No. 12, 5-23.

124. *Daily Telegraph*, September 30, 1926.

125. Roberta Allbert Dayer, *Bankers and Diplomats in China, 1917-1925: The Anglo-American Relationship*, 236.

126. John Carter Vincent, *The Extraterritorial System in China,* 10.

127. These numbers were gathered at the Lenin Library during nine months in 1988-1989, during which time many previously unavailable journals and books on China were opened to outside scholars for the first time since the 1920s. Since the journals specifically dedicated to China were published in tirages of only 1,000-5,000, most never found their way out of the Soviet Union. These journals show just how important the Chinese revolution was to the Soviet Union's hope of spreading revolution to Asia. During 1927, for example, a total of 75 articles in the *Communist International* discussed China; this was out of 289 articles total, or over 25 percent. One journal, entitled *Materials on the Chinese Revolution*, was published by the Sun Yat-sen University in Moscow and was devoted fully to China, while journals like *Bolshevik* and *Problems of China* also featured many articles discussing the revolutionary situation there. In addition, the daily press, which included *Pravda* and *Izvestiia*, often had several articles every day giving updates on the northern expedition's progress. These statistics on China-centered articles and editorials in the *Communist International* alone cast doubt on Donald W. Treadgold's conclusion: "It may be doubted that a policy of even temporary priority for Asia was clearly formulated and adopted before the Chinese Communists stood on the threshold of their post–World War II victory" ("Russia and the Far East," in Ivo J. Lederer, ed. *Russian Foreign Policy*, 554).

128. Sen Katayama (Сен Катаяма), "К положению в Китае" ("On the Position in China). *Коммунистический Интернационал* (*Communist International*), 59 (September 15, 1926): 36-37.

129. "Китайская революция и задачи *Коммунестических партий*" ("The Chinese Revolution and the Problems of the Communist Party"), *Коммунистический Интернационал* (*Communist International*), December 10, 1926, No. 13, 3-8.

130. Yueh Sheng, *Sun Yat-sen University in Moscow and the Chinese Revolution*, 119-120; according to Yueh Sheng, Chinese students became so popular after the taking of Shanghai that Russian girls crowded around them at theaters and the more daring ones "offered themselves as loving wives and asked to be taken back to China."

131. *Ibid.*

132. *Izvestiia*, March 27, 1927.

133. "Новый Этап победоносной революции" ("New Epoch of Victorious Revolution"), *Коммунистический Интернационал* (*Communist International*), April 1, 1927, No. 13, 3-10.

134. *North China Herald,* March 7, 1927.

135. *North China Herald,* March 18, 1927.

136. Sheng, 126-128.

137. *North China Herald*, April 9, 1927.

138. *Советы в Китае–Сборник Материалов и Документов* (*Soviets in China–A Collection of Materials and Documents*), 9.

139. Tetsuya Kataoka, *Resistance and Revolution in China: The Communists and the Second United Front,* 7

140. "Extracts from the Report of Rykov, Chairman of the Council of People's Commissars, to the Fourth Soviet Congress," April 18, 1927, Degras, Vol. 2, 182-192.

141. *British Foreign Policy Documents–Soviet Union*, Vol. 9, Series A, Part II, 48.

142. Many scholars have taken the view that Chiang Kai-shek's coup signified the end of the revolution; for example Harold Isaacs stated: "The defeat of the revolution placed the Kuomintang in power" (Isaacs, 377); also see Lucien Bianco, *Origins of the Chinese Revolution*, 55-57; Jean Chesneaux, Francoise Le Barbier, and Marie-Claire Bergere, *China from the 1911 Revolution to Liberation*, 155-185.

143. Deliusin (Делюсин), *Аграрно-крестьянский Вопрос . . .* (*Agrarian and Peasant Questions. . . .*), 122.

144. Victor A. Yakhontoff, *The Chinese Soviets*, 124.

145. Letter from Maring to Zinoviev, March 8, 1924, Saich, Vol. 2, 708.

146. Edgar Snow, *Red Star Over China,* 102.

147. Ulam, 346-347.

Conclusions

Sino-Soviet diplomatic records from the 1920s show in great detail how the USSR used secret diplomacy to sever Outer Mongolia from China, reclaim control over the CER, and recover virtually all of tsarist Russia's unequal rights and privileges in China, including the Boxer Indemnity, territorial concessions, and extraterritoriality. These records not only reveal that Russia's imperialist foreign policy in China remained remarkably constant both before and after the October Revolution, but they also serve as one of the best indicators of what the USSR sought to accomplish after World War II. Most important, they unveil what the real *status quo* was in Sino-Soviet diplomatic relations; the exact meaning of *status quo* proved extremely important during the Yalta talks in February 1945, and during Sino-Soviet talks from June through August 1945.

Following the end of World War II, the USSR did not renegotiate its unequal treaties with China, but instead resorted once again to secret diplomacy to try to expand its power in China even further. The best example of this Soviet tactic was in Outer Mongolia, which was granted its independence from China on January 1, 1946, following what appeared to be an officially sanctioned plebiscite as outlined by the August 14, 1945 Sino-Soviet Treaty of Friendship and Alliance.

Nationalist China's decision to hold a plebiscite in Outer Mongolia has been universally blamed on the February 11, 1945 Yalta Agreement, in which Roosevelt, Churchill, and Stalin agreed: "The *status quo* in Outer-Mongolia (the Mongolian People's Republic) shall be preserved."[1] As a result, Yalta has been widely criticized for forcing China to give up Outer Mongolia, as well as being the root cause of many of Nationalist China's other postwar problems. One recently published book even described the Sino-Soviet treaty as "a treaty characterized by most Chinese as a mere appendix to Yalta"[2]; a second source claimed that it was the Yalta Agreement that dictated that "a plebiscite to be held in Outer Mongolia"[3]; and a third scholarly work asserted that "Outer Mongolia, as arranged at Yalta, gravitated completely within the Soviet orbit."[4]

Knowledge of the USSR's secret diplomacy during the 1920s allows for an alternative interpretation, however, since Yalta's use of the word *status quo* did not in fact support granting Outer Mongolia its independence from China, but actually meant the continuation of China's juridical sovereignty, as stipulated by the May 31, 1924 Sino-Soviet Treaty. When Roosevelt agreed to support the *status quo* in Outer Mongolia, therefore, he did not intend to betray China's national interests. Instead, Roosevelt tried to support China's continued sovereignty over Outer Mongolia.

This interpretation of the true meaning of *status quo* not only undermines the myth that Roosevelt sacrificed China at Yalta, much in the same way as Woodrow Wilson was falsely accused of sacrificing China at Paris, but also suggests that it was not the Yalta Agreement that forced China into making this decision. In fact, Sino-Soviet negotiating records from 1945 show that it was Chiang Kai-shek who personally decided to recognize Outer Mongolia's independence in a final, and ultimately futile, attempt to stop the USSR from aiding the CCP. In exchange for this sacrifice, Stalin agreed that the Soviet Union would "give to central Chinese Government alone all moral and material support."[5]

It was this Chiang-Stalin secret agreement, not Yalta, that allowed the USSR to encroach on Chinese sovereignty after World War II.[6] As the evidence presented below will show, this agreement was directly based on the USSR's and China's secret diplomacy from the 1920s. Because of these prior agreements, China was also forced once again to cede the Soviet Union control over the CER, transfer to the Soviet government rights over the former tsarist Russian territorial concessions, and renew Russian extraterritoriality.

Knowledge of the secret history of Sino-Soviet relations during 1917-27 suggests that the post–World War II history of Soviet expansionism can perhaps best be portrayed as simply one more episode in the long tradition of Russian imperialism in China. Additional secret Sino-Soviet agreements, signed during August 1945, allowed Stalin to confirm by treaty many of the special rights and privileges that Moscow had formerly secured only indirectly through its secret diplomacy with Peking. As a result, the USSR achieved a dominant vantage point in China from which it could support the CCP's 1949 victory and the creation of the People's Republic of China.

Status Quo and Outer Mongolian Independence

Of the three world leaders who signed the Yalta Agreement, President Roosevelt has been most harshly criticized for undermining China's sovereignty and territorial integrity. One history accused Roosevelt of "not driv[ing] a hard bargain at Yalta"[7]; a second account denounced Roosevelt for granting Stalin's request for "recognition of the independence from China of Outer Mongolia"[8]; and a third castigated Roosevelt for giving Stalin a "powerful pretext" to encroach on China's national interests.[9] These criticisms are based on a misunderstanding of what Yalta meant by the term *status quo*. For example, one historian claimed that: "The *status quo*, i.e., virtual Soviet possession of Outer Mongolia, was also to be included in the future Soviet-Chinese treaty"[10]; another concluded that *status quo* "implied Soviet domination of the area"[11]; and a third condemned President Roosevelt for seeing "nothing imperialistic in giving the Bolsheviks a stranglehold on . . . Outer Mongolia."[12]

By backing the *status quo* in Outer Mongolia, Roosevelt was accused, therefore, of providing Stalin with the leverage necessary to force China to recognize Outer Mongolian independence. In fact, the *status quo* in Outer Mongolia had been legally defined by the May 31, 1924 Sino-Soviet treaty: "The Government of the Union of Soviet Socialist Republics recognizes that Outer Mongolia is an integral part of the Republic of China and respects China's sovereignty therein."[13]

Dr. T. V. Soong, Chiang Kai-shek's brother-in-law, as well as Nationalist China's foreign minister and its official envoy to Moscow during the 1945 Sino-Soviet negotiations, explained that "*status quo* was that juridical sovereignty remains with China. It is true we cannot exercise this sovereignty."[14]

By upholding the Outer Mongolian *status quo* at Yalta, therefore, Roosevelt supported the continuation of China's juridical sovereignty. This interpretation is supported by the 1951 testimony of W. Averell Harriman, the American ambassador to Moscow, to the Senate's committees on armed services and foreign relations. According to Harriman's testimony, on February 10, 1945, Stalin requested Roosevelt's "concurrence also to the *status quo* in Outer Mongolia," but once Sino-Soviet negotiations began, "Stalin, at the outset, made demands that went substantially beyond the Yalta understanding," including the demand that Outer Mongolia be separated from China.[15]

Stalin's intentionally vague use of the term *status quo* at Yalta prepared the way for his demand during subsequent Sino-Soviet talks that China officially grant independence. On July 2, 1945, the first day of the secret negotiations between Stalin and Soong, Stalin suggested that China grant Outer Mongolia its full independence: "It will be better for China and Russia if Outer Mongolia is independent."[16] Thereafter, Stalin informed Soong that preserving the *status quo* meant: "China will recognize independence."[17] Later, he argued that "*Status quo* is [the] formal recognition of independence," and Stalin further insisted that the Yalta Agreement had backed up the Soviet Union's interpretation: "It's our formula. They signed. I am prepared to repeat that."[18]

Soong defended the true definition of *status quo* in his opening discussions with Stalin: "When I left Washington I had no idea that Outer Mongolia question would be a problem. I told Truman that we might settle this question by not discussing it. . . . None of us had any idea that Outer Mongolia would be an obstacle in our discussions." Soong further stated that defining *status quo* as Outer Mongolian independence "was not my understanding when I discussed [it] in Washington," and he reminded Stalin that Outer Mongolia "has many times been recognized by Soviet Union as [an] integral part of China."[19]

But the USSR's foreign minister, V. M. Molotov, threatened that leaving Outer Mongolia's status "indetermined will hamper and spoil the Sino-Soviet relations."[20] Stalin likewise reasoned that Outer Mongolia had really been separate from China since the Red Army's 1921 invasion, and so: "We want that this factual situation [to] be recognized legally."[21] Stalin explained the need for Outer Mongolian independence because of the USSR's geostrategic concerns: "Outer Mongolia has a geographical position from where one can overthrow Soviet Union['s] position in Far East."[22]

Sino-Soviet negotiations quickly deadlocked, resuming only after Soong communicated by telegraph with the Nationalist government in Chungking. Chiang Kai-shek also backed Washington's interpretation of *status quo,* as Soong explained that Chiang: "Agrees with Yalta formula signed by the Three, i.e., preserve *status quo* of Outer Mongolia. We cannot recognize the independence of Outer

Mongolia. Reason simple: self preservation is first law of nature. No Chinese government can last if it signs [an] agreement amputating Outer Mongolia. But we agree to *status quo.*" After consulting directly with "Chiang and his advisers," Soong concluded: "My Government cannot recognize independence and remain in power," and so "cannot recognize independence of Outer Mongolia."[23]

Transcripts of the Sino-Soviet talks clearly show that China was not forced to agree to Outer Mongolian independence by the Yalta Agreement. In fact, Soong only began to shift his position after lamenting to Stalin on July 7, that recognizing Outer Mongolian independence would surely result in the Nationalists' overthrow by the CCP to which Stalin responded: "There is the Kuomintang. Other forces are communists. Can communists overthrow Kuomintang? If China makes alliance with Soviet Union nobody will overthrow [the Nationalist] government."[24]

Only after Stalin indicated his willingness to ally with the KMT against the CCP, did discussions on granting Outer Mongolian independence begin in earnest. Harriman later confirmed that Soong told him that China "was prepared to make concessions which we [the United States government] considered went beyond the Yalta understanding."[25] This important point is also confirmed by the official transcripts, where Soong told Molotov: "Yalta is not sacred. On Outer Mongolia it said quite a different thing. We made a sacrifice."[26]

Forming a Soviet-KMT Alliance

Stalin's strategy for gaining full control over Outer Mongolia after World War II took advantage of the animosity and division between the KMT and the CCP. There is no better example of this strategy in action than Stalin's promise to Chiang Kai-shek that if the Nationalist government granted Outer Mongolia its full independence from China, then the USSR would stop aiding the CCP. As soon as Outer Mongolia held a mock plebiscite and the Nationalist government recognized its independence from China, however, Stalin threw his support behind the CCP in return for Mao's acquiescence to the territorial gains that Stalin had just secured from Chiang.

Even before Soong traveled to Moscow during the summer of 1945, he considered the possibility of forming an alliance between China's Nationalist government and the Soviet Union to oppose the Chinese communists. In fact, two of Soong's advisers even wrote to him recommending that he negotiate a secret agreement with Stalin to ensure that the CCP would be excluded from power in postwar China. Access to Soong's private papers suggest that his attempt to form an alliance with Moscow was not an afterthought, therefore, but was a carefully considered strategy designed to eliminate Soviet support for the CCP.

During September 1944, one of Soong's closest advisors and director of the Nationalist government's department of Russian affairs, Hsu Shu-hsi, predicted that "as soon as Germany is liquidated, the Soviet Union will change her policy and lend-lease the Chinese Red Army, if not also accord it *de jure* recognition." To avoid this eventuality, Hsu warned that the Nationalists would have to make concessions to the USSR and that: "If we can head off Russian intervention, any such measure will be more than justified."[27]

Early in 1945, Hsu further warned Soong: "Conditions for a successful deal with the Soviet Union are not all present, and yet time left for taking up the question with her is running short."[28] Only a week later, however, Hsu was more optimistic: "It seems that since the terms we are prepared to offer are liberal, while those we shall ask for in return would not fetter them in case they should choose to observe this agreement with us only in letter, not in spirit, there is little reason why they should not welcome our approach. . . ."[29]

Lee Wei-kuo, a member of China's delegation to the United Nations Conference on International Organization, also suggested to Soong in late May 1945 that he should visit Moscow as soon as possible, since the USSR "will either make a deal with the National Government, or enter into some kind of arrangement with the Yenan regime. In the light of the friendly gesture made to you by Molotov, however, I have the feeling that Russia is now ready for a deal with us." According to Lee, the Nationalists' best hope of defeating the CCP was to sign a secret pact with Moscow: "If we are able to come to an understanding with Russia, we shall be able also to solve the Communist problem, at least to a large extent, but never vice versa."[30]

Although Soong was willing to use Outer Mongolia as a bargaining chip in his negotiations with Stalin, he first wanted to determine whether Stalin was willing to support the KMT against the CCP. During the very first day of the official negotiations, Soong raised this question with Stalin by confiding the Nationalists' real political goals for China:[31]

> **Soong**: [The] Kuomintang wants to be [a] leading part in Government. Therefore [it] does not want [a] coalition government which may be upset when other parties withdraw.

> **Stalin**: This is [a] rightful wish of Kuomintang. It's obvious from [the] history of China. What other parties?

> **Soong**: To be brutally frank, no other party . . . [the] so-called democratic front: communists, national socialists, [and] youth is only a fiction.

> **Soong further stated**: We want united army, one central government. We don't want . . . warlords or any other party with separate government and army.

Soong's explanation that the Nationalists wanted to eliminate the CCP from any future Chinese government provides a plausible reason for why the KMT was interested in allying with the USSR. This, combined with the fact that the USSR actually controlled Outer Mongolia while the Nationalist military was too weak to retake it, helps explain why Soong was willing to use Outer Mongolian independence as a bargaining chip in his negotiations with Stalin. Finally, Stalin's July 7, 1945 suggestion that the KMT ally with Moscow prompted Soong to telegraph Chiang Kai-shek for his reaction.[32]

The Chiang-Stalin Secret Pact

By July 9, 1945, Chiang Kai-shek's return telegram had arrived in Moscow, and Soong read Chiang's answer to Stalin's request that Outer Mongolia be detached from China (see Document 27). In a message divided into four points, Chiang formally agreed to recognize Outer Mongolia's independence from China, but only in return for Stalin's promise that the Soviet Union would respect China's territorial integrity in Manchuria and Sinkiang, as well as his additional promise that the "Soviet Government to give to central Chinese Government alone all moral and material support." In addition, Chiang specified that "in order to avoid future disputes, [it is necessary] to go through form of plebiscite" in Outer Mongolia, after which he promised the "Chinese Government will declare independence."[33]

Based on Soong's reports to Chungking concerning Stalin's willingness to form an alliance, Chiang agreed that the "Chinese government now willing [to] make [the] greatest sacrifice in the utmost sincerity to find [a] fundamental solution of Chinese/Soviet relations."[34] But, this decision was not made without extracting concessions that Chiang clearly valued even more highly, including Stalin's promise that the USSR would not support the CCP: "Because of [the] Chinese communist administration and army, who are not united within the central government, [I] wish [the] Soviet Government to give to [the] central Chinese Government alone all moral and material support. Any assistance given to China should be confined to the central government.[35]

Stalin promised that he would support only the Nationalists: "As to Communists in China we do not support and don't intend to support [them]. We consider [that] China has one government. If another government calls itself Government it's [a] matter for China. As regards assistance, Chiang told us to send [it] to Central Government. We did so. If we can render help, of course it will be given to [the] government of Chiang. We do not want to play with China. We want to deal honestly with China and allied nations."[36]

Thereafter, when the Sino-Soviet Treaty of Friendship and Alliance was signed on August 14, 1945, Foreign Minister Molotov also signed the following supplementary note: "In accordance with the spirit of the aforementioned treaty, and in order to put into effect its aims and purposes, the Government of the USSR agrees to render to China moral support and aid in military supplies and other material resources, such support and aid to be entirely given to the National Government as the Central Government of China."[37]

1) <u>Sovereignty and administrative integrity of Manchuria</u>. Stalin has expressed his respect of this point for which we are very grateful.

Stalin : Did you expect anything else from me?

Soong : I am translating textually the telegram.

For common interest of China and Russia, China is ready to afford joint use of Port Arthur. Dairen declared an open port for period 20 years. As to administration of Port Arthur and Dairen this should go to China so that China has real sovereignty and administrative integrity in Manchuria.

Molotov : Port Arthur and Dairen, both?

Soong : Yes. Chinese Eastern Railway and South Manchurian Railway main lines to be operated jointly by Soviet Union. Profits to be divided equally. Right of the Railways should belong to China. Branch lines, other enterprises not connected with exploitation of railways not included in joint administration.

Period also 20 years.

2) <u>Sin-kiang</u>. In the last year or so there broke out rebellion in Sin-kiang so that communication between China and Sin-kiang broken : trade and commerce cannot be maintained. We are anxious that Soviet Russia, in accordance with previous agreement, co-operate with us to eliminate trouble so that trade, communication could be resumed. Altai range : originally belonged to Sin-kiang, should continue form part of Sin-kiang.

3) <u>Chinese Government</u>. Because of Chinese communist administration and army, who are not united within the central government, wish Soviet Government to give to central Chinese Government alone all moral and material support. Any assistance given to China should be confined to the central government.

4) <u>Outer Mongolia</u>. Chinese government regards that since Outer Mongolia question is the stumbling block in Sino-Soviet relations, for common interest of Soviet Union and China and lasting peace. is ready. after the defeat of Japan and acceptance of the three points by Soviet Government, to grant Outer Mongolia its independence. On this matter, in order to avoid future disputes, to go through form of plebiscite. After plebiscite Chinese Government will declare independence. As to area of Outer Mongolia should conform former area set out in our maps. Chinese Government deeply hopes Soviet Government can understand the enormous sacrifice and utmost sincerity of the Chinese Government, so as to secure two countries lasting and fundamental co-operation. Will you please communicate to Stalin without any reservation."

Document 27
Chiang Kai-shek's July 9, 1945 Telegram

Although Molotov's note did not specifically allude to Outer Mongolia, minutes of the Sino-Soviet negotiations show that only after Chiang agreed to Outer Mongolia's independence did Stalin agree to this provision. Chiang's decision was risky, since news of Outer Mongolia's separation from China might actually push Chinese public opinion further toward the Communists. Soong was later quoted as expressing surprise over this decision: "Chiang made [a] concession on Outer Mongolia which I did not dare believe he would."[38]

The contents of Chiang Kai-shek's July 9, 1945 telegram, which has only recently become available to historians, proves that Chiang recognized Outer Mongolian independence in exchange for Stalin's promise not to support the CCP. This document contradicts the view that during 1944-45 Mao took it for granted that Stalin would support him and that "CCP-Moscow relations were much closer than we previously assumed."[39] In fact, details of the Sino-Soviet negotiations in Moscow show that the situation was much more complicated, as Stalin allied with Chiang just long enough to legitimize Outer Mongolia's separation from China, and only then did he once again turn to Mao. This diplomatic strategy thereafter allowed the USSR to exert leverage on the PRC to submit to Outer Mongolian independence.

Stalin Retakes the Chinese Eastern Railway

Stalin used similar pressure tactics to regain control over the CER. In the Yalta Agreement, the USSR's "preeminent" interests in the CER were guaranteed. But Yalta intended this to mean that Soviet interests would be greater than other foreign powers; Stalin instead argued that Soviet interests should be preeminent over China's, just as it had been under the tsars. Other aspects of the 1945 Sino-Soviet treaty were also based on tsarist Russia's unequal treaties, as Stalin proposed resetting the tsarist timetable for the CER lease, renewing majority control, and regulating Sino-Soviet relations in Dairen according to the tsarist treaty of 1898. Desperate to keep the Soviet Union out of central China, Soong finally backed down and agreed to most of these points.

During the Soong-Stalin negotiations, Stalin initially stated that the original CER lease was for 80 years, only to have Soong remind him that in: "1924 changed to 60 years." Thereafter, Soong, speaking on behalf of Chiang Kai-shek, stated: "Chiang's views were 20–25 years for Port Arthur and railway," to which Stalin responded "Too short," and proposed a compromise of 40-45 years, after which the railway would return to full Chinese control. Stalin also made it clear that while operation of the Chinese Eastern Railway might be joint, the ownership would not be: "Soviet Union first owner, then China will take over." In addition, the chief of the railway must be a Russian.[40]

Although Yalta further guaranteed the internationalization of the port of Dairen, Stalin demanded full control over Dairen, stating: "What's the use of Chinese Eastern Railway if we do not have certain rights in port?" For this reason, Stalin recommended using the 1898 Sino-Russian treaty, advocating that it would be

"Best to take old treaty and improve."[41] Soong countered, however, by suggesting that "Dairen be administered by China and be an open port," to which Stalin replied: "Then there would be no need to make treaty."[42]

Chiang's July 9 telegram emphasized that China's greatest task was to "secure administrative integrity and territorial sovereignty and real unity in China." To do this, he stated it was necessary to remove "all possible disagreement and rankling unpleasantness so as to secure fundamental co-operation between the two countries in order to complete the will of Dr. Sun Yat-sen which was to co-operate with Soviet Russia." With regard to the CER, he proposed: "Chinese Eastern Railway and South Manchurian Railway main lines to be operated jointly by Soviet Union. Profits to be divided equally. Right of the Railways should belong to China. Branch lines, other enterprises not connected with exploitation of railways not included in joint administration. Period also 20 years."[43]

The offer of twenty years did not satisfy Stalin, however, who immediately argued that the term of the lease should be at least 30 years, not 20: "Re terms for Port Arthur, Dairen and Railways, 20 years do not accommodate us. It's too little. We could accept 30 years. We cannot accept less than 30 years instead of 40. That would be the final solution." Stalin furthermore disputed Chiang Kai-shek's suggestion that Port Arthur and the railways should be controlled by China: "[A]s regards Port Arthur administration is Russian. Someone should be master and command. As regards railway Chinese possession is not correct. Assumption that railway to be Chinese not correct. Russians built it."[44]

On July 10, 1945, Molotov clarified that joint control of the Chinese Eastern Railway did not mean a 50-50 split. Based on the Yalta Agreement's resolution that the Soviet Union was to have a "preeminent" stake in the Chinese Eastern Railway, Molotov proposed that the Soviet Union have four members on the board of directors to China's three. This prompted Soong to remind Molotov: "Preeminent in regard to other powers, not to China. You must be more fair to us," to which Molotov responded "Even 1924 provided for majority of Soviet. I urge you to accept."[45]

This argument continued with Soong insisting that Molotov should be willing to compromise since, unlike the earlier tsarist CER agreement, there was no clause specifying that China could redeem the railway ahead of the thirty-year limit to the lease. Molotov acknowledged this fact, saying "We appreciate it," but reiterated that Yalta gave the Soviet Union preeminent rights over the railway. Still, Soong insisted: "Yalta provides full sovereignty [for China]. But if commonly owned railway is dominated by foreigners there is no sovereignty."[46]

Negotiations on this important point continued the next day, at which time Soong repeated that a 50-50 split on the CER board was necessary. Molotov quickly answered: "The board will not be able to carry on. They may be divided." But, Soong warned that the agreement had to be based on "goodwill and understanding." Stalin then suggested as a compromise that the chairman of the board should have the casting vote.

Negotiations were suspended until July 12, at which time Soong reported the contents of a telegram from Chiang Kai-shek suggesting the following arrangement[47]:

> Railways. Chiang's idea, Chairman should be Chinese. No casting vote. Only courtesy to China. Chinese chairmanship.

> Manager. Russian Manager for Chinese Eastern Railway, Chinese Assistant. South Manchurian Railway: Chinese Manager, Soviet Assistant Manager. Chiang agrees to 30 years.

As this proposal indicated, the Chinese chairman would have no real power, but would merely be a "courtesy to China." In other words, the Chinese chairman would only be a figurehead–as during the 1920s–whose sole purpose was to help China save face. All real power would, once again, rest with the Russian manager of the CER.

It soon became clear that the Soviet Union's definition of "railway" also included much more than the main railway line itself. By taking control over the Chinese Eastern Railway, the Soviet Union hoped to gain much more than just the railway tracks, therefore, it also demanded the subsidiary industries that had traditionally been connected with the railways in Manchuria. This point was first brought up by Molotov, when he explained that these subsidiary industries should include all: "Depot[s], factories, forests allotment."[48]

In addition, Molotov implied that it would be necessary to have control over the branch lines of the CER as well, at least if they were linked to coal mines: "Coal formerly not sufficient. Therefore we suggested that Chinese government ensures supply of coal. Coals mines that we had formerly may have branch lines. Use of the branches is to be reserved." But, according to Soong, the Yalta agreement did not include subsidiaries and branch lines. When he asked Molotov if these would be used only for the railway, Molotov responded: "Yes, exclusively for railway." Soong thereafter telegraphed Chiang, who agreed to this arrangement.[49]

Soviet Territorial Concessions and Extraterritoriality

Sharp differences of opinion also arose during the Sino-Soviet negotiations over the administration of Dairen and Port Arthur, the two major ports in Manchuria. For example, the Soviet proposal would have specified that Dairen was to be an exclusive port for use of Soviet ships and commerce. According to Soong, however, this would have ignored the Soviet promise that Manchuria was fully under Chinese sovereignty. In addition, Molotov called for Port Arthur to be fully administered by the Soviet Union, to which Soong replied that there seemed to be little difference between the Soviet plan and the earlier tsarist lease of Port Arthur.[50] But Soong eventually backed down on these points.

Stalin also demanded, and received, Chinese assurances that extraterritoriality would be continued. Unlike Great Britain and the United States, Stalin clearly felt no moral pressure to eliminate the USSR's own extraterritorial rights. During Sino-Soviet negotiations from June through August 1945, therefore, one of Stalin's top priorities was to renew the USSR's extraterritoriality. Stalin told Soong that all Soviet-operated Manchurian railways must be granted this right[51]:

> **Stalin**: Railway is extraterritorial. Railway bridges, tunnels, stations, to be guarded.
>
> **Soong**: Railway not extraterritorial. You don't want extra-territoriality—we are done with.
>
> **Stalin**: In two years we will see.
>
> **Soong**: Chinese personnel fully adequate. We will send our best men—this is a point I do urge Stalin to consider for us. We do not want foreign troops or gendarmerie in Shanghai or elsewhere. You would help us, the Chinese people, by agreeing to this which Chiang considers as the most essential condition.
>
> **Stalin**: We will think it over.

Later, however, Molotov again insisted that the Red Army guard the railways, a suggestion that Soong opposed, claiming: "Sovereignty in Manchuria would be a doubtful thing if armed foreigners were there."[52]

In late July and early August 1945, the USSR succeeded in renewing extraterritoriality throughout Manchuria when Molotov demanded total control over Port Arthur's harbor: "We cannot accept any regime where civilian administration is not subordinated to military authorities." The Chinese delegate was forced to admit: "If we exclude Port Arthur [from Chinese control] we return to extra-territoriality."[53] Thereafter, on August 13, 1945, the two sides agreed that the Soviet military command would have full control over Port Arthur's port and its facilities, including all rights of extraterritoriality.

To ensure that the Western powers could not interfere, Stalin suggested that all of the USSR's special rights and privileges be included in a secret protocol attached to the final Sino-Soviet treaty.[54] On August 14, 1945, Soong and Molotov met and formally agreed to the contents of this secret protocol that, among other things, renewed extraterritoriality.[55] According to a draft copy of this protocol, the two men agreed that "Russian service courts and authorities will have exclusive jurisdiction over all members of their forces."[56]

"Face" in Sino-Soviet Diplomacy

Although Outer Mongolia has always been portrayed by the USSR and China as an independent country, the minutes of the 1945 Sino-Soviet negotiations reveal that the USSR actually agreed not to annex Outer Mongolia outright in order to save China's face. As discussed above, it was the loss of face associated with the Shantung resolution in 1919 that motivated China to turn to Soviet Russia in the first place. Stalin clearly understood this and realized that it was imperative to preserve China's face in her outward relations with the USSR.

Keeping face was important to the Nationalists, because they once again hoped to use the facade of friendly Sino-Soviet relations to exert leverage over the other powers, the most important being Great Britain. Soong even referred to this policy in a July 2, 1945 conversation with Stalin when he said: "1924 Soviet Union first to relinquish its privileges and gave example to other countries."[57] As a result of this time-honored Chinese policy of playing one "barbarian" off another, Soong offered Stalin the lease to the port of Dairen in exchange for Stalin's agreement that Dairen's administration would appear to remain under Chinese control. Stalin agreed, and even suggested: "Would be well to put in writing on all these points. Port Arthur, Dairen, railways. To be secret, to be known to no one." Soong immediately responded: "Yes."[58]

During negotiations in early August 1945, China's newly appointed foreign minister, Wang Shih-chieh, repeated this argument (see Document 28). He told Stalin: "May I be allowed make a plea to Stalin re Dairen. When I departed from Chungking to Moscow, General Chiang wanted me to state this case to Stalin. Port of Dairen is similar in nature to port of Kowloon. We have been contemplating that after war we will get back Kowloon, perhaps Hong Kong. Therefore we have been so anxious preserve administrative power of Dairen. If not, it will be difficult if not impossible to get back Kowloon and Hong Kong."[59]

Two days later, Wang explained why Port Arthur should appear to remain under China's administration: "Port Arthur only city of 30-40,000 people but we have Kowloon to recover 3/4 million of population. If we yield to you on this we will not recover civil administration of Kowloon. We are going to be allied, take our interest at heart." These minutes then reveal that Molotov agreed that as long as Moscow's actual rights were detailed in a secret protocol, then the published portion of the Sino-Soviet agreement would support China's attempts to recover Kowloon and Hong Kong.[60] Thereafter, on August 14, 1945, Soong and Molotov met and formally agreed to the contents of this secret protocol, which stated that the port of Dairen would "be leased free of charge to Russia."[61]

To save face, it was also Chiang Kai-shek who first suggested holding a plebiscite in Outer Mongolia in his July 9, 1945 telegram, since "Outer Mongolia question is the stumbling block in Sino-Soviet relations, . . . [China] is ready after the defeat of Japan . . . to grant Outer Mongolia its independence. On this matter, in order to avoid future disputes, to go through [the] form of [a] plebiscite. After [the] plebiscite [the] Chinese Government will declare independence."[62]

Molotov : We've got to reach agreement.

Soong   : Anxious to agree before surrender. After we will have more difficulties with our people. Eight years of war. People will say why do you make such concessions.

Stalin   : People will understand and will like an alliance with USSR.

Soong   : Yes, but we have made many concessions, Outer Mongolia, etc.

Stalin   : Outer Mongolia was lost any way - declared war on Japan.

Soong   : Almost one half of China.

Stalin   : It is a desert.

Soong   : Does not look so on map.

Stalin   : Smallest piece of land of Kwangtung is twenty times more valuable.

Soong   : Schoolchildren look at map and see size of Outer Mongolia.

Wang   : May I be allowed make a plea to Stalin re Dairen. When I departed from Chungking to Moscow General Chiang wanted me to state this case to Stalin. Port of Dairen is similar in nature to port of Kowloon. We have been contemplating that after war we will get back Kowloon, perhaps Hong Kong. Therefore we have been so anxious preserve administrative power of Dairen. If not it will be difficult if not impossible to get back Kowloon and Hong Kong.

Stalin   : British consider Hong Kong as theirs. Dairen in 30 years, will be Chinese.

Wang   : Kowloon also leased to Britain. Important to South China as Dairen for Manchuria. Chiang asks Stalin to give sympathetic consideration to this. We are struggling for emancipation of China.

Stalin   : I do not want China to renounce Dairen. What am I called upon to do to satisfy you?

Wang   : Let Dairen to be under Chinese administration, we will use soviet experts. If you accept this we can easier get back Kowloon.

Stalin   : We cannot exclude Dairen from military zone. In case of war we would have to interfere.

Document 28
Wang Shih-chieh's August, 1945 Conversation with Stalin

Later, Soong emphasized why a plebiscite was necessary: "It is more convenient for Chinese Government to confront [the] Chinese people if there is a plebiscite." The following exchange confirms that the plebiscite was just for show[63]:

> **Stalin**: Re Outer Mongolia. How to understand what you said. Not recognize now but after defeat of Japan? We proposed recognize now but [to] publish after defeat of Japan.
>
> **Soong**: Yes. After defeat of Japan [to] go through plebiscite, then recognition. I want Stalin [to] believe me in this: matter of substance is decided now. We can explore the form. We have no intention to evade or be tricky.

Stalin and Soong also took for granted that the plebiscite would result in Outer Mongolia's independence from China, and that this really meant that it was being ceded to the USSR. Soong even admitted that the plebiscite was: "Only a matter of form. The matter is settled."[64] But, in discussions with Molotov, Soong repeated that the final form was all-important. Although it was tacitly understood that Outer Mongolia was Soviet territory, Soong wanted to guarantee that it would be portrayed as an independent country: "It is a question of form and I am sure [the] Soviet government will meet our views re form. Stalin said also Outer Mongolia will not join [the] Soviet Union either. For home consumption, it would be good if [the] Soviet Union say[s] that after independence [the] Soviet Union will respect its territorial integrity." Molotov was agreeable to this suggestion, although he wanted China's immediate recognition, without waiting for a plebiscite. Soong responded: "I assure you there is no catch."[65]

China and the USSR exchanged notes during August 1945, detailing the plebiscite in Outer Mongolia, after which China promised to recognize its independence. Soong's secret negotiations with Stalin show that the plebiscite was merely for form. This fact helps explain why the Nationalists did not dispute the results when it was later reported that 98.14 percent of Outer Mongolia's electorate voted for independence in the hastily arranged plebiscite.[66] Even more unbelievable, Moscow reported that the vote was unanimous–483,291 to 0.[67] As a result of the secret Sino-Soviet agreement, Chiang did not dispute these skewed results and Nationalist China thereafter officially recognized Outer Mongolia's complete independence from China on January 1, 1946.

The existence of these secret protocols detailing the USSR's territorial and extraterritorial rights proves that the KMT government, like the Peking government before it, tried to use its outwardly friendly relations with the USSR to push the British government into giving up its concessions in China. Unlike the 1920s, however, the Kuomintang seriously misjudged the respective strengths of the two groups of competing powers, since, when the Soviet-backed communist forces were on the verge of seizing power throughout mainland China in the late 1940s, the capitalist countries declined to intervene, as they had in 1927.

On February 7, 1948, General Victor W. Odlum, the Canadian ambassador to Turkey, wrote a revealing letter to T. V. Soong, at this point the governor of the Province of Kuangtung, warning him that this policy might fail. In his letter, Odlum warned Soong of the danger that the Soviet Union represented to China, and he specifically advised that China should go "to any amount of trouble to find another Hong Kong into which she could get the Americans to put their foot." Only in this way, could China "have Britain and America pinned down so that they will be more intimately and closely affected by any danger which threatens China."[68]

On April 24, Odlum further recommended that China should attempt to tie its fate more closely to Britain and the United States: "I sincerely hope that whatever may have been the cause for the trouble in Kowloon, a satisfactory solution will be found. I think it would be a tragedy for China if the British were to pull out of Hong Kong. What is more, I believe it would be wise for China if she could find another Hong Kong for the Americans. If China's interests and fate can be tied up irrevocably with those of the two leading democratic groups of the world, it will be a good thing for China and for democracy."[69] China would have profited from this advice.

Soviet Secret Diplomacy and the CCP

The USSR's greatest diplomatic victories in China after World War II resulted from its policy of successfully playing the KMT and the CCP off each other. The outstanding example of this was the Chiang-Stalin secret pact, since as soon as Stalin obtained what he wanted from Chiang, he broke this pact and supported Mao instead. This tactic led the United Nations to censure the USSR on February 1, 1952, for violating its 1945 friendship treaty with the Nationalist government.

Although Chiang Kai-shek clearly expected that his secret pact with Stalin would guarantee the Nationalists' power throughout China, the USSR soon began supporting the CCP once again. But Stalin was careful to wait until after Outer Mongolia's plebiscite was over and after the Nationalist government officially recognized Outer Mongolia's independence from China. Only then did he turn to the CCP. Thereafter, following the 1949 formation of the PRC, Stalin used the fact that China's central government had already recognized Outer Mongolia's independence as leverage to pressure Mao to follow suit. In their 1950 treaty, Stalin and Mao even signed a secret protocol renewing Soviet extraterritoriality.[70]

After 1949, the Outer Mongolian question produced tremendous friction in Soviet-PRC relations when Stalin repeatedly refused to open negotiations with Mao over Outer Mongolia's status. That Mao Tse-tung initially acquiesced to Outer Mongolia's continued independence from China is perhaps best shown by the fact that China's 1950 friendship treaty with the USSR did not even mention Outer Mongolia. But Moscow's failure to live up to the Comintern promise to return Outer Mongolia to a communist-led China convinced Mao that the Bolsheviks had reneged on their 1922 secret agreement with the CCP. In 1964,

Mao even told a foreign interviewer that "the Soviet Union, under the pretext of assuring the independence of Mongolia, actually placed the country under its domination."[71]

Chou En-lai also explained that during January 1957, he had failed to convince Khrushchev to reopen Outer Mongolia border negotiations: "I could not get a satisfactory answer from him then, but the announcement of the issue was kept secret because the Sino-Soviet dispute was not public at that time."[72] Once it became clear that the USSR was unwilling to agree to further negotiations on Outer Mongolia's status, the PRC attempted to act alone. In 1960, for example, Chou carried out talks with Yurii Tsedenbal, the leader of the Mongolian People's Republic. One historian has indicated that Chou's "goal seemed to be separation of the MPR from the Soviet Union rather than a cooperative three-way deal."[73]

This territorial dispute continued to plague Sino-Soviet relations for almost two decades.[74] Sino-Soviet negotiations finally settled the Sino-Mongolian border in 1962, and according to one account: "This is the most meticulously described boundary in the whole of Asia; it stretches for 2,920 miles (4,698 kilometers) and is marked by 678 cement and rock markers located at 639 turning points along the boundary."[75] In response to further tensions, the Soviet Union consolidated its position in Outer Mongolia to the point where: "By the 1970s the Soviet Union had in effect enclosed the MPR completely within its own defense system and extended the de-facto strategic border of the USSR southward to the border between the MPR and China."[76]

The USSR also retained its rights to the CER and its territorial concessions in Manchuria through the mid-1950s, and apparently retained its extraterritorial rights all the way until August 1960, when the last 1,390 Soviet advisers left the PRC. According to one scholarly account, all Soviet advisers were evacuated after the Chinese government demanded that the Soviet government finally carry through on earlier promises to "revise all agreements."[77] Although the Sino-Soviet secret protocol granting extraterritoriality was not specifically mentioned, the sudden and unexpected departure of all Soviet advisers suggests that China's demands probably included the secret agreement on extraterritoriality.

Perhaps more to the point, Soviet sources have estimated that over 10,000 advisers were sent to the PRC between 1950 and 1960. Undoubtedly these advisers enjoyed some form of extraterritoriality. As discussed above, it was at the 1919 Paris Peace Conference that the Chinese delegation first linked abolishing extraterritoriality with safeguarding China's "sovereign rights." It is important to recall this ideological association when one reads the PRC's published denunciations of the "Soviet revisionist social-imperialists," since the PRC specifically accused Moscow of seeking to undermine other countries' "national independence and sovereignty."[78]

Based on this interpretation, it seems plausible to conclude that China's public protests against Soviet violations of its sovereignty referred to the USSR's secret retention of extraterritoriality. The nationalistic fervor with which the PRC carried out this anti-Soviet campaign led one scholar to conclude: "Chinese writing on the question of social imperialism leaves little doubt that there is deep resentment towards the Soviet Union that reflects the political context of Sino-Soviet relations during the 1950's."[79] Only in August 1960, therefore, did the PRC unilaterally rescind the USSR's remaining special rights and privileges, including extraterritorial rights. As a result, Russia's unequal treaties were finally eliminated, a watershed in the chronology of events leading up to the Sino-Soviet split.

The Sino-Soviet Monolith

It was only Peking's decision not to disclose the truth about its negotiations with Moscow that gave the USSR such enormous freedom of action in China. Like the Kuomintang and Chinese communist governments after it, the Peking government used the myth of Sino-Soviet equality in its negotiations with the capitalist nations to convince them to return to China the very rights and privileges that Soviet diplomats had in actuality retained by signing secret agreements. The USSR's secret diplomacy during 1917-27 disproves, once and for all, that the Soviet government treated China better than the other great powers. In fact, the documentary record proves that the opposite was actually the case, providing convincing evidence that within only a few years of the Bolshevik revolution–well before Lenin's illness and eventual death–the Soviet government was carrying out an imperialist policy in China.

Because Peking never released the truth about its secret negotiations with Moscow, the communist propaganda proclaiming that the Soviet Union treated China better than the capitalist countries was assumed to be true. Most important, the Chinese Communist Party was not cognizant of the truth underlying Sino-Soviet relations, and during the summer and fall of 1949, Mao continued to claim that only the Soviet government could provide "genuine and friendly help," and that China should ally with the Soviet Union "in order to wage a life-and-death struggle against imperialism and its running dogs."[80]

Arguably, only after the CCP came to power in China did Mao also discover the bitter truth underlying Sino-Soviet relations. Seen in this light, the CCP's decision to support the USSR during the 1920s backfired, a fact that perhaps explains why later Sino-Soviet territorial disputes were so divisive.[81] The signing of the May 31, 1924 secret protocol was perhaps even the root cause behind why, as late as May 1991, Soviet Foreign Minister Aleksandr Bessmertnykh publicly admitted that 10 percent of the Sino-Soviet border was still in dispute.[82]

What Soviet imperialism gained, China lost. Although tsarist Russia had initially pressured China to grant Outer Mongolia its autonomy in 1915, only in 1945 did Russia achieve its ultimate goal of forcing China to recognize Outer Mongolia's full independence. By means of its secret diplomacy with China, the USSR acquired control over an estimated 600,000 square miles of Chinese territory.[83] This diplomatic victory rivaled the heyday of Russia's nineteenth-century territorial expansion, when China ceded approximately 665,000 square miles of territory to tsarist Russia.[84] Not including Outer Mongolia, the amount of land secured by

Russia during the nineteenth century was approximately five times the area of Japan and more than seven times that of Great Britain; including Outer Mongolia, it exceeded that of India and was more than one-third the size of the United States.[85]

On February 16, 1950, Maxwell Hamilton and Nelson T. Johnson, two State Department Far Eastern experts, wrote a memorandum noting that since as early as 1912 Russia had been attempting to take possession of Outer Mongolia and that the "1945 and 1950 alliances between China and Russia fulfill the Russian objective of detaching Outer Mongolia." They also warned Washington of further outbreaks of Russian expansionism: "The record of the facts in relations between Russia and China makes clear the persistent efforts of the tsarist Russian Government and the Communist Russian Government to expand at the expense of China and neighboring countries. The formulas used in Russian formal documents throughout this period bear striking similarities and show that, no matter what the words, the effort persists."[86]

Hu Shih, the Nationalist government's ambassador to the United States during the 1940s, stressed the importance of secret diplomacy to Russia's success: "What seems to differentiate China from the seemingly much easier conquests in Central Europe and Eastern Europe had been the much greater complexity and difficulty of the conquest, which made it necessary for Stalin to resort to the most cunning forms of secret diplomacy in order to overcome the resistance that Nationalist China had been able to summon for over two decades." Hu Shih thereafter condemned Stalin for "deliberately deceiving . . . Roosevelt" at Yalta, and concluded: "History will not forgive the man who played such deliberate tricks on the generous idealism of a great humanitarian."[87]

Had the Sino-Soviet secret agreements from the 1920s been publicized at the time, the legitimacy of the Chinese Communist Party would have been seriously undermined. This raises grave doubts about whether the CCP would have later been able to rally the Chinese people under its leadership. China's twentieth-century history might have been far less bloody if this had been the case.[88]

In addition, one can only speculate how the U. S. government's reaction to the creation of the Sino-Soviet "monolith" in 1949 might have differed if the true nature of Sino-Soviet relations had been known, especially if one agrees that the cold war "proper" began only after China's communist revolution.[89] Only the recent opening of Asian archives detailing Sino-Soviet relations has clarified, once and for all, just how far the myth of Sino-Soviet friendship and equality differed from the underlying reality.[90]

Notes

1. Yalta resolution on Outer Mongolia, quoted from: Edward R. Stettinius, Jr., *Roosevelt and the Russians,* 351.

2.. Sergei N. Goncharov, John W. Lewis, and Xue Litai, *Uncertain Partners:*

Stalin, Mao, and the Korean War, 3.

3. Walter LaFeber, *America, Russia, and the Cold War, 1945-1966*, 25.

4. Thomas A. Bailey, *America Faces Russia*, 332.

5. "Notes taken at Sino-Soviet Conferences," July 2, 1945–August 14, 1945, Victor Hoo Collection, Hoover Institution Archives, 17.

6. Odd Arne Westad, *Cold War and Revolution: Soviet-American Rivalry and the Origins of the Chinese Civil War*, 36-56.

7. Immanuel C. Y. Hsu, *The Rise of Modern China*, 608.

8. John Lewis Gaddis, *The United States and the Origins of the Cold War, 1941-1947*, 78.

9. Wu Hsiang-hsiang (吳相湘), 俄帝侵略中國史 (*History of Imperial Russia's Aggression in China*), 477.

10. Adam B. Ulam, *Expansion and Coexistence The History of Soviet Foreign Policy, 1917-67*, 371.

11. George A. Lenson, "Yalta and the Far East," in John L. Snell ed., *The Meaning of Yalta*, 157.

12. Felix Wittmer, *The Yalta Betrayal*, 83.

13. "Agreement of the General Principles for the Settlement of the Questions Between the Republic of China and the Union of Soviet Socialist Republics," May 31, 1924, WCTA, 03-32, 495(1).

14. "Notes taken at Sino-Soviet Conferences," July 2, 1945–August 14, 1945, Victor Hoo Collection, Hoover Institution Archives, 16.

15. "Statement of W. Averell Harriman, Special Assistant to the President, regarding our wartime relations with the Soviet Union, particularly as they concern the agreements reached at Yalta," July 13, 1951, Hoover Institution Archives, Maxwell Hamilton collection, Box 3.

16. "Notes taken at Sino-Soviet Conferences," July 2, 1945-August 14, 1945, Victor Hoo Collection, Hoover Institution Archives, 8.

17. *Ibid.*, 13.

18. *Ibid.*

19. *Ibid.*, 3-16.

20. *Ibid.*, 12.

21. *Ibid.*, 18.

22. *Ibid,*, 1.

23. *Ibid.*, 12-14.

24. *Ibid.*, 14.

25. "Statement of W. Averell Harriman . . . ," July 13, 1951.

26. "Notes taken at Sino-Soviet Conferences," July 2, 1945-August 14, 1945, Victor Hoo Collection, Hoover Institution Archives, 28.

27. Memorandum from Hsu Shu-hsi to T. V. Soong, September 28, 1944, Hoover Institution Archives, T. V. Soong collection, Schedule A, Box 30.

28. *Ibid,* memorandum XVII from Hsu Shu-hsi to T. V. Soong, February 22, 1945.

29. *Ibid,* memorandum XVIII from Hsu Shu-hsi to T. V. Soong, February 28, 1945.

30. *Ibid,* letter from Lee Wei-kuo to Soong (underlining in original), May 30, 1945.

31. "Notes taken at Sino-Soviet Conferences," July 2, 1945-August 14, 1945, Victor Hoo Collection, Hoover Institution Archives, 9-10.

32. *Ibid.*

33. *Ibid.*, 16-18.

34. *Ibid.*

35. *Ibid.*

36. *Ibid.*

37. "Statement by United States Delegate John Sherman Cooper in the Political Committee of the United Nations General Assembly in the Discussion of Threats to the Political Independence and Territorial Integrity of China, at Paris, France, January 28, 1952," Hoover Institution Archives, Maxwell Hamilton collection, Box 1.

38. "Notes taken at Sino-Soviet Conferences," July 2, 1945–August 14, 1945, Victor Hoo Collection, Hoover Institution Archives, 34.

39. Michael M. Sheng, "America's Lost Chance in China?" *The Australian Journal of Chinese Affairs,* Issue 29, January 1993, 137n.

40. "Notes taken at Sino-Soviet Conferences," July 2, 1945-August 14, 1945, Victor Hoo Collection, Hoover Institution Archives, 5-7.

41. *Ibid.*

42. *Ibid.*

43. *Ibid.,* 17-19.

44. *Ibid.*

45. *Ibid.,* 26-29.

46. *Ibid.*

47. *Ibid.,* 38.

48. *Ibid.,* 26.

49. *Ibid.*

50. *Ibid,* 29-30.

51. *Ibid,* 21-22.

52. *Ibid,* 27.

53. *Ibid.,* 67.

54. *Ibid.,* 46.

55. "Meeting between Dr. Soong and Mr. Molotov," August 14, 1945, Victor Hoo Collection, Hoover Institution Archives, Box 7, 3.

56. "Treaty of Alliance," August 14, 1945, T. V. Soong Collection, Hoover Institution Archives, Schedule A, Box 25.

57. "Notes taken at Sino-Soviet Conferences," July 2, 1945–August 14, 1945, Victor Hoo Collection, Hoover Institution Archives, 46.

58. *Ibid.*

59. *Ibid.,* 49.

60. *Ibid.,* 66-68.

61. "Meeting between Dr. Soong and Mr. Molotov," August 14, 1945, Hoover Institution Archives, Victor Hoo Collection, Box 7, 3.

62. "Notes taken at Sino-Soviet Conferences," July 2, 1945–August 14, 1945, Victor Hoo Collection, Hoover Institution Archives, 17-19.

63. *Ibid.,* 19-20.

64. *Ibid.*

65. *Ibid.,* 25.

66. Max Beloff, *Soviet Far Eastern Policy Since Yalta,* 9.

67. LaFeber, 25.

68. Personal letter from General Victor W. Odlum to T. V. Soong, 3 pages, February 7, 1948, T. V. Soong Collection, Hoover Institution Archives, Schedule A, Box 6.

69. *Ibid.;* Personal letter from General Victor W. Odlum to T. V. Soong, 3 pages,

April 24, 1948.

70. Goncharov, Lewis, Xue Litai, 125.

71. "Mao's Statement to the Japanese Socialist Delegation," August 11, 1964, Dennis J. Doolin, *Territorial Claims in the Sino-Soviet Conflict*, 43.

72. "An Interview with Zhou Enlai," August 1, 1964, Doolin, 45.

73. Robert Rupen, *How Mongolia Is Really Ruled*, 79.

74. Chou En-lai reportedly asked Khrushchev in January 1957 to discuss territorial concerns, but he refused. "An Interview with Chou En-lai," August 1, 1964, Doolin, 45.

75. J. R. V. Prescott, *Map of Mainland Asia By Treaty*, 90-98.

76. *Ibid.*, 123.

77. Alfred D. Low, *The Sino-Soviet Dispute: An Analysis of the Polemics,* 118-120.

78. Dennis M. Ray, "Chinese Perceptions of Social Imperialism and Economic Dependency: The Impact of Soviet Aid," *Journal of International Studies,* Vol. X, Spring 1975, 36-82.

79. *Ibid.*

80. "On the People's Democratic Dictatorship," June 30, 1949 and "The Bankruptcy of the Idealist Conception of History," September 16, 1949, *Mao Tse-tung Selected Works,* Vol. 5, 417, 457.

81. Donald S. Zagoria, *The Sino-Soviet Conflict, 1956-1961*, 344.

82. S. C. M. Paine, *Imperial Rivals: China, Russia, and Their Disputed Frontier,* 15.

83. *The New Encyclopedia Britannica,* 15th ed., Vol. 12, 362.

84. Alan J. Day, ed. *Border and Territorial Disputes,* 259-261.

85. *The New Encyclopaedia Britannica,* Vol. 10, 34; Vol. 18, 864; Vol. 9, 276; Vol. 18, 905.

86. Memorandum written by Maxwell Hamilton and Nelson T. Johnson, February 16, 1950, Hoover Institution Archives, Maxwell Hamilton Collection, Box 4.

87. Hu Shih, "China in Stalin's Grand Strategy," *Foreign Affairs,* October 1950, 11-40; Hu Shih's opinion is particularly important because he was the Nationalists' ambassador to the United States from 1945-49 and was appointed minister of foreign affairs in 1949. Either one of these positions would have allowed Hu Shih access to documents detailing the Soviet Union's secret diplomacy with China.

88. R. J. Rummel has estimated that between 1900 and 1928, when the Open Door Policy was in place, 737,000 Chinese people died in the turmoil associated with the end of the Ch'ing dynasty, warlordism, and the Republican governments. This yearly average of 26,000 pales by comparison to the average two million casulties per year from 1928 to 1987, during which time Rummel estimated 115 million Chinese people died in the political, economic, and military turmoil ignited by the USSR's struggle to enlarge its sphere of influence in China (*China's Bloody Century: Genocide and Mass Murder Since 1900*).

89. William Taubman has stated that the cold war "proper" did not start until 1949, following the success of the Chinese communist revolution (*Stalin's American Policy From Entente to Détente to Cold War,* 9).

90. Since China never proved otherwise, the USSR's oft-repeated claim that it treated China well created a myth of Sino-Soviet equality that was generally accepted and perpetuated by historians of both China and Russia. See, for example: Nicholas V. Riasanovsky, *A History of Russia,* 568; Edmond O. Clubb, *China and Russia, the "Great Game,"* 210; Immanuel C. Y. Hsu, *The Rise of Modern China,* 515; Jonathan Spence, *The Search for Modern China,* 307.

Appendix A: *The 1925 Soviet-Japanese Secret Agreement on Bessarabia*

Increased accessibility to the Japanese Foreign Ministry Archives in Tokyo has recently produced copies of a secret Soviet-Japanese agreement concerning Bessarabia, signed on January 20, 1925. These documents are important for several reasons: first, because they prove that both the Soviet Union and Japan resorted to secret diplomacy at a relatively early stage in their relations; second, because they show how the Soviet government was able to block successfully all League of Nation attempts to recognize Rumania's 1918 reunion with Bessarabia; and third, because they provide important new insights on how the Soviet Union utilized diplomatic relations with its Far Eastern neighbors, in this case Japan, to influence European affairs.

On August 18, 1916, the Rumanian government declared war on Germany and Austria-Hungary in exchange for an agreement with the Allies that after the war it would receive not only a largely Rumanian-populated Transylvania, but also Bucovina, currently part of Austria-Hungary, as well as the territory of Banat, which was claimed by Serbia.[1] On November 28, 1918, Bucovina voluntarily joined Rumania, while on December 1, 1918, Transylvania followed suit.

After the fall of Imperial Russia, the Moldavian Democratic Republic voted in January 1918 to reunite Bessarabia with Rumania. During March 1918, the Rumanian government justified its decision to accept Bessarabia by arguing that 70.25 percent of the population were Rumanians, 10.75 percent were Ukrainians, and the rest were divided among Jews, Germans, and Turks.[2] Rumania's new borders were recognized by Austria in the Treaty of Saint-Germain in September 1919, by Bulgaria in the Treaty of Neuilly in November 1919, and by Hungary in the Treaty of Trianon in June 1920.[3] Thereafter, on October 28, 1920, Rumania signed the Paris Treaty with Great Britain, France, Italy, and Japan, reaffirming that Bessarabia was part of Rumania; Great Britain and Rumania ratified this agreement soon afterward.

The sole impediment to a unified Rumania was the Bolshevik government, which harshly criticized the annexation of 17,500 square kilometers of what had formerly been Russian territory. As a result, Soviet Russia immediately broke relations with Rumania and impounded its gold reserve in Moscow. The Soviet government then worked through the Comintern's propaganda network to accuse the Rumanian government of "enslaving" a "great many Hungarians and Bessarabians."[4] Later, the Rumanian communists adopted a Comintern resolution that declared that Rumania was an artificial creation of Western imperialism and so refused to recognize that Bessarabia was part of Rumania.[5]

By 1924, it was becoming clear that Rumania's claim to Bessarabia would remain a point of international friction, since only Great Britain and Rumania had ratified the Paris Treaty. Without the additional ratification of France, Italy, and Japan, this agreement would not become internationally recognized or legally binding. In an attempt to negotiate an acceptable settlement, the League of Nations sponsored a conference in Vienna between Rumania and the Soviet Union during the spring of 1924. To exert pressure on the Soviet Union to come to terms, the British government sent a letter to Japan on November 24, 1923, asking whether "the Imperial Japanese Government can see their way to ratify the [Paris] treaty in question at an early date."[6] While Japan did not comply, France did, voting for ratification on April 9, 1924.

When the Vienna conference failed to resolve this conflict, however, the Soviet Union also turned to Japan to try to convince her not to ratify the Paris Treaty. On April 16, 1924, the Soviet envoy to China, Lev Karakhan, initially raised the Bessarabian question with the Japanese minister to Peking, Kenkichi Yoshizawa.[7] Before opening detailed negotiations, however, Karakhan first wanted to be sure that any agreements made with Japan would remain secret. On May 5, 1924, Karakhan wrote a letter to Yoshizawa implying that Japan had already requested this: "Notwithstanding the fact that Soviet Government is opposed to secret negotiations and holds that negotiations between Soviet Government and Japan should be conducted at open and formal conference, nevertheless agreed to first two points of Japanese proposal."[8]

Upon receiving Karakhan's note, Yoshizawa officially denied making any such proposal, as recorded in a letter dated May 5, 1924: "In the first place, your note mentions at the outset three conditions which it is stated were advanced by the Japanese Government as preliminary conditions of the opening of negotiations, but as I verbally pointed out to you at our interview on the 5th, the first two of these so-called conditions were not proposed by the Japanese Government nor did I mention them as condition precedent to the negotiation."[9] In fact, a copy of Yoshizawa's original proposal, dated March 22, 1924, confirms that it was not the Japanese government that first proposed that negotiations be secret.[10]

This evidence suggests that it was the Soviet Union—not Japan—that first proposed carrying out secret negotiations. This is an important point, since after the 1917 October Revolution, the Soviet constituent assembly denounced secret diplomacy as being responsible for "drench[ing] the world in blood."[11] Thereafter, on November 17, 1922, the Soviet envoy to China and Japan, Adolf Joffe, announced that the "Workers and Peasants' Government is opposed on principle to secret diplomacy and never signs secret treaties."[12]

As soon as Yoshizawa agreed to Karakhan's proposal that all negotiations be carried out in secret, Karakhan tried to convince him to sign a comprehensive agreement stating that the Soviet Union and Japan would not interfere with each other's sovereignty.[13] This draft was worded as follows[14]:

>The undersigned, the Plenipotentiaries of the empire of Japan and the U.S.S.R., in proceeding to sign the Basic Agreement relative to the Establishment of Friendly Relations between the Imperial Japanese Government and the Government of the U.S.S.R., hereby severally declare on behalf and in the name of the Empire of Japan and the U.S.S.R. that there exists on the part of their respective Governments no treaty or agreement of military alliance, nor any secret agreement entered into with any third party, which is calculated to infringe upon the sovereignty or territorial rights of or to menace the safety of the other.

That this draft's use of the word "sovereignty" was specifically directed at Bessarabia was clarified in a June 3, 1924 telegram from Yoshizawa to Tokyo.[15]

Since the wording of this draft looked too much like a treaty of alliance, however, negotiations soon turned to drafting a secret agreement whereby Japan would specifically promise not to ratify the 1920 Paris Treaty. This agreement went through many drafts. On January 9, 1925, less than two weeks before the signing of the Soviet-Japanese convention, Karakhan addressed the following confidential message to Yoshizawa: "I have the honor to bring to Your Excellency's knowledge that the ratification of the said [Paris] Treaty by Japan could not be construed by my Government otherwise than [as] an unfriendly act."[16]

On the same day, Yoshizawa responded in a note, also marked "confidential," stating: "I beg to inform Your Excellency in accordance with instructions from my Government that they would refrain from recommending to the throne to ratify the said Treaty so long as it is not ratified by all the European signatory Powers, as they deem it to be dealing with a purely European question."[17]

By wording the Soviet-Japanese secret agreement in such a way, Tokyo tied its own decision to Italy's. If Mussolini decided to ratify the Paris Treaty, then Japan, as the fourth and final signatory, would presumably go along. As long as Italy continued to refuse to ratify the Paris Treaty, however, then Japan was pledged to also support the Soviet Union. Although this solution did not give Moscow the concrete guarantee that it wanted, it did mean that the Paris Treaty could not become official until Italy decided to ratify it. By adopting this method, Japan threw responsibility for the Bessarabian affair back to Europe, where Great Britain and France were even then pressuring Italy to ratify the Paris Treaty over the Soviet Union's firm opposition.

The Soviet Union's negotiations with Italy during the fall of 1924 resulted in a decision by the Italian government not to ratify the Paris Treaty. After the Soviet Union gained Italy's support, the Japanese government became much more willing to follow suit. On January 19, 1925, the Taishō Emperor and Regent Hirohito both signed Yoshizawa's official credentials, giving him permission to sign the Soviet-Japanese convention.[18] This document is especially interesting because it shows that Hirohito, the next emperor of Japan, was cognizant of the Japanese-Soviet secret diplomacy.

The next day, Karakhan and Yoshizawa signed a comprehensive treaty in Peking that included a secret protocol. In his confidential letter to Yoshizawa, Karakhan requested of Japan[19]:

Confidential

Peking, January 20, 1925.

My Dear Minister,

On the 28th of October, 1920, five Powers, including Japan, signed in Paris a Treaty recognizing the annexation by Rumania of the territory of Bessarabia belonging to the Union of Soviet Socialist Republics.

Taking into consideration the restoration of friendly relations between the Union of Soviet Socialist Republics and Japan, my Government trust that the Japanese Government will not proceed to the ratification of the said Treaty, against which the Government of the Union has lodged an energetic protest with the signatory Powers.

Accordingly, under the instructions of my Government, I beg to request Your Excellency to be good enough to acquaint me with the decision of the Government of Japan in this matter for communication to the Government of the Union of Soviet Socialist Republics.

Believe me,
my dear Minister,
yours sincerely
L. Karakhan

Yoshizawa responded in an official note on behalf of the Japanese government agreeing to these terms (see Document 29).[20] A Soviet diplomat, Gregorii Besedovskii, later confirmed that this secret agreement was part of the Soviet-Japanese convention, signed on January 20, 1925.[21]

Due in large part to this 1925 Soviet-Japanese secret agreement, Rumania's international claim to Bessarabia remained unrecognized throughout the 1920s and 1930s. This was especially true after the Italian cabinet voted to ratify the Paris Treaty on March 8, 1927, which put Japan in an extremely difficult position since she alone blocked this treaty from taking effect. On March 19, 1927, Moscow threatened that if the Paris Treaty were given "legal force," then it would perceive Tokyo's action as "decidedly hostile." Moscow furthermore warned: "The friendly relations now existing between the two countries, as well as the prospects of their further development and consolidation will allow public opinion in the U.S.S.R. to hope that the Japanese Government will not follow the example of the Italian Government."[22]

Confidential.

My Dear Ambassador,

    With reference to your letter of the 20th inst.,
on the subject of the Bessarabian Treaty, I beg to
inform Your Excellency in accordance with instructions
from my Government that unless and until the said
Treaty shall have been ratified by all the European
signatory Powers, the Japanese Government have no
intention of proceeding to the steps required for
its ratification, considering that it deals with
an essentially European question.

                Believe me,

                    my dear Ambassador,

                        Yours sincerely

                            (Signed) K. Yoshizawa.

His Excellency
    Mr. Lev Mikhailovitch Karakhan,
        Ambassador of the Union of
            Soviet Socialist Republics.

Document 29
Yoshizawa's January 20, 1925 Confidential Letter to Karakhan

At the same time, the Soviet ambassador privately warned the Japanese Foreign Ministry that ongoing negotiations on a Soviet-Japanese fishing treaty would surely be disrupted if Japan ratified the Paris Treaty.[23] An estimated 20,000 Japanese fishermen were employed in Siberian waters, with an annual catch in excess of $24 million so losing these fishing rights would have been a major blow to Japan, whereas Japan would gain nothing by ratifying the Paris Treaty.[24]

On March 23, 1927, a popular Japanese newspaper, called *The Japan Advertiser*, succinctly outlined Japan's options: "If she ratifies it, she offends Soviet Russia, if she withholds ratification she nullifies the action of Britain, France, and Italy. Whichever step she takes, therefore–ratification or non-ratification–she is bound to hurt the feelings of one country or another, while she herself stands to gain nothing either way; so it only remains for her to decide which of the two conflicting parties she can least afford to offend." But this newspaper clearly did not know of the ongoing Soviet-Japanese fishing negotiations and so falsely predicted that since "the lesser of the two evils in the case of the Bessarabian Treaty appears to be Soviet displeasure, the likelihood is that ratification will be forthcoming in due course."[25]

In fact, the Japanese government decided to continue delaying ratification. On February 3, 1931, a member of the Japanese House of Representatives, Kaju Nakamura, discussed how "Japan alone is burdened by this very great problem, and is in a serious dilemma," advising the government to ratify the Paris Treaty before the constant delays injured Japan's "international honor." But Ryutaro Nagai, the parliamentary vice-minister for foreign affairs, replied that "Japan must take her own position into consideration," and that the Japanese government "is none the less alive to the considerations of Japan's own position."[26] What neither man was willing to admit was that Japan continued to block ratification of the Paris Treaty to avoid upsetting the Soviet Union.

Tokyo's delaying tactics gave Moscow the time it needed to negotiate a second secret agreement with Berlin on August 23, 1939; the Nazi-Soviet Pact's secret protocols stated that Germany would not oppose the Soviet Union's annexation of Bessarabia. After May 1940, Germany's swift military victory over France left Rumania without support. Thereafter, when Stalin demanded on June 26, 1940, that Bessarabia and northern Bucovina be handed over to the Soviet Union, Carol II, the king of Rumania, was forced to concede.[27] Moscow then held a mock plebiscite in Bessarabia to make this action official.

The Soviet Union's efforts to block the ratification of the 1920 Paris Treaty would not have been possible without the secret agreement that it signed with Japan on January 20, 1925. As a result of this secret agreement, Bessarabia's international status remained unresolved throughout the 1920s and 1930s, until a second secret agreement with Germany gave the Soviet Union the opportunity it had been waiting for to retake Bessarabia. Because the Paris Treaty was never ratified, international support for Rumania was ineffectual. On July 4, 1940, Moscow then turned once again to her eastern neighbor and asked Tokyo to recognize Bessarabia as an integral part of the Soviet Union.[28] Bessarabia was thereafter renamed Moldavia and remained an integral part of the Soviet Union until the 1991 dissolution.

Notes

1. Ray Stannard Baker, *Woodrow Wilson and World Settlement*, 55-56.
2. Gaimushō, File B760-2-2.
3. Vlad Georgescu, *The Romanians: A History*, 172.
4. "Theses of the ECCI on the Forthcoming Washington Conference," August 15, 1921, Jane Degras, *The Communist International, 1919-1943: Documents*, Vol. 1, 291.
5. Georgescu, 193.
6. Gaimushō, B760-2.
7. Gaimushō, 251-106-19, 1104-1107.
8. Gaimushō, 251-106-19, 1312.
9. *Ibid.*
10. Gaimushō, 251-106-5-3, Document No. 210683.
11. "Declaration of Rights of the Working and Exploited People," *Pravda*, No. 2, 17 January 1918, reprinted in: *V. I. Lenin On the Foreign Policy of the Soviet State*, 27-29.
12. English-language memorandum from Adolf Joffe to the Peking government, November 17, 1922, WCTA, 03-32, 207(4).
13. Gaimushō, 251-106-19, 1545-1547.
14. Gaimushō, 251-106-19, 2315-2338.
15. Gaimushō, 251-106-19, 2358-2364.
16. Gaimushō, 251-106-5, Document No.230942.
17. Gaimushō, 251-106-5, Document No. 230943.
18. Gaimushō, 251-106-19, 6750-6751; The Taishō Emperor had serious health problems, so although Hirohito was officially only the Regent in 1925, he was, in fact, already responsible for almost all affairs of state.
19. Gaimushō, B760-2.
20. Gaimushō, 2.5.1 106-5, Document No. 230943.
21. Gregorii Besedovskii (Грегории Беседовский), *На путях к термидору* (*On the Path to the Thermidore*), II, 13.
22. "Russians Answer Bessarabia Note," *The Japan Advertiser,* March 19, 1927.
23. Gaimushō, B760-2.
24. K. K. Kawakami, "Japan's Treaty with Russia," *The American Review of Reviews*, April, 1925, 407-410.
25. "Japan and Bessarabia," *The Japan Advertiser,* March 23, 1927.
26. Gaimushō, B760-2.
27. Georgescu, 210.
28. Gaimushō, B100-JR/1.

Appendix B: Essential Information About the Communist Party's Secret Work

During 1992, the Kuomintang archives in Taipei, Taiwan, released a Chinese Communist Party training manual, bearing the translated title: *Essential Information About the Communist Party's Secret Work.* This manual's description of events in China indicates that it was written during the fall of 1926, in the midst of the Northern Expedition to reunite China under the joint leadership of the KMT and the CCP.

According to a handwritten note on the cover, this manual came into the KMT's possession during the summer of 1927, in one of the KMT's anti-communist purges. That this CCP manual was a rare find is perhaps best shown by quoting a warning located at the very end of the volume, stating: "[E]very section (or small group) will only have one copy, and each section's secretary (or leader) should take care of this copy, making sure that it is not lost or its contents revealed."

This CCP training manual has historical importance for three reasons: 1) it provides crucial information on how the CCP was able to recruit new members and quickly train them in how to execute the party's "secret work"; 2) it provides important details on how the CCP used this secret work to expand its influence within the United Front, as well as within China as a whole; 3) it helps fill an important gap in the CCP's history, by providing new perspectives on the CCP's attempts to undermine the KMT's and the CCP's military opponents during the Northern Expedition.

The organization and contents of this 1926 CCP manual confirm that the CCP's efforts to indoctrinate new members into the party were especially important during the two-year period after the beginning of the May Thirtieth Movement in 1925 through until the KMT purges of 1927. During this time it was reported that the CCP's membership expanded a hundredfold; for example, while the CCP's January 1925 fourth party congress reported that there were still fewer than 1,000 members,[1] one Chinese report from 1929 estimated that the party membership perhaps had "no more than 500 intellectuals."[2]

After the May Thirtieth Movement began, however, the CCP's membership soared, with one CCP leader estimating that it quickly grew to 12,000.[3] At the height of the CCP's popularity in early 1927, there were reports that the party had 30,000 members.[4] Finally, even after the beginning of the KMT purges during April 1927, the CCP opened its fifth party congress on May 9, 1927, by claiming a membership of 50,000.[5]

Essential Information About the Communist Party's Secret Work offers to be not only an important new source of information about how the Chinese communists were able to expand and deepen their influence throughout Chinese society, but also how the CCP managed to survive the KMT's later attempts to destroy it. Previously, the question of the CCP's survival during the KMT purges was largely a mystery to scholars. This was because relatively few records were available as to how the CCP arranged its party sections, how it trained its members, and how these members were expected to carry out their duties. This manual answers many of these questions, providing a previously untapped wealth of information describing the CCP's organization, party functions, and cadre preparedness immediately prior to the beginning of the KMT's purges. It was perhaps due to the training outlined in this manual that the KMT purges failed to destroy the Chinese Communist Party.

Notes

1. L. P. Deliusin (Л. П. Делюсин), *Аграрно-крестьянский Вопрос в Политике КПК 1921-1928* (*Agrarian and Peasant Questions in the Policies of the CCP, 1921-1928*), 125.

2. Ts'ai Ho-sen (Цей Хе-сэнь), "История оппортунизма в Коммунистической партии Китая" ("Historial Opportunism in the Chinese Communist Party"), *Проблемы Китая* (*Questions on China*), No. 1, 1929, 73.

3. Tan P'ing-shan, *The Path of Development of the Chinese Revolution,* 52-54.

4. Donald A. Jordan, *The Northern Expedition*, 226.

5. This number also appeared in a letter written by three Comintern advisers in Shanghai, N. Nassonov, N. Fokine, and A. Albrecht, on March 17, 1927 (Leon Trotsky, *Problems of the Chinese Revolution*, 413); this estimate is furthermore supported by James P. Harrison, *The Long March to Power*, 99.

Contents

1. Introduction–The Meaning of "Secret Work"

2. The Organization of Secret Organs

3. Mailing and Preserving Documents

4. Points to Keep in Mind About Communiques, Letters, and Written Materials

5. Points to Keep in Mind About Conferences

6. Points to Keep in Mind About Contacts and Communications

7. Points to Keep in Mind About Renting Houses and Living

8. Points to Keep in Mind About Talking and Answering Questions

9. How to Spread Propaganda to Outsiders, and How to Introduce Comrades

10. Manners Toward the Heads of Organizations and Among Comrades

11. Our Normal Behavior and Dress

12. Points To Keep in Mind About Public Activity

13. Methods for Dealing with Opposition Members and Opposition Organizations

14. Pay Attention to Detectives, and Methods for Dealing with Detectives

15. Points to Keep in Mind When the Organization Is Uncovered, You are Arrested, and You are Serving Your Sentence

16. Other

17. Appendix

1. Introduction–The Meaning of "Secret Work"

The Resolutions of our organization's Second Enlarged Congress says: "The meaning of secret organizational work, while it does not include reducing the scope of our work, halting the advance of our organizations' duties, or decreasing our opportunities for public activities, it does include increasing the secrecy of our organization–to be able to protect ourselves from military, police, and detectives, while at the same time to be able to greatly increase the scope of our work, add to our leadership strength, and form even closer bonds with the masses." But, in the past, there have been local leaders and comrades who have not completely understood this meaning; who have at different times halted our communications; have stopped all of our outside activities; and have been afraid of the masses to the point of not wanting to introduce new comrades; or who have failed to completely destroy all documents to the point where there is not even one left; or leaders who have fled away and brought about the rapid destruction of local organizations. These mistakes all prove that the leaders and comrades do not understand the meaning of secret work, and should be meticulously corrected.

The scope and abilities of the organization's previous work was small, and our organization is still small, which is why our enemies have still not given us their full attention (naturally, the methods of our enemies and detectives are not expert). At the same time, comrades in different places have not considered the true state of affairs, and they have been so presumptuous as to publicly recruit new people to join or they themselves have openly published name cards with their party position listed etc., etc., and have discussed our outside activities without any cares at all. While these matters prove that some of our comrades are immature, at the same time it proves that our organization has not attained a position where the ruling class is afraid of us. But after the May 30 Incident (1925) the national revolutionary movement has been daily expanding and developing, and at every opportunity our organization extends its leadership responsibilities, and base itself ever deeper among the oppressed youth and masses, and so our opponents have united their strength and are daily increasing their attacks. From last September we have statistics which show that during these eight to nine months, more than ten locations were destroyed and many hundreds of comrades have been arrested, killed, or wounded by oppositionists who wish to destroy our local party organizations. But now the warlords and the imperialists are constantly collaborating to completely destroy our organization and so if we aren't careful we won't be able to avoid even more extreme repression. The importance of secret organizational work is incontrovertible.

2. The Organization of Secret Organs

Our organization is a revolutionary organization but it is not the same as secret societies–and is naturally not like kidnappers, swindlers, etc.–but, at the same time, we must adopt methods from other secret organizations in order to support our leading role in the revolution as well as to preserve ourselves from being destroyed by opposition forces. With respect to these points it is not possible to give a precise explanation, but it is to be hoped that comrades everywhere will promote their study. Now the current principles of the Russian party's secret organization, outlined below:

The most important point of the Russian party's secret organization is that all of the organizations are very complicated and have many points of contact (much like the house of a capitalist which has many doors and windows to protect it from thieves and bandits). Therefore, the enemy and detectives have no way of detecting it, such as:

A is the location of an important organization. B, C, D, E, F, G, etc. are all necessary barriers (or check points) to get to A, but C is only known by B and does not know A. D is only known to C and does not know B, E is only known to D and does not know C, F is only know to E and does not know D, and in this way G receives all of the information, without knowing where A, B, C, D, etc. are located. This system was adopted in Russia because they lived under great oppression, and it enabled them to protect their secrets while making it harder for people to uncover them. Our organization ought to now begin to study this kind of organization.

Besides this, every type of organization must be clearly divided up (for example, transportation department, business office, secret documents department, and department responsible for housing comrades, etc.), and it is not permissible to mix them all up. Also you cannot store secret documents outside areas designated for secret documents.

3. Mailing and Preserving Documents

1) All executive levels of the organization ought to store all of their documents in a safe storage place; the fewer the people who know about this storage area, the better. But also it is necessary to pay attention to the fact that if one or two comrades are arrested, there

should still be people who know where this storage area is located. It is necessary to arrange this storage area in accordance with section 7, number 5 in this booklet.

2) After reading communiques and letters which have to do with our organization for a few days or even after only one time, then it ought to destroyed, and you should pay special attention to destroying it completely. But, documents which will endanger your organization cannot be carelessly and incompletely destroyed and put in a waste-paper basket, and you must prevent other people from picking it up and reading it. With regards to having several unimportant theoretical articles, sometimes you can preserve them, but only if they do not refer to particular organizations or particular leaders.

3) Since communiques, letters, and printed materials must often be sent through the mail, which not only is an obstacle and an inconvenience, but also can be quite dangerous, therefore pay attention to the following points:

a) You must find a fellow student or another dependable person to forward letters, and the best solution would be to form a secret communications network and use all kinds of secret ways to forward letters. During particularly serious periods (for example, during military actions, periods of strict government repression, and while being searched while traveling) you must consider how to handle these events, and use the most suitable secret method for delivering messages.

b) It is better to send every document indirectly through a shop or a school than directly to that person or place.

c) If you are sending out many published communiques, etc., you ought to use a variety of envelopes and packages and you must use many different postal boxes.

d) When you mail a document, with regard to the receiver's name and address, you ought to write it very simply and don't use the real surname or name.

e) When you are writing somebody's name and address, write it simply so as not to attract other people's attention.

f) With regard to using the name of a shop or school on an envelope, don't use the same place very long, and you must decide on the kind of false name based on the contents of the letter.

g) You must at all times investigate to make sure whether all the letters have really arrived with the precise numbers, to decide whether to continue using the same method or whether to change it.

h) Sometimes, if you have a report or letter which is too long, you can use a Chinese-style book in which two pages are fastened together and by opening the pages, writing on the reverse side with a pencil, and then reattaching the pages just like the original, it will look just like a religious work, a virtuous tract, a famous novel, or a science book, etc. when it is mailed.

In a word, you should at all times adapt yourself to circumstances to change the methods for sending documents.

4) While carrying and delivering large numbers of propaganda materials and forbidden items, it is best if you are able to hide them in a box. If not, make the package look just like ordinary articles, and the very best method would be to use wrapping paper from a variety of stores, companies, etc. So as not to attract the attention of our enemies, you ought to pay attention to whether the package is securely tied, and make sure that the packages do not fall apart in transit or it could cause a disaster.

4. Points to Keep in Mind About Communiques, Letters, and Written Materials

1) Communiques should avoid being worded too clearly, and should look like a teacher's handout or an advertisement. At the very least, you should use the regulation code lists to put different words in place of the nouns, and if it is an important communique, you should only have someone deliver it by hand or use methods for writing secret letters.

2) When writing a letter you ought to avoid using all kinds of dangerous nouns by using other code words instead. The best method for transmitting

a lengthy letter is to write a convincing false letter, such as a business letter, a letter from the administration of a school, a religious sermon, a letter asking a friend questions, or a letter about family matters, etc. If you are using names or important sentences, then you ought to use headquarters' A and C word conversion list, and if the lists don't have a word then use another word with the same pronunciation or another suitable word. If you have problems with this method, then you can use invisible ink or milk (please look at the secret communique from headquarters about this).

With regards to personal communications you should also use the above methods, but if you are writing to a comrade who is not a leader or to someone who is not a comrade, you should be careful to only repeat theoretical propaganda, and make sure that you do not discuss internal organizational matters.

3) Normally any document related to our work should not be casually discarded, and avoid throwing away anything which might reveal your name, address, or organization's locations, etc. You should not put any of this information in a diary, and it is best to use your memory, otherwise you can use simplified writing, jumble the letters, use a secret number system, or use a secret code.

5. Points to Keep in Mind About Conferences

1) The Executive Committees of each organization should try to avoid holding conferences which have too many people attending (the very best place to hold a conference is to choose a place where there is no contraband) and when the conference is convening, it is important to do all that you can to reduce the number of people and to make sure to absolutely decrease unnecessary coming and going.

2) In the event that it is necessary to assemble a large number of comrades in one room, because they have to get together to discuss various important questions, then pay attention to the following points:

a) Don't issue notification for the meeting either too early or too late so as to avoid other people hearing about the conference or our members not hearing about it in time.

b) Don't publish either the name of the conference or the matter under discussion.

c) After you have given detailed instructions about where the conference will be held, refer to it in simplified form in later communications, and all of our comrades should memorize the relevant information after receiving the first communique.

d) Every comrade must attend the conference on time.

e) After the conference is over, you ought to leave by different roads, one after the other, and while you should not have many people linger behind, at the same time you should not have everyone leave together and use the same road.

f) Everyone speaking should keep their voice as low as possible, and before and after the conference make sure not to waste time chatting in order to avoid unnecessary noise.

g) Make sure that other people cannot either overhear the conference or spy on it.

h) Don't carry unnecessary documents with you, but for those documents which must be carried with you, it is best to keep them concealed and it is best to devise a way so as not to carry the originals.

i) It is important to have a story prepared in advance in case the enemy arrives.

j) When the enemy comes, you must be careful to quickly and carefully destroy all documents (you must at all times carry matches).

k) When you think that the danger is not too great, do not flee in confusion or else our enemy will become suspicious, and be careful not to immediately begin destroying documents or else our enemy will certainly discover us.

l) Pay attention to the escape routes if the enemy comes. Always prepare all kinds of entertainment items and various other research books. Sometimes you can pretend that you are a class of students studying English or French.

6. Points to Keep in Mind About Contacts and Communications

1) When receiving people from other places, you must first check their reference papers, so as to avoid unexpectedly being taken in. When you think you are beginning to talk to a detective, pay attention to his face as well as his questions and answers. Our communications people ought to be able to act according to the situation, and so at all times should be careful to watch out for suspicious-looking people who come and ask questions. Our communications people should be the eyes and ears of our organization.

When you are contacting people regarding our comrades' names or the addresses of organizations, use either a false name or a secret number code. Be careful not to nonchalantly mention their names or addresses, because we ought to be careful to keep this all secret.

2) The executive committees of local groups, sections, and organizations should keep internal communications in written form to a minimum; if you have a matter to transmit it is best to transmit it orally. When you must make contact, then be sure to use only a false name or a secret method of communication–like the number system; or you can temporarily send letters under a false name.

3) When you are coming and going from a comrade's house, from the organization's headquarters, and from your own office, you shouldn't always use the same road and it is best not to go too often (except in times of need).

7. Points to Keep in Mind About Renting Houses and Living

1) The facilities inside the houses should be complete, don't show any flaws, and there should be many furnishings to hide things in so that a detective wandering through won't notice anything and will think that the resident of the house has an ordinary profession and won't be suspicious.

2) Our offices must be absolutely secret, and after you use documents in the office you must put them away carefully–don't just casually throw them on a table or leave them in an obvious place–so that people don't get suspicious, or if something bad were to happen, so that our enemies will easily be able to locate evidence. We must be careful in these small matters. It can save our lives, if we are accidentally arrested

or searched because of suspicion. With regard to newspapers, pamphlets, etc. which concern the organization, you should especially clean up so that if they know about us, it will only appear that we are people who appear to have books and printed matter so as to study philosophy, and it won't be easy for our enemies to attack us. If you can't avoid others suspecting you of distributing books, it is very dangerous, and it is especially so if anyone can just enter the door and see what kind of people we are.

3) Points to keep in mind if you are subletting an apartment:

> a) You must investigate the situations of your landlord and neighbors, to make sure that you are not giving yourself up to a detective or in other ways that would not be advantageous to us.

> b) You must consider your clothing, actions, and friends so as to be sure that they completely conform to your stated profession, and at the same time you must tell comrades who come frequently to your house to avoid giving a story which might conflict with your own.

> c) When a comrade comes to your house to talk with you, make sure no one can overhear you.

> d) When a communication comes for you when you are not at home, be careful that another person doesn't open it and read it.

> e) When you receive letters at your house, make sure that your name is always the same.

> f) After you have read a document which you have no need to keep, you must immediately burn it–don't save it. As for more important documents, you ought to store them safely, don't give them to anyone else to look at.

> g) When you are not at home, make sure that the most important materials are safely locked away in your trunk so that your landlord will not have a chance to see anything by mistake.

4) You shouldn't live too long in the same secret residence; after a certain amount of time you ought to move.

8. Points to Keep in Mind About Talking and Answering Questions

1) The environments in China and in Western European countries like France and Germany are not the same. In Western Europe a regular comrade can publicly announce that he is a member of the Communist Party or the Socialist Youth Corps, can publicly debate with people, and can publicly disseminate propaganda. In Germany, in particular, the Communist Party, the Socialist Youth Corps, and the Socialist Party are all very clearly marked, and they have organized a 200,000-man red army which is always on the streets everywhere fighting hand-to-hand battles with the opposition. But China is not the same, and except in those places which are controlled by the Nationalist Government, if it is simply known that you are a member of the Communist Party or the Socialist Youth Corps, then you can be arrested and shot. Therefore, while we are under the most reactionary rule, our comrades must not tell other people that they have already entered the Chinese Communist Party or the Socialist Youth Corps, because the fact that you have entered the Chinese Communist Party or the Socialist Youth Corps only shows that your responsibilities have increased, and that you are not just some kind of a showoff. If not, you not only might endanger yourself and the party organization, it also shows that you really don't understand the nature of a revolution. The comrades in our organization must fully understand this point.

2) Don't tell anyone that a certain person is a member of the Chinese Communist Party or the Socialist Youth Corps, lest it disclose a comrade's secret, and if you do you must be punished. At the same time it will show people that you are also a member of the Chinese Communist Party or the Socialist Youth Corps, therefore you must clearly understand that this is also extremely dangerous to you yourself. Supposing people ask you whether somebody is or is not a member of the Chinese Communist Party or the Socialist Youth Corps, the best thing to say is that you have no way of knowing; that you only discuss with him someone else's ideas or actions (which, of course, can be openly discussed) or you can decide to say that the matters you consider with him include discussing Marxist philosophy and the policies of the Chinese Communist Party. It's better that you make the listener show sympathy with our organization, or scorn and oppose the reactionaries and the scum who are mistaken as members of the Communist Party or Communist Youth Corps, as well as not reveal our organization's secrets.

3) With the exception of the highest leaders of the organization, you should not discuss with anyone matters which concern our organization (with the exception naturally being when you are training a comrade

and are exchanging experiences with him) and you should not recklessly guess whether they are a member of the Chinese Communist Party or the Socialist Youth Corps; this is a very easy mistake to make. There are some confused comrades who think that Liao Chung-k'ai, Chiang Kai-shek, Wang Ch'ing-wei, Tai Chi-tao, etc. are really our comrades, just as there are those who don't know that Li Han-chun and Chou Fo-hai have already been kicked out, and so incredibly they write letters to them and tell them about our organization's affairs. These kinds of rash actions are not permissible in secret work, just as without a doubt organizational matters cannot be discussed with family members or friends. In the event that this kind of thing takes place, it is the same as an antirevolutionary act. You cannot brag to anyone close to you about important news which pertains to our organization, no matter whether or not your listeners want to destroy our organization; to sum up, by letting one more person know about us, there is one more possibility of revealing our secrets.

4) It is the responsibility of the local leader and section secretary to communicate the decisions of the organization. As long as you have not received a special order to the contrary, then don't pass on orders yourself. For more important matters, it is best not to tell comrades who are not directly involved, and also you should not lightly tell anyone, because the fewer the people who know about it, the easier it will be to keep the secret.

5) Don't talk with a comrade about our organization's special terms in front of someone who is not our comrade; in fact, be careful not to even talk about organizational matters in front of anyone who is not a comrade. If someone is present who is not a comrade, you ought to be especially careful about revealing secrets.

6) As for the names Chinese Communist Party and Socialist Youth Corps, there are some places where you should not publicly use these names and you should use different names instead.

9. How to Spread Propaganda to Outsiders, and How to Introduce Comrades

1) Every comrade should be especially hard-working in spreading propaganda, because if we don't do this we will not be able to enter among the masses and spread our organization. But, among our comrades the majority have committed actions which show leftist infantile illness, to the point where there is a phenomenon where comrades who had

already drawn close to the masses before entering our organization, contrary to expectations leave the masses after entering our organization. Because while he outwardly puts on the face of being a Bolshevik he actually looks down on the masses, and therefore the masses do not want to get closer to him. This mistake is very severe and is one which definitely cannot be permitted.

Among those who are introducing new comrades, there are those who, because of urging from the top of the organization, do not sincerely understand what they are doing and so randomly draw people in, even to the point of introducing oppositionists which means that you are really acting as our enemies' detectives. These are corrupt practices which must definitely be avoided while doing secret work.

Every comrade should, at the same time as he is propagating the content of the philosophy of the Chinese Communist Party and the Socialist Youth Corps to the masses, he should lead the masses in line with the decisions of our leaders so that they will work along with the views of our organization. But you cannot say that these views were presented by the organization and it is best to make it clear that it represents some publicly announced views of the Chinese Communist Party and Socialist Youth Corps.

2) If you run into someone who seems like he is a comrade but he is unfamiliar to you or an old acquaintance, it would be a big mistake to ask him if he is or isn't a comrade or talk with him about organizational matters. Don't treat him as a comrade, just because he said he was a member of the Chinese Communist Party or Socialist Youth Corps. You should be cautious that he may be a detective. We ought to practice our own detective abilities and don't want others to spy on us. If you need to know whether someone is or isn't a comrade, you can contact an organization leader who will send someone to investigate. If someone does not have an introduction from your leader or a leader from a different place, then you ought to continue to treat him as if he is not a comrade.

3) When introducing a new comrade, you ought to use all kinds of methods to test him in our views and in the views of the proletarian world revolution. If you see that he is ready to enter the party, you ought to find another comrade to approach him, jointly observe him and then you can submit a request to the small committee in your section to report to the regional committee and ask for permission for the new comrade to enter, but before the leaders give their permission, you are not allowed to tell him anything which has to do with the

organization's matters or let him see any kind of secret documents, so as to avoid a problem if he is not given permission to enter.

Once the request has been approved, you can slowly tell him that a communist has to work hard and must join a strict and disciplined party in order to test his intention of joining the party, but before he has shown that he is completely sincere and hardworking, you cannot tell him anything that has to do with the organization's affairs or let him see any secret documents (naturally, it is possible to proceed in the meantime with his training on communism and solving problems, etc.). For a new comrade the most important thing is to tell him the significance of keeping secrets, and his training is naturally the responsibility of the organization and those who introduced him.

10. Manners Toward the Heads of Organizations and Among Comrades

1) The more important the leader, the more careful we must be to conceal the identity of our organization's leaders so that our enemies don't find out who they are.

2) When you meet a comrade on the street, if there is no reason to talk to him then don't. We must be especially careful to pay attention to this point since there have been cases when our enemy arrests an comrade and intentionally releases him and lets him walk down the street, just to see who else is in the party.

3) Within the same organization (such as a factory, a school, or a shop) comrades should not be too close to each other and intentionally show others that they are in the same party, and especially with regard to those comrades who outwardly show strong sympathy with communism they ought to be careful to not appear that they are connected with one another, and it would be better to get closer to those masses who are not comrades.

4) When it comes to matters that you don't need to know, you should not ask others, and when you ask and they do not answer, you should not ask again and you should not feel bad about this. Candidates waiting to fill a vacancy should not demand to see documents which they don't need to see.

11. Our Normal Behavior and Dress

1) We don't have to be too fastidious about clothing, we particularly don't have to overdress, but it is also undesirable to have unkempt hair and a dirty face which, on the contrary, will attract people's attention and may imply that we have certain ways of dressing. This is not permitted while engaging in secret work. Our clothing should be chosen according to circumstances, and we should do our best to look ordinary.

2) Although we are doing our secret work well, our enemies are also making progress and we sometimes have trouble in avoiding discovery, therefore, pay particular attention to knowing how to disguise yourself.

12. Points to Keep in Mind About Public Work

1) After you have given a talk in public where you have been handing out propaganda, and after you are released from the police station or the detention house, you should not immediately go to the house of a leading comrade or to a party headquarters, and if you absolutely must go, then make a few more detours. At the same time, pay attention that no one is following you and if someone is following you act according to section 14 below.

2) Even though your public speaking may be very effective, pay attention to the following points:

   a) Comrades who specialize in secret work should not give lectures in public often.

   b) When you are speaking in public don't wear your ordinary clothing.

   c) After speaking in public don't go directly home or to the house of a comrade or to headquarters.

13. Methods for Dealing with Opposition Members and Opposition Organizations

1) If people falsely accuse us and the Soviet Union, we ought to respond that we support the Nationalist Revolution. From the point of view of

the development of the peasant and working classes and their uniting with the world revolution, the Communist Party and the Soviet Union have an important position.

We need to use common sense when correcting gossip about the party; for example, you do not want to let people know that you are a member of the Communist Party. There are times when it is possible to base your comments on fact, especially if these facts have been stated by people who are not members of our organization but who have supported and given evidence on behalf of the Communist Party and the Soviet Union.

2) Points to remember about carrying out secret work within the opposition:

> a) Use all kinds of methods to investigate the opposition organ's content and actions, and then make frequent reports to higher levels of our organization, but pay attention to make sure that the opposition's secret investigators do not know about it.

> b) When you send a nondescript, loyal, active comrade whom the other party doesn't recognize, to get closer to the other party and infiltrate its organization, it is best for them to say that they either don't have any contacts with up or oppose us.

> c) When sending a person to infiltrate it should be a secret decision of the training department, don't announce it to any comrades. If you are sending two comrades, it is best if they don't know each other and then pay attention to see if their reports are accurate.

> d) You ought to be careful to pay attention and to secretly propagandize the other party's progressives, to make them oppose their own party.

> e) If the other party has made a resolution or taken action not helpful to the revolution or to us, our comrades ought to join with other progressives and use both active and passive methods to oppose it.

14. Pay Attention to Detectives, and Methods for Dealing with Detectives

On board a ship or a vehicle, or when you are walking along a street, you ought to always be aware of investigators. If you discover that someone is following you, you need to use our methods to lose him, but don't get afraid too soon by jumping to the conclusion that everyone is a spy, because if you are frightened by your own shadow then you won't know what to do. If you really believe that a detective is following you, keep calm and don't let your fear show on your face. Don't go directly home or to the house of a comrade or to the party headquarters. Instead, you ought to go somewhere where there are many people, like a busy store or an entertainment hall, and mix with the people. Try not to let the other person know that you are trying to lose him, but once you think he is no longer following you then you can return home. After you have returned home, you ought to report immediately and let everyone know that there is a need to be careful.

15. Points To Keep in Mind When the Organization is Uncovered, You are Arrested, and When You are Serving Your Sentence

1) When one of the organizations is uncovered, the comrades who have fled should immediately use a rapid method of informing other organizations which have contacts with theirs and with the leaders, but, at the same time, they should be careful that they are not being followed since they must avoid being an unwitting guide for our enemies.

2) If something goes wrong, don't turn traitor to the party and to the country. Even if you are being tortured, you don't want to destroy the organization by telling the government. Confessing is unpardonable antirevolutionary behavior, and so is the worst crime for someone who is carrying out secret work. If our enemies arrest you and then can prove who you are, they will use you to arrest other comrades and destroy our organization, so, even if you are punished severely, you should only deny their accusations. The small book "What to do when being questioned" includes our comrades' many years of experience, and says (about completely denying accusations) that if you try to avoid punishment by telling them who your comrades are, then your punishment will only get worse, and it then won't do you any good to say that you don't know anything since they will use all kinds of crafty methods to make you answer their questions. So don't be trapped: even when you are in prison also be careful to guard against detectives, and except for completely dependable prison buddies, you cannot trust anyone. If you

are in court it is unacceptable to propagandize, since they undoubtedly won't believe you and will only try to humiliate you. It is best to simply not recognize their questions, and do not turn against the party and be a traitor to the country.

16. Other

1) A comrade who does not have a known profession, will have to assume a fake profession while carrying out secret work.

2) It is a common custom to have pictures taken with friends, but a comrade should take exception to this custom; the fewer pictures of a person carrying out secret work the better, nor should you write your name on the front or write anything else that is suspicious on the photograph.

3) Handing out propaganda is our most important work. When handing out ordinary propaganda a comrade should not be afraid, because even if he is arrested it is not that important. But if a comrade is giving out important propaganda he should be careful to watch for police and investigators and at the same time when handing out propaganda he ought to quickly approach people from behind or from their side, and should take into account the following points:

 a) You cannot carry any documents or a diary with you.

 b) You should be prepared with proper answers if you are arrested (you should always be prepared for this).

 c) Before you go out to hand out propaganda, just in case you are arrested, you should take all of your documents and books and leave them with someone else, or instead of giving your own address you can give the address of a comrade who doesn't have any documents (but you should first inform this other person).

 d) Once you have finished handing out propaganda, you shouldn't go straight home, to the home of a fellow student leader, or to the party headquarters.

e) If you are in an auditorium and two comrades want to figure out whether a third person is or is not a comrade, you can use sign language or can use your own method as long as it is easy for you to understand but not easy for anyone else to notice. At the same time as you are answering the comrades inquiry, use your right hand to touch your collar while looking at the person he is unsure of. If you know that this person is a Communist Party comrade then put one hand over your fist; if he is a comrade of the Socialist Youth Corps then rub your two palms together; if he is not a comrade then intertwine your ten fingers. This is only an example, but be careful not to do it wrong.

f) Female comrades in any type of neighborhood should have long hair; they should not cut their hair.

g) If you go to any kind of mass meeting, no matter whether it seems dangerous or not, you cannot carry any kind of documents, diaries, books, name card, etc. Before going to the meeting, you should check your clothes, and every day when you leave your house you should also check them.

4) To carry out secret work in the military, you should study special books on this topic but this is a short summary:

It is comparatively difficult to carry out secret work within the military, as we know from Russian comrades' experiences working within Russia's military. The shortest time that you can be in the military is one or two years, since if you are there for too short a time you can't get anything done. If you are even a little careless in the military you can be executed, and it is especially difficult to come and go from the army camp during days off and holidays. Since going outside is not easy, we can only do much of our work in the military by approaching the enlisted men. The best way of getting to know the enlisted men is to start asking them about their families, and when it is convenient you should talk about the troubles which people being raised in a family without money experience, since usually money, leggings, shoes, uniforms, etc. are not a big problem for noncommissioned officers, but are a very personal matter to the enlisted men. You also can organize a secret group within the army, but make sure that it is very secret, and you ought to use short and easily passed oral commands which are changed all the time. When there is an insurrection, and the opposition army is attacking the revolutionary movement, we ought to publish propaganda during the night before the action and secretly stuff it into every soldier's boots, so that when they get up they will see it but not know how it got there. These pamphlets and slogans should be simple and understandable as well as geared to excite them easily. If we do it this way then it will certainly be easy to stir them up, and when there is fighting it won't take much to convince the troops not to fight and they will quickly change sides, which is what we hope to achieve with our work.

5) Some of our comrades like to brag about the work they do for the organization, which is a very easy way of causing all kinds of senseless dangers, and so our determined efforts on behalf of the organization are not something that we can brag about.

6) In our organizational work it is not cowardice to always be careful, but we will not allow intentional excuses just to avoid danger, just as we shouldn't stress only carrying out Party work. But even though we always ought to think of methods to avoid danger, naturally there will be times when there will be some danger and we will have to face it in order to carry out the decisions of the organization.

7) There are dangers that we don't want to face and that we must think of ways to avoid; for example, it is very stupid to get arrested for passing out pamphlets from door to door and we don't want to take unnecessary risks; our bodies are the means by which our organization carries out its work and we don't want to casually neglect them, and the more responsibility a person has, the more careful he should be. If we assign someone to do a particular job in a particular situation, or if we call our leaders together for a meeting, they shouldn't use roads that are strictly patrolled or carry too many important documents, and they should make use of the secret methods as outlined in sections 3 and 4 above.

8) Those responsible for carrying out secret work in each area ought to live in that area for a long time, but our experience shows that the longest they ought to live there is two years, because in that time our enemies will never be able to recognize and destroy us.

9) Principles for conducting "public," "semipublic," or "secret" work:

In the present situation, where two powerful governments have formed in the north and in the south, our organization can carry out its work publicly or semipublicly in areas controlled by the Nationalist government, which has had a huge impact on the development of our organization, because for the first time it has been easy to approach a large number of progressive young people and the masses and pull them into our organization as well as preventing them from getting drawn into the right faction and the nationalist faction. But just because we can use public and semipublic methods does not mean we can't use secret work. In fact, we have to work even harder to increase our secret work, because while in this comparatively open environment we can certainly enlarge the scope of our work, the opposition can increase its activities even more: so that even though our opportunities to interact with the masses are greater, our enemy's detectives can take this opportunity to attack us. Therefore, we must make our organization even more secret. We should limit secret work being turned into public or semipublic work to the following situations:

> a) We ought to have a public or semipublic place where we can interact with the masses, but we certainly don't want to put out a sign.

> b) We ought to openly send representatives to mass meetings to give speeches (those public comrades who are able to gain the trust of the masses and are able to talk to them, but this work should not interfere with our secret work).

The above items relating to secret work are all common sense, but we would like to emphasize here several points: if one of our comrades is not careful and talks about revolution or our party matters on the street, this is not only dangerous, it is meaningless. If one of our comrades likes to drink, and after getting drunk gives away our secrets, this must be stopped. It is also not good if comrades frequently change their surname and given name, because while you can change your given name, it is too easy to forget your new surname and people will get suspicious if you don't recognize your new surname, so it is better to change your given name but not your surname.

The sixteen points above are not intended for every comrade, but if your work requires it then you should use them. At the same time you must consider your own surroundings, and every comrade must learn through experience what are the best methods for each place.

17. Appendix

1) Even though our organization's secret work is now still immature, everyone should still pay attention to it. Many local party branches know that they need to be careful, but they don't know how to do it. Usually our comrades' problems and experiences with regard to secret work were not published, and so since our organization has still not collected the best information, it hopes that every branch of the organization will continue to use former principles as well. We should always keep discussing our experiences, so that we never stop increasing our strength against our enemy's detectives as well as increasing the scope of our activities. Furthermore, we hope that as each area realizes that their methods and the principles are not the same as in this small pamphlet, they will discuss them and make changes.

2) This book should be used in each area and by every comrade as a reference book for methods of carrying out secret work. But it is only information for training, and so every section (or small group) will only have one copy, and each section's secretary (or leader) should take care of this copy, making sure that it is not lost or its contents revealed, so that it can be recalled when necessary.

Printed by the Central School Organization

Appendix C: The March 23, 1935 Soviet-Japanese Secret Protocol

During May 1929, the Chinese government in Nanking tried to regain control over the CER by force, demanding the USSR finally sell the railway to China as it had promised to do in 1924. Tensions increased until an undeclared state of war existed. The Soviet victory over China prompted Japan into action, however, and during 1931-32 Japanese forces established the puppet state of Manchukuo. Soviet-Japanese negotiations to transfer the CER opened in 1933 and were completed in 1935. When the final treaty was signed on March 23, 1935, it included a secret protocol that once again proved that the USSR and Japan cooperated in their efforts to divide China.

During May 1929, the Chinese attempted to regain control over the CER. During the subsequent Sino-Soviet conflict, the Soviet Union enjoyed decisive victories over the Chinese troops: by December 1929 the Red Army had taken the Manchurian cities of Hailar and Manchouli.[1] On 22 November 1929, Tsai Yun-shen, the Diplomatic Commissar of Harbin, received the following three Soviet conditions for ending the conflict[2]:

> 1) Official consent by Chinese side to restoration of situation on CER existing prior to conflict on the basis of the 1924 Peking and Mukden Agreements.

> 2) Immediate reinstatement of the manager and assistant manager of the Railway recommended by the Soviet side in accordance with the 1924 Peking and Mukden Agreements.

> 3) Immediate release of all Soviet citizens arrested in connection with the conflict.

On November 26, 1929 the Mukden government accepted these conditions. The Khabarovsk agreement based on these three points was signed on December 22, 1929. Soviet influence throughout northern Manchuria increased, since the agreement specified that: "Restoration of the former proportion of offices held by Soviet and Chinese citizens," including the reinstatement of "Soviet citizens, officers, chiefs and assistant chiefs of departments." Since Soviet citizens had formerly filled 70 percent of the top positions on the railway, this agreement merely returned to the unequal *status quo*. As a result, the Khabarovsk agreement was described as enhancing "Russian prestige and interest in Manchuria."[3]

Sino-Soviet negotiations soon opened in Moscow. In June 1931, it was reported by the Chinese press that Soviet and Chinese diplomats had decided that China would be able to purchase the CER by allowing all Soviet goods into Manchuria duty-free. This solution meant that no money would actually change hands, which was a boon for the cash-strapped Chinese government, while the Soviet goods would now be able to undersell the Japanese goods. As one newspaper noted: "This agreement, if it is completed, will probably arouse protests from the principal trading nations, particularly Japan. But its inventors believe the formula is air-tight, and that protests will be ineffective."[4]

Instead of protesting, Japan proceeded to take control over all of Manchuria, consolidating this control during the winter of 1931-32 by creating the state of Manchukuo. Negotiations between Moscow and Tokyo to transfer the CER were opened on June 26, 1933. The Soviets initially demanded 250 million gold rubles, while Japan offered only 40 million. Although the negotiations stalled numerous times, Manchukuo eventually agreed to pay 140 million paper yen—approximately 112 million gold rubles—for the CER.[5]

The treaty of March 23, 1935 included fifteen articles and, most important, a secret protocol. Most of the major articles in this treaty are well known. Article II transferred the CER to the Manchukuo government. In Article IV the Soviet government assumed responsibility for all claims of "shareholders, bondholders, and creditors of the North Manchurian Railway incurred prior to the Russian Revolution of March 9th, 1917." The Manchukuo government, in turn, accepted responsibility for all claims and obligations after that date.[6]

Article XIII stated that all "treaties, conventions, agreements, and contracts" concluded between the Russian or Soviet governments and any Chinese authority concerning the railway were declared null and void: "[T]he clauses concerning the North Manchuria Railway contained in the Agreement on General Principles for the Settlement of the Questions between the Republic of China and the Union of Soviet Socialist Republics signed at Peking on May 31st, 1924; the whole of the Agreement between China and the Union of Soviet Socialist Republics for the Provisional Management of the CER signed at Peking at the same date; the clauses concerning the North Manchuria Railway contained in the Agreement between the Government of the Union of Soviet Socialist Republics and the Government of the Autonomous Three Eastern Provinces of the Republic of China signed at Mukden on September 20th, 1924, are included in the number of those which are hereby declared null and void."[7]

These fifteen published articles appeared consistent with accepted international practices. Other important decisions were detailed in a secret protocol attached to this treaty (see Document 30). The protocol stated that Moscow would assume responsibility for all demands and claims concerning the railway before May 31, 1924 provided that Manchukuo and the USSR would bear equally the responsibility for all pending lawsuits against the railway that had been brought before the Manchukuo law courts since May 31, 1924. It also stated that the USSR would bear no responsibility for any lawsuits that might be brought before the courts after the signing of the 1935 agreement transferring the CER to Manchukuo.

(Confidential)

In connection with the provisions of the second paragraph of Article IV of the Agreement for the Transfer to Manchoukuo of the Rights of the Union of Soviet Socialist Republics concerning the North Manchuria Railway, signed this day at Tokyo, the Government of the Union of Soviet Socialist Republics agree to assume responsibility for all demands and claims concerning the North Manchuria Railway on the part of any third party, other than those for the fulfilment of the obligations mentioned in the said paragraph, provided that the Governments of Manchoukuo and the Union of Soviet Socialist Republics shall bear in equal shares the obligations that may arise from all pending lawsuits concerning the business of the North Manchuria Railway carried on on and after May 31st, 1924, brought before the Manchoukuo law courts against the North Manchuria Railway up to December 20th, 1934, for which the final judgement of the Manchoukuo law courts may hold the North Manchuria Railway liable.

The Government of the Union of Soviet Socialist Republics further declare that they will not assume responsibility for any lawsuits, which are pending before the Manchoukuo law courts at the time of the coming into force of the said Agreement, or which may be brought before the said courts in future, concerning the business of the North Manchuria Railway as between March 9th, 1917 and May 31st, 1924.

Document 30
March 23, 1935 Soviet-Japanese Secret Protocol

   This secret protocol had a significant impact on China. Even prior to May 31, 1924, the Russo-Asiatic Bank in Paris, which represented the White Russians whose shares in the railway had been canceled in 1921, had begun lawsuits against the CER. According to the secret protocol, therefore, the Soviet government was solely responsible for this litigation. But the protocol determined that the USSR and Japan were jointly responsible for the lawsuit initiated by China's Nationalist government in Nanking, which was initiated after May 31, 1924. The secret protocol reveals that the Soviet Union and Japan continued to cooperate against China, a fact that the Soviet government vehemently denied in its public statements and in its propaganda.

   The secret protocol also contradicted Soviet propaganda that claimed the Soviet Union alone was fighting to protect China's sovereignty and national interests from Japanese imperialism. Although Article XIII stated that all clauses in the May 31, 1924 treaty concerning the CER were null and void, this did not necessarily include the May 31 secret protocol, which did not specify the railway by name. Therefore, in response to Chinese litigation the Soviet government could still refer to this protocol to fight China's claims. By secretly agreeing to work with Japan on all lawsuits arising from the 1924 to 1935 period, the Soviet Union also extended the benefits of the May 31, 1924 protocol to Japan. The USSR's actions were not only equally as imperialist as Japan's, therefore, but the Soviet government actually helped Japan consolidate its position in China.

Notes

   1. Gaimushō, F 192 5-4-1(4).

   2. Gaimushō, File F 192.5-4-1(5).

   3. "Victory of Russian Seen in Protocol," *The Japanese Advertiser,* December 21, 1929.

   4. "Nanking May Buy Eastern Railway," *Shanghai Evening Post,* June 23, 1931.

   5. Jonathan Haslam, *The Soviet Union and the Threat From the East, 1933-41: Moscow, Tokyo and the Prelude to the Pacific War,* 22-24.

   6. *Agreement for the Cession to Manchoukuo of the Rights of the Union of Soviet Socialist Republics Concerning the North Manchuria Railway,* March 23, 1935, Gaimushō, 1674, IMT 345, 142-148.

   7. *Ibid.*

Bibliography

I. Archival Sources

1920 and Before

26 December 1917; WCTA, 03-32 34(2), "Постановление" ("Decree" of the Soviet government); also see *Pravda*, No. 213, 26 December 1917, 3.

31 January 1918, Copy of Russian-language letter No. 245 from Trotsky to Chicherin about the situation in the Far East, Trotsky archives: No. 6.

22 January 1918, WCTA, 03-32 33(1), copy of a Peking government telegram to China's border areas with Russia, warning them that the Bolshevik party might send revolutionaries to China.

1 February 1918, WCTA, 03-32, 33(1), Chinese-language copy of a telegram received from a Correspondent in Heilungkiang.

23 April 1918, WCTA, 03-32, 329(1), English-language letter from the Danish minister in Peking to the Chinese foreign minister, informing him that all Chinese interests in Russia (with the exception of in Irkutsk and Vladivostok) would be looked after by the Danish legations.

14 March 1919, Number Two Historical Archives, Nanking, File 1039(2), No. 437, Vol. 2, "Declarations on the Allied Supervision of the Chinese Eastern and Siberian Railways" (in Russian and English).

22 April 1919, WCTA, 03-32, 329(1), English-language letter from the Danish chargé d'affaires in Peking, informing the Peking government that they owed the Danish Legation in Petrograd 76,000 rubles and 714 Danish crowns for "safeguarding of the Chinese interests in Russia."

5 August 1919, copy of a military report to the Central Committee of the Bolshevik Party marked "Copy. Secret." Trotsky Archives; No. 2956.

20 August 1919, copy of a military report to the Central Committee of the Bolshevik Party marked "Copy. Quite Secret." Trotsky Archives; No. 2957.

13 January 1920, copy of a telegram from Trotsky and Lenin to Smirnov, head of the Siberian Revolution Committee, and marked "Copy. Quite Secret." Trotsky Archives; No. 419.

18 February 1920, copy of a telegram from Trotsky to Smirnov in Irkutsk and marked "Copy. Secret." Trotsky Archives; No. 444.

19 February 1920, copy of a telegram from Lenin to Smirnov and marked "Copy, Quite Secret." Trotsky Archives; No. 446.

26 March 1920, WCTA, 03-32, 463(1), original French-language telegram [seventeen pages] of the July 25, 1919, Karakhan Manifesto, as sent from Irkutsk to the Ministry of Foreign Affairs in Peking. Also a Chinese-language copy of this telegram; WCTA, 03-32, 462(3).

18 May 1920, WCTA, 03-32, 464(1), English-language telegram [thirteen pages] from N. Paltova, secretary of the Ministry of Foreign Affairs of the Far Eastern Republic in Verhne-udinsk, to the Minister for Foreign Affairs of the Chinese Republic, Peking.

3 June 1920, WCTA, 03-32, 464(1), English-language telegram [twenty pages] from "Krasnochekoff," Minister for Foreign Affairs of the Far Eastern Republic in Verhne-udinsk, to the Minister for Foreign Affairs of the Chinese Republic, Peking.

10 June 1920, WCTA, 03-32, 464(1), English-language telegram [three pages] sent from "Maimaichang" [Kiakhta] by "Ignatius Yourin," the "Representative Plenipotentiary of the Ministry for Foreign Affairs of the Far Eastern Republic and Chief of the Diplomatic Mission to China," to the Minister for Foreign Affairs of the Chinese Republic, Peking.

24 June 1920, WCTA, 03-32, 464(1), English-language telegram [three pages] from "Krasnostshoko," Minister for Foreign Affairs of the Far Eastern Republic in Verhne-udinsk, to the Minister for Foreign Affairs of the Chinese Republic, Peking.

1 July 1920, WCTA, 03-32, 464 (2), *aide-memoire*, "Summary of declarations made by Mr. Medvedev, President of the Provisional Government" in Vladivostok, signed by the Assistant Minister for Foreign Affairs, Svirsky.

24 June 1920, WCTA, 03-32, 464(2), English-language telegram [seven pages] from "Chervony," Minister for Foreign Affairs of the Far Eastern Republic in Verhne-udinsk, to the Minister for Foreign Affairs of the Chinese Republic, Peking.

26 July 1920, WCTA, 03-32, 464(3), English-language telegram [three pages] from "Chervony," Minister for Foreign Affairs of the Far Eastern Republic in Verhne-udinsk, to the Minister For Foreign Affairs of the Chinese Republic, Peking.

30 July 1920, Pei-yang Cheng-fu archive document No. 1001, 3483, Nanking Number Two Historical Archive, Vol. 15, 469-474.

24 August 1920, WCTA, 03-32, 432(1), Chinese-language minutes of the Sixth Meeting of the Russian Study Commission.

30 August 1920, WCTA, 03-32, 432(1), Chinese-language minutes of a Meeting Concerning the Status of the Russian Consul.

10 September 1920, WCTA, 03-32, 465(1), Chinese-language minutes of a Meeting Between Chang Ts'an-shih and Iurin on September 10 from 5:00 p.m. until 6:30 p.m."

18 September 1920, WCTA, 03-32, 523(1), internal Chinese-language memo concerning negotiations with Iurin.

18 September 1920, Number Two Historical Archives, Nanking, File 1039, No. 153, Russian-language letter from Prince Kudachev to Foreign Minister Yen.

1 October 1920, WCTA, 03-32, 435(1), Chinese-language telegram from Foreign Minister Yen to Chinese officials in Chilin, the Amur, and along the Chinese Eastern Railway.

2 October 1920, WCTA, 03-32, 479(1), Chinese-language copy of Karakhan's second manifesto, dated September 27, 1920.

5 October 1920, WCTA, 03-32, 438(1), American embassy memo No. 62 and No. 63, signed by the American ambassador to China, Charles R. Crane. Minister Crane was complaining that when the Chinese officials took control of the Russian concession in Tientsin they immediately took over the collection and handling of money from licenses and permits, which made up 70 percent of the Municipal Council's income. Minister Crane was pointing out to the Peking government that most of this money had been paid by Americans and other foreigners, not by Russians, and that he was concerned by the "action of the Chinese authorities in abruptly abrogating the conditions under which American property holders bought property and have paid taxes thereon."

29 October 1920, WCTA, 03-32, 465(1), Russian-language letter from the Vladivostok Provisional government entrusting Iurin with full power to negotiation with Peking in their name.

17 November 1920, WCTA, 03-32, 523(1), English translation of Iurin's Russian-language letter, provided by the Far Eastern Republic's mission and signed by M. Kassanin, the secretary of that mission.

23 November 1920, WCTA, 03-32, 523(1), original Russian-language letter No. 576/a to Foreign Minister Yen and signed by Iurin.

23 November 1920, WCTA, 03-32, 523(1), copy of the original English-language note. This note was hand-written at the top of Iurin's reply on November 24, 1920. The original note stated: "Dear Sir: If you will kindly call at my home . . . on Friday morning at say 10 o'clock (November 26), I shall be glad to talk over various matters with you."

27 November 1920, WCTA, 03-32, 523(1), According to two letters in Russian signed by Iurin—one to Dr. Yen (288/c) and the other to Liu Ching-jen (287/a).

30 November 1920, WCTA, 03-32, 473(3), Chinese-language minutes of the meeting between Iurin and Liu Ching-jen.

13 December 1920, WCTA, 03-32, 466(3), French-language letter to Foreign Minister Yen (300/c), signed and sealed by Iurin; unsigned copies of this same letter are available in 03-32 523(1) and 03-32 524(1).

1921

12 January 1921, WCTA, 03-32, 523(2), official Russian-language letter to Foreign Minister Yen (No. 303/c), signed and sealed by Iurin.

23 February 1921, WCTA, 03-32, 472(2), English-language translation of the Russian original provided by the Soviet legation in London.

7 March 1921, WCTA, 03-32, 471(2), English-language letter from the Peking government to the Soviet government.

26 March 1921, WCTA, 03-32, 471(2), English-language Soviet memorandum No. 898/2 to the Ministry of Foreign Affairs in Peking.

31 March 1921, WCTA, 03-32, 472(2), English-language *aide-memoire* from the Chinese Legation in London to the Soviet government.

2 April 1921, WCTA, 03-32, 473(3), Chinese-language copy of Iurin's letter: "Letter from Iurin."

6 April 1921, WCTA, 03-32, 436(2), two Russian-language letters from the FER Mission in Peking; Official English translations of these two letters are also available: No. 339/c, 03-32 436(2); No 338/c, 03-32 434(1).

12 April 1921, WCTA, 03-32, 523(1), Chinese-language telegram from the Ministry of Foreign Affairs to Wellington Koo in London.

15 April 1921, WCTA, 03-32, 434(1), English-language translation of letter from W. W. Yen to Doyen Batalha de Freitas.

16 April 1921, WCTA, 03-32, 462(4), English-language translation of the Soviet memorandum No. 960/2.

17 April 1921, WCTA, 03-32, 523(2), FER mission's Russian-language memorandum No. 343; see April 18, 1921 for official English-language translation No. 344.

22 April 1921, WCTA, 03-32, 523(2), Russian-language memorandum No. 347/c.

13 May 1921, WCTA, 03-32, 475(1), Chinese-language minutes of Foreign Minister Yen's meeting with Iurin.

13 May 1921, WCTA, 03-32, 524(1), Chinese-language minutes of Foreign Minister Yen's meeting with Iurin.

17 May 1921, WCTA, 03-32, 470(1), Chinese-language telegram from Minister Koo in London to Peking.

15 June 1921, WCTA, 03-32, 462(4), Chinese-language telegram from Consul Ch'en in Moscow to the Peking government.

17 June 1921, WCTA, 03-32, 475(1), Chinese-language telegram to Wellington Koo in London.

17 June 1921, WCTA, 03-32, 462(4), English-language *aide-memoire*, from the Chinese legation in London to the Soviet Government, which repeats the content of the Chinese-language telegram from April 12, 1921.

20 June 1921, WCTA, 03-32, 198(3), English-language note from Peking handed to Russian Trade Commission for transfer to Moscow.

28 June 1921, WCTA, 03-32, 472(2), English-language note from the Soviet official in London, Krassin, to Wellington Koo, answering the *aide-memoire* of June 17, 1921.

July 1921, WCTA, 03-32, 175(1), English-language note from the Soviet official in London, Krassin, to Wellington Koo, concerning Outer Mongolia.

8 July 1921, WCTA, 03-32, 524(2), according to the Chinese-language minutes of a meeting between Foreign Minister Yen and the acting head of the Far Eastern Republic's Mission in Peking, Agrieff.

4 August 1921, WCTA, 03-32, 471(1), Chinese Foreign Ministry telegram to Consul Wellington Koo in London.

3 October 1921, WCTA, 03-32, 466(2), Chinese-language minutes of a meeting between Foreign Minister Yen and Iurin.

4 October 1921, WCTA, 03-32, 466(2), Chinese-language minutes of a meeting between Foreign Minister Yen and Iurin.

5 October 1921, WCTA, 03-32, 466(2), Chinese-language minutes of a meeting between Foreign Minister Yen and Iurin.

15 October 1921, WCTA, 03-32, 470(1), English-language letter No. 741 from the FER to the Peking government.

15 October 1921, WCTA, 03-32, 471(1), Chinese Foreign Ministry telegram to Consul Wellington Koo in London.

18 October 1921, WCTA, 03-32, 474(2), French-language credentials for "Alexandre Constantinowitch Paikes . . . Délégué Extraordinaire de la Republique Socialiste Federative Des Soviets de Russie." This document specified that Paikes was only empowered to discuss the Chinese Eastern Railway, and that any agreement he signed had to be ratified by the Soviet government. Paikes's credentials were then signed by Lenin and Chicherin.

5 November 1921, WCTA, 03-32, 475(1), Russian copy of the Soviet treaty with Outer Mongolia.

16 December 1921, WCTA, 03-32, 523(2), Chinese-language minutes of a meeting between Foreign Minister Yen and Paikes. Additional copies of these minutes are located in WCTA 03-32 465(3).

1922

16 January 1922, WCTA, 03-32, 204(1), Chinese-language minutes of three meetings with Paikes.

2 February 1922, WCTA, 03-32, 475(1), Chinese translation of a January 4, 1922 article in the U.S. magazine *The Nation* which in turn was based on the November 11, 1921 *Izvestiia* article, which was based on the November 5, 1921 Soviet-Mongolia treaty.

4 February 1922, WCTA, 03-32, 482(1), English-language copy of the Washington Conference's resolution on the Chinese Eastern Railway.

7 February 1922, WCTA, 03-32, 204(1), Chinese-language translation of Paikes's letter No. 235 [The hand-written Russian-language letter is at 03-32, 200(3)].

11 March 1922, WCTA, 03-32, 475(1), Chinese-language telegram from the Peking government consul in Chita.

27 March 1922, WCTA, 03-32, 470(2), English-language memorandum No. 311 signed by Paikes, listing the members of the R.S.F.S.R. Mission as follows: "1. Aleksandr K. Paikes–Plenipotentiary Extraordinary. 2. Vladimir D. Vilenskii–Counselor. 3. David E. Sandler–Collaborator. 4. Boris Ph. Bernson–Collaborator. 5. Joseph M. Mussin–Collaborator. 6. Valentine B. Ezierskaia–Collaborator. 7. Charles A. Michelson–Collaborator. 8. Lidia A. Michelson–Collaborator."

24 April 1922, English-language radiogram from Number Two Historical Archives, Nanking, File 1039, No. 437, concerning the decisions of the Washington Conference about the Chinese Eastern Railway.

26 April 1922, WCTA, 03-32, 200(3), Chinese-language minutes of Paikes's meeting with Ministry of Foreign Affairs officials.

15 May 1922, WCTA, 03-32, 475(1), official cabinet letter No. 1035.

23 May 1922, WCTA, 03-32, 163(3), Chinese-language minutes of a meeting between Foreign Minister Yen and Paikes.

29 June 1922, WCTA, 03-32, 200(3), Chinese-language minutes of Paikes's meeting with Chinese Ministry of Foreign Affairs Officials.

29 June 1922, WCTA, 03-32, 462(2), Chinese-language telegram from Moscow.

6 July 1922, WCTA, 03-32, 204(1), Chinese-language minutes of a meeting between Foreign Minister Yen and Paikes.

3 August 1922, WCTA, 03-32, 207(1), English-language memorandum No. 533 from Paikes to the Ministry of Foreign Affairs of the Republic of China.

22 August 1922, WCTA, 03-32, 473(3), Chinese-language minutes of a meeting between Foreign Minister Koo and Joffe.

23 August 1922, WCTA, 03-32, 462(2), Chinese and English lists of the gradually increasing size of the Soviet Mission in Peking dated August 23, 1922, August 31, 1922, September 4, 1922, October 28, 1922, January 15, 1923, February 27, 1923, and June 27, 1923.

24 August 1922, WCTA, 03-32, 472(3), English-language note from Karakhan and Lanson to the Minister of Foreign Affairs of the Imperial Japanese government.

25 August 1922, WCTA, 03-32, 207(1), English-language memorandum from Joffe to Foreign Minister Koo. First rough draft of the opening statement of the Soviet mission in Peking.

31 August 1922, WCTA, 03-32, 481(1), English-language minutes of a conversation between Koo and Joffe.

2 September 1922, WCTA, 03-32, 469(2), English-language memorandum from Joffe to Foreign Minister Koo. Final draft of the opening statement of the Soviet mission in Peking. Additional copies in WCTA, 03-32, 472(3) and 481(1). A Chinese-language version is in WCTA, 03-32, 473(1).

8 September 1922, WCTA, 03-32, 472(3), letter from John C. Ferguson to Foreign Minister Koo.

14 September 1922, WCTA, 03-32, 526(2), letter from T. N. Woo to Foreign Minister Koo.

19 September 1922, WCTA, 03-32, 469(1), American Minister Jacob Gould Schurman's conversation with Foreign Minister Koo.

17 November 1922, WCTA, 03-32, 163(4), Russian-language and English-language memorandum No. 531 from Joffe to Foreign Minister Koo, in which Joffe swore that "the Workers and Peasants' Government is opposed on principle to secret diplomacy and never signs secret treaties." Additional copies of this important document are in WCTA, 03-32, 207(4).

18 November 1922, WCTA, 03-32, 470(2), Russian-language and English-language memorandum No. 549 from Joffe to Foreign Minister Koo, in which Joffe informed Koo that the Far Eastern Republic had become part of the RSFSR.

30 November 1922, WCTA, 03-32, 470(2), Russian-language and English-language notes in which the Soviet mission assigned V. L. Pogodin as special representative to the three Eastern provinces, in Harbin.

6 December 1922, WCTA, 03-32, 470(2), Russian-language and English-language notes in which the Soviet mission answered the Chinese protest and corrected their November 30, 1922 note by admitting that V. L. Pogodin was special representative only to the territory of Harbin and to the adjacent zone of the Chinese Eastern Railway.

11 December 1922, WCTA, 03-32, 204(1), Chinese-language note to the Soviet representative, Joffe, entitled: "An Outline to Workers and Peasants' Representative."

12 December 1922, WCTA, 03-32, 470(2), English-language note No. 758 from the Soviet Mission in Peking to the Waichiaopu.

1923

15 January 1923, WCTA, 03-32, 462(2), Russian-language and English-language notes No. 163 from Joffe to the foreign minister, announcing that his departure to the south was "on the prescription of the physicians . . . for the treatment of my illness." J. C. Davtian was put in charge of the Soviet mission.

30 January 1923, WCTA, 03-32, 470(3), Russian-language and English-language note No. 300 from J. C. Davtian to the foreign minister announcing the Soviet offer to transfer the negotiations to Moscow.

5 February 1923, WCTA, 03-32, 206(5), Chinese-language letter from Wang Hung-nien to the Peking government.

14 February 1923, WCTA, 03-32, 481(5), Chinese-language telegram from the Waichiaopu to Commissioner Ch'en in Moscow.

17 February 1923, WCTA, 03-32, 481(1), English-language note from Wang Wen-pu, member of Parliament, to Joffe in Japan, protesting the Soviet-Japanese negotiations.

20 February 1923, WCTA, 03-32, 481(1), English-language reply from Joffe to Wang Wen-pu, member of Parliament, denying that he was negotiating with Japan.

23 February 1923, WCTA, 03-32, 481(1), Russian-language and English-language note No. 549 from Davtian, in which he acknowledged receiving the Peking government's memorandum No. 155, stating that it would be best to hold the Sino-Soviet conference in Peking, and then repeated that the conference could begin when Joffe returned from his sick leave. This letter also contained an obtuse sentence (both in Russian and in Chinese) in which it was not clear whether the Chinese representative in Moscow–Ch'en–was being blamed for suggesting that the site of the conference be moved from Peking to Moscow, or whether he was simply being given credit for trying to speed up negotiations: "the Russian Government having taken into consideration the desire of the Chinese Government as it was expressed through Mr. [Ch'en], its special Delegate at Moscow, had offered, in order to accelerate the procedure, to start immediate negotiations in Moscow." This caused a minor conflict in Moscow, as Ch'en thought the former and protested directly to Chicherin on March 7, 1923 (WCTA, 03-32, 481(6)) , which prompted Chicherin to send a verbal note (No. 269) refusing to answer Ch'en's letter because it was too impolite (WCTA, 03-32, 481(6)), and then Ch'en once again protested on March 19, 1923 (WCTA, 03-32, 481(6)). These examples merely show that there was much underlying tension in the Sino-Soviet negotiations.

26 March 1923, WCTA, 03-32, 483(3), Chinese-language proclamation making Wang Cheng-t'ing the official Chinese representative at the upcoming Sino-Soviet conference. Two things are particularly important: 1) the date of this announcement was timed exactly three years to the day after the first Karakhan manifesto was received by China, showing that Peking planned to base its negotiations on this document; 2) this proclamation gave Wang the power to sign a treaty in the name of the Peking government only if the government specifically agreed with the treaty under discussion.

31 March 1923, WCTA, 03-32, 481(6), Russian-language and English-language note No. 934 acknowledging Wang's selection as the official Chinese negotiator.

12 May 1923, WCTA, 03-32, 482(1), English-language note from the Waichiaopu to Davtian, asking that the issue of navigation along the Amur River be decided quickly since "the river will be frozen by September."

15 June 1923, WCTA, 03-32, 483(2), English-language note No. 1950 from Davtian to Wang Cheng-t'ing refusing to discuss any questions prior to the convening of the official Sino-Soviet conference: "that my Government does not consider expedient the preliminary settlement of separate questions before the Conference is started."

6 July 1923, WCTA, 03-32, 461(3), English-language copy of the Soviet Union's "Fundamental Law" dated December 30, 1922, but not ratified until July 6, 1923, given to the Waichiaopu by Karakhan on September 5, 1923.

13 July 1923, WCTA, 03-32, 461(3), English-language copy of the official "Declaration of the Union of Soviet Socialist Republics," given to the Waichiaopu by Karakhan on September 5, 1923.

23 July 1923, WCTA, 03-32, 484(3), English-language declaration made by Chang Yuan-chih to Joffe in Japan on behalf of the Peking government (which he received on July 19, 1923), to the effect that "if any thing concerning China [is] negotiated in the Russo-Japanese Conference which is now being held, previous agreement from the Government of China is needed."

27 July 1923, WCTA, 03-32, 481(6), Russian-language and English-language note No. 2574/7 from the Soviet mission in Peking, announcing that Adolf Joffe was being replaced by Lev Karakhan.

28 July 1923, WCTA, 03-32, 512(1), English-language letter from Samuel Gompers, President of the American Federation of Labor, to Sao-Ke Alfred Sze, the Chinese minister to Washington, which included an exchange of letters between Gompers (July 9, 1923) and Secretary of State, Charles Hughes (July 19, 1923). Both Gompers's letter and Hughes's letter denounced the Soviet government for its tyrannical policies toward its own people, as well as attempts to undermine foreign governments.

1 August 1923, WCTA, 03-32, 470(3), French-language copy of Karakhan's credentials, signed by the head of the Central Executive Committee, N. Narimanov, and the Foreign Minister, G. Chicherin.

2 August 1923, WCTA, 03-32, 503(3), Russian-language copy of Karakhan's credentials, signed by the President of the Soviet of People's Commissars, L. Kamenev, and the foreign minister, G. Chicherin.

15 August 1923, WCTA, 03-32, 483(2), Russian-language letter from Lev Karakhan to Wang Cheng-t'ing.

3 September 1923, WCTA, 03-32, 482(3), Chinese-language minutes of the meeting between Karakhan and Wang at 3:00 p.m., No. 21, Kung-chang alley in Peking.

4 September 1923, WCTA, 03-32 467(1), English-language text of Wang's speech welcoming Karakhan to China at a luncheon at Peihai. Russian-language and Chinese-language texts of this speech can be found in WCTA, 03-32, 467(1).

4 September 1923, WCTA, 03-32, 467(1), Russian-language text of Karakhan's speech at the luncheon given by Wang.

5 September 1923, WCTA, 03-32, 461(3), Russian-language and English-language letter from Karakhan, introducing the USSR's Fundamental Law (ratified on July 6, 1923) and the Declaration (July 13, 1923).

8 September 1923, WCTA, 03-32 470(3), Russian-language and English-language copies of Karakhan's letter, mentioning that he was not being given the opportunity to present his credentials directly to the president–an honor given only to representatives of recognized governments–and that he was sending those credentials to the Waichiaopu.

13 September 1923, WCTA, 03-32, 467(2), Chinese-language minutes of the conversation between Karakhan and Chu Ho-hsiang.

14 September 1923, WCTA, 03-32, 483(5), Chinese-language minutes of the conversation between Karakhan and Wang (Wang's official title was Director of the Sino-Soviet negotiations).

4 October 1923, WCTA, 03-32, 477(1), Chinese-language copy of Wang Cheng-t'ing's official negotiating powers. This document was exactly the same as that signed when Wang was selected on March 26, 1923, limiting Wang's powers to signing a final treaty only after the Peking government had agreed to it in advance.

13 October 1923, WCTA, 03-32, 481(5), the official English-language translation of the Chinese-language original, entitled "Draft Agreement for the Resumption of Relations Between China and Russia." This draft had fourteen points.

26 October 1923, WCTA, 03-32, 481(5), English-language "Draft Agreement for the Resumption of Relations Between China and Russia," which included only eleven points.

21 November 1923, WCTA, 03-32, 483(1), Chinese-language note from Wang to Karakhan, explaining that Wang was visiting Japan and hoped to convene the Sino-Soviet conference upon his return.

23 November 1923, WCTA, 03-32, 483(1), English-language reply (No. 7406) from Karakhan to Wang, saying that he would agree to convene the conference only after China recognized the Soviet government.

27 November 1923, WCTA, 03-32, 477(1), Chinese-language copy of Wang's letter to the Waichiaopu.

28 November 1923, WCTA, 03-32, 483(1), Chinese-language copy of Wang's letter to Karakhan.

30 November 1923, WCTA, 03-32, 483(2), Russian-language signed original letter No. 7618 from Karakhan to Wang.

2 December 1923, WCTA, 03-32, 481(3), English-language copies of the 1919 and the 1920 Karakhan Manifestos, provided by the Soviet Mission in Peking and marked "True to the original."

1924

9 January 1924, WCTA, 03-32, 483(1), Chinese-language letter from Wang to Karakhan.

17 January 1924, WCTA, 03-32, 483(2), Russian-language letter from Karakhan to Wang.

18 January 1924, WCTA 03-32, 461(3), Chinese Foreign Ministry report written by Li Chia-ao, the Chinese consul in Moscow, to Foreign Minister Koo, entitled: "Opinion Paper from the Foreign Ministry Official in Moscow."

2 February 1924, WCTA, 03-32, 487(1), Chinese-language minutes of Chu Ho-hsiang's meeting with Karakhan.

24 February 1924, WCTA 03-32, 461(3), Chinese Foreign Ministry report written by Li Chia-ao, the Chinese Consul in Moscow, to Foreign Minister Koo.

27 February 1924, WCTA, 03-32, 487(1), Chinese-language minutes of Chu Ho-hsiang's meeting with Karakhan.

1 March 1924, WCTA, 03-32, 488(1), multiple Chinese-language copies of the draft Sino-Soviet treaty, including suggested changes written on the copies. The most important suggestions came from the ministry of finance and the ministry of education.

4 March 1924, WCTA, 03-32, 487(1), Chinese-language minutes of the conversation between Foreign Minister Koo and the Japanese Minister.

7 March 1924, WCTA, 03-32, 487(1), secret Chinese-language telegram from Wellington Koo to Li Chia-ao in Moscow.

9 March 1924, WCTA, 03-32, 483(1), Chinese-language minutes of a conversation between Li Chia-ao and Chicherin; also see March 11, 1924 telegram No. 732; WCTA, 03-32, 477(1).

9 March 1924, Archives of the Historical Commission of the Central Committee of the Kuomintang Party, Document 433-32. Published copy of Liao Chung-k'ai's speech at Canton Lenin memorial, 中國國民黨周刊 (*Chinese Kuomintang Weekly*).

14 March 1924, WCTA, 03-32, 506(5), English-language original copy of the draft treaty, including the secret protocol. This draft has been signed by Karakhan and Wang, but the dates are not filled in and there are no official seals, which tends to support the Waichiaopu's later claim that this treaty was initialed merely to show agreement between Wang and Karakhan, not as a sign that Wang was signing on behalf of the Peking government.

15 March 1924, WCTA, 03-32, 487(1), Russian-language letter from Chicherin to Li Chia-ao.

16 March 1924, WCTA, 03-32, 487(2), Russian-language letter from Chicherin to Li Chia-ao.

16 March 1924, WCTA, 03-32, 483(2), Russian-language original of Karakhan's signed three-day ultimatum, letter No. 1011.

16 March 1924, Archives of the Historical Commission of the Central Committee of the Kuomintang Party, Document No. 435-33. Sun Yat-sen's directive No. 24.

19 March 1924, WCTA, 03-32, 487(1), English-language original of Karakhan's signed letter No. 1023 to Wellington Koo, including five points.

19 March 1924, WCTA, 03-32, 483(2), Russian-language original of Karakhan's signed letter No. 1037 to Wang, including four points.

19 March 1924, WCTA, 03-32, 487(2), English-language minutes of a meeting between Koo and Karakhan at 10:00 p.m., at Koo's private residence.

25 March 1924, WCTA, 03-32, 487(1), English-language letter No. 1111/11 from Karakhan to Koo; sealed but not signed.

26 March 1924, WCTA, 03-32, 487(2), Chinese-language telegram from Li Chia-ao, Chinese minister to Moscow, to the president of the Republic of China, Ts'ao K'un.

28 March 1924, WCTA, 03-32, 487(2), English-language minutes of a meeting between Koo and "Swasalon," starting at 5:16 p.m.

28 March 1924, WCTA, 03-32, 487(2), English-language minutes of a meeting between Koo and "Schwasalon," starting at 8:45 p.m.

29 March 1924, WCTA, 03-32, 487(2), English-language minutes of a meeting between Koo and "Schwarsalon," starting at 11:00 a.m.

5 April 1924, WCTA, 03-32, 487(3), Chinese-language minutes of a meeting between Li Chia-ao and an unnamed Soviet official, referred to merely as "Du."

12 April 1924, WCTA, 03-32, 537(1), English-language letter from Sir Francis Aglen, Inspectorate General of Customs, to Wellington Koo, informing him that all of the Russian portion of the Boxer Indemnity had already been promised for other uses through 1927.

14 April 1924, WCTA, 03-32, 510(3), English-language letter from Moore-Bennett to Wellington Koo, warning him of a new Germany/Soviet consortium to mine gold in Outer Mongolia.

15 April 1924, WCTA, 03-32, 537(1), English-language letter from Wellington Koo to Aglen, confirming that the text in Aglen's possession appeared to be correct.

3 May 1924, WCTA, 03-32, 268(1), Letter from Jacob Schurman, the U.S. minister to China, to Foreign Minister Wellington Koo.

30 May 1924, WCTA, 03-32, 495(2), English-language copy of the "Certificate of Full Power Given to VI Kyuin Wellington Koo Plenipotentiary," signed by President "Ts'ao K'un" and countersigned by Wellington Koo, as minister for foreign affairs. This certificate stated that Koo was authorized to sign with Karakhan an "Agreement on General Questions . . . (15 Articles)," an "Agreement for the Provisional Management of the Chinese Eastern Railway (11 Articles)," "one Protocol," and then "seven Declarations, and one exchange of Notes."

31 May 1924, WCTA, 03-32, 454(1), Chinese-language copy of the final Sino-Soviet agreement; this version includes the secret protocol with the instructions "Secret Protocol, Do Not Publish." A published English-language copy can be found at WCTA, 03-32, 495(1); this version does not include the secret protocol.

6 June 1924, WCTA, 03-32, 494(1), English-language minutes of the meeting between Karakhan and Koo, at Koo's residence, starting at 5:00 p.m.

7 June 1924, WCTA, 03-32, 455(1), English-language letter to Koo, signed by Karakhan, protesting China's failure to return Russian property to the Soviet government in Shanghai, Chefoo, and at Tientsin.

9 June 1924, WCTA, 03-32, 454(1), English-language letter signed by V. K. Wellington Koo to the Diplomatic Corps' doyen, W. J. Oudendijk, requesting that the Russian consulate in Peking be handed over to Karakhan.

11 June 1924, WCTA, 03-32, 454(1), English-language reply to Foreign Minister Koo, signed by W. J. Oudendijk, announcing that a representative of the Russian government, who was "duly accredited to the Chinese government," should approach the Diplomatic Corps directly.

13 June 1924, WCTA, 03-32, 494(1), English-language minutes of the meeting between Karakhan and Koo, at Koo's residence, starting at 9:00 p.m.

13 June 1924, WCTA, 03-32, 467(3), English-language letter to Foreign Minister Koo, signed by Karakhan, requesting that China allow the Soviet consulate in Peking to be turned into a full embassy, with the Republic of China then having a full embassy in Moscow.

21 June 1924, WCTA, 03-32, 455(4), English-language letter to Foreign Minister Koo, signed by Karakhan, protesting that the Russian consulate in Shanghai had not yet been turned over to Soviet control.

26 June 1924, WCTA, 03-32, 455(4), English-language letter to Foreign Minister Koo, signed by Karakhan, protesting that the Russian consulate in Peking had not yet been handed over to his control.

27 June 1924, WCTA, 03-32, 454(1), English-language copy of Foreign Minister Koo's letter to W. J. Oudenijk, once again requesting that the Russian consulate in Peking be handed over to Karakhan.

27 June 1924, WCTA, 03-32, 488(2), Chinese-language minutes of Li Chia-ao's meetings with Soviet Foreign Minister officials on June 27 and 29, to request that the Sino-Soviet conference be convened on time.

28 June 1924, WCTA, 03-32, 489(1), English-language minutes of the meeting between Karakhan and Koo, at the Ministry of Foreign Affairs, starting at 12:45 p.m.

28 June 1924, WCTA, 03-32, 499(4), English-language letter No. 2524/26 to Foreign Minister Koo, signed by Karakhan, delaying the opening of the official Sino-Soviet conference.

30 June 1924, WCTA, 03-32, 499(4), English-language letter to Karakhan from Wellington Koo, in which he pointed out that June 30 was the last day to convene the Sino-Soviet conference so as to fall within the stipulations of the May 31, 1924 Agreement on General Principles.

7 July 1924, WCTA, 03-32, 455(4), English-language letter No. 2622/29 to Foreign Minister Koo, signed by Karakhan, complaining that White Russians had taken over the Russian consulate in Shanghai.

7 July 1924, WCTA, 03-32, 494(1), English-language minutes of the meeting between Karakhan and Koo, at the Ministry of Foreign Affairs, starting at 11:00 a.m.

8 July 1924, WCTA, 03-32, 455(4), English-language letter No. 2554/27 to Foreign Minister Koo, signed by Karakhan, complaining that the Russian archive in Shanghai had not been turned over to the Soviet mission.

11 July 1924, WCTA, 03-32, 455(1), English-language letter No. 2664/33 to Foreign Minister Koo from Karakhan, complaining that the Russian consulate in Chefoo had not been turned over to the Soviet mission.

12 July 1924, WCTA, 03-32, 455(2), English-language letter No. 2680/34 to Foreign Minister Koo, signed by Karakhan, complaining that the Russian archive in Tientsin had not been turned over to the Soviet mission.

12 July 1924, WCTA, 03-32, 454(1), French-language letter No. 36 to Foreign Minister Koo, signed by Oudendijk.

26 July 1924, WCTA, 03-32, 454(1), English-language letter No. 2875/42 to Foreign Minister Koo, signed by Karakhan, about his meeting with Minister Schurman, the new *doyen* of the Peking diplomatic corps. Including a copy of letter No. 2873 to *doyen* Schurman from Karakhan.

31 July 1924, WCTA, 03-32, 467(3), French-language and English-language notes circulated by the Ministry of Foreign Affairs, stating that Karakhan was the Soviet Union's ambassador to China.

10 August 1924, WCTA, 03-32, 494(1), English-language minutes of the meeting between Karakhan and Koo, at Koo's private residence, starting at 10:00 a.m.

12 August 1924, WCTA, 03-32, 494(1), English-language minutes of the meeting between Karakhan and Koo, at Koo's private residence, starting at 6:00 p.m.

18 August 1924, WCTA, 03-32, 454(1), English-language letter to Foreign Minister Koo, signed by K. Yoshizawa, the Japanese minister to China. Enclosed are two notes to Karakhan from Yoshizawa.

23 August 1924, WCTA, 03-32, 456(1), English-language letter No. 3184/42 to Foreign Minister Koo, signed by Karakhan, discussing the opening of Soviet consulate-generals and consulates in China.

27 August 1924, WCTA, 03-32, 454(1), English-language letter No. 3222/54 to Foreign Minister Koo, signed by Karakhan, which includes a copy of letter No. 3199 of August 25, 1924 to Donald Macleay, the British minister in China.

20 September 1924, Number Two Historical Archives, Nanking, File 1039, No. 99; see page 9, section 6, secret appendix. Supplemental agreements between the USSR and Chang Tso-lin; a signed copy of this treaty is also located at WCTA, 03-32, 491(2).

3 October 1924, Number Two Historical Archives, Nanking, File 1039, No. 437, Vol. 3, 249. French legation in China protest to the Waichiaopu, warning them of the "serious consequences" which would ensue from its "arbitrary action" on the CER that ignored the rights of the Russo-Asiatic Bank.

14 October 1924, WCTA, 03-32, 494(3), Russian-language letter No. 575 to Foreign Minister Chicherin from Li Chia-ao.

6 November 1924, WCTA, 03-32, 489(1), Chinese-language minutes of a conversation between Karakhan and Wang Cheng-t'ing, the new acting foreign minister, during which Karakhan presented three new preconditions that Peking had to meet prior to opening the Sino-Soviet conference.

1925 and After

19 January 1925, WCTA, 03-32, 491(2), Chinese-language letter from Chang Tso-lin to the Peking government's ministry of foreign affairs; including a copy of the September 20, 1924 Supplemental Agreements. This may be the first time that the Waichiaopu knew about the secret protocol giving Chang Tso-lin control over the Chinese half of the Chinese Eastern Railway.

21 February 1925, WCTA, 03-32, 498(1), Chinese-language minutes of a meeting between Li Chia-ao and Chicherin.

26 February 1925, WCTA, 03-32, 497(2), English-language letter No. 35002/21 to Shen Jui-lin, the new foreign minister, signed by Karakhan, stating that the recent reaffirmation of the Portsmouth Peace Treaty did not interfere with China's sovereignty.

February 1925, WCTA, 03-32, 491(1), English-language letter from the Waichiaopu, in response to Karakhan's February 26, 1925 letter; pointed out that China had repeatedly protested the 1915 treaties that Japan had forced on China, and that Karakhan was now supporting.

2 March 1925, WCTA, 03-32, 498(1), Russian-language letter No. 219 to Minister Li Chia-ao from Chicherin.

6 March 1925, WCTA, 03-32, 497(3), English-language letter No. 35002/26 to Foreign Minister Shen Jui-lin from Karakhan, announcing that Red Army troops had withdrawn from Outer Mongolia.

10 March 1925, WCTA, 03-32, 491(1), English-language letter to Foreign Minister Chicherin from Minister Li Chia-ao.

10 April 1925, WCTA, 03-32, 561(1), English-language letter to the Waichiaopu from the Soviet mission in Peking, requesting that all the former Russian property in China be returned to Soviet control. A long list of property is included with this letter.

7 May 1925, WCTA, 03-32, 204(3), Chinese-language transcipts of Li Chia-ao's meeting with Foreign Minister Chicherin, during which Outer Mongolia was discussed.

20 May 1925, WCTA, 03-32, 561(2), English-language letter No. 35002/51 to the Waichiaopu from the Soviet mission in Peking, requesting that all the former Russian property in Tientsin be returned to Soviet control.

21 May 1925, WCTA, 03-32, 265(1), English-language letter No. 35002/52 to the Waichiaopu from the Soviet mission in Peking, claiming that all the CER property must remain under Soviet control.

Spring 1925, WCTA, 03-32, 500(1), English-language draft Sino-Soviet treaty, written by the Waichiaopu, and entitled: "Draft Treaty Between the Republic of China and the Union of Soviet Socialist Republics."

Spring 1925, WCTA, 03-32, 500(1), English-language report on Waichiaopu's goals in the Soviet repayment of damages, entitled "Memorandum on the Russian Issue of the Reorganization Loan of 1913."

2 June 1925, WCTA, 03-32, 204(3), Chinese-language minutes of a May 7 meeting between Minister Li Chia-ao and Foreign Minister Chicherin.

18 June 1925, WCTA, 03-32, 462 (5), English-language letter No. 35002/58 to Foreign Minister Shen, signed by Karakhan, announcing the formation of the Soviet Socialist Republics of Turkestan and Uzbekistan and their "unanimous" decision to join the Soviet Union on February 17 and 20, respectively.

6 July 1925, WCTA, 03-32, 500(3), Russian-language letter from Foreign Minister Chicherin to Minister Li Chia-ao.

8 August 1925, WCTA, 03-32, 461(4), Russian-language letter from Minister Li Chia-ao to Foreign Minister Chicherin.

26 August 1925, WCTA, 03-32, 503(3), English-language minutes of the opening day of the Sino-Soviet conference, entitled "Minutes of the First Meeting of the Sino-Soviet Conference."

10 January 1926, WCTA, 03-32, 536(4), confidential Peking government response to Soviet proposal, entitled "General Observation on the Preliminary Soviet Draft on Trade and Navigation."

26 February 1926, WCTA, 03-32, 540(2), English-language note from the Soviet delegation, entitled: "Answer to the Claims presented by the Chinese delegation to the Soviet delegation for the compensation of the losses sustained by the Chinese Government and its citizens."

25 March 1926, "Вопросы нашей политики в отношении Китая и Японии" ("Questions in Our Policies in Relations with China and Japan"), Trotsky Archives; No. 870.

Spring 1927, Archives of the Historical Commission of the Central Committee of the Kuomintang Party, Document 435-79; a minute book of the executive committee of the Shanghai branch of the Kuomintang.

20 April 1926, WCTA, 03-32, 540(2), English-language note from the Soviet delegation, entitled: "Answer to the Note Presented by the Chinese Delegation on Claims."

1 April 1927, Number Two Historical Archives, Nanking, File 1023, No. 57; minutes of Eighth Meeting of Kuomintang Central Committee Political Commission.

17 May 1927, Archives of the Historical Commission of the Central Committee of the Kuomintang Party, 467-39.

September 1927, Archives of the Historical Commission of the Central Committee of the Kuomintang Party, Document 467-3. Letter from eleven top Kuomintang leaders to Sun Yat-sen protesting Borodin's influence, December 3, 1923; reprinted in *Two Major Documents which Impeach the Chinese Communist Party*, published on the authority of the Central Control Yuan of the Chinese Kuomintang.

November 1929, Archives of the Historical Commission of the Central Committee of the Kuomintang Party, Taiwan; 中俄關於中東路之交涉事略 (*A History of Sino-Russian Negotiations on the Chinese Eastern Railway*), 20-21.

II. Published Secondary Sources

Andrews, Carol Corder. "The Policy of the Chinese Communist Party Towards the Peasant Movement, 1921-1927: The Impact of National on Social Revolution." Columbia University Dissertation, 1978.

Arbatov, G. A. *The Soviet Viewpoint.* London: Zed Books, 1983.

Bailey, Thomas A. *Wilson and the Peacemakers.* New York: Macmillan, 1947.

───────. *America Faces Russia.* Gloucester, MA: Peter Smith, 1964.

Baker, Ray Stannard. *Woodrow Wilson and World Settlement.* Gloucester, MA: Peter Smith, 1960. Two volumes.

Bamba, Nobuya Mark. "Japanese Diplomacy in Dilemma: A Comparative Analysis of Shidehara Kijuro's and Tanaka Giichi's Policies Toward China, 1924-1929." University of California, Berkeley, Dissertation, 1970.

Barmine, Alexandre. *Memoirs of a Soviet Diplomat.* Westport, CT: Hyperion, 1938 reprinted, 1973.

Beloff, Max. *The Foreign Policy of Soviet Russia.* New York: Oxford University Press, 1949.

───────. *Soviet Far Eastern Policy Since Yalta.* New York: Institute of Pacific Relations, 1950.

───────. *Soviet Policy in the Far East, 1944-1951.* New York: Oxford University Press, 1953.

Besedovskii, Gregorii (Беседовский, Грегории). *На путях к термидору (On the Path to the Thermidore).* Paris, 1931.

Bianco, Lucien. *Origins of the Chinese Revolution.* Stanford: Stanford University Press, 1971.

Bibber, Joyce Kathleen. *The Chinese Communists as Viewed by the American Periodical Press, 1920-1937.* Stanford: Stanford University Press, 1969.

Black's Law Dictionary. St. Paul: West Publication Company, 1933.

Borodina, F. S.(Бородина, Ф. С). *В Застенках Китайскых Сатрапов (In the Torture-chambers of the Chinese Satrapies),* Moscow, 1928.

Brandt, Conrad. *Stalin's Failure in China.* New York: Norton, 1958.

Brandt, Conrad, Benjamin Schwartz, and John K. Fairbank, eds. *A Documentary History of Chinese Communism.* Cambridge: Harvard University Press, 1952.

Brockhausen, Terence Elden. "The Boxer Indemnity: Five Decades of Sino-American Dissension." Texas Christian University Dissertation, 1981.

Brown, Zora Anderson. "The Russification of Wang Ming: A Study of the Comintern Career of Chen Shao-yu, 1925-1937. " Mississippi State University Dissertation, 1977.

Campi, Alicia Jean. "The Political Relationship Between the United States and Outer Mongolia, 1915-1927: The Kalgan Consular Records." Indiana University Dissertation, 1988.

Carlton, David, and Herbert M. Levine, eds. *The Cold War Debated.* New York, 1988.

Carr, E. H. *The Bolshevik Revolution.* London: Penguin Books, 1966.

Chan, F. Gilbert, and Thomas H. Etzold eds. *China in the 1920s.* New York: New Viewpoints, 1976.

Chang, Hsu-hsin. "The Kuomintang's Foreign Policy, 1925-1928." University of Wisconsin Dissertation, 1967.

Chang Kuo-t'ao. *The Rise of the Chinese Communist Party, 1921-1927: Volume One of the Autobiography of Chang Kuo-t'ao.* Lawrence: University of Kansas Press, 1971.

Ch'en Kung-po. *The Communist Movement in China: As Essay Written in 1924.* Edited with an Introduction by C. Martin Wilbur. New York: Octagon Books, 1966.

Ch'en Tu-hsiu (陳獨秀). 陈独秀文章选编 (*A Collection of Ch'en Tu-hsiu's Articles*). Peking, 1984.

———, 陳獨秀选集 (*Collection of Chen Duxiu's Works*). Tientsin, 1990.

Chesneaux, Jean, Françoise Le Barbier, and Marie-Claire Bergère. *China From the 1911 Revolution to Liberation.* New York: Pantheon, 1977.

Chih Yu Ju. "The Political Thought of Ch'en Tu-hsiu." Indiana University Dissertation, 1965.

Chiang Kai-shek. *China's Destiny.* New York: Roy Publishers, 1947.

The China White Paper, August 1949. Stanford: Stanford University Press, 1967.

Chow Tse-tung. *The May 4th Movement: Intellectual Revolution in Modern China.* Cambridge: Harvard University Press, 1980.

Chu Chi-hsien. "The Sino-Soviet Conflict in Turkistan." Northeast Missouri State University M.A. Thesis, 1980.

Chu Pao-chin. *V. K. Wellington Koo: A Case Study of China's Diplomat and Diplomacy of Nationalism, 1912-1966.* Hong Kong: Chinese University Press, 1981.

Chu William Tze-fu. "Hu Han-min: A Political Profile (1879-1936)." St. John's University Dissertation, 1978.

Clyde, Paul Hibbert. *United States Policy Toward China.* New York: Russell and Russell, 1964.

Clubb, Edmond O. *China and Russia: The "Great Game."* New York: Columbia University Press, 1971.

Cole, Bernard David. "The United States Navy in China, 1925-1928." Auburn University Dissertation, 1978.

A Collection of Documents of the Chinese Communist Party's Central Committee (中国中央 文件 选集), Vol. 1. Peking, 1989.

Collection of Documents. Relating to the Activities of the Russian Mission in China from November 1, 1917 to December 31, 1920 (Собрание Документов, каскющихся деятельности Российской Миссий в Китай 1 Ноября 1917 г. по 31 Декабря 1920 г.). Peking, 1920.

Collester, Janet Sue. "J. V. A. MacMurray, American Minister to China, 1925-1929: The Failure of a Mission." Indiana University Dissertation, 1977.

The Columbia Encyclopedia. New York: Columbia University Press, 1964.

The Communist International and the Chinese Revolution (Коммунистический Интернационал и китайская революция Документы и материалы). Moscow, 1986.

Cosgrove, Julia Fukuda. *United States Foreign Economic Policy Toward China, 1943-1946.* New York: Garland, 1987.

Curry, Roy Watson. *Woodrow Wilson and Far Eastern Policy, 1913-1921.* New York: Bookman Associates, 1957.

Dalin, Sergei (Далин, Сергей), *В Рядах Китайской Революция* (*In the Ranks of the Chinese Revolution*). Moscow, 1926.

Dallin, Alexander, ed. *Soviet Conduct in World Affairs.* New York: Columbia University Press, 1960.

Dallin, David J. *The Rise of Russia in Asia.* New Haven: Archon Books, 1971.

Day, Alan J., ed. *Border and Territorial Disputes*, Detroit: Gale Research Company, 1982.

Dayer, Roberta Allbert. *Bankers and Diplomats in China, 1917-1925: The Anglo-American Relationship.* Totowa, NJ: F. Cass, 1981.

DeAngelis, Richard C. "Jacob Gould Schurman and American Policy Toward China, 1921-1925." St. John's University Dissertation, 1975.

Degras, Jane, ed. *Soviet Documents on Foreign Policy: Vol. 1, 1917-1924.* New York: Oxford University Press, 1951.

————. *Soviet Documents on Foreign Policy: Vol. 2, 1925-1932,* New York: Oxford University Press, 1952

————. *The Communist International: 1919-1943.* New York: Oxford University Press, 1956. two volumes.

Deliusin, L. P. (Делюсин, Л. П.), *Аграрно-крестьянский Вопрос в Политике КПК 1921-1928 (Agrarian and Peasant Questions in the Policies of the CCP 1921-1928).* Moscow, 1972.

————. and A. S. Kostiaeva (А. С. Костяева). *Революция 1925-1927 гг. в Китае: проблемы и оценки (Revolution of 1925-1927 in China: Problems and Appraisals).* Moscow, 1985.

Dennis, Alfred L. P. *The Foreign Policies of Soviet Russia.* New York: E. P. Dutton, 1924.

Deutscher, Isaac, *Stalin: A Political Biography.* New York: Oxford University Press, 1968.

————. *The Prophet Armed, Trotsky: 1879-1921.* New York: Oxford University Press, 1980.

————. *The Prophet Unarmed, Trotsky: 1921-1929.* New York: Oxford University Press, 1980.

Dictionary of International and Comparative Law. New York: Oceana Publications, 1992.

Dirlik, Arif. *The Origins of Chinese Communism.* New York: Oxford University Press, 1989.

Dockser, Cecile Bahn. "John Dewey and the May Fourth Movement in China." Harvard University Dissertation, 1983.

Documents on Maring in China (马林在中国的关于资料), Peking, 1980.

Doolin, Dennis J. *Territorial Claims in the Sino-Soviet Conflict.* Hoover Institution Studies, No. 7. Stanford: Stanford University Press, 1965.

Dukes, Paul. *The Last Great Game: USA Versus USSR, Events, Conjectures, Structures.* London: Pinter, 1989.

Duus, Peter, Ramon H. Myers, and Mark R. Peattie, eds. *The Japanese Informal Empire in China, 1895-1937.* Princeton: Princeton University Press, 1989.

Ellison, Duane Conan. "The United States and China, 1913-1921: A Study of the Strategy and Tactics of the Open Door Policy." George Washington University Dissertation, 1974.

Encausse, Hélène Carrère and Stuart R. Schram. *Marxism and Asia.* London: Allen Lane, 1969.

Esherick, Joseph W. *The Origins of the Boxer Uprising.* Berkeley: University of California Press, 1987.

Evans, Les, and Block, Russell, eds. *Leon Trotsky on China.* New York: Monad Press, 1976.

Ewing, Thomas. *Between the Hammer and the Anvil? Chinese and Russian Policies in Outer Mongolia, 1911-1921*. Bloomington: University of Indiana Press, 1980.

Eudin, Xenia Joukoff, and Robert C. North. *Soviet Russia and the East 1920-1927: A Documentary Survey*. Stanford: Stanford University Press, 1957.

————. *M. N. Roy's Mission to China: The Communist-Kuomintang Split of 1927*. Berkeley: University of California Press, 1962.

Fairbank, John King, ed. *On the Chinese World Order*. Cambridge: Harvard University Press, 1968.

Falconeri, Gennaro Sylvester. "Reactions to Revolution: Japanese Attitudes and Foreign Policy Toward China, 1924-1927." University of Michigan Dissertation, 1967.

Feigon, Lee. *Chen Duxiu: Founder of the Chinese Communist Party*. Princeton: Princeton University Press, 1983.

Fifield, Russell H. *Woodrow Wilson and the Far East*. New York: Thomas Y. Crowell, 1952.

Fishel, Wesley R. *The End of Extraterritoriality in China*. Berkeley: University of California Press, 1952.

Fischer, Louis. *The Soviets in World Affairs*. Princeton: Princeton University Press, 1951. Two volumes.

Fleming, Denna Frank. *The Cold War and its Origins, 1917-1960*. Garden City, NY: Doubleday, 1961.

Fontaine, André. *History of the Cold War: From the October Revolution to the Korean War, 1917-1950*. New York: Pantheon Books, 1968.

Gaddis, John Lewis. *The United States and the Origins of the Cold War, 1941-1947*. New York: Columbia University Press, 1972.

Gallicchio, Marc. *The Cold War Begins in Asia: American East Asian Policy and the Fall of the Japanese Empire*. New York: Columbia University Press, 1988.

Ganshow, Thomas William. "A Study of Sun Yat-sen's Contacts with the United States Prior to 1922." Indiana University Dissertation, 1971.

George, Brian Thomas. "The Open Door and the Rise of Chinese Nationalism: American Policy and China, 1917-1928." University of New Mexico Dissertation, 1977.

Georgescu, Vlad. *The Romanians: A History*. Columbus: Ohio State University Press, 1991.

Geyer, Dietrich. *Russian Imperialism: The Interaction of Domestic and Foreign Policy, 1860-1914*. New Haven: Yale University Press, 1987.

Gibson, Michael Richard. *Chiang Kai-shek's Central Army, 1924-1938*. George Washington University Dissertation, 1985.

Glaim, Lorne Eugene. "Sino-German Relations, 1919-1925: German Diplomatic, Economic, and Cultural Reentry into China after World War I." Washington State University Dissertation, 1973.

Gluck, Carol. *Japan's Modern Myths, Ideology in the Late Meiji Period*. Princeton: Princeton University Press, 1985.

Glunin, V. I (Глунин, В. И.), *Коминтерн и Восток* (*The Comintern and the East*), Moscow, 1967.

Goldstein, Erik, and John Maurer. *The Washington Conference, 1921-22: Naval Rivalry, East Asian Stability and the Road to Pearl Harbor*. London: Frank Cass, 1994.

Goncharov, Sergei N., and John W. Lewis, Xue Litai, *Uncertain Partners: Stalin, Mao, and the Korean War*. Stanford: Stanford University Press, 1993.

Grabner, Norman A., ed. *The Cold War, A Conflict of Ideology and Power.* Cambridge: Harvard University Press, 1976.

Graves, William S. *America's Siberian Adventure, 1918-1920.* New York: Peter Smith, 1941.

Great Soviet Encyclopedia. New York: Macmillan, 1970.

Griffith, William E. *Cold War and Coexistence: Russia, China and the United States.* Englewood Cliffs, NJ: Prentice-Hall, 1971.

Grimm, E. D. (Гримм Е. Д.). *Сборник договоров и других документов по истории международных отношений на Дальнем Востоке (1842-1925)* (*Collection of Treaties and Other Documents on the History of International Relations in the Far East [1842-1925]*). Moscow, 1927.

Halle, Louis J. *The Cold War as History.* New York: Harper, 1967.

Halliday, Fred. *Cold War, Third World.* London: Hutchinson Radius, 1989.

Hammond, Paul. *Cold War and Détente: The American Foreign Policy Process Since 1945.* New York: Harcourt Brace Jovanovich, 1975.

Harrison, James P. *The Long March to Power.* New York: Praeger, 1972.

Hasiotis, Arthur Christos, Jr. "A Study of Secret Political, Economic, and Military Involvement in Sinkiang from 1928-1949." New York University Dissertation, 1981.

Haslam, Jonathan. *The Soviet Union and the Threat from the East, 1933-41: Moscow, Tokyo and the Prelude to the Pacific War.* Pittsburgh: University of Pittsburgh Press, 1992.

History of the Chinese Revolution (中国革命). Peking, 1989.

Historical Materials from the Chinese Kuomintang's First and Second Party Congress (中国国民党第一，二次全国代表大会会议史料), Edited by the "中国第二历史档案馆" (China's Number Two Historical Archives), Kiangsu, 1986. Two volumes.

A History of Sino-Russian Negotiations on the Chinese Eastern Railway (中俄關於中東路之交涉事略). Nanking, 1929.

Holubnychy, Lydia. *Borodin and the Chinese Revolution, 1923-1925.* Ann Arbor, MI: Published for the East Asian Institute, Columbia University, by University Microfilms International, 1979.

Hou, Chi-ming. *Foreign Investment and Economic Development in China, 1840-1937.* Cambridge: Harvard University Press, 1965.

Hsiang Ch'ing (向青). 共产国际和中国革命关系的历史概述 (*A Historical Summary of Relations between the Communist International and the Chinese Revolution*). Kuangtung, 1984.

Hsu, Immanuel C. Y. *The Rise of Modern China.* New York: Oxford University Press, 1995.

Huang, Chin-Liang Lawrence. "Japan's China Policy Under Premier Tanaka, 1927-1929." New York University Dissertation, 1968.

Huang, Fu-ch'ing. *Chinese Students in Japan in the Late Ch'ing Period.* Tokyo: The Centre for East Asian Cultural Studies, 1982.

Huang, Margaret H. C. "Dr. Sun Yat-sen's Efforts of Modernize China (1894-1925)." Georgetown University Dissertation, 1976.

Hull, Cordell. *The Memoirs of Cordell Hull.* New York: Macmillan, 1948. Two volumes.

Hunt, Michael H. *Frontier Defense and the Open Door.* New Haven: Yale University Press, 1973.

Hyland, William. *The Cold War Is Over.* New York: Random House, 1990.

Iriye, Akira. *After Imperialism: The Search for a New Order in the Far East, 1921-1931.* Cambridge: Harvard University Press, 1965.

————. *The Cold War in Asia: A Historical Introduction.* Princeton: Princeton University Press, 1974.

Isaacs, Harold R. *The Tragedy of the Chinese Revolution.* Stanford: Stanford University Press, 1961.

Jacobs, Dan N. *Borodin: Stalin's Man in China.* Cambridge: Harvard University Press, 1981.

Jakimetz, Gennady Nicholas. "An Interpretation of Czarist-Communist Economic-Political Policy in Sinkiang: With Emphasis on the Years 1851-1955." University of Nevada, Reno, M.A. Thesis, 1981.

Jansen, Marius B. *The Japanese and Sun Yat-sen.* Cambridge: Harvard University Press, 1954.

Jelavich, Barbara. *A Century of Russian Foreign Policy, 1814-1914.* Philadelphia: Lippincott, 1964.

Jordan, Donald A. *The Northern Expedition: China's National Revolution of 1926-1928.* Honolulu: University of Hawaii Press, 1976.

Kagan, Richard Clark. "The Chinese Trotskyist Movement and Ch'en Tu-hsiu; Culture, Revolution and Polity, with an Appended Translation of Ch'en Tu-hsiu's Autobiography." University of Pennsylvania Dissertation, 1969.

Kallinikov, Anatolii (Каллиников, Анатолий). *Революционная Монголия* (*Revolutionary Mongolia*). Moscow, 1926.

Kasanin, Marc. *China in the Twenties.* Moscow, 1973.

Kataoka, Tetsuya. *Resistance and Revolution in China: The Communists and the Second United Front.* Berkeley: University of California Press, 1974.

Kennan, George F. *Soviet-American Relations, 1917-1920: Russia Leaves the War.* Princeton: Princeton University Press, 1956.

————. *Soviet-American Relations, 1917-1920: The Decision to Intervene.* Princeton: Princeton University Press, 1958.

————. *American Diplomacy.* Chicago: University of Chicago Press, 1984.

King, Wunsz. *China at the Washington Conference, 1921-1922.* New York: St. John's University Press, 1963.

Kitts, Charles Roy. "An Inside View of the Kuomintang: Chen Li-fu, 1926-1949." St. John's University Dissertation, 1978.

Koebner, Richard, and Helmut Hans Schmidt. *Imperialism: The Story and Significance of a Political Word, 1840-1960.* London: Cambridge University Press, 1964.

Kotenev, Anatol M. *Shanghai: Its Mixed Court and Council.* Taipei, 1968.

Krebs, Edward Skinner. "Liu Ssu-fu and Chinese Anarchism, 1905-1915." University of Washington Dissertation, 1977.

Ku, Hung-ting. "Urban Mass Politics in Southern China, 1923-1927: Some Case Studies." Ohio State University Dissertation, 1973.

Kuo, Thomas C. *Ch'en Tu-hsiu (1879-1942) and the Chinese Communist Movement.* South Orange, NJ: Seton Hall University Press, 1975 .

LaFeber, Walter. *America, Russia, and the Cold War, 1945-1984.* New York: John Wiley and Sons, 1967.

Langer, William L. *The Diplomacy of Imperialism, 1890-1902 .* New York: Knopf, 1956.

Lederer, Ivo J., ed. *Russian Foreign Policy.* New Haven: Yale University Press, 1962.

Ledovsky, A. *The USSR, the USA, and the People's Revolution in China.* Moscow, 1982.

Lenin, V. I. *On the Foreign Policy of the Soviet State.* Moscow, 1964.

Lensen, George Alexander, ed. *Revelations of a Russian Diplomat: The Memoirs of Dmitri I. Abrikossow.* Seattle: University of Washington Press, 1964.

———. *Russia's Eastward Expansion.* Englewood Cliffs, NJ: Prentice-Hall, 1964.

———. *Japanese Recognition of the U.S.S.R.* Tokyo: Sophia University Press, 1970.

Lentsner, H. (Ленцнер, Н.). *Китайская Революция и Оппозиция (The Chinese Revolution and the Opposition*). Moscow, 1927.

Leong, Sow-Theng. *Sino-Soviet Diplomatic Relations, 1917-1926.* Canberra: Australian National University Press, 1976.

Lerner, Warren. *Karl Radek: The Last Internationist.* Stanford: Stanford University Press, 1970.

Levenson, Joseph R. *Liang Ch'i-ch'ao and the the Mind of Modern China.* Berkeley: University of California Press, 1970.

Levering, Ralph. *The Cold War 1945-1972.* Arlington Heights, Ill: H. Davidson, 1982.

Li, Chien-nung. *The Political History of China, 1840-1928.* Stanford: Stanford University Press, 1956.

Loh, Martin Mun-loong. "American Officials in China, 1923-1927: Their Use of Bolshevism to Explain the Rise of the Kuomintang and Chinese-Anti-Foreignism." University of Washington Dissertation, 1984.

Low, Alfred D. *The Sino-Soviet Dispute: An Analysis of the Polemics.* London: Associated University Presses, 1976.

Lukacs, John. *A New History of the Cold War.* Garden City, NY: Anchor, 1966.

Lynch, Allen. *The Cold War is Over–Again.* Boulder: University of Colorado Press, 1992.

Malia, Martin. *The Soviet Tragedy: A History of Socialism in Russia, 1917-1991.* New York: Free Press, 1994.

Malraux, André. *The Conquerors.* New York: Grove Press, 1977.

Mancall, Mark. *Russian and China.* Cambridge: Harvard University Press, 1971.

Mao Tse-tung. *Dr. Sun Yat-sen Commemorative Articles and Speeches by Mao Tse-tung, Soong Ching Ling, Chou En-lai and Others.* Peking, 1957.

———. *Selected Works of Mao Tse-tung.* Peking, 1965.

———. *Mao Tse-tung Selected Works.* New York: International Publishers, 1961.

Matsuda, Takeshi. "Woodrow Wilson's Dollar Diplomacy in the Far East: The New Chinese Consortium, 1917-1921." University of Wisconsin, Madison, Dissertation, 1979.

Mayer, Arno J. *Political Origins of the New Diplomacy, 1917-1918.* New Haven: Yale University Press, 1959.

McCormack, Gavan. *Chang Tso-lin in Northeast China, 1911-1928.* Stanford: Stanford University Press, 1977.

McKee, Delber L. *Chinese Exclusion Versus the Open Door Policy 1900-1906.* Detroit: Wayne State University Press, 1977.

McLane, Charles, *Soviet Policy and the Chinese Communists, 1931-1946.* New York, 1958.

MacMurray, John V. A. *Treaties and Agreements with and Concerning China, 1894-1919.* London: Oxford University Press, 1921.

McQuilkin, David Karl. "Soviet Attitudes Toward China, 1919-1927." Kent State University Dissertation, 1973.

Medvedev, Roy A. *Let History Judge.* New York: Knopf, 1971.

Megginson, William James, III. "Britain's Response to Chinese Nationalism, 1925-1927: The Foreign Office Search for a New Policy." George Washington University Dissertation, 1973.

Meisner, Maurice. *Li Ta-chao and the Origins of Chinese Marxism.* New York: Atheneum, 1977.

Memorandum of the American Chamber of Commerce of Tientsin Relative to Extraterritoriality in China. Tientsin, 1925.

Metallo, Michael Vincent. "The United States and Sun Yat-en, 1911-1925." New York University Dissertation, 1974.

Mif, Pavel. *Heroic China: Fifteen years of the Communist Party of China.* New York: Workers Library Publishers, 1937.

Miller, Joseph Thomas. "The Politics of Chinese Trotskyism: The Role of a Permanent Opposition China." University of Illinois at Urbana–Champaign Dissertation, 1979.

Moon, Parker Thomas. *Imperialism and World Politics.* New York: Macmillan, 1926.

Moore, Barrington Jr. *Soviet Politics–The Dilemma of Power.* Cambridge: Harvard University Press, 1951.

Morgenthau, Hans H. *Politics Among Nations: The Struggle for Power and Peace.* New York: Knopf, 1948.

Nathan, Andrew J. *Peking Politics, 1918-1923: Factionalism and the Failure of Constitutionalism.* Berkeley: University of California Press, 1976.

Naylor, Thomas. *The Cold War Legacy.* Lexington, MA: Lexington Books, 1991.

North, Robert C. *Kuomintang and Chinese Communist Elites.* Stanford: Stanford University Press, 1952.

————. *Moscow and Chinese Communists.* Stanford; Stanford University Press, 1953.

————. *Chinese Communism.* New York: McGraw-Hill, 1966.

Odani, Akira. "Wang Ching-wei and the Fall of the Chinese Republic, 1905-1935." Brown University Dissertation, 1975.

The Oxford English Dictionary, 2d ed. New York: Oxford University Press. 1989.

Paine, S. C. M. *Imperial Rivals: China, Russia, and Their Disputed Frontier.* Armonk, NY: M. E. Sharpe, 1996.

Pak, Hyobom, ed. *Documents of the Chinese Communist Party, 1927-1930.* Hong Kong, 1971.

Parlett, Sir Harold. *A Brief Account of Diplomatic Events in Manchuria.* London: Oxford University Press, London, 1929.

Pavlovsky, Michel N. *Chinese and Russian Relations.* 1949. Reprint, Westport, CT: Hyperion, 1981

Pipes, Richard. *The Formation of the Soviet Union: Communism and Nationalism 1917-1923.* Cambridge: Harvard University Press, 1964.

Prescott, J. R. V. *Map of Mainland Asia by Treaty.* Melbourne: Melbourne University Press, 1975.

Price, Don C. *Russia and the Roots of the Chinese Revolution, 1896-1911.* Cambridge: Harvard University Press, 1974.

Price, Ernest Batson. *The Russo-Japanese Treaties of 1907-1916 Concerning Manchuria and Mongolia.* Baltimore: The Johns Hopkins Press, 1933.

Pugach, Noel H. *Paul S. Reinsch: Open Door Diplomat in Action.* Millwood, NY: KTO Press, 1979.

Purcell, Victor. *The Boxer Uprising: A Background Study.* Cambridge: Cambridge University Press, 1963.

Quested, R. K. I. *Sino-Russian Relations: A Short History.* Winchester, MA: George, Allen, and Unwin, 1984.

Ramsdell, Daniel Bailey. "Japan's China Policy, 1929-1931: A Fateful Failure." University of Wisconsin Dissertation, 1961.

Reinsch, Paul S. *Secret Diplomacy: How Far Can It Be Eliminated?* New York: Harcourt Brace, 1922.

Riasanovsky, Nicholas V. *A History of Russia.* New York: Oxford University Press, 1963.

Ristaino, Marcia Reynders. "The Chinese Communist Movement, 1927-1928: Organizations, Strategies and Tactics for Making Revolution." Georgetown University Dissertation, 1977.

Roy, M. N. *My Experience in China.* Bombay: Renaissance, 1938.

————. *Revolution and Counter-Revolution in China.* Westport, CT: Hyperion, 1973.

Rossabi, Morris. *China and Inner Asia: From 1368 to the Present Day.* London: Thames and Hudson, 1975.

Rummel, R. J. *China's Bloody Century: Genocide and Mass Murder Since 1900.* New Brunswick, NJ: Transaction Publishers, 1991.

Rupen, Robert. *How Mongolia Is Really Ruled: A Political History of the Mongolian People's Republic, 1900-1978.* Stanford: Stanford University Press, 1979.

Saich, Tony. *The Origins of the First United Front in China: The Role of Sneevliet (Alias Maring).* Leiden: E. J. Brill, 1991.

Scalapino, Robert A., and George T. Yu. *The Chinese Anarchist Movement.* Berkeley: University of California Press, 1961.

Schiffrin, Harold Z. *Sun Yat-sen and the Origins of the Chinese Revolution.* Berkeley: University of California Press, 1968.

————. *Sun Yat-sen: Reluctant Revolutionary.* Boston: Little, Brown, 1980.

Schwarcz, Vera. "From Renaissance to Revolution: An Internal History of the May Fourth Movement and the Birth of the Chinese Intelligentsia." Stanford University Dissertation, 1978.

Schwartz, Benjamin. *Chinese Communism and the Rise of Mao.* Cambridge: Harvard University Press, 1968.

Selected Works of Sun Yat-sen (Сунь Ятсен Избранные произведения). Moscow, 1964.

Seton-Watson, Hugh. *The Russian Empire, 1801-1917.* Oxford: Clarendon, 1967.

Shai, Aron. *Origins of the War in the East Britain, China and Japan 1937-39.* London: Croom Helm, 1976.

Sharman, Lyon. *Sun Yat-sen His Life and Its Meaning.* Stanford: Stanford University Press, 1968.

Sheng, Yueh. *Sun Yat-sen University in Moscow and the Chinese Revolution: A Personal Account.* Center for East Asian Studies, University of Kansas, 1971.

Sheridan, James E. *Chinese Warlord: The Career of Feng Yu-hsiang.* Stanford: Stanford University Press, 1966.

————. *China in Disintegration: The Republican Era in Chinese History, 1912-1949.* New York: Free Press, 1975.

Shirley, James R. "Political Conflict in the Kuomintang: The Career of Wang Ching-wei to 1932." University of California, Berkeley, Dissertation, 1962.

Sicker, Martin. *The Strategy of Soviet Imperialism: Expansion in Eurasia.* New York: Praeger, 1988.

Smith, Joseph. *The Cold War, 1945-1965.* New York: B. Blackwell, 1989.

Snell, John L. ed. *The Meaning of Yalta*. Baton Rouge: Louisiana State University Press, 1956.

Snow, Edgar. *Red Star over China*. London: Gallienz Press, 1938.

Snyder, Louis, ed. *The Dynamics of Nationalism: Readings in its Meaning and Development*. Princeton: Van Nostrand, 1964.

Sokolsky, George. *The Story of the Chinese Eastern Railway*. Shanghai, 1929.

Soviet-Chinese Relations 1917-1957: Documents on the Foreign Policy of the USSR (Советско-китайские отношения 1917-1957 Документы внешней политики СССР), Moscow, 1957.

Soviet-Chinese Relations: 1917-1957, Collection of Documents (*Советско-китайские Отношения 1917-1957 сборник документов*), Moscow, 1959.

Soviets in China–A Collection of Materials and Documents (*Советы в Китае–Сборник Материалов и Документов*), Moscow, nd.

Spector, Ivar. *The First Russian Revolution: Its Impact on Asia*. Englewood Cliffs, NJ: Prentice-Hall, 1962.

Spence, Jonathan. *The Search for Modern China*. New York: W. W. Norton, 1990.

Stettinius, Edward R. Jr. *Roosevelt and the Russians*. Garden City, NY: Doubleday, 1949.

Stremski, Richard. "Britain's China Policy, 1920-1928." University of Wisconsin Dissertation, 1968.

Sullivan, Mark. *Our Times: The Turn of the Century*. New York: C. Scribner's Sons, 1926.

Sun, Yat-sen. *Memoirs of a Chinese Revolutionary*. Taipei, 1953 (1918).

————. *The Vital Problem of China*. Taipei, 1953.

Tan P'ing-shan. *The Path of Development of the Chinese Revolution*. Moscow, 1927.

T'ang Leang-li. *The Inner History of the Chinese Revolution*. London: G. Routledge and Sons, 1930.

————. *Wang Ching-wei: A Political Biography*. Peking, 1931.

Tang, Peter S. H. *Russian and Soviet Policy in Manchuria and Outer Mongolia 1911-1931*. Durham: Duke University Press,1959.

Taubman, William. *Stalin's American Policy from Entente to Détente to Cold War*. New York: W. W. Norton, 1982.

Thornton, A. P. *Imperialism in the Twentieth Century*. Minneapolis: University of Minnesota Press, 1977.

The Treaty of Versailles and After. Washington, 1947.

Trotsky, Leon. *Problems of the Chinese Revolution*. New York: Pioneer, 1932.

————. *The Third International After Lenin*. New York: Pioneer, 1936.

————. *The Stalin School of Falsification*. New York: Pioneer, 1937.

————. *The Revolution Betrayed: What is the Soviet Union and Where is it Going?* New York: Pathfinder, 1972.

Tuan, C. "Russia and the Making of Modern China, 1900-1916." Princeton University Dissertation, 1985.

Tuchman, Barbara W. *Stilwell and the American Experience in China, 1911-45*. New York: Macmillan, 1971.

Tung, William L. *China and the Foreign Powers: The Impact of a Reaction to Unequal Treaties*. Dobbs Ferry, NY: Oceana Publications, 1970.

Uhalley, Stephen. *A History of the Chinese Communist Party*. Stanford: Hoover Institution Press, 1988.

Ulam, Adam B. *Expansion and Coexistence: The History of Soviet Foreign Policy, 1917-67.* New York: Praeger, 1968.

Ullman, Richard H. *Anglo-Soviet Relations, 1917-1921.* Princeton: Princeton University Press, 1968. Two volumes.

Unterberger, Betty Miller. *America's Siberian Expedition, 1918-1920.* Durham: Duke University Press, 1956.

VKP(b), the Comintern and the National-Revolutionary Movement in China, Documents. (ВКП(Б)б Коминтерн и национально-революционное движение в Китае. Документы.). Vol. 1 (1920-1925). Moscow, 1994.

van de Ven, Hans, J. "The Founding of the Chinese Communist Party and the Search for a New Political Order, 1920-1927." Harvard University Dissertation, 1987.

———. *From Friend to Comrade: The Founding of the Chinese Communist Party, 1920-1927.* Berkeley: University of California Press, 1991.

Van Vleck, Bruce G. "Mikhail Borodin: Soviet Adviser to Sun Yat-sen." Florida Atlantic University M.A. Thesis, 1977.

Vernadsky, George. *A History of Russia. Volume 3: The Mongols and Russia.* New Haven: Yale University Press, 1953.

Vilenskii-Sibiriakov, Vladimir Dmitrievich (Виленский-Сибиряков, Владимир Дмитриевиц), *Китай и Советская Россия (China and Soviet Russia).* Moscow, 1919.

Vincent, John Carter. *The Extraterritorial System in China.* Cambridge: Harvard University Press, 1970.

Vishnyakova-Akimova, Vera Vladimirovna. *Two Years in Revolutionary China, 1925-1927.* trans. Steven I. Levine. Cambridge: Harvard University Press, 1971.

Wang, Jonathan C. M. "Sun Yat-sen's New Policy in 1924: The Role of Liao Chung-K'ao." St. John's University Dissertation, 1974.

Wang Ke-wen. "The Kuomintang Transition: Ideology and Factionalism in the National Revolution, 1924-1932." Stanford University Dissertation, 1985.

Wang Shih-han. *China Reconstructs.* Peking, 1962.

Wang Yu-chun (王聿均). 中蘇外交序幕 (*The First Phase of Sino-Soviet Diplomacy*). Taipei, 1978.

Wei Chao. "Foreign Railroad Interests in Manchuria: An Irritant in Chinese-Japanese Relations (1903-1937)." St. John's University Dissertation, 1980.

Wei, Julie Lee, Ramon H. Myers, and Donald G. Gillin. *Prescriptions for Saving China, Selected Writings of Sun Yat-sen.* Stanford: Hoover Institution Press, 1994.

Weigh, Ken Shen. *Russo-Chinese Diplomacy.* Westport, CT: Hyperion, 1981.

Wesley-Smith, Peter. *Unequal Treaty, 1898-1997: China, Great Britain and Hong Kong's New Territories.* Hong Kong: Oxford University Press, 1981.

Westad, Odd Arne. *Cold War and Revolution: Soviet-American Rivalry and the Origins of the Chinese Civil War.* New York: Columbia University Press, 1993.

Whitaker, Urban George, Jr. "Americans and Chinese Political Problems, 1912-1923." University of Washington Dissertation, 1954.

Whiting, Allen S., *Soviet Policies in China, 1917-1924.* New York: Columbia University Press, 1954.

Wilbur, C. Martin. *Sun Yat-sen Frustrated Patriot.* New York: Columbia University Press, 1976.

———. and Julie Lien-ying How. *Documents on Communism, Nationalism, and Soviet Advisers in China 1918-1927: Papers Seized in the 1927 Peking Raid.* New York:

Columbia University Press, 1972.

———. *Missionaries of Revolution: Soviet Advisers and Nationalist China, 1920-1927.* Cambridge: Harvard University Press, 1989.

Williams, William Appleman. *American Russian Relations, 1781-1947.* New York: Rinehart, 1952.

Wilson, David Lee. "The Attitudes of American Consular and Foreign Service Officers Toward Bolshevism in China, 1920-1927." University of Tennessee Dissertation, 1974.

Wittmer, Felix. *The Yalta Betrayal.* Caldwell, ID: Caxton Printers, 1953.

Wong, J. Y. *The Origins of an Heroic Image: Sun Yatsen in London, 1896-1897.* New York: Oxford University Press, 1986.

Woo, T. C. *The Kuomintang and the Future of the Chinese Revolution.* London: George, Allen and Unwin, 1928.

Woodhead, H. G. W. ed. *China Yearbook.* 1921-27. Tientsin, 1922-28.

Wu, Ellsworth Tien-wei. "The Chinese Nationalist and Communist Alliance 1923-1927." University of Maryland Dissertation, 1965.

Wu Hsiang-hsiang (吳相湘). 俄帝侵略中國史 (*History of Imperial Russia's Aggression in China*).1954. Reprint, Taipei, 1986.

Yakhontoff, Victor A. *Russia and the Soviet Union in the Far East.* New York: Coward-McCann, Inc., 1931.

———. *The Chinese Soviets.* New York: Coward-McCann Inc, 1934.

Young, Marilyn. *The Rhetoric of Empire American China Policy, 1895-1901.* Cambridge: Harvard University Press, 1968.

Zagoria, Donald. S. *The Sino-Soviet Conflict: 1956-1961.* Princeton: Princeton University Press, 1962.

Index

About the Author

Bruce A. Elleman completed a bachelor's degree at the University of California at Berkeley, a master's degree in Russian history at Columbia University, a master's degree in International history at London School of Economics, and a doctorate in Russian and Chinese history at Columbia University. Dr. Elleman holds certificates from Columbia University's East Asian Institute and Harriman Institute. Dr. Elleman has spent three years in China and Taiwan, one year in Russia, and one year in Japan engaged in research and language study. He is currently an assistant professor at Texas Christian University.